KU-577-252

SYNONYMS AND ANTONYMS

AN ALPHABETICAL LIST OF WORDS IN COMMON USE GROUPED WITH OTHERS OF SIMILAR AND OPPOSITE MEANING

BY

EDITH B. ORDWAY

GEORGE G. HARRAP & CO. LTD.
LONDON TORONTO BOMBAY SYDNEY

First published July 1918
by George G. Harrap & Co. Ltd.
182 *High Holborn, London, W.C.*1

Reprinted: January 1925; *January* 1927; *June* 1932;
January 1936; *July* 1938; *August* 1942

THIS REPRINT IS IN CONFORMITY WITH
THE AUTHORIZED ECONOMY STANDARDS

Made in Great Britain. Printed by Morrison & Gibb Ltd.,
London and Edinburgh

PREFACE

THE aim in compiling this book has been to make the list of words in common use concise yet full, and authoritative yet suggestive. Above five thousand leading words are given, and the synonyms and antonyms comprise several thousand more different words.

Actual references may be multiplied by looking up a synonym or antonym, as well as by consulting cognate words, such as the corresponding noun, verb, or adjective.

In some cases common words have been omitted, because they were composed of a root word and a prefix, intensive or privative. Their synonyms and antonyms may be found under the root word.

Occasionally within the lists words closely synonymous or antonymic have been grouped within semicolons.

The part of speech of a word is designated by an abbreviation in such cases as are necessary to save confusion.

Synonyms appear immediately after the leading word; antonyms, after the abbreviation "Ant." This order is invariable.

In the effort to make this list authoritative, the standard dictionaries and the acknowledged authorities on the subject have been consulted.

E. B. O.

ABBREVIATIONS

a.	Adjective.
ad.	Adverb.
Ant.	Antonym or Antonyms.
conj.	Conjunction.
interj.	Interjection.
n.	Noun.
p.p.	Past Participle.
prep.	Preposition.
Syn.	Synonym or Synonyms.
v.	Verb.

SYNONYMS AND ANTONYMS

A

Abandon. Desert, leave, forsake, depart from, quit, give up, relinquish, discontinue, abdicate, renounce, repudiate, forswear, withdraw from, vacate, surrender, retract, recant, retire from, cast off, abjure, cede, cease, resign, forego, yield, waive, part with, let go, lay down, evacuate, drop, deliver up.

ANT. *Claim, cherish, defend, keep, hold, maintain, protect, adopt, uphold, advocate, vindicate, occupy, undertake, prosecute, pursue, follow, seek, guard, favor, retain, support, assert, haunt.*

Abandoned. Discarded, rejected *and the p.p. of the syn. of "abandon";* depraved, corrupt, profligate, wicked, unprincipled, shameless, sinful, hardened, impenitent, lost, demoralized, vicious, dissolute, reprobate, graceless, obdurate, licentious, incorrigible, irreclaimable, bad.

ANT. The p.p. of the ant. of "abandon"; *visited, frequented, sociable; virtuous, good, deserving, worthy, commendable, excellent, laudable; reclaimable, penitent; conscientious, correct, upright, righteous, self-controlled, high-principled, steady.*

Abandonment. Desertion, renunciation, surrender, rejection, abandoning, relinquishment, dereliction; cession, resignation, abnegation, demission, abjuration, abdication, defection, abrogation.

ANT. *Solicitude, care, heed, watchfulness, vigilance; hospitality, entertainment, conviviality, welcome, reception; retention, completion, reclamation, support, help, correction, custody, tenacity.*

Abase. Degrade, reduce, lower, discredit, disgrace, dishonor, humble, sink, humiliate, bring low, cast down, stoop, debase, depress, drop, take down, demean.

ANT. *Elevate, exalt, honor, promote, raise, dignify, uplift, aggrandize.*

Abasement. Degradation, humiliation, dishonor, degeneracy, shame, depression, reduction, lowering, fall, deterioration, debasement, degeneration, vitiation, perversion, depravation, abjection, disrepute, discredit, subserviency.

ANT. *Promotion, exaltation, honor, elevation, aggrandizement, dignity, repute, reputation, standing, supremacy.*

Abash. Bewilder, confound, disconcert, discompose, confuse, daunt, humble, dishearten, mortify, shame, humiliate, snub, discountenance.

ANT. *Embolden, cheer, encourage, animate, uphold, rally, countenance, inspirit, abet, incite, buoy.*

Abate. Lessen, lower, reduce, diminish, moderate, decrease, decline, ebb, mitigate, subside, suppress, terminate, remove; temper, assuage, alleviate, appease, pacify; remit, allow; relax, slacken; bate, deduct; soothe, soften, qualify, allay, mollify, compose, tranquilize, quiet, quell, calm, dull, blunt; batter down, beat down, demolish, raze.

ANT. *Increase, prolong, magnify, foment, enlarge, extend, aggravate, continue, develop, revive, raise, enhance, amplify.*

Abatement. Subsidence, decline, lowering, reduction, decrease; allowance, discount, rebate, depreciation, drawback; moderation, lessening, mitigation, assuagement, remission, sinking, settling, waning, fading, ebb, evanishment, declension, deduction, diminution.

ANT. *Increase, augmentation, enlargement, increment, accretion, development, growth, aggrandizement, dilation, accession.*

Abbreviate. Shorten, contract, curtail, reduce, abridge, condense, epitomize, compress.

ANT. *Lengthen, extend, elongate, dilate, expand, amplify, enlarge, produce, stretch, prolong, expatiate.*

Abbreviation. Abridgment, contraction, condensation, compend, abstract, epitome, reduction, summary, curtailment, compression.

ANT. *Expansion, amplification, expatiation, extension, production, enlargement, dilation.*

Abdicate. Resign, relinquish *office (especially of the throne)*, surrender, abandon, vacate, forego, renounce, give up, cede.

ANT. *Retain, claim, occupy, maintain, usurp, seize, grasp.*

Abdomen. Belly, paunch, ventral region, visceral cavity.

Abduct. Take away (*surreptitiously or forcibly*), kidnap, run away with, carry off, spirit away, drag away.

ANT. *Restore, reinstate, adduct.*

Abduction. Withdrawal, drawing away, abstraction, kidnapping, seizure, appropriation.

ANT. *Adduction, replacement, restitution, restoration, surrender, reinstatement.*

Aberrant. Wandering, rambling, divergent, deviating, devious, erratic; irregular, abnormal, unusual, exceptional.

ANT. *Regular, true, consistent, uniform, consecutive, normal, natural, continuous.*

Aberration. Wandering, divergence, irregularity, rambling, disconnectedness, hallucination, illusion, delusion, eccentricity, singularity, peculiarity.

ANT. *Uniformity, consecutiveness, regularity, progression, continuity, order, type, norm.*

Abet. Aid, assist, promote, support, sanction, uphold, countenance, encourage, advocate, incite, instigate, embolden, favor, foment, connive at, coöperate with.

ANT. *Hinder, impede, obstruct, frustrate, baffle, confound, counteract, deter, discourage, thwart, contradict, disconcert, disapprove, denounce, dissuade, expose.*

Abettor. Assistant, helper, aid, ally, coöperator, advocate, confederate, accomplice, accessory, adviser, promoter, instigator, associate, coadjutor.

ANT. *Opponent, foe, adversary, antagonist, rival, dissuader, detector, baffler, disconcerter.*

Abeyance. Suspense, suspension, expectancy, waiting, anticipation, dormancy, intermission, quiescence, suppression, expectation.

ANT. *Renewal, revival, resuscitation, action, operation, exercise, force, possession.*

Abhor. Hate, detest, loathe, shrink from, recoil from, shudder at, abominate, despise, dislike, eschew, nauseate, revolt at.

ANT. *Crave, desire, enjoy, covet, esteem, like, love, relish, admire, approve, affect.*

Abhorrent. Odious, offensive, shocking, repugnant, loathsome, revolting, horrible, repellent, repulsive, nauseating.

ANT. *Admirable, enjoyable, lovely, estimable, desirable.*

Abide. Wait for, await, attend; endure, tolerate, bear, suffer; anticipate, watch for, expect; bide, continue, reside, dwell, sojourn, tarry, lodge, rest, stay, inhabit, remain.

ANT. *Abandon, shun; resist, reject, avoid; deport, migrate, move, journey, continue, proceed, progress.*

Abiding. Lasting, continuing, permanent, durable, constant, stable, immutable, changeless, unchanging.

ANT. *Ephemeral, fickle, changeable, unsubstantial, perishable.*

Ability. Power, force, might, efficiency, vigor, skill, energy, dexterity, adroitness, skilfulness, cleverness, ingenuity, talent, aptitude, facility, knack, expertness, readiness, quickness, strength, capacity, qualification, competency, genius, caliber, capability, capableness, faculty, gift, parts.

ANT. *Incapacity, weakness, inability, unreadiness, maladroitness, imbecility, impotence, disability, inaptitude, inefficiency, incompetence, disqualification, helplessness, stupidity, folly.*

Abject. Base, vile, mean, low, despicable, contemptible, worthless, groveling, fawning, beggarly, servile, cringing, miserable, degraded, menial, ignoble.

ANT. *Dignified, honorable, exalted, worthy, venerable, illustrious, independent, princely, self-assertive, self-reliant, vain, arrogant, insolent, haughty.*

Abjure. Renounce, relinquish, reject, forswear, forego, repudiate, disown, give up, retract, revoke, recant, disavow, disclaim, withdraw, take back, deny, apostatize, discard.

ANT. *Claim, advocate, acknowledge, profess, vindicate, assert, demand, retain, appropriate, avow.*

Able. Accomplished, adroit, talented, clever, ingenious, apt, skilful, efficient, capable, fitted, learned, gifted, masterly, telling, vigorous, strong, proficient, competent, versed, practical, endowed, powerful, mighty.

ANT. *Incapable, ineffective, unqualified, stupid, inept, weak, inefficient, unskilful, silly, incompetent.*

Ablution. Washing, bathing, cleansing, lavation, purification, baptism.

ANT. *Pollution, defilement, dirt, soilure, contamination, taint, stain, abomination, impurity.*

Abnegation. Denial, abjuration, renunciation, rejection, surrender, abandonment, disallowance, abstinence.

ANT. *Assertion, vindication, license, claim, indulgence, concession; affirmation, allegation, statement, declaration, word, averment, deposition; proposal, proffer.*

Abnormal. Singular, unnatural, unusual, irregular, peculiar, exceptional, aberrant, erratic, monstrous, preternatural.

ANT. *Normal, regular, usual, natural, typical, customary, ordinary, common.*

Aboard. On board, on the ship, afloat, inside, within.

ANT. *Ashore, aground.*

Abode. Home, house, place, residence, domicile, habitation, dwelling, lodging, quarters, seat.

ANT. *Halt, tent, bivouac, perch.*

Abolish. Abrogate, annul, destroy, repeal, revoke, suppress, terminate, rescind, cancel, nullify, suppress, overthrow, extirpate, remove, prohibit, set aside, end, stamp out.

ANT. *Establish, support, sustain, cherish, confirm, continue, restore, revive, reinstate, institute, promote, legalize.*

Abominable. Hateful, horrible, loathsome, abhorrent, foul, odious, offensive, detestable, impure, execrable.

ANT. *Desirable, admirable, enjoyable, pleasing, pure, delectable.*

Abomination. Offense, horror, shame, wickedness, abhorrence, aversion, disgust, curse, pollution, iniquity, defilement, corruption, nuisance, annoyance.

ANT. *Acquisition, enjoyment, gratification, blessing, desire, longing, delight, benefit, pleasure, satisfaction.*

Aboriginal. Primitive, primeval, primary, pristine, native, original, indigenous, autochthonous.

ANT. *Subsequent, imported, exotic, recent, modern, late, novel, fresh, immigrant, adventitious.*

Abortion. Failure, miscarriage, disappointment, non-success, vain effort, defect, frustration, blunder.

ANT. *Success, consummation, completion, realization, perfection, achievement, development, exploit, feat.*

Abound. Team, swarm, multiply, swell, increase, flow, luxuriate, flourish, prevail, wanton, revel, exuberate.

ANT. *Waste, lack, wane, vanish, lessen, decrease, die, decay, fall.*

About. Concerning, regarding, touching, relative to, with reference to, in regard to; near, surrounding, around; almost, nearly, well-nigh; ready, on the point of, on the eve of; around, hind part before.

ANT. *Afar, distant, remote; precisely, exactly.*

Above. Overhead, aloft, on high; before, previously; higher, having precedence; over, exceeding, beyond, superior, excessive.

ANT. *Below, beneath, within; later, subsequently; lower; less, diminished.*

Aboveboard. Openly, candidly, frankly, sincerely, fairly, ingenuously, unreservedly, guilelessly.

ANT. *Secretly, elusively, underhand, deceitfully, wilily.*

Above-named. Named before, aforesaid, above-mentioned,

above-cited, above-described, mentioned above.

Ant. *Named below, described below, hereinafter named.*

Abrasion. Rubbing, friction, wearing away *or* off, disintegration, attrition.

Ant. *Accretion, augmentation, increment; supplement, reinforcement.*

Abreast. Alongside, side by side, aligned; against, off, opposite to.

Ant. *Ahead, astern; behind.*

Abridge. Abbreviate, shorten, condense, diminish, reduce, contract, cut down, deprive of, divest of, epitomize, compress.

Ant. *Amplify, expand, spread out, extend, dilate.*

Abridgment. Summary, synopsis, compend, analysis, abstract, abbreviation, epitome, outline, compendium, digest.

Ant. *Amplification, expatiation, exposition, annotation, paraphrase, expansion, comment.*

Abroad. Far away, distant, apart, dispersed, aloof, adrift; distracted, confused, dazed, confounded; forth, out of doors.

Ant. *Near, close, collected, fast, housed; composed, poised, self-contained; within.*

Abrogate. Abolish, cancel, set aside, annul, make void, overrule, invalidate, nullify, repeal.

Ant. *Enact, confirm, enforce, establish, continue, revive.*

Abrogation. Repeal, rescinding, annulment, abolition, revocation, voidance, cancelation, setting aside; discontinuance, disestablishment.

Ant. *Enactment, institution, establishment; sanction, continuance, confirmation.*

Abrupt. Sudden, unexpected, hasty, ill-timed, precipitate; steep, precipitous, craggy, rough, rugged, jagged; short, blunt, curt, unceremonious; stiff, cramped, harsh, disconnected.

Ant. *Easy, gliding; polished, smooth, undulating; expected, courteous, elegant, complaisant, suave.*

Abscond. Depart, steal away, decamp, bolt, disappear, run off, hide, withdraw, retreat, escape, elope, slink *or* sneak off, absent one's self.

Ant. *Show, appear, emerge, issue, present one's self.*

Absence. Non-attendance, non-appearance, non-existence, absenteeism; inattention, abstraction, preoccupation, musing; want, lack, privation, defect, deficiency.

Ant. *Presence, existence, manifestation, evidence, supply; attention, consideration; immanence, inherency.*

Absent. Away, gone; abstracted, preoccupied, inattentive, dreaming.

Ant. *Present, here; attentive, alert.*

Absolute. Perfect, complete, supreme, autocratic, authoritative, commanding, independent, unrestricted, unqualified, unlimited, unconditioned, self-limited, self-existent, self-determined, ideal; despotic, arbitrary, exacting, domineering, tyrannical, imperious, dictatorial, irresponsible; positive, actual, real, veritable, genuine, certain, categorical, unquestionable.

Ant. *Related, responsible, conditioned, limited, qualified, restricted, accountable; ductile, humble, lenient, meek, mild, yielding, compliant, complaisant; dubious, contingent, de-*

fective, deficient, wanting, lacking, mutilated, incomplete.

Absolution. Acquittal, remission, release, deliverance, forgiveness, pardon, shriving, shrift; indulgence, justification.

ANT. *Charge, accusation, condemnation, censure, conviction; penance, purgation, fasting, flagellation.*

Absolve. Acquit, clear, exonerate, forgive, free, liberate, release, pardon, set free, discharge, exempt, exculpate.

ANT. *Accuse, condemn, convict, impeach, charge, compel; obligate, oblige, bind.*

Absorb. Take in, consume, imbibe, swallow, suck up, exhaust; engross, engage, immerse, occupy, arrest, rivet (*of attention*).

ANT. *Give up, disgorge, send out, radiate, throw off, eject; dissipate, distract, disperse.*

Absorption. Absorbing, imbibing, assimilation, destruction, consumption, exhaustion; engrossment, engagement, occupation, immersion.

ANT. *Ejection, rejection, expulsion, discharge; inadvertency, inattention, oversight, disregard.*

Abstain. Refrain, resist, forbear, desist, deny one's self, avoid, cease, stop, withhold, give up, relinquish.

ANT. *Indulge, wanton, revel, yield to, gratify.*

Abstemious. Abstinent, sober, moderate, temperate, sparing, frugal, self-denying, continent.

ANT. *Sensual, self-indulgent, intemperate, greedy.*

Absterge. Wipe off, purge, cleanse, purify, scrub, sponge, scour.

ANT. *Soil, pollute, begrime, contaminate, bespatter, bedaub.*

Abstersive. Cleansing, purging, purifying, scouring; detergent, cathartic.

ANT. *Corruptive, contaminative, offensive.*

Abstinence. Temperance, abstemiousness, self-control, self-restraint, self-denial, sobriety, fasting, continence, moderation, frugality.

ANT. *Excess, intoxication, self-indulgence, sensuality, wantonness, intemperance, greed, gluttony, revelry, dissipation.*

Abstinent. Abstaining, fasting; abstemious, sober, temperate, self-restraining, self-denying, continent, austere.

ANT. *Sensual, self-indulgent, intemperate, epicurean, dissipated, incontinent, debauched.*

Abstract, *n.* Epitome, summary, abridgment, compend, synopsis, syllabus, outline, digest, brief, compendium, gist, drift, contents.

ANT. *Amplification, disquisition, exposition, expansion, expatiation.*

Abstract, *v.* Appropriate, withdraw, remove, separate, take away, detach, purloin, part, eliminate, distract, discriminate, abridge.

ANT. *Add, complete, increase, restore, unite, conjoin, fill up, strengthen, combine.*

Abstracted. Separated, withdrawn, removed; subtle, refined, abstruse; inattentive, preoccupied, dreaming, absent-minded, oblivious, thoughtless, negligent, indifferent, heedless, absorbed, absent.

ANT. *Intelligible, lucid, transparent; attentive, intent, observant, alert, prompt, ready, thoughtful, wide-awake.*

Abstraction. Disconnection, disjunction, removal, isolation, separation; preoccupation, revery, inattention, absorption, absence; taking, abduction, seizure, stealing, appropriation, purloining; classification, generalization.

ANT. *Addition, conjunction, union, restitution, importation, restoration; enumeration, analysis; attention, specification, observation, individualization.*

Abstruse. Hidden, difficult, recondite, profound, deep, curious, occult, dark, obscure, mystical, hard, vague, indefinite, mysterious, abstract, transcendental.

ANT. *Patent, simple, obvious, trite, intelligible, manifest, lucid, clear, easy, plain, popular, superficial.*

Absurd. Ludicrous, monstrous, nonsensical, preposterous, senseless, ridiculous, foolish, irrational, wild, unreasonable.

ANT. *Sensible, rational, reasonable, logical, wise, sagacious, sound, substantial, philosophical, reflective, consistent, true.*

Absurdity. Unreasonableness, irrationality, foolishness, folly, fatuity, idiocy, extravagance, drivel.

ANT. *Reason, possibility; truism, axiom, maxim, adage.*

Abundance. Profusion, wealth, affluence; flow, flood, overflow; copiousness, fertility, richness, largeness, store, plenty, exuberance, plenteousness.

ANT. *Scarcity, deficiency, rarity, scantiness, dearth, failure, poverty.*

Abundant. Abounding, flowing, plentiful, liberal, bountiful, sufficient, lavish, plenteous, much, copious, replete, full, teeming.

ANT. *Rare, scarce, scant, deficient, insufficient, short, niggardly, sparing, impoverished, dry, drained.*

Abuse, *n.* Misuse, dishonor, maltreatment, outrage, reviling, obloquy, defamation, insult, disparagement, reproach, ill usage.

ANT. *Kindness, praise, deference, respect, honor, good treatment, good usage.*

Abuse, *v.* Harm, ill-treat, ill-use, injure, wrong, maltreat, oppress, molest, malign, impose on, ruin, victimize, slander, violate, ravish, defile, disparage, damage, defame, misuse.

ANT. *Cherish, protect, regard, shield, respect, care for, tend, benefit; laud, favor, applaud, extol, eulogize, praise; uphold, sustain, vindicate, conserve.*

Abusive. Insulting, rude, denunciatory, reproachful, injurious, offensive, reviling, insolent, scurrilous, opprobrious.

ANT. *Respectful, attentive, laudatory, kind, flattering, courteous, complimentary, obsequious.*

Abut. Be adjacent, extend, impinge, project, approximate, be contiguous, adjoin; end, border.

ANT. *Diverge, recede, return, retreat, recurve.*

Abutment. Terminal support, buttress.

Abuttal. Adjacency, contiguity, nearness, juxtaposition; boundary, terminus, limit, termination.

ANT. *Interval, separation, gap, chasm, interspace, fissure, breach.*

Abyss. Gulf, gorge, deep, chasm, profound, abysm; the pit.

ANT. *Surface, abutment, adhesion, contact, contiguity; heaven.*

Academical. Scholastic, learned, literary, collegiate, classical.

Ant. *Illiterate, ignorant, unschooled.*

Academy. School, seminary, institute, college, gymnasium, high school; scientific body, association of artists.

Accede. Consent, assent, acquiesce, comply, agree, accept, concur, approve, coincide.

Ant. *Decline, withdraw, refuse, demur, protest, dissent, reject.*

Accelerate. Hasten, quicken, speed, precipitate, despatch, expedite, hurry, urge, push forward, press on; forward, advance, further.

Ant. *Delay, impede, clog, hinder, retard, drag, obstruct.*

Accent, *n.* Stress, beat, emphasis, rhythm, pulsation, intonation, cadence, tone, modulation, ictus.

Ant. *Monotony, equableness, babble, flow, smoothness.*

Accentuate, Accent, *v.* Lay stress upon, put the ictus on; emphasize, mark, make prominent.

Ant. *Make light of, make insignificant, underestimate, ignore.*

Accept. Take, receive; admit, agree to, approve, acknowledge, avow; estimate, regard, value, construe.

Ant. *Refuse, decline, reject, ignore, disown, repudiate.*

Acceptable. Welcome, pleasing, grateful, gratifying, pleasant, agreeable, pleasurable, seasonable, desirable, expedient.

Ant. *Unpleasant, disagreeable, annoying, grievous, ungrateful, unwelcome.*

Acceptance. Reception, taking; acknowledgment, approbation, approval, satisfaction, gratification.

Ant. *Rejection, refusal, repudiation, exclusion.*

Acceptation. Meaning, significance, sense, import, interpretation, construction, understanding; approval, adoption, acceptance.

Access. Entrance, approach, passage, avenue, entry; admission, admittance, audience, interview; addition, increase, gain; accession; attack, onset, fit, paroxysm.

Ant. *Exit, egress, departure; exclusion; repulse, recoil; retirement, retreat; quiescence, inertia, languor, torpor.*

Accessary, *see* **Accessory.**

Accessible. Easy of access, approachable, affable, conversible.

Ant. *Distant, cold, unapproachable, difficult.*

Accession. Addition, increase, enlargement, extension, augmentation; arrival, influx; attainment (*of power*).

Ant. *Abandonment, decrease, ebb, drain, subsidence, departure, resignation, diminution.*

Accessory, *n.* Confederate, assistant, helper, associate, accomplice; detail, accompaniment, subordinate element; companion, partner.

Ant. *Foe, rival, adversary, antagonist, opponent, enemy; principal, instigator.*

Accessory, *a.* Assisting, aiding, abetting, helping, acceding, additional; supplemental, subservient, subsidiary, subordinate, conducive; accompanying, contributory, auxiliary.

Ant. *Essential, inherent; superfluous, irrelevant.*

Accident. Chance, disaster, happening, hazard, incident, misfortune, calamity, adventure, casualty, mishap, possibility.

Ant. *Certainty, provision, plan, intention, appointment,*

calculation, law, necessity, purpose, preparation.

Accidental. Casual, unintended, fortuitous, chance; incidental, immaterial, non-essential; occasional, contingent, adventitious.

ANT. *Intended, purposed, prepared, appointed, certain.*

Acclamation. Applause, cheer, outcry, homage, gratulation, salutation.

ANT. *Censure, execration, denunciation, obloquy, sibilation.*

Acclivity. Rise, incline, ascent, steep, hill, height.

ANT. *Decline, declivity, hollow, descent, depth.*

Accommodate. Oblige, serve, furnish, supply, contain, hold, convenience; adapt, reconcile, adjust, harmonize, suit, conform, arrange.

ANT. *Deprive, aggravate, inconvenience, disturb, disoblige; misfit, incommode.*

Accommodating. Kind, obliging, considerate, unselfish, polite, yielding, conciliatory.

ANT. *Rude, churlish, disobliging, inconsiderate, exacting.*

Accompany. Follow, attend, consort with, go with, escort, convoy.

ANT. *Abandon, leave, quit, avoid, discard, desert.*

Accomplice. Confederate, accessory, abettor, associate, ally, aid, assistant, promoter, coadjutor.

ANT. *Rival, enemy, foe, adversary.*

Accomplish. Complete, finish, achieve, effect, perform, carry out, attain, realize, consummate, execute, perfect, fulfil, do; equip, furnish.

ANT. *Fail, mar, spoil, frustrate, defeat, disconcert, destroy.*

Accomplished. Educated, experienced, practiced, finished, versed, consummate, adroit, expert, apt, skilful, talented, fine, qualified, proficient, polite, elegant; completed, effected, established.

ANT. *Unskilled, unfettered, ignorant, unpolished, uncouth, inefficient, incapable, inexpert, incompetent.*

Accomplishment. Execution, achievement, performance, completion; acquirement, attainment, proficiency, ornament, grace.

ANT. *Failure, blunder, folly, stupidity, incompetency, mismanagement, bungling.*

Accord. Agree, correspond, harmonize; grant, concede, give, yield, deign, vouchsafe, consent, answer.

ANT. *Differ, disagree; withhold, deny, refuse.*

Accordant. Agreeable, suitable, consonant, harmonious, congruous, agreeing, corresponding, conformable.

ANT. *Adverse, inconsistent, discordant.*

Accordingly. Suitably, conformably, agreeably; consequently, therefore, hence, wherefore.

ANT. *Conversely, inconsistently, impertinently.*

Accost. Approach, address, salute, greet, confront, speak to.

ANT. *Depart, rebuff, check, repulse, shun, elude, pass, ignore.*

Account, *n.* Record, register, inventory; bill, charge; count, calculation, enumeration; statement, description, narration, relation, narrative, recital, chronicle, history; explanation, exposition; consideration, regard, motive, reason; importance, worth, dignity, profit, advantage, benefit.

ANT. *Suppression, silence; attempt, project; misannouncement.*

Account, *v.* Esteem, regard, deem, judge, think, hold, believe, consider, view; estimate, reckon, rate; explain, solve.

ANT. *Underrate, undervalue; disesteem, misestimate; mystify, perplex, darken.*

Accountable. Responsible, punishable, answerable, liable, amenable; accredited, delegated.

ANT. *Independent, absolute, supreme, despotic, autocratic.*

Accouter. Equip, furnish, dress, fit out, arm, array.

ANT. *Despoil, impoverish, denude, strip, bare.*

Accredit. Credit, authorize, trust, empower, commission, depute.

ANT. *Recall, supersede, dismiss, discard; disbelieve, distrust, suspect.*

Accredited. Authorized, commissioned, sanctioned; confidential, trusted, believed.

ANT. *Unauthorized, distrusted, discredited.*

Accretion. Growth, accumulation, adhesion, coherence, increase.

ANT. *Abrasion, disintegration, diminution.*

Accrue. Result, arise, issue, ensue, follow, proceed, come, increase, augment.

ANT. *Cause, occasion; reduce, weaken, abate.*

Accumulate. Pile, collect, gather up, bring together; store, amass, garner, treasure, husband, lay by, hoard; aggregate.

ANT. *Separate, dissipate, disperse, scatter, waste, expend.*

Accumulation. Collection, heap, mass, accretion, hoard, store.

ANT. *Separation, segregation; unit, individual; prodigality, leakage, expenditure.*

Accuracy. Exactness, precision, nicety, truth, carefulness, correctness, exactitude, fidelity.

ANT. *Looseness, slovenliness, incorrectness, error, fallacy, misconception, misstatement.*

Accurate. Careful, exact, faithful, precise, truthful, correct, rigorous, close, severe, just, unerring.

ANT. *Inexact, faulty, inaccurate, defective, loose, careless.*

Accusation. Charge, indictment, arraignment, impeachment, imputation, crimination, censure.

ANT. *Discharge, acquittal, vindication, absolution, approval.*

Accuse. Charge, indict, arraign, incriminate, impeach, cite, summon, tax, censure, taunt, blame, reproach.

ANT. *Discharge, acquit, defend, vindicate, exonerate, pardon, absolve, condone, release.*

Accustom. Habituate, use, be wonted, harden, familiarize, train, addict, drill, break in, discipline.

ANT. *Estrange, wean, alienate, dishabituate.*

Acerbity. Sourness, acidity, tartness, bitterness, roughness, harshness, acrimony.

ANT. *Sweetness, mildness, softness, gentleness, smoothness.*

Ache, *n.* Pain, dull *or* continued pain, anguish, suffering, agony.

ANT. *Pleasure, relief, ease, refreshment, delight.*

Achieve. Accomplish, perform, complete, finish, realize, bring to pass, work out, conclude; obtain, acquire, gain, win, get.

ANT. *Neglect, undo, mar, omit; fail of, lose.*

Achievement. Accomplishment, performance, attainment, completion, consummation; exploit, deed, feat.

ANT. *Forfeit, failure, negligence, frustration, blunder.*

Acknowledge. Recognize, be aware of; admit, concede, allow, accept; confess, avow; express thanks for; own *or* profess.

ANT. *Disclaim, disown, deny, repudiate, ignore, disavow.*

Acme. Summit, zenith, climax, top, apex, vertex, pinnacle, culmination.

ANT. *Base, nadir, depth, ground, foundation, foot, root.*

Acquaintance. Association, familiarity; friend; intimacy, companionship, experience, knowledge, friendship, fellowship.

ANT. *Ignorance, inexperience, unfamiliarity, ignoring.*

Acquiesce. Assent, concur, yield, comply, submit, agree, consent.

ANT. *Object, demur, dissent.*

Acquire. Gain, earn, win, reap, obtain, attain, achieve, get, secure; master, learn thoroughly.

ANT. *Lose, surrender, miss, forego, forfeit.*

Acquit. Discharge, exonerate, release, absolve, excuse, pardon, exculpate.

ANT. *Charge, condemn, sentence, compel, indict, imprison.*

Acquittal. Discharge, release, deliverance, liberation, absolution.

ANT. *Judgment, punishment, penalty, trial, retribution, correction, castigation.*

Acrimony. Bitterness, sharpness, sourness, tartness, severity, asperity, hardness, rancor, ill-temper, spite, unkindness.

ANT. *Gentleness, good nature, kindness, sweetness, courtesy.*

Act, *n.* Deed, performance, exploit, accomplishment, achievement, effect, movement, transaction, work.

ANT. *Cessation, inertia, quiescence, inaction, rest, repose, quiet, deliberation.*

Act, *v.* Work, do, perform, execute; behave; play, feign, pretend, dissemble; operate, have effect; be, realize, actualize.

ANT. *Rest, cease, stop, stay; neglect, omit, mar, undo; expose, reveal, vaunt; be quiescent* or *latent; fancy; endure, suffer.*

Action. Exercise, motion, movement, deed, performance; agency, force, operation; battle, conflict; gesture; representation, play; subject, plot; lawsuit, case.

ANT. *Inertia, torpor, languor; quiescence, rest, passiveness; harmony, truce, peace.*

Active. Agile, brisk, alert, lively, quick, prompt, ready, spry; industrious, energetic, busy, diligent.

ANT. *Dull, idle, indolent, lazy, quiet, slow, stupid.*

Actual. Real, true, genuine, certain, absolute, positive, veritable, substantial; present, sensible, perceptible.

ANT. *Possible, fictitious, suppositious, virtual, theoretical, hypothetical, conjectural.*

Acumen. Discernment, penetration, keenness, shrewdness, insight, sharpness, **sagacity,** acuteness.

ANT. *Dulness, obtuseness, stupidity, bluntness.*

Acute. Sharp, pointed, keen, shrewd; violent, intense; high, sudden, severe, distressing; subtile, ingenious, sagacious, discerning.

ANT. *Dull, blunt, obtuse, stupid, heavy; chronic; stolid.*

Adaptation. Adjustment, fitness, conformity, suitableness, aptness, harmony.

ANT. *Incompatibility, incongruity, misfit, discord.*

Add. Sum up, increase, adjoin, append, attach, augment, enlarge, amplify, annex, affix.

ANT. *Deduct, subtract, lessen, reduce remove, diminish.*

Addicted. Habituated, disposed to, inclined, prone, attached to, devoted, given over to, wedded to.

ANT. *Averse, disinclined, unaccustomed, indisposed, divorced from.*

Addition. Accession, enlargement, increase, extension, accretion, augmentation, adjunct.

ANT. *Subtraction, decrease, diminution.*

Address, *n.* Courtesy, manners, politeness, tact, ingenuity, dexterity, discretion, adroitness; discourse, harangue, oration, lecture, speech, appeal, request, suit, solicitation.

ANT. *Clumsiness, rudeness, stupidity, unmannerliness, folly; refusal.*

Address, *v.* Accost, approach, court, greet, hail, salute, speak to.

ANT. *Avoid, elude, ignore, shun, cut, pass, overlook.*

Adduce. Offer, present, advance; cite, quote, introduce, name, mention; allege.

ANT. *Withdraw, except, deduct, suppress, retract.*

Adept. Expert, master, proficient, genius, veteran, professor.

ANT. *Novice, tyro, blunderer, inexpert.*

Adequate. Equal, competent, fitted, qualified, suitable, sufficient, capable, adapted, satisfactory; proportionate, commensurate.

ANT. *Inferior, poor, useless, worthless, unfit, incompetent.*

Adhere. Stick, cling, cohere, hold, cleave; belong, pertain; be attached, fixed, *or* devoted.

ANT. *Part, separate, sunder, sever, give way.*

Adherence. Tenacity, attachment, constancy, fidelity, devotion, partisanship; adhesion.

ANT. *Desertion, separation, disunion, unfaithfulness.*

Adjacent. Near, close, bordering, adjoining, contiguous, beside.

ANT. *Separate, distant, remote, detached, disconnected.*

Adjourn. Postpone, delay, defer; suspend, interrupt, close, end, dissolve.

ANT *Despatch, hasten, conclude, complete, terminate, consummate.*

Adjunct. Addition, appendage, accessory, aid, advantage, help; colleague, associate.

ANT. *Detriment, impediment, hindrance, obstruction, detraction.*

Adjure. Entreat, beseech, pray, supplicate, implore, beg; swear by.

ANT. *Defy, deprecate, remonstrate, dare, expostulate, warn.*

Adjustment. Arrangement, disposal; settlement, agreement, understanding; fitting, adaptation, conformity; regulation, rectification, accommodation.

ANT. *Disturbance, disorder,*

confusion; dissension, divergence; non-conformity.

Administer. Dispense, distribute, supply; direct, manage, control, superintend; offer, proffer, tender.
ANT. *Withhold, refuse, retain; betray, mismanage; repulse, rebuff.*

Admiration. Wonder, approval, love, surprise, astonishment, appreciation, reverence, high regard.
ANT. *Disapproval, contempt, dislike.*

Admire. Honor, esteem, approve, adore, wonder at, venerate, extol, marvel at, applaud, revere, respect.
ANT. *Despise, dislike, execrate, hate, abhor, scorn, detest.*

Admissible. Allowable, lawful, permissible, possible, probable.
ANT. *Absurd, preposterous, improper, wrong, unlawful.*

Admission. Admittance, entrance, access; avowal, acknowledgment, concession, concurrence, allowance.
ANT. *Denial, contradiction, rejection, negation.*

Admit. Receive; accept, acknowledge, own, confess; permit, allow, suffer.
ANT. *Exclude, debar; disown, deny; dismiss, reject, repudiate.*

Admonish. Advise, warn, caution, counsel, censure, rebuke, reprove; forewarn, remind, dissuade; instruct, teach, apprise, acquaint.
ANT. *Encourage, urge, countenance, applaud, abet, instigate.*

Admonition. Caution, warning, advice, counsel, instruction, reminder, hint, reproof, reprehension.
ANT. *Applause, encouragement, incitement, urging, instigation.*

Ado. Trouble, toil, labor, pains; bustle, stir, fuss, noise, turmoil.
ANT. *Quiet, calm, composure, tranquillity.*

Adopt. Appropriate, assume; approve, accept, support, maintain; affiliate, father.
ANT. *Reject, discard; renounce, abandon, disclaim; disown, repudiate.*

Adoration. Worship, devotion, homage, reverence, veneration, idolatry.
ANT. *Execration, disesteem, abomination, abhorrence, hatred, detestation.*

Adorn. Beautify, decorate, embellish, ornament, garnish, illustrate, gild, bedeck, grace, dignify, honor, exalt.
ANT. *Mar, spoil, deface, disfigure, deform, denude, strip.*

Adroit. Dexterous, expert, skilful, apt, handy, quick, clever, ready, deft, ingenious, cunning.
ANT. *Clumsy, unskilful, awkward, bungling, unhandy, maladroit.*

Adulation. Flattery, extravagant compliment, fulsome praise, fawning, sycophancy, blandishment, obsequiousness.
ANT. *Defamation, obloquy, ridicule, satire, sarcasm, detraction, aspersion, libel.*

Adumbrate. Shadow, outline, indicate, hint, trace, delineate; typify, represent, symbolize; darken, obscure, hide, conceal.
ANT. *Fulfil, realize, embody; misrepresent; reveal, illumine.*

Advance, *n.* Progress, improvement, growth; offer, proposal, overture, tender, proposition; rise, appreciation.

ANT. *Regress, return, retrogression; diminution; depreciation.*

Advance, *v.* Push *or* send forward, propel; promote, elevate, dignify, exalt; improve, strengthen, benefit; propose, offer; furnish, lend, loan; increase, augment, raise; proceed, progress; thrive, prosper; accelerate.

ANT. *Retard, hinder, withhold, withdraw; suppress, degrade, depress; oppose, recall, weaken, retreat; lessen, diminish.*

Advantage. Benefit, profit, expediency, favorable opportunity, blessing; behalf, account, interest; privilege, convenience, assistance, utility, service.

ANT. *Loss, disappointment, frustration, difficulty, dilemma.*

Advent. Approach, coming, arrival, accession.

ANT. *Departure, exit, exodus, retirement.*

Adventitious. Accidental, incidental, extrinsic, non-essential, foreign, casual; redundant, superfluous.

ANT. *Intrinsic, pertinent, regular, proper, necessary, appropriate.*

Adventure. Chance, hazard, risk, venture, experiment, trial; event, incident, occurrence, contingency, crisis.

ANT. *Matter-of-fact, matter-of-course; prospect; monotony, routine.*

Adventurous. Bold, daring, venturesome, rash, reckless, headlong; dangerous, perilous, uncertain; fearless, enterprising.

ANT. *Timid, nervous, hesitating, cautious, cowardly.*

Adversary. Foe, enemy, antagonist, opponent, rival, assailant.

ANT. *Ally, helper, assistant, accomplice, aider, abettor, accessory.*

Adverse. Opposite, contrary, conflicting; hostile, injurious, harmful; unlucky, unfortunate, disastrous.

ANT. *Favorable, friendly, propitious, fortunate, lucky.*

Adversity. Calamity, affliction, trouble, disaster, woe, distress, suffering.

ANT. *Success, prosperity, advancement, good luck.*

Advert to. Consider, notice, remark, heed, attend, refer, allude, mention, touch upon; regard.

ANT. *Ignore, pass, drop, overlook, omit.*

Advertent. Mindful, regardful, attentive, watchful, observant, thoughtful, considerate, heedful.

ANT. *Thoughtless, heedless, inconsiderate, inattentive.*

Advertise. Announce, publish, proclaim, declare, circulate, noise abroad; offer for sale; inform, notify, apprise; promulgate.

ANT. *Suppress, ignore, hush, conceal; mislead, misinform.*

Advice. Counsel, suggestion, admonition, instruction, caution; tidings, intelligence, notice; deliberation, care, forethought; recommendation, exhortation, information.

ANT. *Remonstrance, restraint, expostulation, prohibition; deception, delusion.*

Advisable. Judicious, expedient, politic, prudent, desirable, beneficial, profitable; proper, fitting.

ANT. *Imprudent, undesirable, inexpedient, improper, detrimental.*

Advocate. Counsel, lawyer, attorney; defender, promoter, friend, patron, supporter, pleader, maintainer.

ANT. *Accuser, impugner, gainsayer, adversary, opponent.*

Affable. Open, free, frank, unreserved; accessible, familiar; cordial, social, courteous, polite, obliging, urbane, benign, gracious, mild, well-bred; condescending.

ANT. *Distant, unapproachable, inaccessible, haughty, contemptuous, supercilious.*

Affair. Business, concern, function, matter, circumstance, question, subject; event, incident, occurrence, performance; battle, combat, engagement, skirmish, collision, brush, encounter.

ANT. *Detail, item, feature, point.*

Affect. Influence, change, transform, modify, alter; concern, interest, touch, move, impress; crave, yearn, desire, like; assume, adopt, feign, pretend; operate, act on; melt, soften, subdue, overcome.

ANT. *Shun, repel, repudiate, spurn, dislike, eschew.*

Affectation. Airs, mannerism, pretension, pretense, foppery, display.

ANT. *Simplicity, artlessness, naturalness, genuineness.*

Affection. Feeling, passion, attachment, fondness, tenderness, love; propensity, disposition; endearment, devotion, partiality; attribute, quality, characteristic, mark.

ANT. *Indifference, repulsion, disaffection, repugnance.*

Affiance. Trust, confidence, homage, reliance, betrothal, fealty, faith, plighting.

ANT. *Disloyalty, distrust, treason, suspicion, infidelity.*

Affiliate. Associate, adopt, join, connect, incorporate, annex.

ANT. *Sever, transplant, separate, disjoin, dissociate.*

Affinity. Relationship, kin, consanguinity, propinquity; likeness, resemblance, relation, analogy, connection, correspondence; sympathy, attraction.

ANT. *Repugnance, discordance, antipathy, antagonism.*

Affirm. Assert, swear, state, declare, maintain, allege, protest, confirm, ratify, approve, endorse, aver, asseverate, assure, avouch, establish.

ANT. *Deny, doubt, demur, contradict, negative, gainsay, impugn, oppose, dispute.*

Affirmation. Avowal, declaration, statement, assertion, testimony, deposition, confirmation, ratification, approval, endorsement.

ANT. *Doubt, denial, contradiction, disputation, disapproval.*

Affix. Join, annex, attach, fasten, connect to, unite to, append.

ANT. *Remove, detach, separate, unfasten.*

Affliction. Adversity, misfortune, grief, sorrow, distress, tribulation, disaster, trial, misery, calamity, pain, anguish, trouble, hardship.

ANT. *Consolation, relief, blessing, gratification, pleasure.*

Affluence. Wealth, fortune, riches, opulence, abundance, plenty, profusion.

ANT. *Want, scarcity, poverty, penury, lack, indigence.*

Afford. Supply, furnish, contribute, bestow, offer, confer, bear, endure, support, yield, impart, administer.

ANT. *Withhold, deny, retain, stint, grudge, withdraw.*

Affray. Quarrel, tussle, scuffle, scrimmage, collision, brawl, disturbance, fight, rumpus, struggle, contest, strife, encounter, feud, tumult.

ANT. *Peace, amity, friendship, good will.*

Affront. Outrage, insult, abuse, annoyance, displeasure, offense, provocation, wrong, vexation, wound, exasperation, irritation.

ANT. *Courtesy, homage, amends, compliment, apology.*

Afire. Ablaze, burning, ignited, aflame.

ANT. *Out, quenched, extinguished.*

Afloat. Adrift, at sea, abroad, loose; happening, betiding, brewing.

ANT. *Moored, anchored, aground, stranded, fixed, steadfast, firm.*

Afoot. Afloat, preparing, forthcoming, ready, brewing, on hand, astir.

ANT. *Unprepared, unprovided for, inactive, sluggish, latent.*

Aforesaid. Above-mentioned, foregoing, preceding, above-named.

ANT. *Following, subsequent, subjoined, forthcoming, after-cited.*

Afraid. Fearful, timid, apprehensive, anxious, alarmed, terrified, frightened.

ANT. *Fearless, bold, confident, reckless, venturesome, indifferent, secure, hopeful, audacious.*

Afresh. Anew, again, newly, frequently, repeatedly, once more.

ANT. *Uniformly, connectedly, continuously.*

After. Subsequent, later; following, behind, rear, back, posterior; concerning, about, for, in relation to; in imitation of, in the pattern of.

ANT. *Before, preceding, introducing; in front of; opposite; facing; previous* or *prior to, afore; in advance; previously, already.*

Again. Anew, afresh, repeatedly; further, moreover, besides; on the contrary; back, in answer *or* restitution, in return; once more.

ANT. *Once, continuously, uninterruptedly, uniformly.*

Against. Opposite, across, adverse to, counter to, athwart; facing, fronting, close up to, in contact with; for, in preparation for, in expectation of; in compensation for, in requital of, to match.

ANT. *With, for, beside, accompanying, aiding, promoting.*

Agape. Yawning, open-mouthed; wondering, gazing, dazed, amazed; curious, inquisitive, agog, astare, eager.

ANT. *Listless, lukewarm, incurious, indifferent.*

Age. Duration; period, date, epoch, time; maturity, generation; era, century.

ANT. *Infancy, youth, boyhood, childhood; moment, instant.*

Agent. Actor, doer, operator, promoter, performer; cause, force, power; deputy, factor, attorney, representative, substitute; means, instrument.

ANT. *Counteragent, counteractor, opponent, neutralizer; chief, principal; originator, inventor.*

Agglomeration. Accumulation, heap, pile, mass, conglomeration, cluster.

ANT. *Dispersion, division, separation, sifting, dissipation.*

Aggrandize. Exalt, honor, elevate, dignify, promote, advance, enrich, augment.

ANT. *Degrade, impoverish, debase, humiliate, dishonor, lower.*

Aggravate. Exasperate, provoke, wound, make worse, intensify, embitter, heighten.

ANT. *Soothe, assuage, palliate, diminish, conciliate, alleviate.*

Aggregation. Collection, accumulation, mass, heap, pile, amount, total, sum, result, whole, agglomeration.

ANT. *Dispersion, dissipation, separation, division; unit; element, individual, ingredient, item.*

Aggression. Attack, invasion, encroachment, assault, injury, offense, onslaught, provocation, intrusion.

ANT. *Retaliation, repulsion, retreat, resistance, evacuation.*

Aghast. Dismayed, horrified, terrified, frightened; amazed, astounded, startled, astonished, dumfounded.

ANT. *Cool, fearless, indifferent, unmoved, unaffected, unexcited.*

Agile. Nimble, active, lively, smart, prompt, alert, supple, brisk, quick, ready, sprightly, spry.

ANT. *Slow, heavy, clumsy, bulky, awkward, inert, ponderous.*

Agitate. Disturb, trouble, shake, jar, convulse; excite, rouse, ferment; fluster, hurry, disconcert; discuss, controvert, debate, examine, ventilate, investigate; deliberate, contrive, devise, plan.

ANT. *Calm, allay, pacify, smooth, compose, quiet; solve, determine, settle.*

Ago. Past, gone, since.

ANT. *Future, coming, hereafter, hence.*

Agony. Anguish, torture, torment, distress, throe, pangs, pain, suffering, woe, excruciation.

ANT. *Assuagement, comfort, relief, composure, ease, enjoyment.*

Agree. Accept, assent, approve, comply, consent, concur, admit, accede.

ANT. *Contend, disagree, deny; dissent, dispute, protest, oppose, demur, differ; decline.*

Agreeable. Suitable, proper, appropriate, befitting, accordant, conformable, consonant, welcome, amiable, pleasing, gratifying.

ANT. *Unpleasant, disobliging, obnoxious, disagreeable, unwelcome, offensive, inharmonious, unaccommodating.*

Agreement. Contract, compact, bond, bargain, covenant, harmony, unison, obligation, undertaking, treaty.

ANT. *Promise, understanding, parole; discord, dissension.*

Agriculture. Farming, husbandry, cultivation of the soil, tillage.

ANT. *Fallowness, sterility, unproductiveness, waste.*

Aground. Ashore, stranded, not afloat; exhausted in resources.

ANT. *Afloat, loose, abroad, adrift; flush.*

Ahead. In front, forward, onward, in advance.

ANT. *Abaft, astern, back, behind, aft.*

Aid. Help, support, assist, serve, befriend, minister to, relieve, succor; supply, give alms to; foster, protect, encourage, favor.

ANT. *Oppose, discourage, thwart, baffle, deter, confront.*

Ailing. Sick, ill, indisposed, unwell, feeble, infirm, weakly, delicate, unhealthy, pining.

ANT. *Well, healthy, energetic, strong, vigorous.*

Ailment. Disease, malady, indisposition, distemper, complaint.

ANT. *Health, sanity, convalescence, vigor, recovery.*

Aim. Direction, course, tendency, bent, proclivity, bearing; intention, purpose, design, scheme; reason; view, scope, drift, mark, goal, point; endeavor, attempt, aspiration, determination.

ANT. *Deviation, divergence, deflection, digression, aberration; tangent; venture, leap, fluke, chance, hazard, speculation; neglect, avoidance, carelessness, oversight.*

Air. Atmosphere, gas; breeze, vapor, zephyr, wind; weather; appearance, aspect, manner, sort, style, way, behavior, carriage, bearing, expression, look, demeanor, mien, fashion; tune.

Airy. Aërial, thin, rare, ethereal; light, subtle, sublimated; sprightly, buoyant, vivacious, volatile, jolly, jovial, lighthearted; graceful, lithe, pliant, flexible, showy, jaunty, flaunting, garish; windy, empty.

ANT. *Thick, ponderous, heavy, inert, clumsy, dull, sluggish, wooden, slow, cheerless, sullen, doleful, leaden, lugubrious.*

Akin. Related, allied, homogeneous, cognate, similar, congenial, sympathetic.

ANT. *Foreign, alien, hostile, heterogeneous, dissimilar.*

Alacrity. Readiness, briskness, activity, quickness, willingness, promptness, compliance, cheerfulness, eagerness, gaiety, agility.

ANT. *Slowness, reluctance, repugnance, aversion, refusal, shrinking, recoil, disinclination.*

Alarm. Summons, tocsin, distress signal, war-cry; fear, terror, apprehension, consternation, dismay, dread, affright.

ANT. *Lullaby; confidence, quiet, composure, assurance, courage.*

Alert. Lively, prompt, ready, prepared, vigilant, wide-awake, bustling, active, brisk, nimble, watchful, sprightly, agile.

ANT. *Slow, lazy, absent, oblivious, sluggish, dilatory, drowsy.*

Alien, *n.* Foreigner, stranger.

ANT. *Citizen, countryman, native, naturalized person.*

Alien, *a.* Strange, foreign, hostile, remote, distant, contrasted, contrary, unlike, unconnected.

ANT. *Pertinent, essential; domesticated, naturalized; germane, akin, appropriate.*

Alienation. Estrangement, transfer, conveyance, disaffection, variance, rupture, breach; (*relating to the mind*) insanity, aberration, delusion, lunacy, delirium, mania, imbecility.

ANT. *Confederacy, coalition, alliance, league, union; sanity, soundness, sobriety, rationality.*

Alight. Perch, settle, drop, lodge; dismount, descend.

ANT. *Soar, spring, ascend, start, mount.*

Alike. Similar, kindred, same, resembling, equivalent, homogeneous, identical, analogous, uniform, akin, allied.

ANT. *Different, unequal, dissimilar, unlike, heterogeneous, distinct, various.*

Aliment. Food, nourishment, subsistence, fare, diet, regimen, nutriment, viands, meat, sustenance.

ANT. *Poison, bane; starva-*

tion, exhaustion; venom, scourge.

Alive. Living, quick, subsisting, animate, alert, active, breathing; sensitive, susceptible; operative; cheerful, joyous; brisk.

ANT. *Dead, defunct, lifeless, deceased; inanimate, dull; departed, cold; dispirited.*

All, *n.* Whole, totality.

ANT. *Part, piece, share, portion.*

All, *a.* Whole, entire, complete, total; each, every.

ANT. *Some, part.*

Allay. Repress, restrain, check, subdue, silence, still, hush, soothe, compose, calm, appease, lull, alleviate, mitigate, solace, abate, relieve, palliate.

ANT. *Aggravate, arouse, excite, stir, kindle, fan, provoke.*

Allege. Declare, affirm, claim, maintain, state, asseverate; advance, aver, introduce; profess, cite.

ANT. *Contradict, gainsay, refute, deny, disprove, quash.*

Allegiance. Fealty, loyalty, devotion, homage, faithfulness, obedience.

ANT. *Treason, rebellion, sedition, disloyalty, disaffection.*

Allegory. Parable, fable, myth, story, tale, apologue, metaphor, illustration, simile.

ANT. *History, fact, narrative, chronicle, record.*

Alleviate. Abate, mitigate, reduce, relieve, lessen, assuage, remove, soften, moderate, lighten.

ANT. *Augment, increase, heighten, intensify, magnify, aggravate, enhance, embitter.*

Alliance. Connection, relationship, affinity; confederacy, league, union, treaty, copartnership, coalition; affiliation, similarity.

ANT. *Separation, estrangement, divorce; antagonism, disruption, enmity, hostility, schism, secession.*

Allot. Divide, apportion, distribute, deal out, dispense; assign, grant, give, appoint, destine.

ANT. *Refuse, retain, misdeal, deny, confiscate, appropriate, seize, withhold.*

Allow. Grant, own, confess, admit; permit, let, authorize; suffer, tolerate, endure; yield, give, grant; approve, sanction, abate, remit.

ANT. *Protest, refuse, deny, disapprove, forbid, disallow, reject, withstand, resist.*

Allowance. Leave, permission, sanction, approval; admission, acknowledgment, assent; commission; qualification, exception; ration.

ANT. *Refusal, disapproval, denial; ratification, confirmation.*

Alloy, *n.* Admixture, adulteration, deterioration, debasement, disparagement, drawback.

ANT. *Genuineness, enhancement, purity, integrity.*

Allude. Intimate, insinuate, point, refer, suggest, signify, hint, imply, indicate, mention.

ANT. *Demonstrate, specify, declare.*

Allure. Decoy, entice, coax, attract, tempt, inveigle, seduce.

ANT. *Dissuade, repel, warn, chill, damp, drive away, deter, alarm, terrify.*

Allusion. Hint, suggestion, intimation, reference, implication, innuendo.

ANT. *Mention, demonstration, specification.*

Ally, *n.* Assistant, helper, aider, friend, associate, colleague, partner, accessory, accomplice.

ANT. *Opponent, adversary, foe, enemy, antagonist.*

Aloft. Above, skyward, heavenward, overhead, in the air.

ANT. *Beneath, earthward, below.*

Alone. Solitary, sole, single, isolated.

ANT. *Accompanied, associated.*

Along. Lengthwise, onward, forward; together, beside, simultaneously.

ANT. *Across, sidewise* or *sideways, lateral; apart, tandem.*

Aloof. Apart, distant, away, off.

ANT. *Close, near, together, unitedly.*

Aloud. Distinctly, audibly, vociferously, clamorously, sonorously.

ANT. *Softly, silently, inaudibly.*

Also. As well, likewise, too, similarly, withal, besides, in addition, in like manner.

ANT. *Nevertheless, notwithstanding, on the contrary, but, yet, in spite of, on the other hand.*

Alter. Change, turn, vary, modify, shift, substitute, remodel, transform, convert.

ANT. *Conserve, perpetuate, preserve, arrest, solidify, retain.*

Alteration. Change, variation, modification, shifting, mutation.

ANT. *Changelessness, identity, fixity, permanence.*

Altercation. Dispute, contention, controversy, difference, quarrel, wrangle, dissension.

ANT. *Concord, agreement, compromise, reconciliation, unanimity, harmony, consonance.*

Alternate. Reciprocal, every other one, one after another, in turn, interchangeable, mutual.

ANT. *Continuous, successive, consequent, proximate, sequent.*

Alternative. Choice, option, preference, election, pick, resource.

ANT. *Compulsion, quandary, necessity; fixity, changelessness.*

Although. Albeit, even if, supposing, grant that.

ANT. *Yet, notwithstanding.*

Altitude. Height, elevation, loftiness, ascent, eminence.

ANT. *Depth, declivity, descent, abasement.*

Altogether. Collectively, conjointly, wholly, quite, completely, totally, utterly, entirely, thoroughly, fully, in the mass.

ANT. *Partially, piecemeal, by instalments, partly, incompletely, by halves, wanting; individually, separately.*

Altruism. Philanthropy, unselfishness, public spirit, devotion to others, self-sacrifice, self-forgetfulness, generosity.

ANT. *Selfishness, self-indulgence, worldliness, meanness; egoism.*

Always. Ever, forever, eternally, for aye, evermore, everlastingly, perpetually; uniformly, invariably, generally, habitually.

ANT. *Now, momently, instantly, suddenly; sometimes, occasionally.*

Amalgamate. Mix, commingle, unite, combine, blend, compound, incorporate, join, fuse, consolidate.

ANT. *Disintegrate, decompose, disperse, separate, dissipate, analyze.*

Amaranthine. Of the amaranth; fadeless, imperishable, undying, immortal, perennial; purplish, amethystine.

ANT. *Ephemeral, perishable, mortal, fading.*

Amass. Accumulate, heap up, collect, gather, hoard, store up.

ANT. *Disperse, divide, scatter, spend, squander, waste, dissipate; portion, distribute, parcel.*

Amateur. Lover, votary, devotee; beginner, neophyte, novice, tyro, dilettante.

Amazement. Astonishment, bewilderment, wonder, marvel, stupefaction, confusion, perplexity, awe.

ANT. *Anticipation, calmness, coolness, familiarity, preparation, stoicism, self-possession, steadiness, composure.*

Amazing. Astonishing, astounding, wonderful, surprising, marvelous, prodigious, strange, miraculous, stupendous, extraordinary.

ANT. *Common, familiar, trivial, commonplace, frequent, hackneyed, usual, customary.*

Ambagious. Winding, devious, sinuous; tortuous, indirect, evasive, circuitous; diffuse, dull, tedious; dubious, enigmatical, vague.

ANT. *Direct, straight, frank, open, simple, straightforward, plain, clear, lucid, unmistakable.*

Ambassador. Minister, envoy, legate, deputy, plenipotentiary.

Ambient. Surrounding, encompassing, enfolding, circling, investing.

ANT. *Penetrating, infiltrating, permeating, intervening.*

Ambiguous. Doubtful, dubious, uncertain, indefinite, vague, obscure, indistinct, equivocal, enigmatical.

ANT. *Obvious, plain, clear, lucid, unmistakable.*

Ambition. Emulation, rivalry, aspiration, competition, opposition.

ANT. *Contentment, moderation, indifference, satisfaction.*

Amelioration. Amendment, improvement, promotion, bettering, elevation.

ANT. *Degeneration, deterioration, injury, detriment.*

Amenable. Liable, responsible, answerable, accountable; open, impressible, pliant, docile.

ANT. *Obstinate, irresponsible, independent, autocratic.*

Amend. Improve, mend, repair, ameliorate, reform, correct, rectify.

ANT. *Harm, corrupt, spoil, debase, aggravate.*

Amends. Compensation, atonement, expiation, recompense, indemnity.

ANT. *Insult, injury, fault, offense.*

Amenity. Softness, mildness, suavity, gentleness, refinement, amiability.

ANT. *Austerity, ungraciousness, discourtesy, moroseness.*

Amiable. Agreeable, gentle, good-natured, pleasing, winsome, attractive, charming, lovable.

ANT. *Crusty, hateful, sullen, surly, crabbed, cruel, unlovely, gruff, disagreeable, ill-tempered.*

Amicable. Cordial, kind, friendly, harmonious, peaceable, propitious, favorable, sociable, amiable.

ANT. *Unkind, cold, distant, hostile, adverse, unfriendly.*

Amid. Among, between, in the midst of, betwixt, surrounded by.

ANT. *Outside, without, beyond, afar from, away from.*

Amiss. Wrong, improper, faulty, incorrect, inaccurate, inopportune.

ANT. *Correct, right, faultless, perfect, effective, true.*

Amount, *n.* Sum, total, aggregate, whole; effect, substance, purport.

ANT. *Portion, instalment, part; failure, deficiency.*

Ample. Liberal, large, spacious, plentiful, copious, lavish, exuberant, bountiful, generous.

ANT. *Niggardly, stingy, scant, mean, narrow, insufficient.*

Amplify. Augment, enlarge, expand, expatiate, increase, develop, widen, dilate, extend.

ANT. *Abbreviate, condense, reduce, abridge, amputate, epitomize, summarize.*

Amusement. Diversion, sport, play, fun, entertainment, merriment, pastime, game, frolic, relaxation.

ANT. *Weariness, disgust, satiety, tedium, monotony, strenuosity.*

Analogy. Likeness, relation, resemblance, similitude, comparison.

ANT. *Unlikeness, incongruity, disproportion, disagreement.*

Analysis. Separation, dissection, investigation, partition.

ANT. *Synthesis, composition, aggregation, combination, coherence.*

Anarchy. Misrule, disorder, lawlessness, violence, confusion.

ANT. *Law, order, government, control, organization, subjection.*

Anatomy. Analysis, dissection; skeleton; dismemberment.

ANT. *Synthesis, organization, union, construction; body.*

Ancient. Old, antique, antiquated, obsolete, primeval, aged.

ANT. *Modern, young, fresh, new, juvenile, upstart.*

Ancillary. Auxiliary, helping, instrumental; subsidiary, subordinate, subservient.

ANT. *Alien, adverse, redundant, obstructive, impertinent, irrelative, counteractive.*

Angelic. Seraphic, celestial, pure, ethereal, adorable, rapturous, heavenly, divine, spiritual.

ANT. *Demoniac, demoniacal, diabolical, hellish, fiendish, foul.*

Anger. Fury, ire, offense, passion, choler, indignation, rage, temper, vexation, displeasure, animosity, wrath, resentment.

ANT. *Patience, self-control, self-restraint, forbearance, leniency, mildness, forgiveness, giveness, charity, love.*

Angry. Provoked, indignant, exasperated, irritated, wrathful, furious, resentful, mad, passionate, sulky, piqued, galled.

ANT. *Calm, unresentful, peaceful, self-controlled, good-tempered, forgiving, lenient.*

Anguish. Agony, torture, torment, pang, acute distress, extreme suffering.

ANT. *Ease, pleasure, relief, solace, assuagement, ecstasy.*

Animal. Brute, beast, living organism, sentient being; fauna.

ANT. *Man; vegetable; angel; inanimate object, substance; soul, spirit.*

Animate. Enliven, vivify, quicken, invigorate, revive, stimulate, waken, rouse, excite, provoke, encourage, inspire, elate.

ANT. *Deaden, discourage, deter, depress, dishearten, stifle.*

Animation. Life, vitality, spirit, vivacity, energy, exhilaration, sprightliness, courage, force, buoyancy, vigor, liveliness.

ANT. *Dulness, deadness,*

spiritlessness, inertness, stolidity.

Animosity. Hatred, enmity, malignity, antipathy, aversion, acrimony, strife, bitterness, hostility, dissension, malice, anger.

ANT. *Congeniality, unanimity, friendship, companionship, harmony, concord, regard, alliance, kindness, sympathy.*

Annals. Chronicles, records, registers, rolls, archives.

ANT. *Romance, tradition, hearsay, legend, lays.*

Annex. Add, affix, attach, adjoin, append, subjoin, tag, join, unite, connect.

ANT. *Detach, disconnect, withdraw, separate, remove, disengage.*

Annihilation. Extermination, obliteration, eradication, destruction; non-existence; oblivion, non-being, eternal blank; Nirvâna.

ANT. *Perpetuation, immortality; genesis, evolution, development.*

Annotation. Note, comment, remark, observation, gloss, scholium, explanation, illustration, elucidation.

ANT. *Narrative, text, assertion, proposition, statement.*

Announce. Proclaim, publish, report, herald, make known, state, reveal, tell, declare, communicate, promulgate, circulate, enunciate.

ANT. *Suppress, secrete, hide, cover up, conceal, bury, withhold.*

Announcement. Notice, proclamation, declaration, advertisement, notification, manifesto, promulgation.

ANT. *Suppression, concealment, secrecy, equivocation, ambiguity, insinuation.*

Annoyance. Trouble, discomfort, vexation, torment, infliction, nuisance, irritation.

ANT. *Gratification, delight, ease, pleasure, relief.*

Annual, *n.* Yearly publication, year-book, annals; plant living but a year.

ANT. *Perennial, biennial, triennial; exotic.*

Annul. Cancel, abrogate, recall, repeal, revoke, countermand, reverse, rescind, abolish, nullify, supersede, invalidate.

ANT. *Conserve, confirm, maintain, enact, establish.*

Anomalous. Abnormal, unnatural, irregular, peculiar, exceptional, aberrant, unusual, singular, eccentric, erratic.

ANT. *Normal, regular, usual, ordinary, common, wonted.*

Anon. Soon, shortly, forthwith, immediately, instantly, directly, ere long; afterward, presently, again.

ANT. *Herewith, now; already, previously.*

Anonymous. Nameless, unacknowledged, of unknown authorship.

ANT. *Identified, authorized, authenticated, attested, signed.*

Answer, *v.* Reply, rejoin, respond; be accountable, responsible, *or* liable, go surety; correspond, be similar; do, serve, suit, pass; refute, defend; satisfy, fulfil.

ANT. *Challenge, defy, question, interrogate, query, summon.*

Answerable. Refutable, responsible, amenable, liable, accountable; corresponding, correlative, suitable, proportionate.

ANT. *Independent, irresponsible, irrefutable; unsuitable, dissimilar, different.*

Antagonism. Opposition, contradiction, hostility, animosity, enmity.

ANT. *Amity, alliance, association.*

Antecedent, *a.* Preceding, previous, prior, foregoing, anterior, precursory.

ANT. *Subsequent, posterior, sequent, following.*

Antedate. Date before the true time; anticipate, forestall, foretaste.

ANT. *Postdate, follow, succeed, supervene.*

Anticipate. Forestall, expect, foretaste, antedate, forecast, apprehend, hope for, look forward to.

ANT. *Postdate, follow; reflect upon, recall, recollect, remember; despair of, doubt, dread, fear.*

Anticipation. Expectation, prospect, hope, trust, contemplation, abeyance, foreboding, apprehension, presentiment; prescience, prevision, forethought.

ANT. *Realization, consummation, despair, enjoyment, surprise, doubt, dread, wonder, fear.*

Antipathy. Repugnance, repulsion, aversion, detestation, abhorrence, hatred, hostility, loathing.

ANT. *Attraction, affinity, congeniality, sympathy, harmony.*

Antiquated. Quaint, obsolete, bygone, ancient, archaic, old-fashioned.

ANT. *Modern, modish, new, recent, stylish, fashionable, fresh.*

Antiquity. Ancient times, eld, early days; ancients, people of early days; great age; (*pl.*) relics of ancient days, archeology.

ANT. *Modernity; futurity, eventuality, posterity; the present, to-day.*

Anxiety. Perplexity, apprehension, care, concern, solicitude, worry, dread, trouble, foreboding, misgiving, eagerness, diffidence.

ANT. *Ease, confidence, contentment, apathy, acquiescence, calmness, nonchalance, assurance.*

Apathy. Stoicism, calmness, composure, lethargy, unconcern, indifference, insensibility, immobility, quietude, phlegm, stillness.

ANT. *Fury, frenzy, susceptibility, sensitiveness, anxiety, excitement, agitation, feeling, passion, vehemence, emotion.*

Ape, *v.* Mimic, imitate, counterfeit, copy, affect, personate, represent.

ANT. *Vary, modify, change.*

Aperture. Opening, hole, gap, rift, chasm, loophole, orifice, cleft.

ANT. *Closure, blank wall; seclusion, imperviousness.*

Apex. Acme, vertex, pinnacle, summit.

ANT. *Base, nadir, foot, root.*

Aphorism. Adage, maxim, proverb, saying, dictum, apothegm, saw.

ANT. *Lecture, disquisition, discourse, sermon.*

Apiece. Each, individually, severally, distributively, separately.

ANT. *Together, collectively, synthetically, in the aggregate.*

Apocalyptic. In *or* from "The Revelation of St. John the Divine"; prophetic, mystical, mysterious; manifesting, revealing, unveiling.

ANT. *Concealing, obscuring, shrouding, eclipsing.*

Apocryphal. Unauthentic, uncanonical, legendary, fictitious, false, equivocal, doubtful, spurious.

Ant. *Palpable, authorized, accepted, authentic, genuine, current, verified, attested.*

Apology. Plea, excuse, defense, confession, acknowledgment, justification, vindication, explanation, extenuation.

Ant. *Charge, censure, imputation, condemnation, insult, complaint, offense, wrong.*

Apostate. Renegade, turncoat, backslider, deserter, pervert, traitor.

Ant. *Adherent, supporter, zealot, dogmatist, fanatic.*

Apothegm. Saying, dictum, proverb, aphorism, precept, byword.

Ant. *Sermon, discourse, tirade, harangue.*

Appall. Terrify, frighten, dismay, shock, daunt, alarm, affright.

Ant. *Reassure, embolden.*

Apparel. Clothes, dress, raiment, attire, costume, habit, guise, garments, robes, vesture, wardrobe, equipment, trappings.

Ant. *Nudity, deshabille, rags, tatters.*

Apparent. Seeming, probable, likely, obvious, conspicuous, manifest, clear, patent, evident. plain, legible, specious.

Ant. *Real, hidden, dubious, improbable, doubtful, unimaginable, unsupposable, minute.*

Appeal. Address, invoke, entreat, implore, supplicate, sue, petition.

Ant. *Protest, defy, abjure, disdain, deprecate, repudiate.*

Appearance. Semblance, look, show, pretense, guise, fashion; arrival, advent, apparition; demeanor, air, complexion, manner.

Ant. *Disappearance, evanition, departure, vanishing.*

Appease. Calm, pacify, soothe, quell, mollify, mitigate, lull; propitiate, placate, satisfy, reconcile.

Ant. *Aggravate, exasperate, provoke, inflame, incense, excite.*

Appellation. Epithet, title, description, designation, name.

Ant. *Anonymousness, namelessness.*

Appendage, Appendix. Attachment, addition, adjunct, supplement.

Ant. *Main body, original, whole, total.*

Appertain. Belong, inhere, adhere, regard, concern, touch, relate.

Ant. *Be remote, far-fetched,* or *forced, have no bearing upon.*

Appetite. Longing, craving, desire, relish, gust, zest, liking.

Ant. *Aversion, loathing, repugnance, antipathy, disgust.*

Applause. Praise, approbation, commendation, compliment, plaudit, acclamation, éclat, clapping of hands.

Ant. *Denunciation, censure, blame, sibilation, vituperation, hissing.*

Appliances, *n. pl.* Means, instruments, appointments, appurtenances, tools, adjuncts, equipment; resources, steps, measures, ways; contrivances.

Applicable. Fit, appropriate, suitable, pertinent, apt, proper, relevant, germane; adjustable.

Ant. *Irrelevant, useless, unavailable, impertinent.*

Applicant. Petitioner, solicitor, suitor, candidate, aspirant.

Apply. Use, employ, exercise, appropriate; execute, carry out, practice; devote, engage, dedicate; request, petition.

Ant. *Divert, misuse, discard, divorce.*

Appoint. Determine, establish, fix; assign, allot, designate; nominate, name, create; equip, supply, furnish; direct, command, decree, enjoin, impose, require, ordain.

Ant. *Reserve, cancel, disarrange, reverse, withhold, retain, undo, suspend, recall, withdraw.*

Appointment. Assignation, assignment, agreement, arrangement; meeting, tryst; station, position, office, place; decree, command, order, edict, ordinance, mandate, requirement, law.

Apportion. Appoint, allot, appropriate, divide, distribute, share, grant, dispense, assign, deal.

Ant. *Retain, collect, consolidate, receive, gather, divert.*

Apposite. Apt, pertinent, suitable, seasonable, apropos, fit, applicable, adapted.

Ant. *Untimely, irrelevant, unfitting, impertinent, misplaced.*

Appraise. Estimate, prize, value, rate, fix a price for, survey, assess, assize.

Ant. *Undervalue, discard, misprize; discount, rebate, allow.*

Appreciate. Estimate justly, value highly, esteem, prize, raise the value of; recognize, respect.

Ant. *Undervalue, misjudge, ignore, misconceive; depreciate, disdain.*

Apprehend. Arrest, seize, take, catch, capture; imagine, conceive, regard; perceive, realize, understand, appreciate; fear, forebode.

Ant. *Miss, lose, misunderstand, ignore, misconceive.*

Apprehension. Arrest, capture; understanding, intelligence, mind, reason; notice, cognizance; conception, imagination; knowledge, discernment, perception, sense; opinion, fancy, sentiment, notion, fear, suspicion, anxiety.

Ant. *Escape, non-detection; sensibility, emotion; apathy, lethargy; illiteracy, stupidity, stolidity; confidence, nonchalance.*

Apprise. Give notice, inform, tell, publish, advise, acquaint.

Ant. *Deceive, mislead, hoodwink, mystify.*

Approach, *v.* Advance, draw near, bring near, go near, push; broach, address confidentially; resemble closely, be like, similar, *or* equal.

Ant. *Diverge, retreat, go back; retard, restrain; be unlike.*

Approbation. Praise, commendation, approval, liking; support, consent, sanction, indorsement, concurrence, assent.

Ant. *Censure, protest, denial, disapproval, dissatisfaction.*

Approve. Praise, commend, sanction, support, encourage, authorize.

Ant. *Disparage, condemn, disown, repudiate, dislike.*

Approximation. Approach, nearness, similarity, likeness, contiguity, resemblance, propinquity, neighborhood.

Ant. *Remoteness, variation, distance, difference, divergence.*

Appurtenant. Belonging, connected, appended, attached, coordinate.

ANT. *Isolated, detached, unallied, independent.*

A priori. Theoretically; necessarily, apodictically, constitutionally, absolutely, primordially, inductively.

ANT. *A posteriori; practically, according to experience; deductively from facts.*

Apropos. Opportune, seasonable, apposite, timely, apt, suitable.

ANT. *Inopportune, irrelevant, untimely, inapt, unsuitable.*

Aptitude. Disposition, knack, endowment, tendency, inclination, fitness, suitability, bias, propensity.

ANT. *Unreadiness, unskilfulness, repugnance, incongruity.*

Arbiter. Umpire, judge, referee; controller, master, lord.

ANT. *Appellant, claimant, litigant, disputant.*

Arbitrary. Despotic, autocratic, tyrannical, overbearing, peremptory; capricious, wilful, fanciful; imperious, dictatorial.

ANT. *Considerate, lenient, obliging, equitable.*

Arbitration. Mediation, intercession, interposition, intervention; arbitrament, umpirage, trial, judgment, decision.

ANT. *Litigation, contention, disputation, appeal, dissension.*

Ardent. Passionate, fervent, intense, vehement, fierce, fiery; hot, burning; zealous, enthusiastic, strenuous.

ANT. *Cool, cold, indifferent, torpid, apathetic, dispassionate, phlegmatic.*

Argument. Reasoning, proof, evidence, controversy, discussion, debate; subject, topic, theme, thesis; summary, abstract, outline.

ANT. *Assertion, assumption; dogma.*

Aridity. Dryness, parchedness, sterility, unfertility, barrenness; dulness, indifference, torpidity, insensibility.

ANT. *Moisture, fertility, verdancy, luxuriance, productivity.*

Arise. Ascend, mount, get up, stand up; rebel, revolt; result, eventuate.

ANT. *Descend, dismount; submit, cower; cause, instigate.*

Aristocracy. Government of nobles; nobility, peerage, gentry.

ANT. *Democracy; people, populace, masses, rabble.*

Arm, *v.* Equip, array, furnish, gird, accouter, provide; fortify, cover, protect, guard; prepare.

ANT. *Divest, disarm; expose.*

Army. Soldiery, legion, armament, forces, host, phalanx, troops.

ANT. *Individual; citizens.*

Aromatic. Fragrant, spicy, balmy, redolent, odoriferous, ambrosial.

ANT. *Scentless, malodorous, fetid, offensive, noisome, rank.*

Arouse. Excite, provoke, instigate, stimulate, animate, kindle, warm, whet, summon, awaken.

ANT. *Allay, mitigate, moderate, still, quiet, assuage, quell.*

Arraign. Accuse, charge, indict, impeach, denounce; prosecute.

ANT. *Acquit, discharge, condone, release.*

Arrange. Settle, determine, adjust; dispose, group, marshall, rank, range, distribute, place; plan, contrive, project, devise, construct, organize.

ANT. *Confuse, disturb, jumble, disperse, disorder, derange.*

Array, *n.* Order, parade, show, exhibition, collection, arrangement, line of battle, disposition.

ANT. *Disorder, confusion, jumble.*

Arrest. Apprehend, capture, seize, detain, hold, take prisoner; stop.

ANT. *Liberate, free, dismiss, release, discharge; expedite.*

Arrival. Advent, coming; comer, person *or* thing arrived.

ANT. *Departure, going.*

Arrive. Reach, get to, come; attain, touch, overtake; happen.

ANT. *Depart, set out* or *forth, be gone.*

Arrogant. Haughty, insolent, proud, lordly, disdainful, supercilious, self-important, egoistic, overbearing, dogmatic, imperious.

ANT. *Humble, diffident, polite, bashful, servile, considerate.*

Art. Craft, business, calling, employment, trade; practical knowledge; creation of beauty; skill, dexterity, sagacity, aptitude, cleverness, ingenuity; cunning, artifice, deceit, guile.

ANT. *Misrepresentation, caricature; candor, simplicity; incompetency, inability.*

Article. Thing, substance, commodity, part, portion, particular, point, item, member; essay, paper, monograph, brochure.

ANT. *Nothing, nullity, cipher; totality, entirety, unity, integer.*

Articulate. Join, unite, connect, fasten together; enunciate, utter distinctly, pronounce.

ANT. *Disperse, separate, rend, dissect, disjoin, disconnect; whisper; render mute, silence, muzzle.*

Artifice. Cunning, craft, machination, stratagem, guile, device, contrivance, cheat, imposture, trick, ruse, maneuver, wile.

ANT. *Fairness, frankness, candor, openness, sincerity, truth, honesty, artlessness, ingenuousness, simplicity.*

Artificial. Unnatural, factitious; feigned, counterfeit, fictitious, spurious, sham; affected, forced, strained.

ANT. *Natural, genuine, spontaneous, transparent, artless, unaffected.*

Artist. Designer, contriver, skilled workman, artisan; mechanic, operative; painter; sculptor, carver; master, master-hand.

Ascend. Rise, mount, soar, aspire, go up, tower.

ANT. *Descend, fall, sink.*

Ascendancy. Power, authority, sway, dominion, rule, mastery, control, government, influence.

ANT. *Subordination, servility.*

Ascertain. Determine, establish, settle, fix, define, verify; discover, find out, get at.

ANT. *Guess, surmise, suppose, presume, conjecture.*

Ascetic. Austere, rigid, severe, self-denying, abstinent, stern, puritanical.

ANT. *Lenient, indulgent, epicurean, pampered, mild, tolerant.*

Ascribe. Impute, attribute, assign, refer, charge, set down.

ANT. *Dissociate, exclude; deny, refuse; disconnect.*

Ask. Request, petition, solicit, entreat, beg, beseech, supplicate, require of, crave, demand.

ANT. *Refuse, reject, deny; command, claim, exact, extort, enforce, insist.*

Aspect. Air, mien, look, countenance, expression, feature, bearing; state, attitude, posture, condition, appearance; direction, outlook, prospect.

Asperity. Acrimony, sourness, sharpness; sternness, severity,

bitterness, sullenness, ill-temper; roughness, unevenness.
ANT. *Sweetness, pleasantness; gentleness, mildness; smoothness.*

Asperse. Slander, calumniate, traduce, vilify, attack, abuse, blemish, besmirch, vituperate, disparage, censure, slur, malign.
ANT. *Eulogize, vindicate, clear, defend, extol, praise, shield.*

Aspiration. Pronouncing with the rough breathing; yearning, longing, ardent desire, craving, spiritual ambition.
ANT. *Apathy, inertia, indifference, dulness, aversion, repudiation, avoidance.*

Assault. Attack, invasion, charge, onset, onslaught, aggression.
ANT. *Resistance, defense, repulsion, retaliation, undermining.*

Assemble. Gather, collect, convene, congregate, meet, come together.
ANT. *Disperse, scatter, dismiss.*

Assembly. Concourse, company, gathering, congregation, assemblage, meeting, convocation, throng; congress, parliament, legislature, synod, diet, council, convention; ball, dance, dancing party.
ANT. *Dispersion, dismissal, disunion, disruption.*

Assent, *n.* Acquiescence, acknowledgment, approval, concurrence, approbation, accord, consent, agreement, compliance.
ANT. *Disagreement, dissent, difference, protest, declension.*

Assertion. Asseveration, protestation, allegation; position, statement, word, declaration; vindication, defense, maintenance.
ANT. *Denial, contradiction, abandonment, protest, disavowal, retraction, repudiation, confutation, abjuration.*

Assess. Tax, value, appraise, estimate, compute, fix, assign, determine, impose.
ANT. *Discount, rebate, allow.*

Assiduous. Diligent, industrious, untiring, indefatigable, devoted, constant, attentive, painstaking, laborious, persistent, active.
ANT. *Indolent, remiss, inattentive, lazy, desultory, inconstant.*

Assignment. Appointment, allotment; specification, fixing, determination, offer, presentation; transfer, allowance.
ANT. *Withdrawal, refusal; acceptance, reception.*

Assimilate. Make similar, cause to resemble; digest, appropriate, incorporate, absorb.
ANT. *Contrast, reject, separate, segregate.*

Assist. Help, aid, succor, relieve, support, befriend, serve; speed, sustain, promote, further, coöperate with, patronize.
ANT. *Hinder, oppose, antagonize, prevent, resist, counteract.*

Associate, *n.* Companion, comrade, chum, friend, helpmate, partner, colleague, coadjutor, accomplice, ally, consort, confederate, peer.
ANT. *Antagonist, enemy, foe, opponent, rival, stranger, opposer.*

Association. Federation, fellowship, alliance, companionship, society, union, partnership, lodge, company, confederacy, corporation, fraternity, club.
ANT. *Solitude; disintegration; independence, separation.*

disunion, estrangement, disruption, avoidance; individuality.

Assortment. Arrangement, allotment, distribution; set, class, group, parcel, collection; variety, miscellany.

ANT. *Disarrangement, displacement, misplacement; conglomeration.*

Assuage. Soothe, pacify, mitigate, ease, alleviate, abate, calm.

ANT. *Excite, inflame, provoke, aggravate, exasperate.*

Assume. Arrogate, feign, pretend, take, usurp, accept, affect, appropriate, claim.

ANT. *Waive, allow, surrender; doff; concede, grant, abandon, resign; demonstrate, prove, argue.*

Assumption. Presumption, hypothesis, theory, postulate, conjecture; acceptance of, responsibility for; usurpation, arrogance, haughtiness, conceit, lordliness, impudence, effrontery.

ANT. *Truth, fact; timidity, distrust, misgiving, consternation.*

Assurance. Confidence, effrontery, presumption, assumption, arrogance, impudence, self-reliance, boldness, assertion; pledge.

ANT. *Doubt, distrust, hesitancy, misgiving, timidity, confusion, dismay, shyness.*

Astonish. Amaze, startle, surprise, astound, stupefy, stagger.

ANT. *Encourage, embolden, assure.*

Astute. Keen, discerning, acute, sagacious, shrewd, sharp, cunning, subtle, discriminating, knowing, perspicacious, crafty.

ANT. *Stupid, unintelligent, imbecile, dull, idiotic, shortsighted, shallow.*

Atrocious. Infamous, outrageous, nefarious, villainous, diabolical, heinous, flagrant, horrible.

ANT. *Humane, noble, honorable, admirable, chivalrous, generous.*

Attachment. Adherence, friendship, regard, tenderness, love, esteem, affection, devotion, inclination, union.

ANT. *Alienation, aversion, coolness, distance, estrangement, indifference, antipathy, animosity, dislike, enmity, divorce.*

Attack, *v.* Assault, storm, assail, invade, charge, rush upon, spring upon; censure, criticize; combat, besiege, beset.

ANT. *Withstand, defend, resist, support, shield, aid, uphold, shelter, vindicate, protest.*

Attain. Achieve, accomplish, gain, master, secure, earn, obtain, win, acquire, accomplish.

ANT. *Lose, fail of, forfeit, give up, abandon, let go, miss.*

Attainment. Winning, getting, accomplishing, securing; erudition, acquirement, wisdom, accomplishment, mental resources, information, learning, enlightenment.

ANT. *Inspiration, intuition, genius; ignorance.*

Attempt. Try, undertake, seek, endeavor, essay, attack, strive.

ANT. *Abandon, shun, drop, dismiss, neglect.*

Attendance. Presence; persons present; train, retinue; ministration, service, waiting on.

ANT. *Absence; non-attendance; neglect, abandonment.*

Attention. Care, notice, observation, consideration, watchfulness, alertness; study, reflection, application; respect, courtesy, politeness, civility, regard; courtship, devotion, wooing.

ANT. *Indifference, carelessness, heedlessness, abstraction, distraction, absence of mind; neglect, preoccupation, ignoring.*

Attenuate. Rarefy, thin, reduce, diminish, make slender, slim, *or* spare, lessen.

ANT. *Amplify, dilate, swell, develop, enlarge, broaden, expand, increase.*

Attest. Bear witness, certify, indorse, corroborate, support, authenticate; invoke, adjure; prove, show, manifest, exhibit.

ANT. *Controvert, contradict, disprove, deny, upset, refute; conceal; vitiate.*

Attire. Dress, apparel, robes, garments, habiliments, habit, raiment, uniform, costume, livery.

ANT. *Nudity, nakedness.*

Attitude. Position, pose, posture, situation, standing, aspect.

ANT. *State, condition, essence; amorphism.*

Attraction. Drawing, allurement, lure, fascination, charm, enticement, witchery, grace.

ANT. *Repulsion, aversion, disinclination, repugnance.*

Attribute, *n.* Quality, property, characteristic, peculiarity, mark.

ANT. *Essence, substance, nature, being.*

Attribute, *v.* Ascribe, assign, impute, refer, charge, connect, associate.

ANT. *Separate, sever, sunder, disconnect, deny, dissociate.*

Audacious. Bold, daring, fearless, courageous, venturesome, intrepid, dauntless; presumptuous, forward, assuming, impudent, impertinent, insolent.

ANT. *Timid, cowardly, cautious; unenterprising; retiring.*

Augur, *v.* Foretell, portend, predict, presage, prophesy, divine, prognosticate, betoken.

ANT. *Demonstrate, establish, settle, prove, warrant, calculate.*

August. Awful, imposing, majestic, stately, grand, regal, kingly, princely, noble, dignified.

ANT. *Mean, common, vulgar, beggarly, commonplace, paltry.*

Auspicious. Successful, fortunate, lucky, happy, prosperous; propitious, promising, opportune, favorable.

ANT. *Hopeless, abortive, unpromising, unsatisfactory, discouraging.*

Austere. Severe, hard, stiff, stern, uncompromising, unrelenting, ascetic, rigid, formal.

ANT. *Affable, kindly, indulgent, genial, bland, mild, tender.*

Authentic. Genuine, trustworthy, veritable, accepted, authorized, certain, accredited, sure, true, reliable, original, legitimate.

ANT. *False, fictitious, spurious, unauthorized, apocryphal, fabulous, counterfeit.*

Author. Creator, maker, contriver, originator, inventor; writer, composer.

ANT. *Destroyer, demolisher, spoiler, annihilator.*

Authority. Power, government, empire, dominion; supremacy, control, influence, interest; order, precept, sanction, liberty, warranty; expert, master, connoisseur.

ANT. *Anarchy, license, insubordination, misrule, lynch law; embargo, restriction, hindrance, proscription, prohibition, injunction, interdiction; weakness, wrong, usurpation.*

Autocratic. Absolute, unlimited, tyrannical, oppressive, disdainful, overbearing, arrogant.

Ant. *Subordinate, dependent, responsible, constitutional.*

Automatic. Self-moving, self-acting.

Ant. *Voluntary, free, optional.*

Auxiliary, *n.* Assistant, helper, confederate, aid, ally, accessory, promoter, subordinate.

Ant. *Opponent, antagonist, hinderer, opposer.*

Available. Serviceable, useful, profitable, beneficial, advantageous.

Ant. *Useless, inappropriate, irrelevant, inoperative.*

Avaricious. Grasping, sordid, greedy, covetous, miserly, stingy.

Ant. *Liberal, bountiful, extravagant, wasteful, prodigal, unselfish.*

Avenge. Punish, retaliate, revenge, vindicate.

Ant. *Forgive, pardon, overlook, condone, waive, forego, remit.*

Avenue. Access, entrance, entry, approach, passage; alley, walk, street, road; route, channel.

Aver. Assert, declare, say, protest, affirm, asseverate, allege.

Ant. *Deny, contradict, disavow.*

Average. Medium, medial, middling, ordinary, tolerable, moderate, mediocre, passable.

Ant. *Extreme, excessive, perfect, extraordinary, excellent.*

Aversion. Dislike, hatred, repugnance, disgust, loathing, antipathy, abhorrence, detestation, unwillingness.

Ant. *Sympathy, congeniality, ardor, eagerness, avidity, love, desire, affection.*

Avidity. Eagerness, longing, desire, yearning; rapacity, craving, greediness.

Ant. *Apathy, indifference, coldness, aversion, loathing.*

Avoid. Quit, shun, abandon, escape, elude, withdraw, forsake, dodge.

Ant. *Seek, court, approach, accost, address, affect.*

Avouch. Assert, affirm, declare, protest, profess, asseverate.

Ant. *Deny, contradict, gainsay.*

Avow. Confess, own, acknowledge, admit, profess, proclaim, testify.

Ant. *Disavow, repudiate, deny, contradict, disclaim, ignore.*

Awaken. Rouse, kindle, excite, provoke.

Ant. *Allay, quiet, subdue.*

Award. Grant, allot, accord, distribute, assign, decree, determine.

Ant. *Refuse, withhold, retain, misappropriate, deny.*

Aware. Conscious, sensible, cognizant, knowing, apprised, mindful.

Ant. *Unconscious, ignorant, insensible.*

Awe. Fear, dread, reverence, veneration, terror, wonder.

Ant. *Contempt, familiarity, irreverence, disrespect, insolence.*

Awful. Dread, grand, imposing, majestic, noble, portentous, appalling, august, alarming, horrible, frightful, shocking, terrible.

Ant. *Commonplace, contemptible, despicable, vulgar, undignified.*

Awkward. Clumsy, bungling, ungainly, uncouth, rough, unskilful.

Ant. *Clever, skilful, handy, dexterous, adroit.*

Awry. Oblique, slanting, twisted, crooked, distorted, athwart.
ANT. *Straight, direct, true, right.*

Axiom. Truism, postulate, self-evident proposition, necessary truth.
ANT. *Paradox, sophism, contradiction, nonsense, absurdity.*

Azure. Blue, sky-color, cerulean.

B

Babble. Chatter, prattle, jibber; prate, gossip, tattle; tell secrets, blab, blurt out; murmur.
ANT. *Hush, suppress; enunciate.*

Babel. Tumult, disorder, clamor, confusion, discord, din, pother.
ANT. *Silence; articulation, distinctness, enunciation; monotony.*

Back, *a.* and *ad.* Remote, hindmost, in the rear; again, return.
ANT. *Near, foremost, in advance.*

Back, *v.* Support, aid, second, sustain, assist; retire, retreat, withdraw; move backward, cause to go backward.
ANT. *Fail, disappoint; advance, push.*

Backbiter. Slanderer, defamer, traducer, calumniator, detractor, cynic.
ANT. *Advocate, upholder, defender, vindicator.*

Backslider. Recreant, apostate, renegade, deserter, abjurer.
ANT. *Confessor, zealot, bigot, adherent.*

Backward. Averse, indisposed, reluctant, loath, unwilling, hesitating, wavering; dull, slow, stupid, stolid; late, tardy.
ANT. *Forward, eager, willing, ready, prompt; quick, bright; previous, antecedent, prior.*

Bad. Evil, wicked, depraved, abandoned, corrupt, immoral, unfair, unprincipled, villainous; pernicious, mischievous, hurtful, injurious, detrimental, unwholesome; unlucky, unfortunate; sad, unwelcome, distressing, disappointing; sorry, mean, shabby, vile, wretched, abominable; poor, imperfect; serious, hard, severe.
ANT. *Good, perfect, right, holy, beautiful, pleasant.*

Baffle. Frustrate, thwart, defeat, circumvent, checkmate, undermine; bewilder, perplex, confound, disconcert.
ANT. *Aid, assist, advance, encourage, promote.*

Balance. Poise, hold in equilibrium; weigh, compare, estimate; neutralize, counteract, compensate; equalize, square, adjust.
ANT. *Upset, cant, tilt, overbalance, subvert.*

Bald. Bare, hairless; treeless, unsheltered, naked, verdureless; unadorned, prosaic, dull, vapid, tame, inelegant; literal, unvarnished; mere, unsupported, uncorroborated.
ANT. *Adorned, periwigged; forested, shaded; bright, elegant, rhetorical; ornate, polished, witty, scintillating.*

Baleful. Harmful, hurtful, injurious, baneful, pernicious, deadly, ruinous.
ANT. *Innocent, beneficial, salutary, advantageous.*

Balk. Frustrate, defeat, foil.

Ant. *Aid, promote, instigate.*

Banish. Dismiss, drive out, eject, expel, exile, ostracize, evict, expatriate.

Ant. *Welcome, admit, protect, domesticate, harbor.*

Banquet. Feast, treat, regalement, entertainment, festivity, carousal, cheer.

Ant. *Fast, starvation, abstinence.*

Banter, *n.* Badinage, irony, raillery, ridicule, satire, chaff, mockery, jeering, derision.

Ant. *Discourse, discussion.*

Barbarous. Brutal, atrocious, cruel, inhuman, merciless, savage, barbaric, barbarian.

Ant. *Civilized, humane, polite, refined, tender, delicate, cultured, elegant, nice, courtly.*

Bare. Nude, naked, unclothed, exposed; sheer, simple, mere; bald, unadorned, meager; poor, destitute, indigent, empty.

Ant. *Dressed, protected; rich, luxurious, costly.*

Bargain. Agreement, contract, stipulation, transaction; purchase, speculation, haggling, getting, proceeds; cheap purchase.

Ant. *Loss, misprofit; cheat.*

Barren. Sterile, childless, unprolific; unfertile, unproductive; uninstructive, ineffectual.

Ant. *Productive, fertile, luxuriant, fecund; profitable, useful.*

Barrier. Obstruction, hindrance, obstacle, bar, barricade, rampart; restraint, restriction.

Ant. *Thoroughfare, entrance, admittance, opening, passage.*

Base. Cheap, worthless, inferior; vulgar, humble, unknown; mean, contemptible, servile; shameful, scandalous, vile.

Ant. *Noble, honored, exalted, pure, valued, lofty, esteemed, refined.*

Bashful. Modest, shy, retiring, reserved, diffident.

Ant. *Bold, forward, pert, impudent, confident, conceited, egoistic.*

Basis. Base, foundation, groundwork.

Ant. *Apex, top, superstructure.*

Bathe. Wash, lave, cover, flood, immerse, suffuse.

Ant. *Dry, expose.*

Battle, *n.* Fight, contest, skirmish, combat, encounter, bout, engagement, strife, action, conflict.

Ant. *Armistice, truce, concord.*

Bauble. Trifle, toy, plaything, trinket, gimcrack, knickknack.

Ant. *Valuable, jewel, ornament, decoration, gem, possession.*

Bays. Crown, wreath, garland, chaplet; honors, renown, plaudits, praise, glory, applause.

Ant. *Disgrace, contumely, stigma, brand.*

Beach. Shore, strand, margin, sands, marge, rim, coast, seashore, seaboard.

Ant. *Ocean, sea, deep, main.*

Beacon, *n.* Signal fire, mark, sign, guide, light, flame.

Ant. *Shadow; dark; will-o'-the-wisp, ignis fatuus.*

Beam, *v.* Shine, emit rays, beacon, gleam, glitter, be radiant.

Ant. *Die out, grow dark, go out.*

Bear. Support, sustain, hold up, carry; have, hold, possess; suffer, undergo, endure, tolerate, submit to; permit, allow; maintain, cherish, harbor; be responsible for; produce, yield, give birth to; generate.

ANT. *Drop, drag; release, give up; protest, resist, rebel, resent, reject.*

Bearing. Behavior, deportment, demeanor, appearance, aspect, position, carriage, mien, air; relation, connection; patience, endurance; direction, course, aim; effect, force, meaning, scope; producing; bed, socket.

ANT. *Misbehavior; disconnection, independence, irrelevancy; pendency, suspension; diversion, deflection; inanity, absurdity.*

Beat. Strike, thrash, flog, cudgel, pound, scourge, whip, batter, smite, pommel, overcome, chastise, conquer, defeat, castigate, bruise, bastinado, belabor, switch, spank, worst, vanquish.

ANT. *Soothe, stroke, caress, pat, shield, protect, mollify, heal.*

Beatific. Ravishing, enrapturing, enchanting, transporting, ecstatic.

ANT. *Tormenting, disgusting, obnoxious.*

Beatitude. Bliss, felicity, blessedness.

ANT. *Suffering, tribulation, pain, dolor.*

Beautiful. Handsome, lovely, charming, fair, pretty, graceful, exquisite, beauteous, bewitching, attractive, picturesque, comely.

ANT. *Hideous, repulsive, ugly, deformed, frightful, ghastly, grim.*

Because. Since, inasmuch as, for, as.

ANT. *Yet, notwithstanding, however, although, nevertheless.*

Beckon. Signal, sign, call by gesture, nod.

ANT. *Ignore, repulse.*

Become. Suit, adorn, fit, set off, be appropriate to; get *or* grow to, turn to, change into; befall, bechance, happen to.

ANT. *Disagree, clash, mismatch.*

Becoming. Befitting, beseeming, fit, graceful, proper, neat, suitable, congruous, worthy.

ANT. *Unseemly, indecent, derogatory, unsuitable.*

Befall. Happen, occur, chance, betide.

ANT. *Impend, threaten, loom.*

Befitting. Decent, becoming, suitable, proper, appropriate, expedient.

ANT. *Compulsory, obligatory; improper, inexpedient.*

Before. Preceding, in front of; prior to, previous; in advance of, ahead of; hitherto; above, in a former place *or* previous passage; formerly, of old, already; under the judgment *or* control of.

ANT. *Behind, after, subsequently, later.*

Beg. Beseech, pray, ask, request, supplicate, solicit, sue, implore, importune.

ANT. *Require, demand, extort, exact, insist; refuse.*

Beggar. Mendicant, supplicant, pauper, suitor, applicant.

ANT. *Bestower, giver, benefactor.*

Beggary. Want, penury, indigence, destitution.

ANT. *Riches, wealth, affluence, abundance, plenty.*

Beginning. Origin, commencement, fountain, source, spring, start, opening, initiation, arising, outset, rise, inception, inauguration.

ANT. *End, finish, fulfilment, outcome, conclusion, termination, result, effect, expiration, completion.*

Beguile. Cheat, deceive, befool; amuse, entertain, cheer, solace.

ANT. *Enlighten, advise; weary, bore.*

Behavior. Conduct, deportment, manners, breeding, carriage, bearing, action, demeanor, life.

ANT. *Misconduct, misdemeanor.*

Behest. Command, injunction, charge, precept.

ANT. *Option, liberty.*

Behind. Back, astern, rearward.

ANT. *Before, in front of.*

Behold. See, look, discern, gaze, scan, observe, contemplate.

ANT. *Ignore, miss, wink, overlook, disregard, connive.*

Behoof. Advantage, profit.

ANT. *Loss, detriment, disadvantage.*

Being. Reality, existence, actuality; essence, inmost nature, substance, life, vital principle, root, heart.

ANT. *Nonentity, nullity, nonexistence.*

Beleaguer. Desiege, beset, blockade, invest; compass, block up, surround, obstruct, environ.

ANT. *Abandon; conquer, subdue.*

Belief. Trust, confidence, conviction, credence, persuasion, reliance, assurance; dogma, creed, tenets, opinion, view; credit, acceptance, assent, currency.

ANT. *Distrust, denial, discredit, dissent, rejection, disavowal.*

Belligerent. Warlike, contending, conflicting, hostile, rival, opposed, adverse, antagonistic, pugnacious, contentious, quarrelsome.

ANT. *Peaceful, friendly, forbearing, pacific, neutral.*

Belonging, *n.* Quality, gift, endowment, attribute; property, goods, estate, chattel, possession; appendage, appurtenance, accessory.

Belonging, *a.* Related, connected, appertaining, congenial, cognate, accompanying.

ANT. *Alien, optional, independent, irrelevant.*

Below. Under, beneath, underneath, hereinafter.

ANT. *Above, beforementioned, previously.*

Bend. Curve, twist, crook, bow, deflect, deviate, diverge, twine; influence, persuade, incline, submit.

ANT. *Straighten, stiffen, direct; resist, break, crush.*

Beneath. Below, under, underneath; unworthy of, unbefitting.

ANT. *Above, superior to; over, aloft.*

Benediction. Benison, blessing, beatitude; gratitude, thanks, praise; benefit, grace, boon.

ANT. *Curse, censure, execration, ingratitude.*

Benefactor. Patron, supporter, upholder, friend, contributor.

ANT. *Destroyer, enemy, oppressor, brute.*

Beneficence. Charity, bounty, liberality, benevolence.

ANT. *Malevolence, hatred, stinginess, miserliness, niggardliness.*

Benefit. Boon, service, advantage, profit, favor, blessing.

ANT. *Evil, loss, damage, calamity, injury, privation.*

Benevolence. Kindness, humaneness, charitableness, good will, altruism, beneficence, liberality, philanthropy, benignity, bounty, humanity, sympathy, munificence, generosity, unselfishness, kind-heartedness.

ANT. *Malevolence, malignity, selfishness, stinginess, unkindness, brutality, churlish-*

ness, barbarity, illiberality, self-seeking, niggardliness, harshness.

Benign. Kind, gracious, amiable, gentle, friendly, benevolent, humane, obliging, good.
ANT. *Hateful, harsh, brutal, churlish.*

Bequeath. Will, leave, devise; hand down, transmit, impart.
ANT. *Withhold, alienate, disinherit.*

Bereavement. Deprivation, loss, destitution, affliction, forlorn condition, desolation.
ANT. *Blessing, compensation, reparation, consolation, restitution, restoration, substitution.*

Bereft. Stripped, despoiled, deprived.
ANT. *Endowed, blessed, enriched, compensated.*

Beseech. Beg, implore, pray, ask, solicit, entreat, petition, importune.
ANT. *Grant, requite, confer; disdain, defy.*

Beset. Surround, circle, hem in, besiege, beleaguer; embarrass.
ANT. *Defend, defy, repel.*

Beside. Near, close together; aside from; out of.
ANT. *Far, distant.*

Besides or **Beside.** Except, save, distinct from; moreover, furthermore, else, beyond that.
ANT. *Apart, separate from; exclusively; finally.*

Bestow. Give, present, award, grant, confer; place, stow, store.
ANT. *Receive; seize, appropriate, usurp; disperse, throw away.*

Bet. Stake, wager, pledge.
ANT. *Plan, calculate, dispose.*

Betide. Happen, bechance, befall, come to pass, occur, take place.
ANT. *Result, be destined* or *doomed.*

Betimes. Seasonably, in good time *or* season.
ANT. *Inopportune, late, tardy, unseasonable.*

Betoken. Signify, denote, indicate, represent, imply, prove, show, augur; presage, prefigure, foretell, portend.
ANT. *Mask, hide, mislead, belie, misrepresent.*

Betray. Reveal, expose, divulge, deliver up, deceive; manifest, show, indicate; lure, ensnare, entrap, beguile; seduce, ruin, corrupt.
ANT. *Protect, preserve, foster, cherish, conceal, suppress, guard.*

Betrothal. Engagement, plighting, affiancing.

Better. Amend, ameliorate, improve, correct, advance, reform.
ANT. *Make worse, degrade, wreck, weaken, cripple, impair, injure.*

Between. Amid, among, betwixt.
ANT. *Outside, beyond, without.*

Bewail. Bemoan, lament, sorrow, grieve.
ANT. *Rejoice, joy, exult.*

Beware. Take care, be cautious, be wary, look out, mind.
ANT. *Be reckless, careless; neglect, ignore.*

Bewilderment. Confusion, embarrassment, daze, maze, perplexity, mystification.
ANT. *Enlightenment, self-possession, calmness, discernment, perspicacity.*

Bewitch. Charm, enchant, fascinate, captivate.
ANT. *Repulse, avoid, recoil, annoy, harass.*

Beyond. Over, across, remote, farther than, before; yonder, above, exceeding.
ANT. *Beside, near, at hand,*

close; behind, back; below, less than.

Bias. Bent, inclination, tendency, leaning, proneness, proclivity, propensity, partiality, predilection.

ANT. *Repulsion, reaction, repugnance.*

Bicker. Wrangle, quarrel, dispute, squabble.

ANT. *Agree, sympathize, understand, harmonize.*

Bidding. Command, order, direction, appointment, mandate; offer, bid, proposal.

ANT. *Request, solicitation; refusal, rebuff.*

Bide. Dwell, stay, reside, wait, tarry, remain; endure, bear.

ANT. *Depart, go, move, migrate; resist, rebel, protest.*

Big. Large, great, wide, bulky, huge, gross, fat; proud, arrogant, haughty, pompous.

ANT. *Small, little, least, thin, narrow; humble, subservient, unassuming.*

Bigot. Zealot, fanatic, dogmatist, devotee.

ANT. *Skeptic, liberal, apostate, proselyte, doubter, agnostic.*

Bigoted. Intolerant, opinionated, prejudiced, dogmatical, narrow-minded, one-sided.

ANT. *Liberal, broad-minded, open to conviction.*

Bill. Account, charge, score, amount due, reckoning; draft of law; poster, placard, advertisement.

Bind. Fetter, tie, fasten, shackle, restrict, restrain, secure; compel, oblige, engage.

ANT. *Free, loose, set free, untie.*

Birth. Family, parentage, origin, source, lineage, nativity, descent, extraction, race; rise.

ANT. *Death, extinction.*

Bit. Part, piece, fragment, morsel.

ANT. *Whole, mass, aggregation.*

Biting. Gnawing, sharp, severe, sardonic, censorious, piercing, sarcastic, trenchant.

ANT. *Pleasant, gentle, soothing, genial, flattering.*

Bitter. Harsh, caustic, cutting, savage, acidulous, acrimonious, irate, sharp, sour, stinging, pungent, virulent.

ANT. *Sweet, honeyed, nectared, luscious, dulcet, saccharine.*

Blacken. Slander, malign, defame, daub, bespatter, befoul, asperse, traduce, vilify, decry, calumniate.

ANT. *Clear, eulogize, vindicate, whiten, whitewash.*

Blackguard. Rascal, scoundrel, villain.

ANT. *Gentleman.*

Blame. Censure, rebuke, chide, reprove, reproach, condemn, vituperate, reprobate, reprehend, dispraise.

ANT. *Approve, praise, exonerate, acquit, exculpate.*

Blameless. Pure, innocent, irresponsible, without fault.

ANT. *Guilty, implicated, blameworthy, faulty.*

Blanch. Bleach, whiten, whitewash.

ANT. *Blacken, stain, dye, darken, color.*

Bland. Soft, gentle, mild, affable, gracious, tender, benign, courteous, complaisant.

ANT. *Harsh, abrupt, rough, biting, savage, severe, impolite.*

Blandishment. Flattery, coaxing, fascination, wheedling, attraction, charm, fawning, cajolery.

ANT. *Bluntness, unmannerliness, roughness, scolding, severity, sternness.*

Blank. Bare, drear, bleak, void, empty; utter, pure, simple, mere, unqualified, unmitigated; amazed, astonished, confused, disconcerted.

ANT. *Full, replete; complex; modified, qualified; composed, controlled, self-possessed, cognizant, intelligent.*

Blasphemy. Profanity, sacrilege, impiety, swearing.

ANT. *Reverence, godliness, veneration.*

Blast. Shrivel, destroy, blight, kill, ruin, wither, annihilate; explode, rend, burst.

ANT. *Restore, expand, swell.*

Blazon. Exhibit, show off, blaze, blare, trumpet, proclaim, publish.

ANT. *Conceal, hush, cover, hide, suppress, shroud, bury.*

Bleach. Blanch, whiten.

ANT. *Blacken, darken, soil, stain.*

Bleak. Windy, exposed, bare; cold, chill, raw, desolate, comfortless, cheerless.

ANT. *Sheltered, protected, warm, balmy, cheerful, comfortable.*

Blemish. Blot, spot, flaw, fault, imperfection, stain; defacement, tarnish, disfigurement, disgrace, defect, dishonor, stigma, taint.

ANT. *Purity, unsulliedness, honor, integrity, wholeness.*

Blend. Mix, unite, fuse, merge, mingle, amalgamate, combine, coalesce, harmonize.

ANT. *Separate, run, dissociate, divide.*

Bless. Delight, gladden, make happy, thank, glorify, exalt, praise, extol, felicitate, cheer.

ANT. *Curse, anathematize, sadden, grieve.*

Blessing. Benediction, benison; good, benefit, happiness, profit, boon, gain; glory, praise, gratitude.

ANT. *Malediction, curse; bereavement, impoverishment, calamity, deprivation, disaster, damage, detriment.*

Blight. Pestilence, withering, blast, destruction,

ANT. *Development, maturity.*

Blind. Sightless, unseeing, eyeless, undiscerning, ignorant, unconscious, uninformed.

ANT. *Clear-sighted, far-seeing, discerning, penetrating, conscious, keen, aware, sensitive.*

Blink. Wink, ignore, connive, overlook.

ANT. *Notice, note, mark.*

Bliss. Blessedness, happiness, joy, ecstasy, rapture, felicity, beatitude.

ANT. *Torment, woe, suffering, misery, accursedness.*

Blithe. Merry, joyous, cheerful, gay, lively, airy, sportive, blithesome, mirthful, jocund, elated, vivacious, joyful.

ANT. *Dejected, heavy, dull, sullen.*

Block. Obstruct, arrest, stop, fill.

ANT. *Free, open, clear.*

Blockhead. Dunce, dolt, stupid fellow, numskull, ninny, simpleton, ignoramus, dullard, booby.

ANT. *Sage, adept, savant, philosopher, schoolman, luminary.*

Blood-thirsty. Cruel, savage, ferocious, murderous, bloody, bloody-minded, gory, barbarous, inhuman, ruthless, sanguinary.

ANT. *Humane, kind, merciful, mild, tender, compassionate.*

Bloom, *n.* Blossom, flower, flowering, efflorescence; flush, freshness, prime, vigor, glow; delicacy, innocence.

ANT. *Decay, decadence, blight, blast, roughness, toughness, ghastliness, superannuation, cadaverousness, coarseness.*

Bloom, *v.* Blossom, bud, flower, germinate, sprout, blow, develop.

ANT. *Blight, be blasted, wither.*

Blooming. Flourishing, flowering; young, beautiful, fair, fresh.

ANT. *Fading, waning, old, unsightly, deformed, blasted, withered.*

Blot. Sully, spot, tarnish, spoil, discolor, pollute, stain, erase, blur, blotch, smear, smutch, obliterate.

ANT. *Cleanse, clear, whiten, blanch; perpetuate, preserve.*

Blot out. Erase, cancel, expunge, obliterate, efface, destroy, wipe out.

ANT. *Restore, replace.*

Blow, *n.* Knock, thump, stroke, box, buffet, calamity, cuff, cut, concussion, disaster, lash, misfortune, rap, shock, stroke, wound, affliction, blast, gale, gust; disappointment.

ANT. *Relief, comfort, blessing, consolation, assuagement.*

Bluff. Abrupt, blunt, inconsiderate, open, rough, unmannerly, uncivil, blustering, bold, brusque, coarse, discourteous, frank, impolite, plain-spoken, rude.

ANT. *Bland, courteous, genial, polite, refined, reserved, urbane, polished.*

Blunder. Error, mistake, misunderstanding, fault, slip, oversight, inaccuracy, delusion.

ANT. *Accuracy, correctness, truthfulness, exactness, ratification, foresight, achievement, success, correction.*

Blunt, *a.* Obtuse, dull, pointless, edgeless, brusk, abrupt, plain, informal, stupid, stolid.

ANT. *Sharp, keen, acute, sensitive, polished, courteous, refined.*

Blunt, *v.* Subdue, numb, harden, dull, make dull, deaden, paralyze, stupefy; moderate, allay, mitigate, assuage.

ANT. *Quicken, sharpen, instigate, excite, stimulate, animate, vitalize.*

Blush, *n.* Bloom, color, reddening, carnation, complexion; shame, confusion, guiltiness.

ANT. *Pallor; innocence, purity, unconsciousness; boldness, effrontery.*

Bluster. Storm, rage, insult, roar, swagger, vaunt, boast.

ANT. *Cringe, whine, whimper.*

Boast. Vaunt, brag, swagger, magnify, make much of, swell, bluster, triumph, glory, vapor.

ANT. *Whine, cringe; minimize, apologize.*

Bodily. Corporeally; completely, wholly, altogether, entirely, collectively, unitedly.

ANT. *Spiritually, ghostly; piecemeal, partially, gradually, fragmentarily.*

Body. Material *or* physical substance; carcass, corpse; trunk, stem, bulk, main part; person, individual, mortal, creature, being; company, society, corporation; system; consistency, substance; ashes, form, dust, frame, remains, clay.

ANT. *Intellect, intelligence, soul, spirit, mind; branch, limb; world, universe; mass, conglomeration.*

Boil. Bubble, rage, effervesce, explode, fume.

ANT. *Calm, subside, cool, recover.*

Boisterous. Loud, unrestrained, stormy, noisy, furious, violent, clamorous.
ANT. *Quiet, silent, unostentatious, mild, gentle, peaceful, calm, serene, self-possessed.*

Bold. Courageous, fearless, adventurous, brave, intrepid, dauntless, audacious, daring, valiant.
ANT. *Timorous, fearful, retiring, shy, bashful.*

Bolster. Support, prop, help, sustain, aid, buoy, patch, defend, maintain.
ANT. *Depress, fail, relax.*

Bombast. Bluster, pomposity, fustian, braggadocio, rhodomontade.
ANT. *Modesty, humility, veracity, moderation, temperance.*

Bond. Tie, fastening, manacle, fetter; compact, obligation, security.
ANT. *Option, freedom, parole, honor, discretion.*

Bondage. Servitude, slavery, imprisonment, captivity, incarceration, subjection, serfdom, confinement, thraldom.
ANT. *Liberty, freedom, manumission, independence.*

Bondsman. Slave, serf, captive, vassal, prisoner.
ANT. *Freeman, gentleman, master, lord.*

Bonny. Fair, pretty, pleasant, handsome, shapely, buxom.
ANT. *Homely, ugly, unseemly, deformed, ill-favored.*

Bonus. Premium, douceur, boon, benefit.
ANT. *Fine, penalty, discount, mulct.*

Booby. Dunce, idiot, numskull.
ANT. *Wiseacre, solon, oracle.*

Bookish. Pedantic, studious, learned, erudite, educated.
ANT. *Illiterate, ignorant.*

Boor. Rustic, clown, lout, peasant, countryman, plowman, swain, bumpkin.
ANT. *Gentleman, courtier.*

Boorish. Rude, rustic, clownish, loutish, ungainly, awkward, coarse, rough, gawky.
ANT. *Polite, civil, polished, urbane, courtly, affable, gracious.*

Bootless. Useless, unavailing, unprofitable, profitless, vain.
ANT. *Effectual, profitable, useful, effective.*

Booty. Plunder, prey, spoil, pillage, loot.
ANT. *Restitution, fine, forfeiture, confiscation, penalty.*

Border. Edge, limit, boundary, brink, rim, verge, enclosure, confine, band.
ANT. *Land, tract, interior, center, space, substance.*

Bore. Pierce, perforate, penetrate, drill; weary, plague, trouble, vex, worry, annoy.
ANT. *Delight, gratify, please.*

Bosom. Breast, heart, affection; hollow, depths, midst, inmost recesses; retreat, retirement, quiet, privacy.
ANT. *Surface, exterior, expanse; manner, deportment, demeanor.*

Both. Twain, two.
ANT. *Either, each, every, neither, none, not any, no one.*

Bother. Worry, pester, perplex, harass, plague, tease, vex, molest, annoy, excite.
ANT. *Aid, assist, calm, quiet, compose.*

Bottom. Deep, profound, base, foot; foundation, basis, groundwork; valley, meadow; ship, vessel; seat; grounds, lees, sediments; stamina, power of endurance.
ANT. *Top, height, acme, apex, summit, crown, brow; surface.*

Bound, *v.* Skip, leap, frisk, jump, spring; confine, limit, circumscribe, terminate, restrict, restrain.
ANT. *Hobble, limp, crawl, creep, shamble; enlarge, open, extend, spread out.*

Boundary. Margin, limit, confines, border, bound, frontier, line, marge, verge, termination, term, barrier, bourn, edge, enclosure, landmark; circumference.
ANT. *Land, region, estate, interior, territory; center, citadel; inside.*

Boundless. Unlimited, illimitable, unbounded, measureless, infinite.
ANT. *Narrow, restricted, confined, circumscribed.*

Bountiful. Liberal, generous, benevolent, unselfish, munificent.
ANT. *Miserly, selfish, stingy, niggardly.*

Bounty. Liberality, gift, generosity, charity, benefaction, benignity, benevolence, munificence, donation; premium, reward, bonus.
ANT. *Closeness, stinginess, niggardliness, miserliness.*

Bower. Recess, arbor, retreat, alcove, summerhouse.
ANT. *Open place.*

Brag. Boast, vaunt, bully, swagger.
ANT. *Cringe, whine, whimper.*

Braid. Bind, weave, plait, tie.
ANT. *Unbind, dishevel.*

Branch. Member, bough, limb, shoot, arm, twig, scion, offshoot, ramification; section, department, division; article, part, portion; tributary; derivative line, cognate stock.
ANT. *Trunk, stock, stem; race, family, house.*

Brand, *v.* Denounce, mark, stigmatize, disgrace.
ANT. *Honor, decorate, distinguish.*

Brandish. Flourish, wield, whisk, shake, wave.
ANT. *Suspend, stay, arrest.*

Bravado. Boasting, bragging, bluster.
ANT. *Diffidence, reserve, concealment, modesty.*

Brave. Fearless, heroic, undaunted, undismayed, adventurous, bold, courageous, daring, dauntless, gallant, intrepid, valiant, venturesome, doughty, chivalrous, chivalric, splendid, courteous.
ANT. *Afraid, cringing, fearful, shrinking, timid, timorous, frightened, cowardly, faint-hearted, pusillanimous, churlish, discourteous, fearsome.*

Brawny. Muscular, strong, powerful, athletic, sinewy, herculean, robust, stout.
ANT. *Weak, fragile, delicate, feeble, effeminate, lean.*

Breach. Break, rupture, opening, fracture, flaw, fissure, rent; violation, infringement, nonobservance; quarrel, difference, variance, dissension, schism, alienation.
ANT. *Integrity, wholeness, flawlessness, completeness; reconciliation, healing; conservation, observance; inviolateness; union, fidelity, amalgamation.*

Break. Fracture, rend, part, sever, shatter, smash, shiver; weaken, impair, enfeeble, enervate; tame; make bankrupt; dismiss, discard, degrade, cashier; mitigate, assuage; interrupt, stop, cut short; open, unfold; destroy, sunder, burst, rive, crack, crush, demolish, rupture, split, transgress.
ANT. *Fasten, join, mend, se-*

cure, unite, weld, attach, bind, solder, heal, piece, conjoin, rejoin; protect, conserve; encourage, strengthen, preserve; observe, obey.

Breast. Bosom, heart, affection, conscience.

Breathless. Out of breath; lifeless, dead; exhausted, eager, absorbed, attentive, fascinated; astonished, astounded, bewildered.

ANT. *Calm, collected, cool, composed; indifferent, uninterested.*

Breed, *n.* Lineage, race, pedigree, progeny, stock, line, family, extraction, strain.

ANT. *Ancestor, source, original, origin.*

Breed, *v.* Bring forth, bear, beget, produce; nurture, foster, nourish; discipline, educate, instruct, train, teach, school; occasion, originate, generate, procreate, propagate, cause, evolve.

ANT. *Destroy, extirpate, stifle, extinguish.*

Breeding. Discipline, instruction, education, nurture, training, schooling; manners, deportment.

ANT. *Ill manners, misbehavior; ignorance, illiteracy.*

Brevity. Shortness, terseness, conciseness, compression, pithiness, succinctness, pointedness; abbreviation, abridgment.

ANT. *Prolixity, diffuseness, verbosity, length, protraction, elongation, extension, tediousness.*

Brew. Concoct, compound, mix, hatch, foment, excite; prepare, collect, gather, grow; threaten, impend; form.

ANT. *Disperse, break, spoil, mar, miscompound.*

Bridle, *v.* Restrain, curb, control, govern, check; bristle, ruffle; master, moderate, compress, repress.

ANT. *Relax, loosen, give vent, liberate, discharge; soothe, calm.*

Brief. Short, concise, succinct.

ANT. *Long, tedious, diffuse.*

Bright, Shining, resplendent, luminous, glowing, lustrous, beaming, gleaming, glistening, blazing, flaming, flashing, radiant, ruddy, refulgent, brilliant, dazzling, sparkling, scintillating, burnished; lucid, clear, transparent, pellucid, lambent, cloudless, limpid; glorious, famous, illustrious; intelligent, acute, discerning, keen, ingenious; auspicious, promising, propitious, favorable, inspiring; cheerful, merry, lively, happy, animated.

ANT. *Opaque, dull, dark, gloomy, black, ebon, shadowy, rayless, sunless, murky, cloudy, overcast, pitchy, lurid; obscure, mysterious, enigmatical, mystic, unintelligible, occult, recondite, abstruse, cabalistic, transcendental; disheartening, discouraging, dismal, cheerless; ignorant, unlettered, untaught, imbecile, rude, benighted; foul, infamous, horrible, damnable, vile, infernal, wicked, sullen, atrocious, dejected.*

Brilliant. Bright, radiant, flashing, lustrous, glorious, luminous, effulgent, beaming, sparkling; illustrious, distinguished, celebrated, famous, renowned, eminent.

ANT. *Dark, dull, stupid, gloomy; notorious, infamous; obscure, insignificant.*

Bring. Bear, fetch, convey; conduct, guide, lead, attend, accompany, convoy; obtain, gain, procure, produce; induce, prevail upon.

ANT. *Remove, export, send, exclude, debar, transport, abstract, subtract.*

Brisk. Lively, quick, vivacious, active, alert, animated, prompt, sprightly, nimble, spry, agile.

ANT. *Slow, heavy, dull, sluggish, indolent, inactive, unenergetic, stagnant.*

Bristling. Full, crowded, swarming, stocked, multifarious, multitudinous; bristly, standing on end like bristles; ruffled, roughened, corrugated, bespined; bridled, angered, offended.

ANT. *Smooth, soothed, allayed; prone; bare, nude, scant, devoid, vacant.*

Brittle. Fragile, crumbling, shivery, frail, easily broken.

ANT. *Tough, stout, strong, hardy.*

Broach. Open, pierce, tap; suggest, hint, approach, break; utter, publish, proclaim, give out; originate, propound.

ANT. *Repress, cork, bottle, secrete, conceal, hide.*

Broad. Wide; large, ample, extensive, vast, spacious, capacious; liberal, tolerant, free, hospitable; spread, diffused, open; gross, vulgar, indecent, coarse.

ANT. *Narrow; contracted, restricted, confined, limited; prejudiced, illiberal, bigoted, reserved; veiled, enigmatical, shrouded, shaded; refined, delicate, sketchy; specific, pointed.*

Broil. Affray, quarrel, contention.

Brook. Tolerate, bear, suffer, endure, abide, submit to, undergo, permit.

ANT. *Resist, resent, reject.*

Brotherhood. Fraternity, fellowship, association, sodality, society.

Browbeat. Bully, intimidate, bulldoze, overawe.

ANT. *Rally, support.*

Bruise. Pommel, crush, squeeze, break, pound, batter, deface.

ANT. *Heal, soothe.*

Brunt. Shock, attack, impulse, onslaught, onset, assault.

ANT. *Repulse, resistance, endurance.*

Brutal. Brutish, animal, beastly, bestial; savage, ferocious, cruel, harsh, uncivil, rude, rough, gruff, impolite, brusque; sensual, carnal.

ANT. *Humane, self-controlled, civilized, enlightened, elevated, noble, refined, intelligent, grand.*

Bubble. Toy, trifle, fancy, conceit, dream, vision, froth, trash.

ANT. *Prize, treasure, reality, substance, jewel, good, advantage.*

Buffoon. Wag, clown, jester, mountebank, harlequin, droll, punch, fool.

ANT. *Wit, genius, pedant, philosopher.*

Build. Make, form, shape, figure, model; construct, erect, raise.

ANT. *Demolish, overthrow, destroy.*

Building. Architecture, edifice, structure, fabric, pile, erection.

ANT. *Ruin, demolition, dilapidation, dismantlement.*

Bulk. Magnitude, size, volume, mass; greatness, amplitude, massiveness; majority, major part, most, principal part; dimension.

ANT. *Portion, section, atom, particle; diminution, tenuity, contraction, dismemberment, disintegration.*

Bulwark. Rampart, fortress, fortification, stronghold, intrenchment, bastion, parapet, citadel.

ANT. *Siege, bombardment, cannonade, boarding, storming.*

Bungler. Botcher, clown, fumbler, clumsy workman, novice.
ANT. *Adept, adroit, master, artist, proficient workman, professor.*

Buoy, *v.* Float, support, sustain; elevate, inspire, assure, animate, cheer.
ANT. *Sink, drown, depress, swamp; crush, betray, fail, deject, overcome.*

Buoyant. Light; cheerful, hopeful, sprightly, vivacious, joyous, blithesome, jocund, sportive, jubilant, elastic, floating.
ANT. *Heavy, dejected, depressed, moody, joyless, cheerless, desponding.*

Burden. Load, weight; cargo, freight; capacity, tonnage; impediment, incubus, grievance, trial, trouble, affliction, sorrow; chorus, refrain; topic, drift, tenor, point, substance.
ANT. *Ease, lightness; facility, airiness, light-heartedness; consolation, assuagement, alleviation, liberation, mitigation.*

Burial. Interment, sepulture, entombment, burying.
ANT. *Exhumation, disinterment.*

Burlcsque. Parody, travesty, caricature, ridicule, farce.
ANT. *Classic, history, fact.*

Burn. Char, consume, cremate, scorch, set on fire, singe, ignite, incinerate, kindle, blaze, cauterize, glow, smolder.
ANT. *Smother, stifle, subdue, extinguish, cool, put out; subside, glimmer, lower, pale.*

Burnish. Brighten, polish, make to glisten, glaze, gloss.
ANT. *Dull, bedim, cloud, scratch, abrade.*

Burst. Break, open, explode, blow up, rend, split, crack, discharge, shatter, disrupt.
ANT. *Cohere, hold, stand, stick together, adhere.*

Bury. Inter, cover up, entomb, inearth, inhume, inurn; shroud, conceal, secrete, hide; immure, confine; cancel, compose, hush, cover with oblivion.
ANT. *Resurrect, exhume, disinter, excavate, expose, resuscitate; publish, announce, advertise.*

Business. Employment, craft, trade, commerce, handicraft, traffic, transaction, work, vocation, job, affairs, avocation, profession, occupation, calling, concern, duty, office, interest.
ANT. *Stagnation, leisure, inactivity.*

Bustle. Activity, stir, commotion, excitement, haste, hurry, energy, eagerness, flurry.
ANT. *Idleness, inactivity, vacation, stagnation, quiet, indolence, indifference, unconcern.*

Busy. Engaged, employed, occupied; diligent, industrious, active, working, sedulous; brisk, stirring, bustling, agile, spry, nimble; meddling, officious.
ANT. *Idle, lazy, indolent, slothful.*

But. Save, except, furthermore, barely, besides, however, just, only, notwithstanding, though, unless, yet, still, merely, nevertheless, provided, moreover.

Buxom. Bonny, blithe, shapely.
ANT. *Lean, slender, ill-shaped.*

Buy. Purchase, bargain, acquire; bribe, corrupt, pervert, suborn, subsidize.
ANT. *Sell, hawk, retail, vend.*

By. Through, with; at, on; from, according to; near, close by; past; along, over; before, in the sight of, in the name of; per, at.

C

Cabal. Confederacy, conspiracy, conclave, combination, faction, crew, junto, gang, coterie, plot, political intrigue, league.

Cadaverous. Bloodless, pallid, pale, wan, ghastly, deathlike, ashy.

ANT. *Rosy, blushing, sanguine, incarnadine.*

Cage, *v.* Imprison, immure, confine, incarcerate.

ANT. *Liberate, free, dismiss, unbar.*

Caitiff. Rascal, miscreant, villain, wretch, coward, sneak, traitor, scoundrel, vagabond.

ANT. *Gentleman, patriot, philanthropist.*

Cajole. Coax, wheedle, flatter, fawn upon, blandish; deceive, entrap, beguile, inveigle, impose upon.

ANT. *Scold, chide, warn.*

Calamitous. Disastrous, unfortunate, unlucky, adverse, untoward, deplorable, ruinous, inauspicious, wretched, distressing, grievous, ill-starred, troublous, hapless, ill-omened.

ANT. *Fortunate, auspicious, felicitous, propitious, favorable, advantageous.*

Calamity. Disaster, misfortune, catastrophe, mishap, trial, trouble, affliction, adversity, distress, hardship, ill luck, visitation.

ANT. *Blessing, boon, advantage, good fortune, benefaction.*

Calculate. Number, reckon, sum up, count, compute, account, estimate, enumerate, rate; consider, deem, apportion, investigate.

ANT. *Guess, risk, chance, conjecture, stake.*

Calculating. Wary, cautious, scheming, crafty, cool, hard, selfish; careful, circumspect, sagacious, farsighted.

ANT. *Shortsighted, improvident, rash, careless.*

Calculation. Reckoning, computation; expectation, anticipation, prospect; foresight, forethought, caution, wariness, discretion, prudence, deliberation.

ANT. *Omission, carelessness, imprudence, indiscretion, inconsideration.*

Caliber. Diameter, gage, capacity; faculty, scope, talent, ability, gifts, parts, endowment.

ANT. *Smallness, thinness; imbecility, incapacity, puerility.*

Call. Cry, bellow, clamor, ejaculate, scream, roar, shout, shriek, bawl, yell, exclaim, vociferate; invite, summon, send for, bid; assemble, convene, muster; elect, ordain, appoint; invoke, appeal to.

ANT. *Be silent, hush, list, listen, harken, be still; ignore; disperse; disdain, defy.*

Calm. Composed, peaceful, placid, quiet, still, tranquil, self-possessed, serene, undisturbed, dispassionate, sedate, collected, imperturbable, unruffled.

ANT. *Frantic, frenzied, passionate, furious, raging, stormy, violent, boisterous, agitated, excited, fierce, turbulent, wild, heated, wrathful, disturbed.*

Calumniate. Slander, traduce, defame, vilify, revile, asperse.

ANT. *Praise, commend, vindicate, laud, honor, eulogize; shield.*

Calumny. Slander, aspersion,

defamation, detraction, abuse, obloquy.
ANT. *Vindication, justification; eulogy, panegyric.*

Camp. Encampment, bivouac.

Cancel. Obliterate, scratch out, erase, efface, expunge, cross off; abolish, abrogate, nullify, annul, revoke, rescind, make void, repeal.
ANT. *Confirm, enact, perpetuate, approve, enforce, uphold, sustain, maintain, establish, record, write.*

Candid. Honest, open, straightforward, transparent, unbiased, artless, frank, guileless, ingenuous, naive, sincere, impartial, innocent, unprejudiced, aboveboard, simple, truthful, unsophisticated, fair.
ANT. *Deceitful, designing, foxy, sharp, shrewd, crafty, artful, sly, tricky, subtle, adroit, cunning, insincere, diplomatic, intriguing, wily.*

Candidate. Aspirant, solicitant, petitioner, canvasser, claimant, solicitor.
ANT. *Non-competitor; resigner, abandoner, abjurer.*

Canvass. Debate, discuss, dispute, agitate; examine, investigate, scrutinize, sift, study, consider; solicit votes from, apply for.
ANT. *Admit, pass, misexamine, allow, ignore, disregard.*

Capability. Capacity, ability, skill, power, competency, efficiency, caliber, force, faculty, scope, brains, talent.
ANT. *Dulness, inability, inaptitude, difficulty, awkwardness.*

Capacity. Space, magnitude, volume, dimensions, extent, size, tonnage, caliber; faculty, gift, talent, genius, competency, capability, discernment, cleverness, skill, aptitude; sphere, office, province, character, function.
ANT. *Restriction, narrowness, contractedness, incapacity; incompetency, inefficiency, inability.*

Capital, *n.* Metropolis; large letter; stock, sum invested; head of a column *or* pillar; mental, physical, *or* financial resources.

Capital, *a.* Chief, principal, essential, leading, cardinal; fatal, forfeiting life; excellent, prime, first-class, first-rate, consummate, high, important.
ANT. *Subordinate, inferior, unimportant, minor; defective, mean.*

Capitulate. Surrender, yield, submit, stipulate.
ANT. *Resist, contend, struggle.*

Caprice. Vagary, freak, whim, fancy, crotchet.
ANT. *Purpose, plan, determination, conviction, seriousness.*

Capricious. Wayward, fanciful, freakish, whimsical, inconstant, uncertain, fitful, fickle, changeable.
ANT. *Firm, inflexible, unswerving, constant, decided, serious.*

Captious. Carping, hypercritical, censorious; crabbed, snappish, touchy, cross, snarling, acrimonious, contentious; insidious, ensnaring.
ANT. *Appreciative, commendatory, complimentary, encouraging, flattering, laudatory, approving.*

Captivate. Charm, enchant, fascinate, enamor, bewitch, please highly, lead captive, win, catch.
ANT. *Disenchant, disillusionize; disgust.*

Captivity. Thraldom, confinement, duress, imprisonment, bondage, subjection, slavery, servitude, durance.

ANT. *Freedom, liberty, independence.*

Capture. Seize, catch, arrest, apprehend, make captive; prize.

ANT. *Liberate, free, release; acquit.*

Care. Anxiety, trouble, solicitude, concern, vigilance, worry, charge, caution, attention, heed, forethought, management, perplexity, watchfulness, wariness, precaution, oversight, prudence.

ANT. *Indifference, heedlessness, negligence, oversight, remissness, slight, recklessness, disregard, carelessness, inattention.*

Career. Course, line of achievement, passage, race, flight, procedure, conduct, progress, active life, success.

Careful. Thoughtful, provident, considerate, reflective, heedful, diligent, pensive, regardful, contemplative.

ANT. *Careless, thoughtless, improvident, unthinking, heedless, inconsiderate, rash, wanton, idle, dreamy, trifling.*

Caress, *v.* Embrace, fondle, kiss, pet, pamper, coddle, court, flatter.

ANT. *Vex, tease, affront, annoy, provoke, persecute.*

Cargo. Freight, load, goods, lading, consignment, merchandise.

Caricature. Imitation, mimicry, parody, travesty, burlesque, exaggeration, extravaganza, take-off, farce, monstrosity.

ANT. *Portraiture, resemblance, representation, reproduction.*

Carnage. Massacre, bloodshed, slaughter, havoc, butchery.

ANT. *Deliverance, ransom, quarter, redemption.*

Carnal. Sensual, fleshly, lustful, lascivious; natural, unregenerate, earthly, temporal.

ANT. *Spiritual, ethereal, refined, pure, exalted, temperate, self-controlled.*

Carnival. Festival, revel, masquerade, rout.

ANT. *Fast, retirement, Lent, penance, mortification.*

Carol. Sing, warble, chirp, twitter, chant, whistle, hum; hymn.

ANT. *Whine, lament, dirge, cry, croak, weep, groan, moan.*

Carousal. Feast, festival, banquet, revel, debauch, wassail, orgies.

ANT. *Fast, abstinence, starvation; temperance, moderation; self-denial.*

Carp. Cavil, find fault, object to, pick flaws, challenge, censure, hypercriticize.

ANT. *Concede, admit, compliment, approve, applaud, acquiesce, assent.*

Carpet. Covering for floor; table or board (*metaphorical*), consideration, consultation.

ANT. *Shelf* (metaphorical), *rejection, oblivion, disposal.*

Carry. Convey, move, transport, lift, bring, bear, transmit, support, sustain, take; impel, urge, push forward; signify, infer, involve, implicate.

ANT. *Drop, let go, throw down, fall under, shake off; retard, impede; leave, be separate from.*

Case. Box; covering, sheathe; state, condition, plight, predicament; instance, example, occurrence; circumstance, event, contingency; suit, action, process, trial, cause; question, subject of discussion; form, inflection.

ANT. *Hypothesis, supposition, fancy, theory, conjecture;*

generalization, principle, universality.

Cash. Coin, money, specie, currency, capital.

ANT. *Paper money, greenbacks, bills.*

Cast. Hurl, throw, pitch, fling, drive, thrust, sling, toss; shed, lay aside; calculate, compute, reckon; found, form; direct, turn; assign, appoint, allot; impart, shed, diffuse, communicate.

ANT. *Raise, elevate, erect; accept, approve, retain, carry; miscalculate; break, dismember, dissipate.*

Caste. Grade, rank, order, lineage, dignity, respect.

ANT. *Abasement, degradation, disrepute, taboo, reproach, ostracism.*

Castigate. Whip, flagellate, cane.

ANT. *Reward, encourage, caress, pat.*

Casual. Accidental, incidental, fortuitous, chance, contingent.

ANT. *Regular, certain, fixed, ordinary, periodic, systematic.*

Casuistry. Sophistry, fallacy, quibble; refinement.

ANT. *Reason, common sense, conscience.*

Catalogue. List, register, index, enrolment, entry, record, roll, inventory, schedule.

ANT. *Non-registration, obliteration, oblivion, forgetfulness; non-entry, oversight, omission.*

Catastrophe. Revolution, disaster, mishap, misfortune, calamity, cataclysm, blow, visitation.

ANT. *Victory, triumph, benefit, ovation, success, felicitation, blessing.*

Catch. Grasp, seize, clutch, capture, clasp, secure, snatch, take, arrest, ensnare, entrap, grip, lay hold; comprehend, apprehend, understand.

ANT. *Lose, miss, fail of, let go, give up, release, restore.*

Categorical. Plain, absolute, distinct, positive, declaratory, affirmative.

ANT. *Obscure, ambiguous, dubious, hypothetical, contingent, mystical, enigmatical.*

Category. Class, division, order, rank; universal aspect, primitive relation.

ANT. *Essence, truth, being, substance, nature.*

Causality. Causation, potentiality, eventuality, operativeness.

ANT. *Counteractivity, barrenness, sterility; finality.*

Cause. Agent, origin, source, creator, spring; reason, power; designer, antecedent, originator, author, producer; condition, principle.

ANT. *Effect, result, end, production, issue, accomplishment, development, consequence, creation, fruit, event, outcome, outgrowth.*

Caution. Care, heed, wariness, circumspection, forethought, discretion; warning, admonition, advice, counsel.

ANT. *Temerity, heedlessness, unguardedness, improvidence, imprudence.*

Cavalier, *a.* Arrogant, haughty, overbearing, insolent, disdainful.

ANT. *Courteous; subservient, servile; civil, polite.*

Cavil. Carp, object, censure.

ANT. *Approve, allow, concede.*

Cavity. Opening, gap, aperture, hole, fissure.

ANT. *Obstruction, filling.*

Cease. End, finish, desist, leave off, quit, stop, refrain, abstain, discontinue, pause, terminate.

ANT. *Begin, commence, con-*

tinue, originate, inaugurate, start, set going, set in operation.

Celebrated. Famous, renowned, distinguished, famed, illustrious, eminent, glorious, notable, exalted.

Ant. *Obscure, unknown, unnotable, mean, insignificant, inconspicuous.*

Celebration. Solemnization, observance, commemoration, laudation, praise, commendation.

Ant. *Oblivion, desuetude, non-observance.*

Celebrity. Fame, renown, reputation, glory, honor, repute, eminence, distinction; person of note, "lion."

Ant. *Obscurity, ignominy, disgrace, contempt, meanness; infamy; oblivion.*

Celerity. Rapidity, speed, haste, velocity, swiftness, fleetness, despatch.

Ant. *Slowness, tardiness, inertness.*

Celestial. Heavenly, angelic, supernal, ethereal, atmospheric, immortal, seraphic, divine, godlike.

Ant. *Earthly, terrestrial; human, mortal; infernal.*

Censure. Blame, disapproval, reproach, disapprobation, reprimand, condemnation, remonstrance, rebuke.

Ant. *Praise, approval, eulogy, commendation, encouragement.*

Center. Middle, midst.

Ant. *Perimeter, rim, bound, circumference, boundary.*

Central. Convenient, medial, accessible.

Ant. *Remote, inaccessible, inconvenient.*

Centralize. Concentrate, collect, localize.

Ant. *Disperse, distribute.*

Ceremonial, *n.* Ritual, rites, formalities, etiquette.

Ceremonial, *a.* Ritualistic, formal, official, ministerial, pompous, sumptuous, scenic, functional.

Ant. *Private, unostentatious, undramatic, unimposing, unassuming.*

Ceremonious. Stately, lofty, courtly; formal, studied, punctilious; prim, precise.

Ant. *Brusk, blunt, supercilious, plain, simple.*

Certain. Sure, infallible, positive, undeniable, unfailing; assured, fixed, regular, established; true, accurate, unmistakable.

Ant. *Dubious, irregular, undecided, doubtful, exceptional, casual.*

Certainty. Assurance, conviction, confidence, positiveness.

Ant. *Hesitation, doubt, misgiving, conjecture, indecision.*

Certify. Acknowledge, avow, declare, prove, inform, assure, attest.

Ant. *Disavow, misinform, disprove.*

Cessation. Stop, pause, abeyance, suspension, lull, respite.

Ant. *Incessancy, continuity, continuance.*

Chafe. Vex, irritate, gall, rub, chagrin, tease, worry, harass, annoy, fret; rage, fume; nettle, exasperate, anger.

Ant. *Soothe, coax, calm, console, humor; submit, endure, succumb.*

Chaff. Banter, badinage, nonsense, frivolity; refuse, trash.

Ant. *Sense, reason, pith, gist, seriousness, substance.*

Chagrin. Humiliation, shame, mortification, confusion, discomposure, dismay, disappointment.

ANT. *Delight, glory, exultation, triumph, rejoicing.*

Challenge, *v.* Dare, brave, defy; demand, require, claim; object to, take exceptions.

ANT. *Pass, allow, grant, concede, permit; retract, retreat.*

Champion. Defender, protector, vindicator; hero, winner, chief, victor, combatant.

ANT. *Renegade, traitor, deserter, coward; adversary, opponent.*

Chance. Hazard, casualty, accident, luck, fortune.

ANT. *Law, sequence, purpose, design, intention, causation, certainty.*

Change, *n.* Transformation, variation, transition, conversion, innovation, diversion, novelty, variety, vicissitude, alteration, transmutation.

ANT. *Fixity, identity, constancy, uniformity, firmness, permanence, persistence, steadiness.*

Change, *v.* Alter, transform, vary, turn, veer, shift, qualify, modify, exchange, diversify, convert, metamorphose, substitute.

ANT. *Continue, endure, stay, hold, keep, retain, abide, remain, persist.*

Changeless. Stationary, undeviating, immovable, reliable, consistent.

ANT. *Fluctuating, vacillating, capricious, variable, plastic.*

Character. Mark, figure, sign, symbol, emblem, letter; constitution, nature, disposition, turn, cast, bent; temperament, moral qualities, personality, traits, habits; person, individual; repute, reputation.

ANT. *Anonymousness; disrepute; vagueness; indefiniteness.*

Characteristic. Attribute, peculiarity, trait, sign, indication, mark, feature, distinction, singularity, property, idiosyncrasy.

ANT. *Nondescript, generality, miscellany, commonness.*

Charge, *v.* Load, freight, burden; intrust; impute, ascribe; accuse, impeach, incriminate, arraign, indict; command, order, require, bid; attack, assault.

ANT. *Free, acquit, liberate, discharge.*

Charitable. Benign, bountiful, liberal; lenient, mild, considerate.

ANT. *Selfish, harsh, exacting, revengeful, churlish, censorious.*

Charity. Benevolence, liberality, bounty, generosity, philanthropy.

ANT. *Harshness, ill will, malignity, malevolence.*

Charlatan. Quack, mountebank, impostor, pretender, humbug, cheat.

ANT. *Victim, dupe, gull.*

Charm. Spell, incantation, enchantment; fascination, attraction, allurement; witchery, sorcery, magic, necromancy.

ANT. *Fear, repulsion, disenchantment, disillusion.*

Chary. Careful, cautious, wary; frugal, sparing, saving, reluctant.

ANT. *Liberal, lavish, profuse, extravagant.*

Chase. Pursue, track, hunt, follow, prosecute; emboss, enchase.

ANT. *Flee, shun, elude, evade; abandon, relinquish.*

Chaste. Pure, spotless, immaculate, modest, virtuous, simple; refined, classic, elegant.

ANT. *Corrupt, impure, flashy, gaudy; coarse, inelegant.*

Chasten. Discipline, chastise, subdue, afflict, punish, soften, try.

ANT. *Indulge, pamper, spoil, demoralize.*

Chattels. Goods, wares, effects, furniture.

ANT. *Freehold.*

Cheap. Common, inexpensive, mean, worthless, vile, paltry, low-priced, poor, indifferent.

ANT. *Rare, costly, expensive, high, precious.*

Cheat, *n.* Fraud, trick, artifice, swindle, deceit, fiction, imposture.

ANT. *Truth, reality, fact, honesty, authenticity, certainty, openness, sincerity.*

Check, *v.* Restrain, curb, stop, bridle, hinder, impede, inhibit; reprove, chide, reprimand, rebuke.

ANT. *License, indulge, allow, loose, liberate, abet, instigate.*

Cheer, *n.* Gladness, joy, gaiety, mirth, merriment, cheerfulness, happiness, hope, conviviality, plenty, hospitality.

ANT. *Gloom, dearth, sullenness, niggardliness, unsociableness.*

Cheerful. Glad, lively, mirthful, animated, jocund, jolly, blithe, buoyant, merry, joyous.

ANT. *Gloomy, dejected, unhappy, lifeless, dull, depressing, melancholy, joyless, dispiriting.*

Cherish. Foster, nurture, protect, shelter, treasure, comfort, cheer.

ANT. *Abandon, afflict, check, discourage.*

Chief, *a.* Head, important, excellent, high, principal, consummate.

ANT. *Subordinate, minor, inferior.*

Chieftain. Captain, commander, general, leader, chief.

ANT. *Vassal, minion, adherent, retainer, attendant, follower.*

Childish. Puerile, weak, infantine; silly, foolish, trivial, trifling.

ANT. *Manly, strong, wise, sagacious; important, momentous.*

Chimerical. Visionary, imaginary, unreal, dreamy, fanciful, fabulous.

ANT. *Real, actual, substantial, veritable.*

Chivalrous. Knightly, gallant, gentlemanly, heroic, valiant, spirited.

ANT. *Dastardly, recreant, sneaking.*

Choice, *n.* Option, preference, alternative, selection, election, free will.

ANT. *Necessity, compulsion; refusal; force; fate, predestination.*

Choice, *a.* Select, dainty, rare, valuable, cherished, exquisite, precious.

ANT. *Common, ordinary, despicable, cheap, inferior.*

Choose. Select, pick out, cull, prefer, elect.

ANT. *Cast away, reject, decline, refuse, leave, throw aside.*

Chronicle. Annals, records, register, memorials, archives, history.

ANT. *Legend, romance, tradition.*

Cipher. Zero, nothing, nonentity, naught; character, symbol, device, monogram; secret character, private alphabet; nobody, person of no account.

ANT. *Infinity; somebody, celebrity, star, notability, colossus.*

Circular. Round, annular, spherical, ring-shaped.
Ant. *Linear, direct, straight.*

Circulate. Move in a circle; diffuse, spread, disseminate, promulgate, propagate, publish, notify; travel.
Ant. *Suppress, hush, cease, stagnate; center, monopolize, appropriate.*

Circumference. Periphery, circuit, boundary, outline, enclosure.
Ant. *Center, interior.*

Circumlocution. Verbosity, prolixity, wordiness, diffuseness, periphrasis, redundance, tautology.
Ant. *Brevity, compression, condensation, shortness, succinctness, terseness, compactness, conciseness, directness, plainness.*

Circumscribe. Define, limit, delineate, enclose, confine, restrict.
Ant. *Distend, dilate, expand, amplify, enlarge, extend.*

Circumspect. Cautious, wary, heedful, attentive, careful, prudent, watchful, scrupulous, vigilant.
Ant. *Careless, reckless, incautious, heedless, unwary.*

Circumstance. Event, situation, occurrence, position, detail, incident, feature, accompaniment, particular, point, item, condition.
Ant. *Deed, case, transaction, business, affair.*

Cite. Call, summon, name, select, refer to, quote, mention.
Ant. *Discard, dismiss, dispute, contradict, reject, challenge, disprove.*

Citizen. Inhabitant, dweller, townsman, burgher, resident, subject, denizen.
Ant. *Foreigner, alien, exile, visitor, tramp, transient, tourist, sight-seer.*

Civilization. Culture, cultivation, refinement, amelioration, humanization.
Ant. *Demoralization, savagery, barbarism, rudeness.*

Claim, *n.* Assertion, requisition, demand, call; title, privilege, right, pretension.
Ant. *Disclaimer, surrender, abjuration, waiver.*

Claim, *v.* Demand, ask, require, call for, assert, insist, request, maintain, pretend.
Ant. *Repudiate, waive, concede, forego, abjure.*

Clamor, *n.* Noise, uproar, hubbub, outcry, vociferation, exclamation.
Ant. *Silence, reticence, acquiescence; repression, stifling.*

Clandestine. Secret, private, furtive, stealthy, underhand, sly, surreptitious, hidden.
Ant. *Open, aboveboard, sincere, frank.*

Class. Company, grade, order, rank, caste, clan, circle, association, club, clique, coterie, set.

Classical. Refined, elegant, polished, chaste, pure.
Ant. *Corrupt, barbarous, uncouth, debased, inelegant.*

Classification. Grouping, disposition, arrangement, distribution, category, genus, designation, order, species, nature, character; homogeneity.
Ant. *Individuality, speciality, singularity, distinction, heterogeneity.*

Clause. Portion, section, passage, paragraph, stipulation, article, chapter, provision.
Ant. *Document, instrument, writing.*

Clean, *a.* Pure, neat, clear, spotless, cleansed, untarnished, upright.

ANT. *Foul, impure, untidy, hampered, unclean.*

Cleanse. Purify, wash, clean, disinfect, lave, scour, sponge, scrub, sweep, wipe, rinse, dust, purge.

ANT. *Defile, pollute, stain, deprave, sully, taint, befoul, contaminate, corrupt, vitiate.*

Clear, *a.* Pure, bright, transparent, free, serene, unclouded, obvious, manifest, pellucid, unadorned, plain, distinct, evident, lucid, intelligible, explicit, straightforward, perspicuous.

ANT. *Mysterious, unintelligible, vague, opaque, foggy, dim, cloudy, dubious, turbid, ambiguous.*

Clever. Gifted, expert, capable, apt, bright, ingenious, quick-witted, skilful, adroit, dexterous, intellectual, happy, smart, talented, keen, knowing, intelligent, quick, sharp.

ANT. *Foolish, slow, stupid, idiotic, thickheaded, witless, bungling, awkward, dull, ignorant, clumsy, senseless.*

Climax. Acme, top, summit, culmination, height, consummation, zenith, head.

ANT. *Base, floor, nadir, anticlimax, depth; bathos.*

Cling. Stick, cleave, fasten, hold, adhere.

ANT. *Drop, relax, swerve, let go.*

Close. Packed, condensed, compressed, narrow, restricted, solid; secret, reserved; niggardly.

ANT. *Ample, wide, open, spacious, patent, public, advertised; open-handed, free, liberal.*

Clownish. Rude, rustic, boorish, awkward, clumsy, bucolic, cloddish.

ANT. *Polite, affable, civil, urbane.*

Clumsy. Awkward, inexpert, uncouth, bungling, unskilful, unwieldly.

ANT. *Neat, skilful, clever, expert, adroit, dexterous, workmanlike.*

Coalesce. Blend, mix, harmonize, unite, consolidate, combine, adhere.

ANT. *Disagree, sunder, separate, sever.*

Coalition. League, union, alliance, confederacy, combination, compact, amalgamation.

ANT. *Disruption, rebellion, disagreement, sedition, mutiny.*

Coarse. Of large fibers, crude, rough, gross; indecent, indelicate, unrefined, unpolished, vulgar, common, ordinary.

ANT. *Fine, choice, delicate, gentle.*

Coax. Wheedle, flatter, cajole, fawn, allure, seduce, circumvent.

ANT. *Coerce, impel, drive, intimidate.*

Coerce. Impel, restrain, inhibit, force, compel, drive, check, intimidate.

ANT. *Persuade, coax, permit, urge, induce, tempt.*

Coexistent. Contemporary, concurrent, coincident, simultaneous.

ANT. *Preceding* or *succeeding.*

Cogent. Forcible, powerful, effective, irresistible, convincing, conclusive, persuasive, potent, urgent.

ANT. *Weak, feeble, powerless, ineffectual.*

Cogitate. Meditate, think, reflect, consider, ponder, contemplate.

ANT. *Dream, idle, wish.*

Cognizance. Knowledge, observation, notice, recognition, experience.

ANT. *Ignorance, oversight, neglect.*

Coherent. Compact, consecutive, close, logical, consistent.

ANT. *Rambling, loose, discursive, aberrant.*

Coincidence. Chance, fortuity, harmony, agreement, casualty, concurrence, contemporaneousness.

ANT. *Design, purpose, asynchronism, anachronism, difference.*

Cold. Frigid, chilly, frosty, icy, polar, wintry; dull, lifeless, unimpassioned, sluggish, apathetic, indifferent, spiritless.

ANT. *Hot, warm, ardent, impassioned, fiery, burning, fervid, vehement, passionate.*

Colleague. Associate, coadjutor, collaborator, helper, companion, partner, assistant, ally, confederate.

ANT. *Opponent, rival, antagonist, competitor.*

Collect. Gather, glean, amass, garner, muster, congregate, assemble, convoke, accumulate.

ANT. *Distribute, dispense, divide, assort, deal.*

Collision. Clash, shock, impact, concussion, encounter, contact, opposition, conflict.

ANT. *Divergence; concord, harmony, agreement, coincidence, concert, unity, amity, unison.*

Colloquy. Dialogue, conversation, talk, discourse, consultation, conference.

ANT. *Babel, tumult, outcry, clamor; silence, taciturnity.*

Collusion. Connivance, accompliceship, confederacy.

ANT. *Frustration, betrayal, exposure.*

Color. Hue, tint, tinge, shade, complexion; pigment, paint; pretense, speciousness, varnish, appearance, semblance, excuse, makeshift.

ANT. *Paleness; transparency, openness.*

Combat. Conflict, encounter, battle, struggle, contest, contention.

ANT. *Truce, surrender, mediation.*

Combination. Association, connection, union; alliance, league; mixture, compound.

ANT. *Division, disruption, analysis, dissolution.*

Comfortable. Agreeable, satisfactory, pleasant, convenient, commodious, snug, genial.

ANT. *Miserable, distressed, forlorn, wretched, cheerless.*

Comic. Laughable, droll, funny, comical, farcical, ludicrous, ridiculous.

ANT. *Serious, solemn, grave, tragic, melancholy.*

Command. Order, direct, bid, instruct, charge, enjoin; rule, govern.

ANT. *Beg, petition, supplicate, entreat; obey, yield, comply.*

Commemorate. Celebrate, observe, perpetuate.

ANT. *Forget, abolish, ignore.*

Commence. Begin, start, inaugurate, undertake.

ANT. *Finish, conclude, terminate.*

Commend. Approve, encourage, applaud, praise.

ANT. *Blame, condemn, censure, denounce.*

Comment. Remark, observe, explain, note, expound, interpret, illustrate.

ANT. *Confuse, obscure, mystify, confound, misrepresent.*

Commerce. Trade, traffic, business, exchange.

ANT. *Embargo, inactivity, boycott.*

Commit. Assign, confide, trust, relegate, entrust, consign.
ANT. *Omit, let pass, disregard, misconsign.*

Commodious. Ample, spacious, convenient, comfortable, suitable.
ANT. *Narrow, cramped, ill-contrived.*

Commodity. Staple, ware, stock, produce, article.
ANT. *Drug, refuse.*

Common. Ordinary, habitual, everyday, familiar, frequent; coarse, vulgar, mean, low.
ANT. *Exceptional, scarce, refined, rare.*

Commotion. Excitement, disturbance, agitation, turmoil, tumult, disorder.
ANT. *Quiet, tranquillity, calm, subsidence, pacification.*

Communicate. Divulge, impart, disclose, tell, announce, publish.
ANT. *Secrete, suppress, conceal, withhold, reserve; repress; disavow.*

Communion. Fellowship, intercourse, participation.
ANT. *Alienation, exclusion, deprivation, ostracism.*

Community. Aggregation, society, commonwealth, neighborhood; fraternity, similarity, sympathy, homogeneity.
ANT. *Hostility, animosity, heterogeneity.*

Commute. Exchange, replace, barter, compensate, mitigate, modify, lessen, diminish.
ANT. *Disallow; charge; increase, enlarge.*

Compact, *n.* Agreement, bond, contract, treaty, covenant.
ANT. *Promise, intention.*

Compact, *a.* Dense, close, solid, firm, compressed; concise, terse, pithy, short, brief, laconic, compendious, succinct, sententious.
ANT. *Diffuse; sparse, straggling; broadspread, unshapely; prolix, verbose.*

Companion. Associate, partner, mate, comrade, colleague.
ANT. *Rival, antagonist, adversary.*

Companionable. Sociable, pleasant, affable, genial, friendly, agreeable.
ANT. *Reserved, haughty, distant, cold, solitary, inaccessible.*

Company. Concourse, gathering, crowd, throng, meeting, multitude, assembly, conclave, conference, congregation, convention, convocation.
ANT. *Privacy, retirement, solitude, dispersion, loneliness, seclusion.*

Compare. Collate, estimate, declare similar, liken, parallel.
ANT. *Contrast, disconnect, pit, distinguish.*

Compass. Surround, enclose; effect, achieve, consummate, complete.
ANT. *Expand, liberate; fail, bungle, mismanage.*

Compassion. Pity, sympathy, condolence, kindness, clemency, mercy.
ANT. *Cruelty, antipathy, retaliation, vindictiveness.*

Compatible. Consistent, accordant, congruous, congenial, harmonious.
ANT. *Hostile, adverse, impossible, destructive, contradictory.*

Compel. Force, oblige, make necessary, coerce, constrain, necessitate.
ANT. *Hinder, prevent, delay, block, hamper, encumber.*

Compensation. Recompense, reward, requital, satisfaction, reparation, amends, indemnification.
ANT. *Damage, injury, deprivation.*

Compete. Contend, rival, strive, struggle.
Ant. *Share, participate.*

Competence. Ability, capableness; sufficiency, enough, adequacy.
Ant. *Inability, weakness; poverty, want, indigence.*

Competition. Rivalry, emulation, contest.
Ant. *Alliance, co-partnership.*

Complacent. Pleased, satisfied, contented, amiable, pleasant, affable.
Ant. *Morose, austere, unmannerly.*

Complain. Murmur, grumble, remonstrate, find fault, repine, lament, grieve, expostulate.
Ant. *Approve, commend, applaud, congratulate, rejoice.*

Complement. Fulfilment, totality, counterpart, supply, correlative.
Ant. *Deficit, abatement, deficiency.*

Complete, *a.* Perfect, finished, total, whole, entire; concluded, consummated, ended; adequate, exhaustive, thorough.
Ant. *Partial, inadequate, imperfect, unfinished.*

Complex. Confused, involved, mixed, entangled, complicated, composite, manifold, mingled, intricate, obscure.
Ant. *Direct, obvious, plain, uniform, simple, homogeneous, unraveled.*

Complexion. Face, feature, appearance, look, hue, character, indication.
Ant. *Heart, core; reticence, concealment, inexpression.*

Compliance. Yielding, submission, acquiescence, docility, obedience.
Ant. *Resistance, repulsion, refusal.*

Compliment. Flattery, praise, homage, commendation, encomium.
Ant. *Insult, contempt, discourtesy.*

Complimentary. Commendatory, flattering, laudatory.
Ant. *Disparaging, abusive, defamatory, denunciatory*

Component. Constituent, factor, element, ingredient.
Ant. *Compound, entirety, sum, aggregate.*

Comport. Conduct, behave, demean; accord, agree, harmonize.
Ant. *Contrast, militate, differ; misdemean, misconduct.*

Compose. Compile, construct, constitute; soothe, allay, calm; write.
Ant. *Analyze, dissect; irritate, excite; criticize.*

Composition. Formation, making; compound, mixture; arrangement, union, combination; writing, invention; agreement, compromise.
Ant. *Examination, analysis, criticism; disturbance; segregation.*

Composure. Tranquillity, calm, repose, self-possession, serenity.
Ant. *Restlessness, perturbation.*

Compound, *n.* Mixture, combination, amalgamation, coalescence, synthesis.
Ant. *Analysis, dissolution, resolution.*

Comprehend. Understand, conceive, grasp; include, enclose, embrace.
Ant. *Misunderstand, misconstrue; except, exclude.*

Comprehension. Conception, understanding, perception, apprehension, capacity, intellect, reason, mind, intelligence.
Ant. *Idiocy, nescience, misunderstanding, misconception.*

Comprehensive. Ample, wide, inclusive, extensive, capacious, compendious.
ANT. *Narrow, shallow, restricted.*

Compress. Condense, squeeze, contract, epitomize, abridge.
ANT. *Expand, diffuse, dilate.*

Comprise. Include, involve, contain, comprehend, embrace, imply.
ANT. *Except, bar out, omit, reject.*

Compromise. Adjust, arbitrate, settle; engage, pledge, commit; implicate, involve, endanger.
ANT. *Contend, fight; repudiate, disallow; exonerate, extricate.*

Compulsion. Force, coercion, constraint, control.
ANT. *Coaxing, persuasion, inducement.*

Compunction. Regret, remorse, contrition, penitence.
ANT. *Assurance, self-complacency, satisfaction.*

Compute. Number, calculate, reckon, count; value, estimate, appraise.
ANT. *Guess, conjecture, surmise.*

Comrade. Companion, compeer, colleague, associate, partner, friend.
ANT. *Opponent; stranger, alien.*

Concatenation. Connection, continuity; series, chain, succession.
ANT. *Intermission, severing, disconnection.*

Concave. Hollow, depressed, excavated.
ANT. *Convex, protuberant, tumular.*

Conceal. Hide, suppress, secrete, disguise.
ANT. *Reveal, expose, make manifest, lay bare, confess, publish, divulge.*

Concede. Surrender, admit, resign, yield, allow.
ANT. *Refuse, claim, contend, contradict, deny, contest.*

Conceit. Notion, whim, vagary, idea, abstraction, affectation, imagination.
ANT. *Reality, fact, substance; simplicity, humility.*

Conceited. Egoistical, opinionated, vain.
ANT. *Simple, unassuming, unaffected.*

Conceive. Imagine, apprehend, believe, design, think, understand.
ANT. *Express, produce, execute.*

Concentrate. Convene, assemble, congregate, muster, centralize.
ANT. *Scatter, disperse, dispense, dismiss.*

Concern. Interest, anxiety, solicitude; affair, matter, institution.
ANT. *Indifference, carelessness, disregard.*

Concerning. About, regarding, in relation to, respecting, in respect to, relative to, of.
ANT. *Disregarding, omitting.*

Concert. Agreement, harmony, concord, concordance, combination, union, association.
ANT. *Opposition, disagreement, discord.*

Concession. Surrender, grant, boon, acknowledgment, admission.
ANT. *Refusal, denial, withdrawal.*

Conciliate. Win, gain, pacify, reconcile, propitiate.
ANT. *Alienate, irritate, estrange, lose, antagonize.*

Concise. Succinct, condensed, terse, pregnant, pointed, brief, short, laconic.

ANT. *Prolix, verbose, diffuse, discursive, rambling, pointless.*

Conclave. Assembly, synod, cabinet, council, bureau.
ANT. *Throng, mob, populace, concourse, crowd.*

Conclude. Close, end, terminate, finish; decide, determine.
ANT. *Begin, commence, undertake, initiate; prolong, protract.*

Conclusion. End, termination, finale, finis.
ANT. *Commencement, beginning, initiation.*

Conclusive. Final, decisive, positive, definitive, indisputable.
ANT. *Dubious, vague, uncertain, problematical, theoretical, indeterminate.*

Concoct. Brew, prepare, compound, mix.
ANT. *Spoil, upset, overbrew.*

Concoction. Compound, brew, mixture; scheme, fiction.
ANT. *Rawness, crudity; simplicity.*

Concomitant. Attending, coincident, attendant, synchronous.
ANT. *Antecedent; diverse, unconnected; subsequent.*

Concord. Harmony, agreement, friendship, unanimity, accord.
ANT. *Variance, animosity, discord.*

Concourse. Assembly, throng, crowd, mob, assemblage, gathering, multitude.
ANT. *Conclave, cabal, cabinet; desert, solitude.*

Concrete. Solid, firm, compact; complex, conglomerate; individualized, specific, particular.
ANT. *Loose, shifting, yielding, unresisting; abstract, general.*

Concur. Approve, harmonize, agree; help, combine, conspire.
ANT. *Disagree, dissent, part, differ, disapprove, separate.*

Concussion. Collision, encounter, crash, impact, percussion.
ANT. *Inter-divergence; escape; tangency; failure, missing.*

Condemn. Blame, censure, denounce, convict, sentence, reprove, doom.
ANT. *Acquit, exonerate, absolve, pardon, justify, praise, approve.*

Condense. Concentrate, abridge, shorten.
ANT. *Expand, amplify, enlarge.*

Condescend. Deign, vouchsafe, stoop.
ANT. *Scorn, spurn, disdain.*

Condescension. Graciousness, favor.
ANT. *Arrogance, haughtiness, pride.*

Condign. Adequate, deserved, merited, suitable, meet, just.
ANT. *Unmerited, inadequate; excessive* or *scant.*

Condiment. Sauce, seasoning, preserve, pickle, relish, appetizer.

Condition. Situation, case, circumstances, plight; rank, estate, grade; proviso, consideration, stipulation.
ANT. *Concession, adaptation; relation, dependence.*

Conditionally. Provided, provisionally, hypothetically, contingently.
ANT. *Absolutely, positively, categorically.*

Condole. Console, commiserate, sympathize.
ANT. *Congratulate, rally, exhilarate.*

Condone. Pardon, overlook, forgive.
ANT. *Atone, expiate, satisfy.*

Conduce. Subserve, promote, forward, advance, contribute to, aid.

ANT. *Defeat; counteract, neutralize.*

Conduct. Lead, direct, guide, convoy, escort; command, govern; manage, regulate; rule, superintend.

ANT. *Mislead; mismanage; follow.*

Confection. Candy, cake, condiment, concoction, sweetmeat.

Confederacy, Confederation. Alliance, league, treaty, union, coalition, federation, compact.

ANT. *Secession, disruption, disunion.*

Conference. Discourse, conversation, talk; interview, colloquy, parley, consultation; convention, convocation, meeting.

ANT. *Silence; monologue; dispersion.*

Confess. Acknowledge, admit, disclose, own, allow, grant, concede, avow.

ANT. *Deny, conceal, repudiate, disavow, hide, dissemble.*

Confession. Admission, avowal, acknowledgment; creed, doctrines, tenets, catechism, subscription.

ANT. *Heresy, apostasy, protest, refutation, renunciation, abjuration.*

Confide. Trust, rely, lean, hope, depend, believe, put confidence in.

ANT. *Doubt, mistrust, disbelieve, disprove, despair of.*

Confident. Assured, sure, positive, certain; bold, presumptuous, impudent, sanguine.

ANT. *Dubious, doubtful, undecided, vacillating.*

Confidential. Intimate, secret, private; trusty, faithful.

ANT. *Public, patent, open; treacherous, insidious, traitorous.*

Configuration. Outline, shape, form, contour.

ANT. *Shapelessness, indeterminateness; distortion, deformity.*

Confine, *v.* Limit, bound, imprison, restrict, circumscribe, enclose.

ANT. *Widen, expand, liberate, unfasten, loosen, extend, dilate.*

Confirm. Sanction, uphold, assure, establish, strengthen, substantiate, settle, corroborate.

ANT. *Shatter, weaken, upset, annul, abrogate, cancel, destroy, shake.*

Confiscate. Forfeit, seize, escheat, condemn, sequestrate.

ANT. *Release, restore, refund.*

Conflagration. Fire, arson, ignition, incendiarism, combustion.

ANT. *Extinction, quenching; smoldering.*

Conflict. Contest, battle, struggle, encounter; clashing, interference, disagreement, discord.

ANT. *Amity, reconciliation, pacification, arbitration.*

Conform. Agree, consent, harmonize, comply, correspond, comport.

ANT. *Dissent, disagree; antagonize, secede; vary, differ.*

Confound. Confuse, perplex, bewilder, mystify; surprise, astonish, astound, startle; destroy, ruin, overwhelm; disconcert, abash, shame.

ANT. *Clear, set right, arrange, enlighten; save, protect; calm, console, soothe, restore.*

Confront. Oppose, threaten, encounter, challenge, face, intimidate.

ANT. *Encourage, abet, countenance.*

Confuse. Mingle, confound; derange, disturb, perplex, embarrass, obscure, mortify.

ANT. *Arrange; relieve, assist, allay; calm, restore.*

Congeal. Freeze, convert to ice, benumb.

ANT. *Melt, thaw, dissolve.*

Congenial. Kindred, similar, sympathetic, suited, natural, proper, agreeable.

ANT. *Disagreeable, abhorrent, unnatural, alien, dissimilar, unsuited, unsympathetic.*

Congenital. Coeval, connatural, innate, inherent, ingenerate.

ANT. *Unnatural, assumed, extraneous, acquired, artificial, adventitious.*

Congeries, Congestion. Conglomeration, aggregation, accumulation, plethora, repletion.

ANT. *Dissipation, diffusion, clearance, dispersion.*

Congratulate. Felicitate, compliment, rejoice with.

ANT. *Console, condole with, commiserate.*

Congregate. Assemble, collect, meet, convene, gather, throng.

ANT. *Disperse, disappear, separate, part, scatter.*

Congregation. Assembly, meeting, audience, conference.

ANT. *Dispersion, dismissal.*

Congress. Parliament, conclave, cabinet, council, assembly, legislature, synod, convention, conference.

ANT. *Cabal, sedition, uprising, mob; intrigue.*

Congruous. Accordant, agreeing, harmonious, coherent, suitable, consistent, proper, appropriate.

ANT. *Discordant, heterogeneous, inharmonious, improper, unsuitable.*

Conjecture, *n.* Supposition, surmise, guess, hypothesis, theory, notion, divination.

ANT. *Calculation, inference, deduction, proof; fact, surety, certainty, security.*

Conjuncture. Combination, concurrence; emergency, crisis, exigency, juncture.

ANT. *Provision, preparation, arrangement.*

Connection. Conjunction, combination, union, association, dependence.

ANT. *Independence, disjunction, dissociation, dissolution.*

Conquer. Overcome, subjugate, master, vanquish, subdue, rout, defeat, overpower, overthrow, prevail, over, reduce, win, surmount, worst, checkmate, beat, crush, down, discomfit.

ANT. *Surrender, capitulate, cede, forfeit, fly, yield, retreat, withdraw, retire, submit, succumb, fall, lose, resign, fail.*

Conquest. Victory, subjugation, triumph.

ANT. *Defeat, failure, surrender, submission.*

Conscience. Moral sense, intuition, integrity, principle.

ANT. *Irresponsibility, laxity, undutifulness, unscrupulousness.*

Conscientious. Scrupulous, exact, upright, high-principled, honest, honorable, equitable, incorruptible, fair, faithful.

ANT. *Lax, unprincipled, unscrupulous, reprobate, dishonorable, faithless.*

Conscious. Sensible, cognizant, aware, intelligent, advised, apprised, assured, sure, certain, informed; thinking, reflecting, rational, intellectual.

ANT. *Insensible, unaware, ignorant, dead, cold, deaf; irrational, thoughtless.*

Conscription. Drafting, impressment.

ANT. *Volunteering, enlistment.*

Consecrate. Dedicate, ordain; sanctify, hallow.
ANT. *Desecrate, defile.*

Consecutive. Sequent, continuous, orderly, following.
ANT. *Disordered, rambling, discursive, illogical.*

Consent. Assent, approve, agree, yield, comply, acquiesce.
ANT. *Refuse, resist, decline, dissent.*

Consequence. Result, issue, sequel, effect, outgrowth, event, end, upshot; importance, dignity, moment.
ANT. *Cause, occasion, origin; axiom, postulate, premise, antecedence; insignificance, paltriness.*

Consequential. Following, resulting, coherent, cogent, connected; pompous, self-conceited, arrogant, vainglorious.
ANT. *Incoherent, illogical; affable, accessible, humble, considerate.*

Conservation. Protection, perpetuation, preservation, maintenance.
ANT. *Neglect, exposure, destruction, abolition.*

Conservative. Stationary, traditional, opposed to change.
ANT. *Radical, progressive, changeable, transitional, modifiable, innovating.*

Consider. Think, ponder, meditate, reflect, investigate, weigh, deliberate, observe, attend, regard.
ANT. *Guess, conjecture, ignore, chance, hazard.*

Considerate. Kindly, thoughtful, reflective, careful, prudent, deliberate, serious, charitable, forbearing, cautious.
ANT. *Rash, careless, imprudent, thoughtless, rude, selfish, overbearing, injudicious.*

Consignment. Custody, commission, delegation; sending, shipping.
ANT. *Miscommitment.*

Consistency. Density, solidity, compactness, coherence; agreement, congruity, correspondence, uniformity, harmony, invariableness.
ANT. *Tenuity, subtility, volatility; incoherence, incongruity, contrariety, contradiction.*

Console. Comfort, condole with, sympathize, encourage, soothe, assuage, solace.
ANT. *Distress, grieve, disturb, annoy, sadden, trouble, wound, hurt.*

Consolidate. Solidify, harden, condense, compress, compact; thicken, strengthen, solder, cement, fuse; conjoin, combine.
ANT. *Dissolve, melt, vaporize, weaken, dissipate, sublimate, pulverize; dissect, disjoin.*

Conspicuous. Visible, apparent, discernible, plain, clear, perceptible, noticeable; eminent, distinguished, prominent, famous, noted, manifest.
ANT. *Invisible, microscopic, hidden, imperceptible, unseen; ordinary, mediocre, commonplace.*

Conspiracy. Intrigue, treason, cabal, plot, machination, combination; sedition.
ANT. *Legislation, congress, parliament, synod.*

Constant. Fixed, immutable, invariable, unchanging, permanent, perpetual; resolute, firm, steady; persevering, assiduous; incessant, unbroken, continuous; faithful, true, loyal, devoted.
ANT. *Irregular, exceptional, casual, incidental, fickle, faithless, broken, treacherous, untrustworthy, false.*

Consternation. Amazement, terror, alarm, dismay, panic, bewilderment.

ANT. *Fearlessness, boldness, composure, presence of mind.*

Constituent. Elector, patron, voter, supporter, sender; ingredient, component, element.

ANT. *Representative, nominee; constitution, system, compound, whole.*

Constitution. Organization, formation; quality, character, temperament, peculiarity, characteristic; charter, law.

ANT. *Conspiracy, rebellion, tyranny, anarchy, despotism, destruction, disorganization; disposition, mood, frame of mind, temper.*

Construct. Build, erect, invent, form, shape, combine.

ANT. *Demolish, overthrow, destroy, derange.*

Construction. Building, erection, composition, fabrication; structure, formation, form, figure; explanation, version, rendering, interpretation.

ANT. *Dislocation, dismemberment, dissolution; misunderstanding, misconception.*

Consult. Deliberate, take counsel, confer, advise with, canvass, question, consider, regard.

ANT. *Dictate, counteract, contradict.*

Consume. Eat up, devour; destroy, lavish, dissipate, waste, spend.

ANT. *Discard, reject, throw aside; preserve, replenish, supply, provide.*

Consummate, *a.* Perfect, excellent, supreme, finished, complete.

ANT. *Common, faulty, defective, ordinary, mediocre.*

Consummation. Achievement, attainment, completion, termination, accomplishment, fulfilment, realization, close, finish, finale.

ANT. *Beginning, attempt, inception, initiation, source, origin.*

Consumption. Expenditure, use, waste, extinction, destruction.

ANT. *Development, increase, growth, enlargement, augmentation.*

Contact. Touch, junction, contiguity, closeness, union.

ANT. *Adjacence, proximity; separation, distance, isolation.*

Contagion. Infection; contamination, taint, pestilence, corruption.

ANT. *Prevention; antisepsis, disinfection.*

Contain. Include, embody, comprehend, comprise, embrace; restrain, hold.

ANT. *Omit, exclude, drop, discharge; yield, give way.*

Contaminate. Taint, defile, corrupt, sully.

ANT. *Cleanse, purify.*

Contemn. Despise, scorn, disdain, slight.

ANT. *Venerate, respect.*

Contemplate. Meditate, study, ponder, survey, reflect; intend, design.

ANT. *Overlook, waive, abandon; execute, complete, do.*

Contemptible. Despicable, abject, base, worthless, mean, low.

ANT. *Respectable, venerable; worthy, estimable, important, grave.*

Contend. Strive, fight, struggle, combat; debate, argue, dispute; affirm, assert, maintain, claim.

ANT. *Concede, allow, surrender.*

Content. Satisfied, pleased, easy, willing, resigned, gratified.

ANT. *Reluctant, unwilling, unsatisfied, rebellious, discontent.*

Contention. Strife, dissension, quarrel, rupture, dispute, debate, controversy, altercation.
ANT. *Peace, amity, harmony, concord, reconciliation.*

Contingent, *a.* Casual, happening, fortuitous, dependent, incidental, provisional, uncertain.
ANT. *Independent, absolute, positive, uncontrolled, uninfluenced, unaffected.*

Continual. Incessant, ceaseless, invariable, perpetual, constant, uninterrupted, unbroken, unremitting, continuous.
ANT. *Exceptional, irregular, casual, contingent, intermittent, interrupted, suspended.*

Continually. Constantly, perpetually, ever, always, repeatedly, frequently, continuously.
ANT. *Occasionally, rarely, sometimes.*

Continue. Remain, endure, persist; abide, stay, tarry; persevere, be constant *or* steadfast.
ANT. *Stop, cease, fail, pause.*

Contract, *n.* Compact, stipulation, agreement, arrangement, bargain, covenant, pact, obligation, pledge, engagement, bond.
ANT. *Promise, parole, assurance, understanding, assumption.*

Contract, *v.* Narrow, abbreviate, abridge, lessen, reduce, compress; shrivel, shrink; agree, stipulate, bargain.
ANT. *Expand, amplify, dilate; reverse, cancel, abandon.*

Contradict. Deny, gainsay, dispute, impugn, controvert; oppose, counteract, annul, thwart, abrogate.
ANT. *Maintain, argue, confirm, state, affirm, endorse.*

Contrary. Opposite, opposed, adverse, counter; conflicting, contradictory, antagonistic, repugnant; perverse, obstinate, stubborn, headstrong.
ANT. *Compatible, agreeing, kindred, compliant, submissive; consistent.*

Contrast, *v.* Differentiate, discriminate, oppose, compare.
ANT. *Resemble, be like* or *similar, liken, harmonize.*

Contribute. Add, give, coöperate, assist, subscribe, supply.
ANT. *Refuse, withhold, deny.*

Contribution. Donation, offering, gift, subscription, subsidy, aid, assistance.
ANT. *Withholding, retention, reservation.*

Contrive. Plan, design, devise, invent, project, form, frame, scheme, plot, consider; manage, make out; concert, adjust.
ANT. *Hit, chance, venture, bungle, hazard; mismanage, miscontrive.*

Control, *v.* Direct, manage, rule, command, sway, superintend; hinder, repress, restrain, curb, check.
ANT. *License, free; neglect, abandon; mismanage, misconduct.*

Controversy. Dispute, altercation, contention, disagreement.
ANT. *Agreement, unanimity, coincidence.*

Contumacy. Obstinacy, stubbornness, perverseness, pertinacity, obduracy; disobedience, insolence.
ANT. *Docility, tractableness, flattering, fawning, servility.*

Contumely. Obloquy, reproach, opprobrium, insolence, abuse, contempt, scorn, disdain, arrogance.
ANT. *Regard, consideration, adulation, obsequiousness.*

Convene. Assemble, meet, congregate, summon, master, collect.

ANT. *Dismiss, disperse, disband, dissipate.*

Convenient. Suitable, fit, appropriate, proper, adapted; advantageous, commodious, comfortable, useful, serviceable.

ANT. *Inconvenient, useless, awkward, superfluous; inopportune.*

Convention. Assemblage, conference, meeting, concourse, session, synod, congress, convocation; treaty, compact.

ANT. *Recess, dissolution, prorogation; dispersion, scattering; promise, understanding, parole.*

Conventional. Usual, customary, ordinary, habitual, regular, wonted, prevalent, social, everyday; stipulated.

ANT. *Unusual, erratic, extraordinary; legal, compulsory.*

Conversant. Familiar, skilled, acquainted, proficient, versed.

ANT. *Strange, ignorant, unversed, unlearned.*

Conversation. Converse, communion, intercourse, parley, talk, chat, conference, communication, discourse, colloquy, dialogue.

ANT. *Speech, oration, harangue, soliloquy, apostrophe, monologue, silence, taciturnity.*

Converse, *a.* Opposite, reverse, contrary, counter, contradictory.

ANT. *Identical, one, same, indistinguishable; direct, primary.*

Conversion. Alteration, transmutation, change, transformation.

ANT. *Permanence, identity, persistence, conservation.*

Convertible. Equivalent, interchangeable, identical; reversible.

ANT. *Variant, contrary, incommensurate.*

Convey. Take, transfer, move, change, carry, shift, transmit, transport, remove, consign, relegate.

ANT. *Retain, preserve, hold, cling to, possess.*

Conviction. Belief, assurance, persuasion; confutation, refutation; proof, detection.

ANT. *Doubt, disbelief, misgiving; vindication, justification.*

Convince. Persuade, satisfy, enlighten, indoctrinate, inoculate.

ANT. *Mislead, mystify, perplex, puzzle, unsettle, upset; turn, convert.*

Convivial. Social, festive, hospitable, jovial, jolly, companionable, gay.

ANT. *Inhospitable, unsocial, unneighborly, churlish; abstemious, ascetic, austere.*

Convocation. Convention, congress, assemblage, council, synod.

ANT. *Dispersion, disruption, dismission, dismissal.*

Convolution. Coil, involution, spiral, twist, contortion.

ANT. *Unfolding, evolution, unraveling, explication.*

Convoy. Escort, guard, attendance, protection.

ANT. *Capture, betrayal, onset, onslaught, hold-up.*

Convulse. Disturb, shake, agitate.

ANT. *Calm, compose, soothe, assuage.*

Cool. Somewhat cold, chilling, frigid, freezing; unimpassioned, composed, collected, unruffled, self-possessed, sedate, placid, quiet; indifferent, unconcerned, apathetic.

ANT. *Hot, warm, burning, heated, excitable, ardent, eager.*

Coöperate. Assist, abet, help, conspire, concur, colabor.
ANT. *Oppose, thwart, rival, counteract, conflict, hinder, defeat, frustrate.*

Coördinate. Equal, equivalent, proportionate, commensurate, tantamount, equipollent.
ANT. *Subordinate; disparate, extraneous; inferior, superior.*

Copy. Portraiture, facsimile, duplicate, imitation, likeness, image, transcript, counterfeit.
ANT. *Model, original, pattern, example, prototype, archetype, exemplar.*

Cordial. Earnest, warm, hearty, ardent, affectionate, sincere, invigorating, refreshing, pleasing, grateful.
ANT. *Cool, formal, ceremonious, distant, reserved, disinclined.*

Corner. Angle, bend, crotch, knee; nook, recess, niche, retreat.
ANT. *Abutment, protrusion, prominence, convexity, projection.*

Corollary. Inference, conclusion, deduction, consequence.
ANT. *Problem, proposition.*

Corporal, Corporeal. Fleshly, bodily, material, physical.
ANT. *Spiritual, mental, intellectual, moral, ethereal, immaterial.*

Corps. Body of troops, division of army, squadron, band, company.
ANT. *Aggregate, army, host, mass, force, organization.*

Corpse. Remains, dead body, cadaver, carcass, dust.
ANT. *Soul, spirit, individual, personality, mentality.*

Corpulent. Fat, fleshy, plump, obese, portly, round, stout.
ANT. *Lean, thin, attenuated, emaciated, slight, slender, frail.*

Correct. True, exact, accurate, proper, faultless, right.
ANT. *False, untrue, wrong, inexact, inaccurate, fallacious, defective.*

Corrective. Regulative, preventive, alterative, preservative, rectifying, modifying, improving, reformatory.
ANT. *Confirmative, stimulative, intensitive, provocative, conducive.*

Correlation. Interrelation, correspondence, apposition, interdependence, mutuality, reciprocation, interchange, reciprocity.
ANT. *Contradiction, independence, opposition, inconsistency, incongruity.*

Correspond. Agree, suit, match, fit, tally, harmonize, answer, correlate, stand counter; communicate, write.
ANT. *Vary, disagree, clash, jar; ignore, disregard, neglect.*

Correspondence. Adaptation, agreement, congruity; writing, letter, despatches, communication.
ANT. *Conversation; withdrawal, non-intercourse; incongruity, discord, disagreement.*

Corroborate. Strengthen, establish, sustain, support, confirm.
ANT. *Weaken, confute, rebut, invalidate, shake, enfeeble, overthrow.*

Corrode. Consume, eat away, waste, impair, rust, canker, wear, crumble.
ANT. *Renew, restore.*

Corrupt, *v.* Defile, pollute, infect, taint, vitiate, demoralize, contaminate, debase, spoil, deteriorate.
ANT. *Cleanse, purify, better, correct, ameliorate.*

Corruption. Decay, decomposition, pollution, defilement, infection, contamination, adulteration; depravity, immorality, laxity, wickedness; dishonesty, bribery.

Cost. Price, worth, expenditure, expense, charge, disbursement, outlay; preciousness, richness, splendor; loss, damage, pain.

Costume. Dress, livery, robes, uniform.

ANT. *Disguise, incognito; nudity, nakedness.*

Council. Cabinet, bureau, chamber, conclave, synod, convocation, meeting, conference, parliament, consultation, convention.

ANT. *Cabal, league, conspiracy; multitude, mob.*

Counsel. Advice, consultation, opinion, suggestion, recommendation, instruction, caution, admonition; deliberation, forethought; plan, design, scheme; purpose; lawyer, barrister, attorney.

Count. Compute, reckon, add, tell, estimate, number, enumerate, sum, calculate.

ANT. *Guess, conjecture, surmise, think, fancy.*

Countenance, *v.* Approve, support, sanction, help, aid, abet, encourage, patronize, befriend, assist, favor.

ANT. *Oppose, confront, discourage, browbeat, face, compare, disparage.*

Counter. Contrary, opposed, opposite, against.

ANT. *Accordant with, coincident, consonant.*

Counteract. Oppose, foil, baffle, thwart, hinder, rival, resist, defeat, cross, frustrate, neutralize.

ANT. *Aid, coöperate, subserve, promote, advance, assist.*

Counterfeit, *n.* Forgery, fraudulent copy, cheat, artifice, pretense, sham, fabrication.

ANT. *Exposure, detection; verity, fact, truth, reality.*

Countermand. Abrogate, annul, revoke, rescind, recall, make void.

ANT. *Order, command, bid, charge, enjoin, direct, instruct.*

Counterpart. Duplicate, copy; correlative, complement, supplement, obverse; match, mate, tally, twin.

ANT. *Antithesis, contradiction, contrast.*

Countervail. Balance, compensate, make up, counterbalance, offset.

ANT. *Overthrow, unbalance, weigh down.*

Countryman. Rustic, agriculturist, farmer, swain, yeoman, laborer, peasant, husbandman; clown, boor.

ANT. *Citizen, townsman; alien.*

Couple, *v.* Link, unite, connect, join, clasp, tie, yoke, buckle, pair, splice, button; marry, wed.

ANT. *Loose, part, separate, detach, isolate, unclasp; divorce.*

Courage. Bravery, valor, fearlessness, spirit, heroism, fortitude, hardihood, boldness, daring, mettle, pluck, resolution, intrepidity.

ANT. *Cowardice, timidity, fear, dread, terror, dismay, consternation.*

Course. Route, way, road, track, race; direction, bearing, progress, process; career; succession, order, regularity; deportment, conduct; series, system.

ANT. *Deviation; disorder, discursion; hindrance, error.*

Court, *v.* Woo, flatter, seek, invite, solicit.

ANT. *Avoid, shun, repudiate, repel, antagonize.*

Courtesy. Politeness, affability, urbanity, civility, complaisance.

ANT. *Rudeness, incivility, churlishness, ungraciousness.*

Courtly. Polished, elegant, polite, ceremonious, formal, respectful.

ANT. *Undignified, unrefined, coarse, awkward, boorish, plebeian.*

Covenant. Agreement, stipulation, bond, compact, contract, bargain, arrangement, concordant, pact, treaty.

ANT. *Promise, understanding, assurance, parole.*

Cover, *v.* Hide, conceal, overspread, overlay, secrete, cloak, veil, screen, mask, shroud, disguise; invest, clothe, wrap; protect, shelter, shield, guard, defend; comprehend, comprise, embrace; balance, compensate, countervail.

ANT. *Expose, reveal, produce, exhibit; betray, divulge; omit, exclude.*

Covet. Desire, long for, wish for, aim after, aspire to.

ANT. *Dislike, despise; undervalue.*

Covetous. Eager, avaricious, desirous, greedy, grasping, acquisitive, rapacious.

ANT. *Liberal, unselfish, generous, bountiful.*

Coward. Craven, recreant, dastard.

ANT. *Hero, champion; daredevil, desperado.*

Coy. Bashful, shy, modest, reserved, retreating, shrinking.

ANT. *Bold, forward, impertinent, pert, brazen, flippant.*

Crack. Split, break, chop, rend, cleave, snap; craze, madden.

ANT. *Mend, unite, repair; restore, heal.*

Craft. Skill, ability, power, talent, dexterity, aptitude, tact; artifice, shrewdness, guile, deception, cunning, deceit; art, trade, employment, vocation, calling; vessel.

ANT. *Inaptitude, tactlessness; fairness, openness, candor, sincerity, frankness, ingenuousness, straightforwardness.*

Cramp. Restrain, hinder, check, confine, hamper, clog, fetter, cripple.

ANT. *Free, liberate, loose, expand, ease, relieve, extricate.*

Crash. Jar, uproar, clash, rending, noise, clang, resonance.

ANT. *Murmur, whisper; silence.*

Crassitude. Grossness, thickness, density, corpulence, obesity.

ANT. *Tenuity, agility, activity; spareness, slightness.*

Crave. Intreat, beg, beseech, implore, supplicate, desire, long for, hunger for, yearn.

ANT. *Demand, insist, require.*

Crazy. Shattered, broken, tottering; distracted, mad, lunatic, insane, delirious, cracked, demented, deranged.

ANT. *Sound, robust, vigorous, sane, whole.*

Create. Form, produce, make, originate, cause, occasion, appoint, constitute; beget, engender, generate; imagine, compose, fashion, design.

ANT. *Destroy, demolish, annihilate.*

Creature. Created being, being, animal, man, person; dependent, vassal, parasite; wretch, miscreant.

ANT. *Chimera, ghost, hallucination, fantasy, phantom, conceit, crotchet.*

Credence. Belief, trust, faith, acceptance, confidence, reliance.
ANT. *Denial, distrust, disbelief, doubt, skepticism.*

Credentials. Diploma, missive, title, warrant, vouchers, certificates, testimonials.

Credible. Probable, possible, reliable, trustworthy, likely.
ANT. *Improbable, unlikely, incredible, unreliable, untrustworthy.*

Credit. Trust, belief, faith, confidence, credence, reliance; reputation, influence, power; esteem, regard; loan, securities.
ANT. *Insecurity; distrust; shame, disgrace, censure.*

Credulity. Gullibility, credulousness, simplicity.
ANT. *Skepticism, suspiciousness, incredulity, shrewdness.*

Creed. Belief, catechism, confession, articles of faith, tenets, dogmas, doctrines.
ANT. *Protest, abjuration, disbelief, recantation, retraction.*

Crestfallen. Downcast, dispirited, dejected, disheartened, depressed, desponding, low-spirited, down-hearted.
ANT. *Exuberant, elated, confident, inspirited.*

Crew. Gang, set, band, horde, crowd, mob, throng.
ANT. *Supercargo; bevy, galaxy, cream, élite.*

Crime. Offense, misdeed, wrong, felony, sin, iniquity, misdemeanor, enormity, transgression, wickedness, delinquency.
ANT. *Good deed, well-doing, exploit, achievement, duty, service, benefit, benefaction, heroism.*

Criminal, *a.* Immoral, iniquitous, sinful, unlawful, wicked, wrong, vile, nefarious, culpable, abominable, illegal, vicious.
ANT. *Virtuous, moral, innocent, just, honorable, praiseworthy, lawful, legal, right, meritorious.*

Criminate. Charge, accuse, arraign, impeach.
ANT. *Acquit, absolve, extricate.*

Cripple, *v.* Weaken, disable, impair, break down, cramp, curtail.
ANT. *Renovate, strengthen, augment, liberate, ease, expedite.*

Criterion. Standard, test, rule, touchstone, measure, canon, proof.
ANT. *Eye, glance; intention, conjecture.*

Critic. Judge, censor, reviewer, connoisseur; caviller, carper; arbiter, savant.
ANT. *Artist, author, writer, performer, maker, poet, composer.*

Critical. Accurate, nice, exact; decisive, crucial, determining, important; dangerous, hazardous, imminent, momentous, dubious, precarious.
ANT. *Inexact, loose, undiscriminating; unimportant, inconclusive; safe, sure, settled, decided, retrieved, redressed.*

Criticism. Censure, stricture, animadversion, review, critique.
ANT. *Approbation, praise, approval.*

Criticize. Examine, estimate, judge, discuss, analyze, anatomize, scan, animadvert.
ANT. *Survey, overlook, slur, skim, slight, neglect.*

Crooked. Bent, curved, bowed; distorted, twisted, wry, askew, deformed, disfigured; perverse, contumacious, capricious; dishonest, unfair, unscrupulous, knavish, deceitful, tricky.
ANT. *Straight, linear, up-*

right, direct, honest, straightforward.

Cross. Fretful, petulant, peevish, snappish, touchy, morose, ill-natured, sullen, snarling, cynical, sour, out of humor, captious, crabbed, sulky.

ANT. *Amiable, genial, good-tempered, good-natured, blithesome, charming, winsome, attractive, benign.*

Crowd. Throng, multitude, concourse, press, horde, herd, host, rabble, mob, populace.

ANT. *Cream, élite, bevy, constellation, galaxy; solitude, solitariness.*

Crown, *n.* Diadem, coronet, garland, chaplet, wreath, laurel, bays; reward, honor, distinction, dignity; summit, crest, top, head, brow, apex.

ANT. *Base, bottom, floor, foot, pedestal, foundation, sole; infamy, shame.*

Crown, *v.* Complete, consummate, conclude, seal, achieve, accomplish.

ANT. *Mar, spoil, frustrate, fail.*

Crucial. Severe, trying, searching, decisive, critical, momentous, strategic.

ANT. *Superficial, indifferent, mild, lenient, lax, unimportant.*

Crude. Raw, immature, unripe; coarse, unrefined; undigested, unconsidered, unpolished, uncouth, awkward.

ANT. *Mature; refined, sensitive; well-considered, finished, classical, highly wrought, elaborate.*

Cruel. Inhuman, merciless, unfeeling, dire, ruthless, pitiless, relentless, savage, brutal, ferocious, blood-thirsty, sanguinary; severe, sharp, bitter, hard.

ANT. *Gentle, mild, merciful, humane, forbearing, generous.*

Crush. Pound, crumble, demolish, overpower, squeeze, compress, bruise, shatter, raze, pulverize.

ANT. *Consolidate, compact, amalgamate, solidify, stabilitate.*

Culmination. Zenith, success, consummation, acme, completion, apex.

ANT. *Failure, downfall, defeat, descent, decline.*

Culpable. Blameworthy, blamable, censurable, reprehensible, faulty, wrong.

ANT. *Innocent, blameless, laudable, praiseworthy.*

Culprit. Criminal, delinquent, felon, malefactor, offender.

ANT. *Hero, example, pattern, model, saint, upright man.*

Cultivate. Till; fertilize; improve, refine, train, discipline, develop; study, pursue, investigate; nourish, foster, cherish, promote.

ANT. *Neglect, blight, blast; uproot, eradicate, extirpate; stifle, abandon, prevent, discourage.*

Cunning. Craft, artifice, deceit, intrigue, subtlety, chicane.

ANT. *Candor, guilelessness, sincerity.*

Cupidity. Longing, greed, lust; covetousness, avarice, acquisitiveness, stinginess.

ANT. *Prodigality, liberality, generosity, extravagance.*

Curb. Restrain, check, control, repress, bridle.

ANT. *Indulge, emancipate, loose, release, free, liberate.*

Cure, *n.* Remedy, antidote, restorative, corrective, help, specific; healing, restoration, convalescence, alleviation, renovation.

ANT. *Complaint, contagion, disease, ailment; aggravation, confirmation; inoculation.*

Curiosity. Inquisitiveness, wonder, marvel, rarity, celebrity; inquiry, investigation, scrutiny, research.

ANT. *Indifference, heedlessness, disregard, abstraction; apathy.*

Curious. Prying, meddling, inquisitive, searching, scrutinizing; rare, singular, strange; elegant, finished.

ANT. *Indifferent, uninterested; trite, common, usual.*

Current. Common, general, prevalent, present, floating, popular, ordinary, vulgar.

ANT. *Obsolete, rejected, exploded; private, secret; confined.*

Curse, *n.* Execration, malediction, anathema, denunciation; scourge, plague, torment, affliction, trouble; imprecation, ban, oath.

ANT. *Blessing, benediction, joy, crown; prosperity, welfare, luck, success.*

Cursory. Hasty, superficial, desultory, careless, slight, rapid.

ANT. *Elaborate, searching, minute, profound.*

Custody. Care, keeping, protection; confinement, duress, imprisonment.

ANT. *Neglect, betrayal, exposure, desertion; liberation, discharge.*

Custom. Usage, habit, fashion, practice, rule; form, formality, observance; patronage; duty, tax.

ANT. *Law, regulation, command; disuse, non-observance, desuetude.*

Cutting. Sharp, keen; sarcastic, severe, satirical, wounding, piercing, trenchant, stinging, sardonic, cruel.

ANT. *Mild, soothing, flattering, indulgent, consoling, gratifying.*

Cynical. Censorious, churlish, carping, cross, peevish; derisive, contemptuous, scornful, pessimistic, misanthropic.

ANT. *Genial, lenient; optimistic, philanthropic.*

D

Dainty. Exquisite, choice, rare, refined; savory, palatable, delicious, toothsome, tasty, epicurean; fastidious, luxurious.

ANT. *Common, dirty, vulgar, coarse, defiled, nasty, foul, filthy.*

Damage. Hurt, injury, detriment, loss, mischief, impairment.

ANT. *Benefit, compensation, advantage, blessing, reparation.*

Danger. Peril, risk, hazard, venture, insecurity, liability, jeopardy.

ANT. *Safety, security, precaution, defense.*

Daring. Adventurous, fearless, risky, brave, courageous, dauntless, intrepid, valorous.

ANT. *Cautious, timid, wary, fearful.*

Dark. Black, swarthy, opaque, obscure, shadowy, lurid, sunless, murky, cloudy, overcast, ebon, pitchy, secret; mysterious, enigmatical, unintelligible, occult, abstruse; gloomy, disheartening, cheerless, dismal; ignorant, rude, untaught, benighted; wicked, foul, horrible, damnable, vile, artocious, infernal; joyless, mournful, sad, sorrowful.

ANT. *White, fair, light, radiant, bright, clear, buoyant, plain, brilliant, glaring, crystalline, transparent, dazzling, luminous, illumed; happy, joyful, festive.*

Darling. Sweetheart, love, pet, favorite, idol, dear.

Dash. Strike, hurl, cast, throw, drive, send, speed, dart; alloy, adulterate; suffuse, overspread, color; disappoint, ruin, frustrate; surprise, abash.

ANT. *Raise, erect, reinstate; creep, crawl; fulfil, realize, effect.*

Dastard. Coward, craven, recreant.

ANT. *Hero, champion; daredevil.*

Data. Facts, basis, grounds, postulates, premises, given conditions.

ANT. *Conjectures, assumptions, inferences, deductions.*

Date. Time, era, epoch, period, age.

ANT. *Non-duration; eternity.*

Daub. Smear, plaster, sully, begrime, soil, deface, defile.

ANT. *Embellish, decorate; cleanse, whiten.*

Daunt. Terrify, alarm, intimidate, appal, frighten off, tame.

ANT. *Rally, inspirit, encourage.*

Dauntless. Valiant, fearless, intrepid, bold, indomitable, unconquerable, valorous, chivalrous, heroic, brave, daring.

ANT. *Cowardly, timid, cautious, fearful, afraid, faint-hearted, shrinking.*

Dawn. Appear, begin, open; break, grow light, rise.

ANT. *Wane, set, sink, close.*

Dazzle. Daze, blind; astonish, surprise, overpower, bewilder, confuse.

ANT. *Enlighten, illumine, illuminate; make clear, instruct.*

Dead. Lifeless, breathless, inanimate, deceased, defunct, departed; dull, cold, frigid, inert, indifferent; tasteless, insipid, flat; insensible, heavy, unconscious, spiritless, still, torpid.

ANT. *Quick, live, living, animate, alive, stirring, vivacious.*

Deadly. Mortal, fatal, destructive, noxious, murderous, malignant, pernicious, baneful, venomous.

ANT. *Vital, wholesome, life-giving.*

Deaf. Hard of hearing; dull, insensible, heedless; inexorable, averse, disinclined; inaudible.

ANT. *Acute, listening, attentive, willing, susceptible.*

Deal. Bargain, chaffer, trade, traffic, do business; distribute, allot, divide, share, mete out.

ANT. *Close, stop, fail; collect, gather, glean, muster.*

Dear. Costly, high-priced, expensive, precious; beloved, valued.

ANT. *Cheap, common, inexpensive; hated, abhorred.*

Dearth. Lack, want, scarcity, poverty.

ANT. *Plenty, abundance, luxury.*

Death. Decease, dying, dissolution, departure, exit, expiration.

ANT. *Life, birth, rise, vitality, growth, activity.*

Debar. Exclude, bar out, stop, prevent, prohibit, restrain, hinder.

ANT. *Admit, enclose, embrace; allow, indulge, permit, entitle.*

Debase. Degrade, deprave, corrupt, alloy, deteriorate, lower, impair.

ANT. *Raise, enhance, exalt, honor, purify, improve, ameliorate.*

Debate, *n.* Discussion, dispute, controversy, contention, altercation, contest.
ANT. *Compliance, surrender, withdrawal of opposition.*

Debatable. Dubious, doubtful, uncertain, disputable, problematical.
ANT. *Sure, certain, incontestable, self-evident.*

Debauch. Seduce, corrupt, vitiate, defile.
ANT. *Purify, elevate.*

Debility. Infirmity, weakness, languor, exhaustion, feebleness.
ANT. *Vigor, strength, nerve, energy, tone, vitality.*

Debt. Liability, obligation, default, claim, score.
ANT. *Liquidation, assets, accommodation, credit.*

Debtor. Borrower, mortgagor.
ANT. *Creditor, lender, mortgagee.*

Decay, *v.* Corrupt, putrefy, decompose, rot, spoil, molder, wither, perish.
ANT. *Flourish, luxuriate, expand, vegetate, grow, increase.*

Deceit. Fraud, deception, cheating, artifice, imposition, guile.
ANT. *Honesty, openness, fair dealing, frankness, truth, verity.*

Deceive. Cheat, dupe, delude, beguile, fool, trick, impose upon, disappoint, mislead, circumvent, entrap.
ANT. *Enlighten, guide, disabuse, deliver.*

Deception. Craft, cunning, lying, fraud, hypocrisy, trickery, delusion, duplicity, deceitfulness, falsehood, prevarication.
ANT. *Candor, honesty, sincerity, truth, veracity, guilelessness, frankness, simplicity.*

Decide. Determine, settle, conclude, close, terminate, end, resolve.
ANT. *Waver, hesitate, vacillate, fluctuate, be irresolute.*

Decipher. Reveal, explain, unravel, unfold.
ANT. *Puzzle, mystify.*

Decision. Determination, sentence, conclusion, judgment; firmness, resolution.
ANT. *Vacillation, vagueness, uncertainty.*

Decisive. Conclusive, positive, final, definitive, indisputable.
ANT. *Vague, hypothetical, indeterminate, dubious, problematical.*

Deck. Adorn, dress, ornament.
ANT. *Strip, despoil; deform, deface.*

Declaim. Recite, speak, debate, harangue.
ANT. *Study, compose, elaborate.*

Declamation. Harangue, effusion, debate, oratory, elocution.
ANT. *Hesitation, stammering.*

Declaration. Assertion, affirmation, avowal; publication, proclamation, official announcement.
ANT. *Denial; concealment; recantation, disavowal, retraction.*

Declare. Announce, publish, advertise, reveal, proclaim.
ANT. *Suppress, withhold, conceal.*

Decline. Fall, decay, decadence, degeneration; refusal, rejection, repudiation.
ANT. *Rise, advancement, improvement; acceptance.*

Declivity. Fall, slope, descent.
ANT. *Ascent, rise.*

Decoction. Concoction, mixture, mess.
ANT. *Rawness, crudity.*

Decompose. Analyze, dissolve, resolve; decay, putrefy, become corrupt.
ANT. *Compound, mix, organize, compose.*

Decorate. Adorn, embellish, improve.
ANT. *Spoil, mar, denude, deface.*

Decorum. Dignity, order, propriety, seemliness.
ANT. *Disorder, disturbance, unseemliness.*

Decrease. Lessen, diminish, subside, want, dwindle, curtail, retrench, reduce, lower.
ANT. *Increase, grow, augment, expand.*

Decree. Decision, determination, law, edict, mandate, manifesto.
ANT. *Suggestion, request, hint.*

Decrepit. Weak, infirm, tottering, aged.
ANT. *Strong, youthful.*

Decry. Disparage, detract, depreciate, denounce, abase, traduce.
ANT. *Extol, praise, eulogize, laud.*

Dedicate. Devote, hallow, sanctify, consecrate; address, inscribe; assign, apply, set apart.
ANT. *Desecrate, misuse, alienate.*

Deduce. Infer, draw, derive, conclude.
ANT. *Induce, state, conjecture, guess, anticipate, foresee.*

Deed. Performance, act, action, exploit; reality, fact, truth; document, instrument.
ANT. *Omission, failure, invalidation, reversal, recall; undoing.*

Deep. Profound; difficult, mysterious, hard, intricate; penetrating, sagacious, astute, intelligent, discerning, shrewd; heartfelt, intense, thorough.
ANT. *Shallow; superficial, artless, undesigning; indifferent.*

Default. Neglect, failure, omission; want, destitution, lack; lapse, forfeit, delinquency, absence.
ANT. *Satisfaction; appearance, plea; maintenance, supply; presence.*

Defeat. Overthrow, frustration, discomfiture.
ANT. *Success, triumph, victory.*

Defect. Fault, flaw, imperfection; omission, want, shortcoming.
ANT. *Emendation, perfection; supply, sufficiency.*

Defense. Apology, justification, vindication; shelter, shield, protection, guard, resistance, rampart, fortress, safeguard, bulwark.
ANT. *Surrender, betrayal, exposure, hazard; challenge.*

Defer. Delay, postpone, procrastinate, adjourn, put off; yield to, respect.
ANT. *Hasten, hurry, expedite, quicken, overdrive; slight, disregard.*

Deference. Respect, consideration, esteem, veneration, homage.
ANT. *Disrespect, contumely, impudence, defiance, disobedience.*

Defile. Contaminate, spoil, pollute, vitiate, infect, taint, befoul.
ANT. *Purify, cleanse, disinfect, wash, hallow, sanctify.*

Definition. Description, exposition, comment, explanation, interpretation, rendering, translation.
ANT. *Misstatement.*

Deformity. Ugliness, malforma-

tion, distortion, disfigurement, abnormity, hideousness.
ANT. *Grace, beauty, regularity, symmetry.*

Defrayment. Payment, settlement, liquidation, discharge.
ANT. *Failure, insolvency, repudiation, embezzlement, nonpayment.*

Defy. Challenge, dare, provoke, scorn, brave.
ANT. *Dread, cower, shrink, shun.*

Degeneracy. Degradation, deterioration, growing worse, decay, decline; inferiority, meanness.
ANT. *Improvement, advancement.*

Degree. Grade, rank, step, station, stage, quality, standing; measure, interval, space.
ANT. *Mass, magnitude, size, numbers.*

Dejected. Disheartened, discouraged, depressed, downcast, despondent, gloomy, melancholy, low-spirited.
ANT. *Cheerful, elated, gay, blithe, inspirited, joyous, jovial, merry.*

Delay. Postponement, procrastination; hindrance, impediment.
ANT. *Hurry, despatch, quickening, urgency; assistance, furtherance.*

Delegate, *n.* Substitute, proxy, representative, legate, deputy.

Delegate, *v.* Depute, commission, appoint, empower, constitute, ordain.
ANT. *Relegate, recall, supersede, remove.*

Deleterious. Destructive, noxious, deadly, poisonous; hurtful, harmful, injurious, pernicious, unwholesome.
ANT. *Wholesome, healthy, beneficial, sanitary, salubrious, nutritious.*

Deliberate, *v.* Meditate, ponder, debate, confer, consider, reflect, consult, weigh, cogitate.
ANT. *Shelve, dismiss, discard, put aside; hazard, chance, risk.*

Deliberate, *a.* Cautious, careful, wary; well-advised, purposed, studied; slow, leisurely; intentional, earnest, unbiased.
ANT. *Facetious, playful; irresolute, hesitant, faltering, vacillating; impulsive, rash, hasty; prejudiced.*

Delicacy. Dainty, morsel, tidbit, relish; refinement, luxury, nicety, elegance; frailty, weakness; fastidiousness, scrupulousness; purity, sensibility.
ANT. *Necessaries, commons, fare; coarseness, roughness, rudeness; vigor, strength; grossness.*

Delicious. Dainty, savory, delightful, luscious, exquisite.
ANT. *Nauseous, repulsive, bitter, loathsome, unpalatable, acrid.*

Delight. Joy, gladness, charm, rapture, transport, satisfaction, pleasure, ecstasy, happiness, enjoyment, bliss.
ANT. *Pain, suffering, sorrow, misery, discomfort, dejection, melancholy, discontent, trouble, distress, depression.*

Delightful. Agreeable, congenial, grateful, pleasant, refreshing, welcome, satisfying, delicious, acceptable, pleasurable.
ANT. *Miserable, depressing, disappointing, horrible, melancholy, painful, woful, wretched, mournful, saddening.*

Delineate. Describe, figure, represent, sketch, draw, portray, depict, paint.
ANT. *Caricature, misrepresent, exaggerate.*

Delinquent. Offender, culprit, criminal, miscreant, malefactor.

ANT. *Worthy, model, paragon, pattern,* beau ideal.

Deliver. Free, liberate, release; save, rescue; give, hand over, transfer; yield, grant, resign, surrender; pronounce, declare, speak; discharge, deal.

ANT. *Confine, capture; suppress, retain; withdraw, betray; appropriate.*

Deluge. Inundation, flood, overflow, rush, cataclysm.

ANT. *Drought, dearth, aridity; mist, moisture; subsidence, ebb, abatement.*

Delusion. Error, fallacy, illusion, hallucination, trick, snare, fraud, deception, imposture.

ANT. *Fact, certainty, verity, actuality, truth, reality.*

Demand. Require, ask, call for, insist, exact, challenge.

ANT. *Request, petition, supplicate; disclaim, forego, waive.*

Demarcation. Outline, sketch, limit, boundary, division, enclosure, separation, distinction.

ANT. *Openness, space, expanse, extent.*

Demean. Behave, comport, act, conduct one's self.

ANT. *Misbehave.*

Demerit. Fault, delinquency, misdeed, failure.

ANT. *Credit, merit, worth, excellence, desert.*

Democratic. Popular, representative, republican, radical.

ANT. *Imperial, aristocratic, regal, oligarchical, autocratic, despotic, tyrannical, constitutional, conservative.*

Demolish. Overthrow, destroy, overturn, raze, ruin.

ANT. *Restore, repair; build, construct, make.*

Demonstration. Exhibition, exemplification; manifestation, illustration; evidence, proof, certainty, conclusion, consequence, induction, inference, deduction.

ANT. *Concealment, secrecy; theory, supposition.*

Demoralize. Corrupt, deprave, vitiate, undermine, subvert.

ANT. *Stimulate, impel, promote, incite, reassure, animate, uplift.*

Demure. Sedate, staid, modest, prudish, discreet.

ANT. *Lively, vivacious, facetious, wanton, wild.*

Denial. Refusal; contradiction, negation, disavowal.

ANT. *Affirmation, avowal, admission, concession.*

Denizen. Citizen, subject, inhabitant, dweller, sojourner.

ANT. *Foreigner, alien, traveler, stranger, transient.*

Denomination. Name, designation, description, appellation, class, sect, school.

ANT. *Misnomer.*

Denounce. Brand, defame, stigmatize, decry; accuse; menace, threaten; proscribe, vituperate.

ANT. *Eulogize, applaud, uphold, vindicate.*

Dense. Thick, slow, compact, solid, close, thickset.

ANT. *Sparse, thin, scattered; quick, intelligent, clever, alert, ready.*

Denunciation. Censure, arraignment; threat, menace; exposure.

ANT. *Vindication, defense, apology, plea, excuse.*

Deny. Refuse, withhold; contradict, gainsay; renounce, abjure, disown.

ANT. *Affirm, grant, accept, concede; indulge, yield, admit.*

Depart. Leave, go, start, sally, retire, disappear, vanish, bid farewell; die, decease.

ANT. *Arrive, alight; stay, remain, cling.*

Department. Division, section, portion; function, office, duty, station; province, branch, line.
ANT. *Organization, whole, body.*

Dependent. Hanging, resting, contingent, conditioned, relying, subject, relative.
ANT. *Independent, free, absolute, irrespective.*

Depict. Portray, draw, paint, delineate.
ANT. *Caricature, parody.*

Deplorable. Lamentable, pitiable, sad, mournful, disastrous, calamitous, grievous, distressing, melancholy.
ANT. *Acceptable, felicitous, happy, welcome, glad, joyous, beneficent, pleasing.*

Deportment. Conduct, carriage, behavior, demeanor, character.
ANT. *Misbehavior, misconduct.*

Depose. Dethrone, debase, degrade, dismiss, oust, displace.
ANT. *Enthrone, install, initiate, elevate, exalt, invest with power.*

Deprecate. Regret, disapprove, lament; intercede, expostulate.
ANT. *Rejoice in, approve; invoke, imprecate, curse.*

Depreciate. Disparage, decry, undervalue, detract, underestimate.
ANT. *Appreciate, value, esteem.*

Depredation. Robbery, pillage, plunder, spoliation, theft, invasion, trespass, havoc, encroachment.
ANT. *Restitution, compensation, restoration, amends, reparation.*

Depression. Lowering, degradation, abasement, perversion, depreciation, dejection, discouragement; hollow, valley, decline.
ANT. *Elevation, raising, exaltation, promotion, amelioration, preferment, prominence, eminence.*

Deprive. Bereave, rob, divest, strip, despoil, dispossess, depose; prevent, hinder.
ANT. *Endow, enrich, invest, compensate, present, indemnify.*

Deputy. Lieutenant, agent, representative, envoy, legate, substitute, vicegerent, proxy, delegate.
ANT. *Master, principal, governor, chief, sovereign, ruler.*

Derangement. Disorder, confusion, disarrangement; disturbance, discomposure; madness, lunacy, insanity, mania, delirium, alienation, aberration.
ANT. *Order, arrangement, regulation; calmness; sanity, poise, rationality.*

Derision. Scorn, contempt, ridicule, mockery, contumely, scoffing.
ANT. *Admiration, respect, reverence, regard, esteem, veneration.*

Derivation. Source, origin, genesis, fountain, descent, root, etymology.
ANT. *Result, issue, termination, effect, application, use.*

Derogate. Detract, depreciate, disparage, compromise, lessen.
ANT. *Esteem, value, overestimate, enhance, extol.*

Descendant. Offspring, posterity, progeny, stock, family, lineage, scion, branch, issue.
ANT. *Ancestry, progenitor, origin, root, source, founder, parent.*

Describe. Trace, draw, portray, mark out, represent, depict, recount, narrate, illustrate, define, explain, characterize.
ANT. *Caricature, misrepre-*

sent, distort; mystify, perplex, confuse.

Descry. Perceive, discern, recognize, discover, espy, see, behold, detect, find out.

ANT. *Overlook, miss, neglect.*

Desecrate. Profane, pollute, pervert, abuse, secularize, prostitute.

ANT. *Hallow, sanctify, respect, esteem, dedicate, devote.*

Desert. Solitude, wild, wilderness, waste.

ANT. *Oasis, pasture, meadow.*

Deserter. Renegade, turncoat, recanter, backslider, abjurer, traitor, apostate.

ANT. *Adherent, devotee, supporter, bigot, disciple, ally.*

Deserve. Merit, earn, win, be entitled to.

ANT. *Forfeit, lose, miss, fail of.*

Desideratum. Very desirable thing, requisite, want, essential.

ANT. *Superfluity, surplus, perquisite.*

Design, *n.* Intention, purpose, aim, end, scheme, proposal, project, object, plan, device, purport, meaning, drift, scope, mark; delineation, sketch, artifice, drawing, draft; invention, contrivance; cunning, guile.

ANT. *Execution, performance, structure, construction, issue, result; candor, openness, sincerity; chance, accident.*

Design, *v.* Intend, plan, prepare, project, contrive, scheme, purpose, mean, propose; draw, delineate, sketch; contemplate, outline, plot.

ANT. *Risk, guess, conjecture, chance; misconceive, misinterpret, misrepresent.*

Designate. Specify, particularize; describe, define, denominate, name, call, style, christen, dub; appoint, allot.

ANT. *Misname, miscall; generalize; misrepresent.*

Desirable. Eligible, expedient, advantageous, beneficial, advisable, valuable, profitable, enviable, proper, judicious.

ANT. *Inexpedient, disadvantageous, harmful, inadvisable, evil.*

Desire. Appetite, inclination, longing, proclivity, craving, impulse, hankering, coveting, propensity, wish; aspiration, will.

ANT. *Loathing, disgust, aversion, hate, repugnance, horror.*

Desolate, *a.* Bereaved, comfortless, forlorn, cheerless, lonely, solitary; uninhabited, forsaken, unfrequented, waste, dreary, wild.

ANT. *Peopled, colonized, developed, cultivated; populous, crowded, frequented.*

Despair. Desperation, discouragement, hopelessness, despondency.

ANT. *Courage, hope, expectation, anticipation, assurance, confidence, elation, cheer, trust, hopefulness, encouragement.*

Despatch, *v.* Expedite, speed, accelerate, quicken, hasten; kill, slay.

ANT. *Delay, retard, impede, obstruct; preserve, save, spare.*

Desperate. Wild, reckless, despondent, hopeless, wretched, forlorn, lost; heroic, extreme, defiant; precipitate, headlong, frantic.

ANT. *Cautious, timid, shy; hopeful, promising, propitious.*

Despise. Contemn, scorn, slight, disdain, spurn.

ANT. *Respect, esteem, venerate, regard, revere.*

Despoil. Strip, denude, ravage; rob, plunder, pillage, devastate.

ANT. *Adorn, enrich, rehabilitate.*

Despotic. Tyrannical, absolute, imperious, autocratic, arrogant.
ANT. *Conciliatory, humane, merciful; constitutional, democratic, representative.*

Destination. Aim, end, object, purpose, design; goal, harbor.
ANT. *Action, movement; initiation, project, effort.*

Destiny. Fate, lot, doom, star, fortune, necessity, end, predestination.
ANT. *Choice, will, freedom, volition, free will.*

Destructive. Ruinous, injurious, pernicious, deleterious, baneful, detrimental, hurtful, noxious.
ANT. *Constructive, restorative, beneficial, wholesome, preservative.*

Desuetude. Disuse, non-observance, obsolescence.
ANT. *Use, custom, practice, exercise, operation.*

Desultory. Rambling, irregular, capricious, wandering, roving, discursive, cursory, erratic, spasmodic, unsystematic.
ANT. *Methodical, continuous, unperiodical, diligent, exact, untiring, persevering, earnest, serious, settled, consecutive.*

Detail. Account, narrative, recital; detachment; individual, particular, item, specialty, element, point, component.
ANT. *Totality, whole, generality, aggregation, mass, bulk.*

Detention. Hindrance, retaining, restraint, stopping.
ANT. *Relinquishment, abandonment, letting go, release, liberation.*

Deter. Hinder, discourage, prevent, restrain, withhold, terrify, scare, dishearten, dissuade.
ANT. *Incite, provoke, allure, tempt, seduce, prompt, persuade.*

Deteriorate. Impair, degrade, debase; decline, degenerate.
ANT. *Ameliorate, promote, advance, rectify.*

Determine. Settle, adjust, decide; ascertain, verify; influence, lead, incline; resolve.
ANT. *Vacillate, waver, unsettle, doubt.*

Detest. Abominate, abhor, execrate, loathe, shrink from.
ANT. *Like, approve, appreciate, praise, love.*

Dethrone. Depose, uncrown, drive out of power, cause to abdicate.
ANT. *Crown, enthrone, exalt.*

Detract. Depreciate, disparage, lessen, derogate, calumniate, slander, defame, decry, vilify.
ANT. *Enhance, augment, increase, flatter, compliment.*

Detriment. Loss, damage, injury, harm, evil, prejudice, disadvantage, impairment, inconvenience.
ANT. *Enhancement, remedy, augmentation, improvement, repair, reinstatement.*

Develop. Evolve, unfold, educe, disclose, unravel, exhibit, expand, enlarge; open, grow, mature.
ANT. *Envelop, wrap, conceal, contract, compress; stunt, dwarf, hinder, prevent.*

Deviate. Digress, wander, deflect, veer, diverge; depart, err, stray, swerve; differ, vary.
ANT. *Cohere, coincide; accompany, continue, remain; advance; converge; agree, assimilate.*

Device. Contrivance, invention, design, project, plan, scheme, expedient, resource; wile, artifice, stratagem, evasion, fraud; emblem, symbol, type.
ANT. *Fortune, luck, hazard,*

hit; openness, frankness, candor.

Devious. Erratic, wandering, deviating, crooked, circuitous, misleading, treacherous, roundabout.

ANT. *Direct, plain, straightforward, frequented.*

Devise. Plan, design, contrive, imagine, scheme, project, concoct; bequeath, leave.

ANT. *Mismanage, miscontrive; inherit.*

Devoid. Void, wanting, empty, destitute, vacant, unprovided for.

ANT. *Full, supplied, provided, replete, furnished, abundant, plentiful, sufficient.*

Devolve. Transfer, consign, convey, demise, devise, deliver; impose, place, attach, commission, charge, depute; fall, pass, be transferred.

ANT. *Deprive, withhold, recall, cancel, alienate, skip, pass, miss.*

Devotion. Dedication, consecration, piety, religion, sanctity, holiness, worship, adoration; attachment, affection, love; ardor, earnestness, zeal, eagerness, self-sacrifice.

ANT. *Impiety, profanity, sacrilege, irreverence; aversion, alienation, antipathy, indifference, apathy.*

Devour. Consume, gorge, eat ravenously, swallow; destroy, annihilate, waste, swallow up, expend.

ANT. *Disgorge, vomit; save, conserve.*

Dexterity. Aptitude, skill, expertness, readiness, adroitness.

ANT. *Ineptitude, inability, weakness, awkwardness, clumsiness.*

Diadem. Crown, chaplet, fillet, wreath, tiara, circlet.

Diagnosis. Investigation, determination, analysis.

ANT. *Misjudgment, error.*

Diagnostic. Symptom, feature, sign, cue, indication, mark, index.

ANT. *Development, consummation, crisis, head, formation.*

Dialect. Language, phraseology, tongue, speech, provincialism, idiom, accent.

Dialogue. Conversation between two people, colloquy, discourse, tête-à-tête.

ANT. *Monologue, soliloquy, apostrophe, oration.*

Dictate. Direct, ordain, command, prescribe, order, bid, require, decree; utter; prompt, suggest, enjoin, instruct.

ANT. *Follow, repeat, obey, answer; accept.*

Dictation. Injunction, precept, command, rule, maxim, direction, utterance.

ANT. *Consultation, conference, council; advice, recommendation.*

Dictatorial. Imperious, imperative, domineering, arbitrary, absolute, unlimited, authoritative, unrestricted, overbearing.

ANT. *Condescending, supplicatory, affable, suppliant, unassuming, persuasive.*

Diction. Expression, language, phrase, phraseology, style, verbiage, vocabulary, wording.

ANT. *Provincialism, barbarism, solecism.*

Dictionary. Lexicon, word-book, glossary, vocabulary.

Didactic. Instructive, perceptive, moral, directive, educative.

ANT. *Unsound, misleading, erroneous, uninstructive, pernicious.*

Die. Expire, decease, depart; wither, perish, decay, decline, fade; cease, vanish, disappear; sink, faint, fall; subside.

ANT. *Live, recover, be born; survive, exist; originate, develop, grow, strengthen, flourish, luxuriate, vegetate.*

Diet. Food, victuals, nourishment, aliment, nutriment, provision, viands, rations, fare, subsistence; assembly, parliament, congress.

ANT. *Starvation, fasting, abstinence, fast; gluttony, omnivorousness.*

Difference. Contrast, diversity, variation, variety, discrepancy, disagreement, disparity, distinction, divergence, unlikeness.

ANT. *Agreement, uniformity, unity, consonance, identity, likeness, resemblance, harmony, sameness, similarity.*

Differentiate. Discriminate, individualize, distinguish, particularize, specify, segregate, identify.

ANT. *Generalize, classify, confuse, amalgamate.*

Difficult. Arduous, exhausting, severe, onerous, trying, toilsome, hard, laborious; intricate, involved, obscure, enigmatical; unmanageable, reserved, opposed, unamenable.

ANT. *Easy, facile, trifling, slight, trivial, pleasant, light; simple, plain, clear, manifest; approachable, amenable, pliant.*

Diffident. Modest, doubtful, reluctant, hesitating; bashful, timid, shy, self-distrustful.

ANT. *Bold, aggressive, forward, arrogant, self-conceited.*

Diffuse, *a.* Prolix, loose, copious, rambling, verbose, long-winded, diluted.

ANT. *Epigrammatic, laconic, terse, condensed.*

Digest. Methodize, systematize, arrange, classify, codify; study, ponder, consider, contemplate, meditate, con; master, assimilate.

ANT. *Confound, complicate, disorder, derange, disturb; reject, refuse.*

Dignified. Stately, noble, grand, majestic, self-respecting, imposing, decorous, august, lofty, exalted, pompous.

ANT. *Stunted, low, mean, unimposing, depressed, ordinary, self-accusing.*

Dignify. Advance, promote, exalt, ennoble, prefer; grace, honor, adorn; elevate, aggrandize.

ANT. *Humiliate, debase, degrade.*

Digress. Deviate, ramble, wander; differ.

ANT. *Proceed, advance; harmonize, agree.*

Dilapidation. Ruin, decay, disintegration, downfall, demolition.

ANT. *Construction, reparation; soundness, solidity; fabrication, building.*

Dilate. Stretch wide, expand, enlarge, widen, distend.

ANT. *Compress, compact, restrict, narrow, condense, concentrate.*

Dilatory. Slow, loitering, tardy, procrastinating, dawdling, lagging, lingering, sluggish.

ANT. *Prompt, vigilant, alert, eager, earnest.*

Diligence. Industry, assiduity, activity, perseverance, application, attention, care, heed.

ANT. *Neglect, carelessness, idleness, inertness, inattention, desultoriness.*

Dim. Obscure, dark, covered, hidden, dusky, indistinct, uncertain.

ANT. *Bright, clear, manifest, light.*

Dimension. Measurement, bulk, mass, extent; (*pl.*) size, capacity, amplitude, massiveness, greatness.

ANT. *Segment, section, portion, part.*

Diminish. Lessen, reduce, decrease, abate, subside, shorten, dwarf, retrench.

ANT. *Augment, amplify, increase, magnify, expand.*

Din. Racket, clamor, noise, uproar.

ANT. *Crash, explosion; silence.*

Dingy. Dirty, dull, soiled, tarnished, dim, obscure, somber.

ANT. *Bright, burnished, radiant, glittering, gleaming, luminous.*

Dip. Immerse, plunge, inundate, soak, steep, drown, submerge.

ANT. *Dry, drain, parch; air, ventilate, evaporate, vaporize.*

Diplomacy. Negotiation, indirection, tact, artful management, contrivance, circumvention; embassage, ministry, ambassadorship.

ANT. *Dismissal, congé, recall; candor, naïveté, ingenuousness; mismanagement, maladministration; self-defeat.*

Diplomatic. Prudent, wise, tactful, astute, politic, sagacious, judicious, discreet.

ANT. *Blundering, tactless, injudicious.*

Direct, *a.* Unswerving, straight, rectilinear, undeviating.

ANT. *Meandering, crooked, roundabout, circuitous.*

Direction. Course, tendency, aim, bearing; oversight, management, control, superintendence, conduct; order, command; address, superscription.

ANT. *Deviation, aberration; miscontrol.*

Directly. Straightly, immediately, forthwith, soon, speedily, instantly, promptly, presently, quickly. straightway, at once.

ANT. *Secondarily, by-and-by; remotely, obliquely, circuitously.*

Dirge. Requiem, elegy, lament, wake, threnody, coronach.

ANT. *Anthem, Te Deum, Jubilate, pœan, jubilee, halleluiah.*

Dirt. Filth, uncleanness, dung, foulness, meanness, filthiness, defilement.

ANT. *Cleanness, purity, ablution; innocence, spotlessness.*

Dis-. The prefix *dis-* has usually a negative, sometimes an intensive, force. Therefore, for words beginning with it look under the antonyms of the root words. When its force is intensive, however, they will be found under the synonyms of the root words. Only a few of derived significance are here given.

Disability. Unfitness, inability, incompetence, incapacity, disqualification.

ANT. *Merit, fitness, recommendation, qualification, capability.*

Disabuse. Undeceive, set right, correct, enlighten, inform, rectify.

ANT. *Deceive, delude, hoodwink.*

Disappoint. Frustrate, foil, defeat, baffle, disconcert, mortify, vex, betray, tantalize.

ANT. *Fulfil, realize, satisfy, gratify, encourage, verify, support.*

Disaster. Misfortune, mishap, reverse, calamity, catastrophe.

ANT. *Blessing, benefit, good fortune, profit, gain, boon.*

Disburse. Spend, expend, consume, waste, use, lay out, pay.

ANT. *Save, economize, hoard, husband.*

Discern. Observe, discriminate, distinguish, perceive, see, descry, behold, espy, discover, penetrate, differentiate.

ANT. *Overlook, neglect, miss.*

Discernible. Discoverable, perceptible, visible, apparent, conspicuous, palpable, plain, manifest, evident.

ANT. *Obscure, minute, invisible, microscopic, impalpable.*

Discernment. Sagacity, perception, discrimination, brightness, astuteness, insight, intelligence, perspicacity, penetration, acuteness, judgment, ingenuity.

ANT. *Blindness, inattention, dulness, density.*

Discharge, *v.* Unburden, unload; expel, eject; shoot, fire; release, exonerate, acquit, liberate, free; dismiss, discard, cashier; remove, destroy; perform, execute, observe.

ANT. *Confine, charge, load, burden, contain; detain, check, delay, stop; preserve; ignore.*

Disciple. Follower, student, believer, pupil, learner, scholar, supporter, adherent, votary.

ANT. *Master, teacher, professor, leader, rabbi.*

Discipline. Training, teaching, drill, exercise; control, regulation, subjection, government; punishment, correction, coercion, chastisement.

ANT. *Laxity, latitude, negligence; reward, encouragement; disorganization, mutiny, rebellion, confusion, disorder.*

Discomfit. Defeat, overpower, conquer; foil, disconcert.

ANT. *Encourage, rally, aid, assist.*

Disconcert. Frustrate, balk, defeat, thwart, baffle; discompose, embarrass, disturb, upset, perplex, abash, confuse, bewilder.

ANT. *Assist, countenance, encourage, compose, calm, appease, pacify, tranquilize.*

Disconsolate. Inconsolable, sorrowful, heart-broken, comfortless, melancholy, desolate, forlorn, sad.

ANT. *Joyous, cheerful, glad, merry, jovial, happy, blithe.*

Discordance. Disagreement, discord, dissonance, conflict, opposition.

ANT. *Accordance, harmony, concord.*

Discover. Find, detect, discern, ferret out, invent, expose, ascertain, descry, disclose, betray, indicate, manifest.

ANT. *Hide, conceal, cover, secrete, bury, suppress, withhold.*

Discreet. Discerning, wise, sagacious, prudent, cautious, judicious, considerate, circumspect.

ANT. *Foolish, heedless, reckless, silly, imprudent, undiscerning, unrestrained.*

Discrepancy. Dissonance, discord, discordance, difference, variation, disagreement.

ANT. *Agreement, harmony, correspondence.*

Discrimination. Acuteness, penetration, sagacity, discernment, shrewdness, insight.

ANT. *Dulness, shortsightedness.*

Discursive. Reasoning, argumentative; roving, wandering, rambling, desultory, inconsequent.

ANT. *Orderly, coherent, continuous; condensed, succinct, concise; strategic.*

Discuss. Debate, argue, reason, agitate, deliberate upon, consider.

ANT. *Confound, obscure; assert, dogmatize.*

Disdain, *n.* Contempt, scorn, disregard, haughtiness, arrogance.

ANT. *Reverence, respect, esteem, considerateness, humility.*

Disease. Infirmity, ailment, distemper, complaint, illness, sickness, malady, indisposition, unsoundness, affection.

ANT. *Health, strength, robustness, soundness, sturdiness, vigor; convalescence; sanity, salubrity.*

Disgust, *n.* Distaste, loathing, dislike, repugnance, aversion, abhorrence.

ANT. *Partiality, desire, liking, relish, fondness.*

Dismal. Dark, gloomy, cheerless, dull, dreary, melancholy, lonesome, somber, sad, doleful, funereal; horrible, terrible, frightful.

ANT. *Cheerful, bright, inviting, cordial, gay, propitious, promising.*

Dismay. Affright, terrify, appal, alarm, intimidate, daunt.

ANT. *Rally, inspirit, assure, encourage, hearten.*

Dismember. Disintegrate, mutilate, separate, rend asunder, sever.

ANT. *Integrate, incorporate; constitute, construct.*

Dismiss. Banish, discard, discharge, remove.

ANT. *Recall, welcome.*

Disparage. Depreciate, decry, undervalue, underrate; defame, reproach.

ANT. *Appreciate, overestimate, extol, praise, exaggerate.*

Dispel. Drive away, disperse, dissipate, banish, scatter.

ANT. *Collect, summon, accumulate.*

Dispensation. Apportionment, allotment, distribution; administration; exemption; system, scheme, plan, régime.

ANT. *Retention, restriction, reservation, injunction, prohibition; enforcement.*

Disperse. Dispel, scatter, separate; diffuse, spread, disseminate.

ANT. *Gather, collect, concentrate; recall, summon.*

Display. Expand, unfold, extend, uncover, open, spread; exhibit, show, parade.

ANT. *Conceal, hide, wrap, dissemble, suppress.*

Disposition. Arrangement, location, placing, grouping; management, control, regulation, direction; tendency, inclination, propensity; temper, character, nature, humor; willingness; distribution.

ANT. *Confusion, inversion, disorder; mismanagement, laxity; antipathy, repulsion; obstinacy; mood; agglomeration, collection.*

Disputant. Litigant, debater, arguer, controversialist, competitor, claimant.

ANT. *Advocate, auxiliary, partner.*

Dispute, *v.* Quarrel, wrangle; debate, argue, discuss, agitate, ventilate; impugn, deny, contradict, oppose, contest.

ANT. *Allow, concede, grant, forego, relinquish.*

Disquisition. Treatise, dissertation, discourse, essay, discussion.

ANT. *Effusion, tirade, diatribe, rhodomontade.*

Dissect. Anatomize, scrutinize, analyze, explore, investigate, examine, sift.

ANT. *Integrate, organize, compound, grasp; comprehend, discern, diagnose.*

Dissemble. Conceal, disguise, cloak, hide, restrain, smother.
ANT. *Reveal, confess, manifest, expose, vaunt, profess.*

Dissent. Differ, disagree, decline.
ANT. *Assent, consent, agree.*

Dissertation. Disquisition, discussion, treatise.

Dissipate. Scatter, vanish, disperse, disappear, waste, squander.
ANT. *Hoard, save, gather, conserve.*

Dissociate. Separate, sever, disjoin, divide, part, sunder, disconnect.
ANT. *Associate, join, affiliate.*

Dissolute. Abandoned, corrupt, loose, profligate, reprobate, dissipated.
ANT. *Upright, honest, conscientious, self-controlled.*

Distance. Remoteness, space, interval; absence, separation; reserve, coldness, stiffness.
ANT. *Proximity, contiguity, nearness, presence, neighborhood, contact.*

Distend. Dilate, extend, spread, stretch.
ANT. *Contract, narrow, constrict, condense.*

Distil. Drop, extract, separate; percolate, emanate, drip.
ANT. *Condense, retain; suck; hold.*

Distinct. Separate, definite, different, clear, plain, unmistakable.
ANT. *Blurred, dim, indefinite, confused, conjoined, obscure.*

Distinguish. Discern, perceive, tell, discriminate; differentiate; characterize, mark; separate, divide; signalize, make famous *or* celebrated.
ANT. *Confound, miss, confuse.*

Distinguished. Illustrious, famous, celebrated, noted, eminent, marked, conspicuous, supreme, extraordinary, consummate.
ANT. *Obscure, inconspicuous, hidden; infamous, notorious.*

Distortion. Deformity, twist, perversion, falsification, misrepresentation, sophistry, corruption.
ANT. *Regularity, shapeliness, symmetry; right, truth, verification, rectification.*

Distract. Divert, perplex, confuse, disconcert, bewilder, confound, derange, craze.
ANT. *Unite, fix, compose, concentrate, collect.*

Distraction. Confusion, perplexity, abstraction, disturbance, perturbation, agitation; inattention; absence, frenzy, madness; alienation, aberration; delirium, mania, derangement, lunacy.
ANT. *Attention, composure, self-possession, tranquillity.*

Distress, *n.* Affliction, calamity, adversity, misery, perplexity, misfortune; agony, suffering, anguish; privation, destitution, poverty, indigence.
ANT. *Consolation, relief, assuagement, alleviation; boon, blessing, pleasure.*

Distribute. Dispense, scatter, allot, apportion, grant, appoint.
ANT. *Restrict, retain, collect, gather, hold, reserve, keep.*

District. Region, tract, territory, province, circuit, quarter.

Disturb. Agitate, shake, stir, disorder, confuse, derange; molest, annoy, plague, trouble, vex, worry; interrupt, hinder.
ANT. *Soothe, quiet, assist, compose, pacify; arrange, order.*

Diversion. Detour, deviation, divergence; recreation, amusement, enjoyment, pastime.

ANT. *Directness, business, procedure, continuity, task, labor.*

Diversify. Vary, change, alter, modify; variegate, streak, spot.

ANT. *Settle, fix, stereotype, arrest.*

Diversity. Difference, dissimilitude, variation, unlikeness, divergence, dissonance, heterogeneousness, multiformity.

ANT. *Identity, similarity, uniformity, consonance, homogeneousness, coincidence.*

Divest. Dismantle, strip, unclothe, undress, unrobe, deprive.

ANT. *Clothe, invest, shroud, indue, encumber.*

Divide. Sever, part, separate, disunite, sunder; alienate, estrange; distribute, allot, apportion, assign, share, dispense.

ANT. *Unite, commingle, collocate, congregate, convene.*

Divination. Magic, foretelling, augury, prophecy, presage, prediction.

ANT. *Investigation, study; information; analysis.*

Divorce, *v.* Separate, part, sunder, alienate, disunite.

ANT. *Marry, wed, betroth, consort.*

Do. Accomplish, achieve, bring to pass, complete, effect, realize, discharge, perpetuate, perform, commit, consummate, actualize; execute, finish, fulfil; work out, transact.

ANT. *Neglect, ruin, spoil, defeat, destroy, mar, miscarry, fail, frustrate, baffle, omit, come short.*

Docile. Manageable, amenable, compliant, gentle, tame, submissive, yielding, tractable, pliable, obedient.

ANT. *Obstinate, firm, inflexible, stubborn, self-willed, wilful, determined, dogged, resolute, opinionated.*

Doctrine. Tenet, dogma, opinion, belief, precept, principle, teaching, creed.

ANT. *Duty, practice, action, conduct, operation, application.*

Dogmatic. Arrogant, authoritative, imperious, domineering, positive, self-opinionated, doctrinal, magisterial, dictatorial.

ANT. *Practical, active, modest, diffident, vacillating, considerate.*

Domestic. Private, family, familiar, homelike.

ANT. *Public, foreign, alien, strange.*

Domicile. Home, abode, house, residence, mansion, dwelling.

ANT. *World, wilderness; estrangement, migration, travel, exile.*

Dominance, Domination. Superiority, lordship, mastery, sway, supremacy, command, ascendancy, government.

ANT. *Servility, subjection, inferiority, weakness, minority, subordination.*

Domineer. Lord, tyrannize, dictate, bully, swagger.

ANT. *Submit, yield, bow, defer, patronize, succumb; resist, contend.*

Dominion. Government, domination, supremacy, sway, dominance, control, authority, domain, territory, sovereignty.

ANT. *Submission, subjugation, servitude.*

Doom, *n.* Condemnation, fate, sentence, judgment, destiny, verdict.

ANT. *Liberation, respite, escape, acquittal, discharge.*

Dormant. Sleeping, latent, inert, quiescent.

ANT. *Active, operative, vigilant, awake, alert.*

Doubt, *n.* Distrust, skepticism, disbelief, suspicion, suspense, hesitation, incredulity, irresolution, misgiving, unbelief, perplexity, uncertainty.

ANT. *Conviction, certainty, assurance; belief, confidence; determination, resolution, resolve.*

Downwards. Below, beneath, down.

ANT. *Upwards, above, aloft.*

Drag. Draw, pull, haul, bring.

ANT. *Carry, push, propel, raise.*

Drain. Empty, exhaust, draw, strain, dry.

ANT. *Fill, supply, replenish, moisten, drench.*

Draw. Haul, lead, pull, drag, lure, entice, attract, incline, induce.

ANT. *Repel, repulse, rebuff, alienate, estrange, reject.*

Dread, *n.* Fear, terror, awe, apprehension, horror, alarm.

ANT. *Confidence, courage; familiarity.*

Dream. Reverie, fancy, vision, delusion, conceit, hallucination, romance, trance, vagary.

ANT. *Fact, reality, realization, verity, certainty, substance.*

Dreary. Dismal, gloomy, dark, lonesome, solitary, cheerless.

ANT. *Cheerful, bright, promising, inviting.*

Dress. Clothing, garments, apparel, garb, array, uniform, attire, costume, raiment, habiliments, vesture, robes, habit, vestments.

ANT. *Nakedness, disarray, nudity, bareness, deshabille, exposure, undress.*

Drift, *n.* Direction, bearing, course; aim, purpose, intention, scope, tendency, design; rush, impulse, current; heap, mass.

ANT. *Aimlessness, vagueness, aberrancy, indefiniteness.*

Drink. Swallow, imbibe, quaff, drain, absorb, suck in.

ANT. *Pour, exude, disgorge, water, moisten.*

Drive. Impel, propel, compel, push, thrust, urge; repulse, repel, resist; ride.

ANT. *Draw, attract, invite, summon.*

Droll. Whimsical, comical, ludicrous, funny, ridiculous, odd, queer, facetious.

ANT. *Sober, solemn, tragic, funereal.*

Droop. Languish, sink, decline, flag, pine, wither, fade, wilt.

ANT. *Prosper, revive, rally, flourish, raise, luxuriate.*

Drown. Sink, immerse, swamp, overwhelm, overflow, inundate, deluge, flood, overcome, overpower.

ANT. *Dry, drain, air, ventilate, expose.*

Dry. Arid, parched; thirsty, craving drink; barren, meager, dull, dreary, tedious, plain; severe, sarcastic, sharp, keen.

ANT. *Moist, fresh, juicy; lively, entertaining; fulsome, florid.*

Due. Proper, fitting, suitable, appropriate, becoming; owing, obligatory.

ANT. *Improper, unsuitable, independent; unfair, extravagant, deficient.*

Dull. Heavy, stupid, unintelligent, apathetic, insensible, callous, dead; inert, lifeless, inactive, slow, torpid; blunt, obtuse; gloomy, sad, dismal; dim, obscure; wearisome, dreary, tedious.

ANT. *Bright, light, spark-*

ling, brilliant, quick, interesting, lively, keen, witty, cheery, inviting, entertaining.

Dumb. Speechless, mute, silent, still, inarticulate.

ANT. *Talkative, chatty, loquacious.*

Duplicate. Copy, counterpart, facsimile, imitation, likeness, replica, reproduction, double, transcript.

ANT. *Original, pattern, prototype, archetype, model.*

Duplicity. Deceit, deception, circumvention, guile, artifice, hypocrisy, fraud, dishonesty.

ANT. *Candor, straightforwardness, frankness, sincerity, honesty.*

Duration. Continuance, term, period, protraction, prolongation (*in time*).

ANT. *Brevity, momentariness; infinity, eternity.*

Duty. Office, responsibility, obligation, function, business, accountability, right, righteousness.

ANT. *Immunity, freedom, license, exemption, dispensation.*

Dwell. Live, reside, rest, stop, stay, abide, lodge, sojourn.

ANT. *Visit, migrate, hasten, flit, roam, depart, travel.*

E

Eager. Impatient, anxious, desirous, longing, yearning, ardent, enthusiastic, earnest, animated, fervent, impetuous, vehement.

ANT. *Torpid, sluggish, slow, backward, belated, late, tardy.*

Earn. Acquire, merit, win, get, gain, procure, deserve, achieve, obtain, realize.

ANT. *Waste, lose, spend, forfeit, squander.*

Earnest. Eager, zealous, fervent; steady, intent, fixed; sincere, serious, true; important, momentous.

ANT. *Indifferent, irresolute, sportive, jesting, flippant.*

Ease. Facility, knack, readiness, expertness, easiness, satisfaction, contentment, comfort, repose, refreshment, relief.

ANT. *Perplexity, irritation, annoyance, constraint, disquiet, trouble, vexation, difficulty, uneasiness, awkwardness, worry.*

Easy Quiet, comfortable, tranquil, compliant, facile, complacent, submissive; unaffected, natural, smooth; moderate, affluent.

ANT. *Disturbed, uncomfortable, hard, difficult, anxious, exacting.*

Ebb. Retire, recede, abate, decrease, subside, wane, sink.

ANT. *Flow, swell, increase, flood, inundate, deluge.*

Eccentric. Irregular, abnormal, uncommon, peculiar, singular, wayward, strange, aberrant, erratic, whimsical.

ANT. *Normal, conventional, common, usual, regular, customary.*

Echo. Resonance, repetition, reverberation, imitation, answer.

ANT. *Sound, voice, original, tone, noise, speech.*

Eclipse, *n.* Obscuration, dimming, obscurity, hiding, shrouding, concealment, vanishing, extinction, obliteration, annihilation, destruction.

ANT. *Illumination, enlightenment, revelation; perpetuation; radiation; unveiling, discovery.*

Economics. Science of wealth, public *or* political economy; household management, household economy, housewifery.

Economize. Save, husband, retrench, manage frugally, be frugal *or* prudent, practice economy, avoid waste; develop resources, utilize.

ANT. *Waste, misuse, sacrifice, be lavish, profuse,* or *extravagant; squander, dissipate.*

Economy. Thrift, thriftiness, frugality, providence, good husbandry; management, arrangement, regulation, administration; plan, system, established order, dispensation.

ANT. *Prodigality, wastefulness, extravagance, lavishness.*

Ecstasy. Transport, rapture, inspiration, fervor, frenzy, emotion, delight, enthusiasm, happiness.

ANT. *Coolness, dulness, ennui, weariness, tedium, indifference.*

Edge. Border, margin, brink, rim, brim, verge; sharpness, keenness, intensity, animation, zest.

ANT. *Center, interior; dulness, bluntness, flatness; inertness, inactivity.*

Edible. Eatable, esculent, wholesome, culinary.

ANT. *Poisonous, deleterious, harmful, dangerous, noxious, uneatable.*

Edict. Decree, command, order, proclamation, mandate, ordinance.

ANT. *Hoax, canard; request, wish.*

Edifice. Building, tenement, fabric, structure.

ANT. *Ruin, heap, demolition, destruction.*

Edify. Build up, enlighten, improve, stimulate, strengthen, nurture.

ANT. *Defile, debase, mislead, misguide, pervert, corrupt.*

Edit. Revise, correct, prepare for the press, annotate, emend; bring out; conduct, manage.

ANT. *Distort, pervert, falsify, garble, mutilate.*

Educate. Discipline, teach, instruct, train, nurture, breed, develop.

ANT. *Dwarf, stunt, hinder; pervert, corrupt.*

Education. Training, teaching, tuition, instruction, schooling, discipline, cultivation, breeding, development, nurture, information, knowledge, learning, reading, study.

ANT. *Ignorance, illiteracy, nescience, blindness, darkness.*

Educe. Draw out, extract, elicit, evolve, produce.

ANT. *Adduce, cite, allege, quote, advance, name, mention; apply, insert, deposit, bestow.*

Efface. Obliterate, erase, blot out, destroy, cancel, eradicate, expunge.

ANT. *Restore, revive, delineate, imprint, portray, replace, reinstate, renew.*

Effect, *n.* Result, consequence, event, issue; force, efficiency, validity, weight, power; purport, drift, tenor, meaning; fact, reality, truth; impression, appearance, *ensemble;* (*pl.*) chattels, goods, commodities, property, movables.

ANT. *Cause, motive, source, incentive; origin.*

Effect, *v.* Cause, produce, accomplish, change, achieve, create, execute, perform, realize, compass, effectuate, consummate, fulfil.

ANT. *Obviate, frustrate, prevent, mar, hinder; deter, deflect.*

Effective. Adequate, competent, effectual, sufficient; potent, cogent, efficacious, forcible, energetic, powerful; active, efficient, operative; conducive; serviceable, able, talented.

ANT. *Weak, futile, nugatory, inconducive, inoperative, inadequate, impotent, incompetent, powerless.*

Effectuate. Accomplish, effect, execute, achieve, secure, fulfil.

ANT. *Prevent, hinder, abolish, defeat, nullify, stifle, blight.*

Effeminate. Feminine, womanly, delicate; womanish, feeble, unmanly, timorous, enervated, soft, weak, emasculated.

ANT. *Strong, manly, masculine, virile, manlike, vigorous, hardy, robust.*

Effervesce. Boil, bubble, froth, foam, ferment, sparkle; *express irrepressible emotion.*

ANT. *Subside; acquiesce, refrain, bear, brook, digest.*

Effete. Barren, unfruitful; decayed, spent, exhausted, worn, wasted, decrepit.

ANT. *Vigorous, fertile, prolific, productive, exuberant, luxuriant, rank.*

Efficacious. Effectual, effective, active, operative, powerful, adequate, cogent.

ANT. *Insufficient, inadequate, ineffectual.*

Efficacy. Power, potency, force, competency, strength, effectiveness, vigor, energy, usefulness.

ANT. *Inefficacy, incompetency.*

Efficiency. Power, strength, capabilty, virtue, energy, usefulness, productiveness, effectiveness; attentiveness, aptitude, skill, ingenuity, competence, inventiveness, readiness, ingeniousness, faculty, cleverness, genius, acuteness.

ANT. *Weakness, inability incompetence, unproductivity, inattention, awkwardness, absence of mind, thoughtlessness preoccupation, distraction, laziness, stupidity.*

Efficient. Operative, active, potent, efficacious, effective, effectual; able, skilled, ready, energetic, proficient, competent.

ANT. *Inactive, impotent, ineffective, abortive; dull, inert, indolent, sluggish, senseless, stupid.*

Effigy. Image, representation, figure, statue, likeness; dummy.

ANT. *Caricature, misrepresentation, distortion; bust, portrait.*

Efflorescence. Flowering, blooming, blossoming, budding; outburst; bloom, luxuriance.

ANT. *Deflorescence, fading, waning, blasting, withering; nudity, bareness, denudation; absorption, desiccation.*

Effluence. Emanation, flow, effusion, efflux; issue, outpouring; emission, discharge; abundance, overflow.

ANT. *Influx, infusion, refluence, ebb; exhaustion; absorption, retention.*

Effluvium. Exhalation, emanation, malaria, miasma, stink, noxious vapor.

ANT. *Ventilation, scent, disinfectant; zephyr, aroma, balm.*

Effort. Endeavor, attempt, trial, exertion, struggle, essay, strain, striving, stretch.

ANT. *Failure, frustration, futility, weakness, deficiency, misadventure; ease, inactivity, spontaneity, facility.*

Effrontery. Assurance, impudence, audacity, shamelessness, presumption, hardihood, boldness, brass; insolence, sauciness.

ANT. *Modesty, coyness, shyness, diffidence, sensitiveness, shrinking, timidity, bashfulness.*

Effulgence. Brilliancy, splendor, luster, brightness, radiance, refulgence, glory, flame, luminosity, resplendence.
ANT. *Darkness, tenebrosity, obscuration, gloom, opaqueness, shade.*

Effuse, *a.* Profuse, poured forth freely, lavish, prodigal, copious, abundant, effluent.
ANT. *Dry, scanty, sparing, meager, thin.*

Effusion. Outpouring, effluence, discharge, emission; abundance; speech, address, oration; waste, shedding, spilling.
ANT. *Infusion, absorption; essay, reading, document, instrument; influx; retention.*

Effusive. Lavish, generous, profuse, prodigal, gushing; spread widely, diffused.
ANT. *Sparing; taciturn, laconic, curt, brief.*

Egoism. Selfishness, self-assurance, self-conceit, self-consciousness, self-confidence, self-esteem, conceit, vanity, self-assertion, self-praise, self-admiration, self-love, self-exaltation.
ANT. *Self-abnegation, deference, self-forgetfulness, diffidence, bashfulness, humility, modesty, self-distrust, shyness, unobtrusiveness, considerateness, unostentatiousness.*

Egregious. Surpassing, extraordinary, remarkable, enormous, monstrous, outrageous, tremendous, prodigious, peculiar; flagrant, gross.
ANT. *Ordinary, usual, commonplace, mediocre, everyday.*

Egress. Exit, way out, departure, going out, outlet; sally.
ANT. *Entrance, avenue, approach, inlet; inroad, incursion, invasion.*

Either. One *or* the other of two; each, both.
ANT. *Neither, not any one of two.*

Ejaculation. Exclamation, cry, utterance; expletive.
ANT. *Silence, speechlessness, dumfounderment; drawl; oration, speech.*

Eject. Cast out, emit, vomit, void, evacuate; expel, dismiss, discharge, oust; reject, banish, throw aside, cast away.
ANT. *Retain, absorb; accept, receive, house, store, admit, accommodate, welcome; introduce, inject.*

Eke out. Add to, supply, increase, stretch, raise, augment, help.
ANT. *Stint, drain, withhold, diminish, exhaust.*

Elaborate. Improve, refine, develop, mature, execute, forge, prepare, concoct, work upon, labor over.
ANT. *Slight, neglect, disregard, overlook; miscontrive, mismanage; chance, hit, guess, conjecture, extemporize.*

Elapse. Pass, slip, glide away, lapse; intervene.
ANT. *Wait, abide, halt, hold; continue, endure; grasp, seize.*

Elastic. Flexible, springy, resilient, extensile, ductile, buoyant; alterable, modifiable; rebounding, recoiling.
ANT. *Rigid, tough, inflexible; crystallized, unchangeable; dull, inert.*

Elated. Cheered, excited, exhilarated, animated, flushed, inspirited, inflated.
ANT. *Depressed, dejected, discouraged, dispirited, humiliated, abashed, confounded.*

Elder. Senior, older, more ancient, earlier born; superior; precedent.

ANT. *Younger, junior, juvenile.*

Elect, *a.* Picked, selected, chosen, choice; appointed, delegated; redeemed, saved; élite, accepted.

ANT. *Rejected, doomed, reprobate; abandoned, depraved.*

Election. Selection, preference, choice; appointment by vote; alternative, free will, freedom, power to choose; discrimination, discernment, distinction; predestination.

ANT. *Postponement; rejection, reprobation, abandonment.*

Electric. Charged with electricity, relating to electricity; inspiring, inspiriting, stimulating; lightninglike, swift, flashing, thrilling, stirring, exciting.

Electrify. Charge with electricity, render electric; rouse, excite, thrill, stir, astonish, astound, amaze, appal.

ANT. "*Kill*" (of something charged, from which the electricity is suddenly removed); *disconnect, sever* (of apparatus for carrying electricity); *stupefy, soothe, deaden, calm, mesmerize.*

Elegance. Grace, beauty, propriety, symmetry; polish, politeness, refinement, gentility, gracefulness, taste.

ANT. *Deformity, awkwardness, coarseness, rudeness, disproportion.*

Elegant. Graceful, well-formed, symmetrical, lovely, handsome, comely, refined, tasteful, ornamental, accomplished, polished.

ANT. *Awkward, deformed, ill-proportioned, misshapen, ungraceful, hideous, coarse, rude.*

Elegy. Dirge, threnody, lament, jeremiad, requiem, coronach, funeral song; serious *or* melancholy poem.

ANT. *Pæan, jubilee, halleluiah, anthem.*

Element. Constituent, component, ingredient, part, principle, atom; (*pl.*) rudiments, outlines, essential parts.

ANT. *Whole, mass, aggregate, total, totality, gross, sum, amount.*

Elementary. Simple, uncompounded, rudimentary, primary; physical, material, natural; ultimate, component, constituent.

ANT. *Compounded, collective, aggregate, developed, organized; immaterial, incorporeal, impalpable.*

Elevate. Raise, lift up, exalt, promote, advance, aggrandize; improve, dignify, ennoble, refine, inspire, greaten; animate, elate, cheer, excite, exhilarate.

ANT. *Lower, degrade, debase, depress, demean, humble, humiliate.*

Elevation. Raising, elevating; promotion, aggrandizement, exaltation; dignity, refinement, improvement; amelioration; hill, height, altitude, superiority, eminence, loftiness, tallness.

ANT. *Degradation, debasement, depression, decline, fall, depth; deterioration, inferiority; shortness, stuntedness.*

Elicit. Draw out, evoke, educe, call forth, bring out, deduce, bring to light; express, extract, evolve, worm out, extort.

ANT. *Insert, implant, introduce, inoculate, inject, infuse, instill, incorporate, insinuate; suggest.*

Eligible. Desirable, preferable, worthy of choice, qualified, capable, suitable, prime, choice.

ANT. *Worthless, ordinary, indifferent, unprofitable, undesirable.*

Elimination. Expulsion, exclusion, discharge, removal, rejection, eradication, erasure, riddance, obliteration.

ANT. *Inclusion, retention; approval; preservation, conservation.*

Elision. Omission, ejection, ellipsis, abridgment, excerption.

ANT. *Insertion, inoculation, introduction, implantation; inclusion; augmentation.*

Elliptical. Contracted, abbreviated; suggestive, latent, allusive; significant, pregnant; defective, incomplete.

ANT. *Explanatory, categorical, full; expository, declaratory, enunciative.*

Elocution. Speech, power of expression, utterance, delivery, declamatory art; eloquence, oratory.

ANT. *Reading, lection.*

Elongation. Protraction, extension, production, drawing out, continuation; withdrawal, distance.

ANT. *Apocope, elision, curtailment, abridgment, contraction.*

Eloquence. Oratory, graceful utterance, appropriate expression, impassioned speech.

ANT. *Verbosity, wordiness, prolixity, tediousness; grandiloquence, bombast, fustian.*

Elucidate. Explain, illustrate, clear, make manifest, unfold, make plain, expound.

ANT. *Confuse, mystify, obscure, puzzle, bewilder, befog.*

Elucidation. Explanation, exposition, illustration, demonstration; comment, annotation, commentary, gloss, scholium.

ANT. *Mystification, confusion; obscurity, ambiguity.*

Elude. Escape, avoid, shun, slip away; baffle, foil, thwart, disappoint, disconcert, balk, frustrate, evade, mock.

ANT. *Meet, encounter, confront; dare, defy; court, invite, challenge.*

Elusive, Elusory. Evasive, delusive, equivocating, deceptive, fraudulent, fallacious, deceitful, illusory; shuffling, shifting, slippery, fugitive; shadowy, unsubstantial, intangible.

ANT. *Persistent, staple, certain, solid; true, sure, unequivocal.*

Em-, or en-. A prefix meaning *in* or *into*, sometimes interchangeable with *in-*. The form *em-* is used before words beginning with *p*, *b*, or *m*. The prefix has also a causal force. Words beginning with this prefix, whose original meaning is simply the meaning of the root word plus that of the prefix, are omitted here, for their synonyms and antonyms may be readily formed from those of the root word.

Emaciation. Leanness, lankness, thinness, tenuity, attenuation, wasting, gauntness, skinniness, meagerness.

ANT. *Obesity, fatness, corpulence.*

Emanate. Flow forth continuously, issue, arise, spring, proceed, emerge.

ANT. *End, terminate, culminate, eventuate, cease; dry up.*

Emancipate. Free, enfranchise, liberate, rescue, release, manumit, unfetter, unchain, disenthrall, set free.

ANT. *Subjugate, enslave, enthrall, bind; disqualify, incapacitate.*

Embalm. Preserve, cherish, enshrine, keep; scent, perfume, make fragrant; treasure, store, consecrate.

ANT. *Abandon, desecrate, expose, vulgarize, violate, profane.*

Embargo. Prohibition, ban, restraint, hindrance, restriction; detention, stoppage.

ANT. *Permit, permission, release, discharge, congé, liberation, dismissal.*

Embark. Ship; engage, enlist, put in, invest; launch, enter, start.

ANT. *Land, arrive, anchor, disembark, go ashore.*

Embarrass. Entangle, perplex, make intricate *or* difficult; distress, trouble, harass, hamper, confuse, disconcert, clog, puzzle, abash, confound, encumber.

ANT. *Extricate, relieve, disentangle, liberate, deliver; expedite, facilitate, accelerate, assist; calm, compose, tranquilize.*

Embellish. Adorn, decorate, ornament, deck, beautify.

ANT. *Detract, diminish, derogate from, strip, destroy, denude.*

Embezzle. Appropriate, steal, purloin, peculate; falsify, forge, counterfeit.

ANT. *Square, clear, balance; restore, refund, retrieve.*

Embitter. Make bitter, aggravate, exacerbate, exasperate, enrage, anger, madden; molest, provoke, excite.

ANT. *Alleviate, soothe; compose, quiet, pacify; sweeten; delight, please, comfort.*

Emblem. Figure, image, sign, symbol, token, type, attribute; device, cognizance, representation; badge, mark, signal.

ANT. *Disguise, decoy, incognito, ruse, blind, domino, mask.*

Embody. Incorporate, make corporeal, concentrate, compact, integrate, combine, collect; systematize, codify; comprehend, include, embrace, comprise, contain.

ANT. *Analyze, dismember, disband, disintegrate, dissipate.*

Embolden. Encourage, animate, reassure, inspirit, incite, urge, stimulate.

ANT. *Intimidate, frighten, alarm, deter, overwhelm, discourage.*

Embosomed. Concealed, enveloped, surrounded, encircled, enfolded.

ANT. *Exposed, open, unconcealed, revealed.*

Embrace. Clasp, hug, press; seize, welcome, accept; comprehend, include, cover, contain, embody, take in.

ANT. *Cast off, reject; exclude, except.*

Embroider. Embellish, enrich, emboss, adorn with needlework.

ANT. *Darn, botch, patch, repair.*

Embroil. Implicate, entangle, ensnarl, involve; disturb, perplex, confuse, distract, trouble.

ANT. *Extricate, separate, remove; compose, pacify, arrange, calm.*

Embryo. Germ, rudiment, nucleus, origin.

ANT. *Development, completion, maturity, fulfilment.*

Emendation. Amendment, correction, rectification, reformation, improvement.

ANT. *Error, defect, fault, incorrectness, inaccuracy.*

Emerge. Rise, issue, emanate, escape; appear, become visible.

ANT. *Disappear, sink; retreat, abscond, recede; enter; depart.*

Emergency. Exigency, urgency,

necessity, crisis, difficulty, extremity, strait; juncture, turn of events; unforeseen occasion; embarrassment, difficulty, casualty.

ANT. *Rescue, deliverance, solution, provision, arrangement, anticipation, foresight, climax.*

Emigration. Removal, exodus, migration from, colonization; departure.

ANT. *Immigration, migration to* or *into; settlement, sojourn, abode, stay; domiciliation, domestication.*

Eminence. Prominence, projection, elevation, protuberance, hill, high point; distinction, celebrity, reputation, renown, repute, fame, preferment; note, conspicuousness; superiority.

ANT. *Debasement, degradation, lowliness, decline; infamy, disgrace, shame, obloquy, opprobrium, scandal.*

Eminent. High, lofty, elevated; celebrated, distinguished, prominent, illustrious, remarkable, renowned, conspicuous, famous, reputed.

ANT. *Mediocre, worthless; infamous, notorious; egregious, outrageous.*

Emission. Ejection, expulsion, issue; issuance, putting into circulation.

ANT. *Injection, admission, entrance.*

Emit. Eject, expel, throw out; issue, decree, discharge; put into circulation.

ANT. *Inject; retain, withhold.*

Emollient. Softening, laxative, balsamic, soothing, palliative.

ANT. *Irritant, astringent, irritating, galling.*

Emolument. Gain, pay, profit, remuneration, wages, salary, income, hire, stipend, lucre, compensation; advantage, benefit; gratuity, perquisite.

ANT. *Loss, damage, waste; disadvantage.*

Emotion. Feeling, passion, excitement, agitation, sensibility, perturbation, tremor, trepidation.

ANT. *Indifference, insensibility, impassiveness, stoicism, imperturbability.*

Emphasis. Stress, force, ictus; weight, significance, impressiveness.

ANT. *Elision, monotony, uniformity.*

Emphatic. Significant, expressive, strong, forcible, positive, energetic, decided, distinct, unequivocal, earnest, important, special.

ANT. *Mild, ordinary, usual, unimportant, commonplace, unnoticeable, cool, unimpassioned, undemonstrative.*

Empire. Dominion, supremacy, sovereignty, authority, government, command, control, sway, rule, kingdom.

ANT. *Independence, insurrection, anarchy, mutiny, sedition, uprising.*

Empiric, Empirical. Tentative, experimental, provisional, hypothetic, experiential; quackish.

ANT. *Regular, scientific, uniform, constant, inductive, categorical.*

Employ. Engage, call, hire, use, engross, busy, exercise; apply, enlist, entrust, occupy, economize.

ANT. *Discard, dismiss, misuse.*

Employment. Business, vocation, pursuit, calling, profession, craft, trade, occupation; service, agency, office, employ; application, engrossment.

ANT. *Leisure, laziness, indolence; recreation, vacation.*

Empower. Commission, authorize, warrant, qualify; enable, encourage; delegate, sanction, direct.

ANT. *Hinder, prevent, discourage, disqualify, disable; recall, revoke, withdraw.*

Empty, *a.* Void, without contents, vacant, unoccupied; destitute, devoid; unsupplied, unfurnished, unfilled; unsatisfactory, vain, hollow, unsubstantial; desolate, waste, deserted, uninhabited; senseless, weak, frivolous; clear, unencumbered, unobstructed, vacuous, untenanted, evacuated; silly, idle, deficient.

ANT. *Full, occupied, inhabited, colonized, obstructed, encumbered; cultivated, informed, well-instructed, sensible, experienced; significant, important, forcible, substantial.*

Emulation. Rivalry, desire to excel, exceed, *or* surpass, competition; jealousy, envy, contention; vying, aspiration, contest.

ANT. *Stagnation, inactivity, dulness; contempt, disregard, disdain, disaffection; abandonment, resignation, discouragement.*

Enable. Empower, strengthen, qualify, make capable, capacitate, invigorate.

ANT. *Weaken, disqualify, incapacitate, disable, hinder.*

Enact. Decree, establish by law, ordain; play, personate, represent, act, feign, dissimulate; pass

ANT. *Abolish, abrogate, annul, cancel, repeal, rescind, expunge.*

Enamor. Charm, captivate, fascinate, inflame with love, enslave, endear, bewitch, enchain.

ANT. *Disenthrall, repel, estrange, disgust, disenchant, horrify.*

Encamp. Bivouac, pitch, settle, quarter, camp.

ANT. *March, decamp, retire, retreat, advance, charge.*

Enchain. Bind with chains, fetter, manacle, enslave.

ANT. *Loose, liberate, manumit, extricate, free.*

Enchant. Charm, fascinate, bewitch, enamor, captivate, win, catch, lead captive; enrapture, ravish, transport, beatify, delight.

ANT. *Repel, estrange, disgust, horrify, shock, alienate.*

Enchantment. Incantation, fascination, charm, conjuration, necromancy, magic, witchery, sorcery, spell; delight, rapture, ravishment, transport, bliss.

ANT. *Disillusionment, repulsion, shock, alienation.*

Encircle. Surround, encompass, environ, gird, enclose; embrace, fold, clasp; hem in, beset, circumscribe.

Enclose. Encompass, encircle, shut, include, environ, envelop, wrap, circumscribe.

Enclosure. Space enclosed, compass, circle; yard, compound; fence, ring, limit, park, field, boundary, precinct.

ANT. *Space, waste, desert, wild, open, prairie, wilderness, stretch, void, clearing.*

Encomium. Eulogy, praise, eulogium, panegyric, commendation, laudation, pæan, compliment, good word.

ANT. *Invective, taunt, vituperation, obloquy, vilification, slander.*

Encompass. Encircle, enclose, gird, hem in, surround, circumscribe.

Encounter. Meet, confront, face.

withstand; assault, combat, engage, fight, attack, contend, compete with; fall upon.

ANT. *Elude, avoid, escape, shun, miss, flee, frustrate.*

Encourage. Inspirit, animate, embolden, hearten, incite, stimulate; cheer, comfort, console; support, countenance, reassure; advance, further; foster, abet, aid, help, patronize; prompt, urge.

ANT. *Deter, discourage, dishearten, dissuade; depress, deject; provoke, incite, exasperate; retard, hinder, prevent.*

Encroach. Intrude, trespass, infringe, invade; creep, advance stealthily; transgress.

ANT. *Respect, recognize, observe; protect; refrain.*

Encumber. Clog, load, impede, obstruct, hinder, burden, overload; embarrass, perplex, involve, entangle, complicate.

ANT. *Free, liberate; assist, aid, help; relieve, straighten.*

Encumbrance. Load, impediment, hindrance; debt, claim, liability.

ANT. *Aid, assistance; relief; cancelation.*

End, *n.* Limit, outcome, period, extremity, extent, bound, conclusion, boundary, completion, close, effect, expiration, finish, finis, finale; issue, goal, intent, fulfilment, purpose, point, result, termination, terminus; utmost, uttermost; accomplishment, achievement; cessation, consummation, design, consequence; fragment, scrap, remnant.

ANT. *Commencement, origin, beginning, source, spring, start, fountain, arising, inception, opening, initiation, outset, rise.*

End, *v.* Cease, break off, close, complete, conclude, stop, quit, desist, terminate, finish, expire, wind up; destroy, kill, put to death.

ANT. *Begin, commence, initiate, start, open; restore, revivify.*

Endanger. Hazard, risk, peril; commit, compromise, expose to danger, jeopardize.

ANT. *Protect, shield, save, defend, cover, screen, preserve.*

Endear. Make dear, attach, secure the affection of, gain; conciliate.

ANT. *Estrange, alienate, embitter, antagonize.*

Endeavor, *v.* Attempt, essay, try, strive, undertake, make effort, labor, aim, exert one's self.

ANT. *Neglect, omit, abandon, drop, dismiss, pass by, let go, give up, throw away, up,* or *over, overlook.*

Endless. Interminable, boundless, limitless, infinite, immeasurable, illimitable; everlasting, perpetual, eternal, unending, without end; incessant, ceaseless, uninterrupted, continual, continuous; immortal, deathless, undying, imperishable.

ANT. *Limited, brief, temporary, periodic, transient, fugitive, finite, ephemeral, transitory, temporal.*

Endow. Furnish with dowry, enrich, endue, put on, invest, present, furnish, qualify, supply, clothe.

ANT. *Denude, deprive, divest, spoliate, strip, impoverish, despoil.*

Endowment. Grant, gift, bequest, bounty, present, largess, boon; property, fund, revenue; talent, faculty, power, quality, capability, aptitude, parts, genius, qualification, ability; attainment, provision, benefaction.

ANT. *Poverty, lack, incapacity, impoverishment, spoliation.*

Endure. Suffer, submit, bear, tolerate, allow, sustain, support, undergo, abide, afford, brook; experience; continue, remain, persist, be permanent.

ANT. *Fail, sink, succumb, surrender, yield, break down, despair, droop, faint, fall, falter, give out, give up.*

Enemy. Adversary, competitor, foe, opponent, rival, antagonist.

ANT. *Abettor, ally, friend, accomplice, supporter, helper, accessory, associate, companion, familiar, confidant, adherent.*

Energetic. Vigorous, active, forcible, powerful, effective, potent, efficacious, efficient, able, capable.

ANT. *Weak, languid, faint, drooping, pining, exhausted, feeble; listless, spiritless, inactive.*

Energy. Agility, activity, force, power, potency, strength, intensity, vigor, might, efficacy, efficiency; spirit, animation, life, manliness, animal spirits, zeal.

ANT. *Indolence, slowness, sloth, clumsiness, lassitude, inactivity, sluggishness, heaviness, inertness, laziness.*

Enervate. Unnerve, weaken, enfeeble, debilitate, effeminate; break, paralyze; incapacitate.

ANT. *Invigorate, strengthen, harden, nerve, brace, empower.*

Enfeeble. Enervate, weaken, debilitate, unnerve.

ANT. *Strengthen, nerve, invigorate, brace.*

Enfold. Envelop, wrap, enclose, embrace, encircle, encompass.

ANT. *Disclose, unwrap, develop, reveal, expose.*

Enforce. Urge, impress, compel, constrain, oblige, force, require, exact, exert, strain.

ANT. *Relax, abandon, remit, waive, forego.*

Enforcement. Inculcation, execution, sanction, constraint, compulsion.

ANT. *Relaxation, abandonment, remission.*

Enfranchise. Endow with franchise *or* suffrage; free, emancipate, release, qualify, manumit.

ANT. *Disenfranchise, disqualify.*

Engage. Promise, bind, pledge, commit; plight, affiance, betroth; enlist, induce to serve; attract, allure, gain, win, entertain; arrest, fix, occupy, busy, employ, engross; encounter, attack, fight with, battle with; contend, struggle, contest; involve; stipulate, agree; adopt.

ANT. *Decline, refuse, withdraw, extricate, disengage, dismiss, discard; retreat, retract.*

Engagement. Promise, stipulation, contract, obligation, assurance, pledge; betrothal, affiancing; employment, occupation, business, vocation; combat, battle, contest, fight, encounter, action, conflict.

ANT. *Release, liberation; dismissal; excuse.*

Engaging. Attractive, winning, charming, pleasing, interesting, delightful.

ANT. *Repulsive, unattractive, disagreeable.*

Engender. Beget, generate, create, breed, produce, cause, occasion, propagate.

ANT. *Stifle, destroy, extinguish, blight, prevent, neutralize.*

Engrave. Carve, cut, chisel, imprint, cut in, infix, grave, impress deeply; sculpture, stereotype.
ANT. *Erase, obliterate, wear out, efface, destroy; carve in relief.*

Engross. Absorb, engage, monopolize, engulf, occupy, forestall; copy.
ANT. *Distract, disperse, dissipate, scatter, vanish.*

Enhance. Heighten, swell, raise the price of, advance; augment, increase; aggrandize.
ANT. *Undervalue, depreciate, disparage, detract, underestimate.*

Enigmatic, Enigmatical. Obscure, puzzling, hidden, mysterious, perplexing, unintelligible, ambiguous, recondite, incomprehensible, mystical, occult.
ANT. *Plain, clear, manifest, self-evident, lucid, explanatory, open, intelligible.*

Enjoin. Urge, admonish, advise, order, direct, command, bid, require; prohibit, restrain; commission, ordain, oblige, prescribe.
ANT. *Dissuade; remit, absolve, exonerate; recall, dispense with, disqualify.*

Enjoy. Possess; delight in, like, be pleased with.
ANT. *Dislike, loathe, endure, tolerate, lose, disrelish.*

Enjoyment. Pleasure, delight, happiness, gratification; fruition; possession; satisfaction, gladness, felicity.
ANT. *Misery, wretchedness, grief, affliction, suffering, calamity.*

Enlarge. Amplify, augment, increase, extend, expand, magnify; make greater, ennoble; dilate, descant, expatiate; swell, grow.
ANT. *Contract, narrow, reduce, diminish, restrict, lessen, curtail.*

Enlighten. Illuminate, light up; inform, teach, edify, make intelligent, instruct.
ANT. *Darken, obscure; mystify, mislead, perplex, confound.*

Enlist. Enroll, register, incorporate, enter, embody, record, chronicle, muster.
ANT. *Erase, expunge, withdraw, dismiss, disband, muster out.*

Enliven. Amuse, quicken, animate, rouse, invigorate, inspire, inspirit, cheer, delight, gladden, exhilarate.
ANT. *Depress, dispirit, subdue, sober, moderate, oppress, weary, paralyze, deaden, tire, stupefy.*

Enmity. Hatred, hostility, malice, rancor, animosity, antagonism, acrimony, bitterness, ill will, malevolence, spite, malignity, maliciousness, opposition, asperity, aversion, hate, discord.
ANT. *Friendship, love, affection, esteem, cordiality, amity, alliance, concord, agreement, regard, harmony, sympathy, kindliness, kindness.*

Ennoble. Dignify, elevate, exalt, ameliorate, enlarge, make great.
ANT. *Debase, degrade, deteriorate, depress, deprave, corrupt, vitiate.*

Enormity. Depravity, atrocity, wickedness, villainy, outrageousness, heinousness, nefariousness, abomination, perpetration, sin.
ANT. *Innocence, righteousness, guilelessness, inoffensiveness.*

Enormous. Huge, vast, immense,

immoderate, inordinate, abnormal, exceptional, monstrous, gigantic, colossal, prodigious, elephantine; heinous, depraved, nefarious.

ANT. *Trivial, insignificant, ordinary, average, diminutive, moderate.*

Enough. Sufficient, plenty, satisfactory, ample, abundant.

ANT. *Insufficient, short, inadequate, scant, ill-supplied, bare.*

Enrage. Exasperate, provoke, irritate, madden, incite, incense, inflame, infuriate, excite, aggravate, anger.

ANT. *Soothe, conciliate, allay, tame, quiet, mollify, appease, pacify, tranquilize.*

Enrapture. Enchant, entrance, enravish, delight, transport, beatify, satisfy, please, gladden, fascinate, bewitch, captivate, charm, attract, enamor, enslave.

ANT. *Disgust, nauseate, repel, torment, torture, horrify.*

Enrich. Aggrandize, enhance, endow, augment, store, supply; adorn, decorate, ornament, embellish; fertilize.

ANT. *Impoverish, rob, denude, fleece, reduce, beggar, despoil, strip.*

Enroll. Enlist, register, record, chronicle, embody, list, catalogue.

ANT. *Erase, expunge, withdraw.*

Enrolment. Registration; register, record.

ANT. *Omission; withdrawal; erasure.*

Enshrine. Treasure, preserve, cherish, embalm, consecrate.

ANT. *Lose, misplace, expose, destroy, desecrate.*

Enslave. Captivate, charm, enthral, subjugate, master, dominate, bewitch, delight, fascinate.

ANT. *Repel, disgust, alienate; free.*

Ensue. Follow, result, eventuate, succeed, befall, accrue, happen, take place, supervene; issue, arise, spring, come.

ANT. *Precede, herald, introduce; forewarn, threaten, premonish, caution.*

Entail. Transfer, transmit, fix, devolve, involve, bequeath, demise, leave, induce, necessitate.

ANT. *Prevent, obviate, nullify; neutralize; estrange, alienate, supersede.*

Entangle. Implicate, involve, compromise, entrap, knot, perplex, embarrass, confuse, intertwist, interweave, intertwine.

ANT. *Straighten, extricate, disentangle, unravel, deliver.*

Enter. Go *or* come into; pierce, penetrate; begin, commence; enroll, inscribe, chronicle, note, register, record; engage in; embark, enlist, join; invade.

ANT. *Depart, leave, issue, quit, vacate; go out; finish, end; withdraw from, retire, resign.*

Enterprise. Adventure, undertaking, effort, attempt, essay, endeavor, trial, experiment; energy, activity, readiness, willingness; progress.

ANT. *Routine, monotony, humdrum, matter-of-fact, unprogressiveness; caution, inactivity.*

Enterprising. Venturesome, adventurous, daring, audacious, bold; prompt, alert, active, energetic, efficient, spirited, strenuous, eager, zealous, stirring; progressive, speculative.

ANT. *Timid, cautious, inactive, fearful, cowardly; conservative; wary, prudent, dis-*

creet, anxious, careful, thoughtful; indolent, unenterprising, inactive, unready, laggard.

Entertain. Amuse, interest, divert, cheer, delight, recreate, beguile, please, occupy, gratify, enliven, disport; consider, ponder; lodge, treat hospitably, cherish, harbor, hold, receive.

ANT. *Annoy, tire, bore, disturb, weary, distract, disquiet; refuse, reject, deny, debar, exclude, eject.*

Entertainment. Delight, diversion, amusement, cheer, enjoyment, pastime, fun, merriment, pleasure, recreation, sport, hospitality, frolic, reception, lodging.

ANT. *Weariness, work, toil, ennui, labor, fatigue, disturbance; refusal, rejection.*

Enthrone. Crown, instal, exalt, elevate, invest with power.

ANT. *Dethrone, depose, debase, degrade.*

Enthusiasm. Ardor, earnestness, excitement, inspiration, frenzy, vehemence, warmth, ecstasy, passion, zeal, rapture, eagerness, devotion, fervency, fanaticism, fervor, intensity, transport.

ANT. *Indifference, caution, calmness, prudence, timidity, policy, coldness, dulness, calculation, lukewarmness, deadness, callousness.*

Entice. Lure, attract, seduce, coax, persuade, wheedle, cajole, delude, entrap, decoy, inveigle, lead astray, induce.

ANT. *Warn, hinder, deter, repel, admonish, caution, make aware.*

Entire. Whole, complete, perfect, unimpaired, unbroken, undiminished, undivided; full, integral, thorough, solid, unalloyed, plenary; unmixed, sheer, mere, unmitigated, pure; total, absolute.

ANT. *Partial, incomplete, broken, impaired, alloyed, limited, divided, defective, mixed; relative.*

Entitle. Name, designate, denominate, call, style, characterize; christen; enable, fit, empower, qualify.

ANT. *Disable, disqualify.*

Entity. Being, essence, existence.

ANT. *Nonentity, chimera, phantom, fantasy, hallucination.*

Entomb. Bury, inter, inhume.

ANT. *Exhume, disinter.*

Entrance. Approach, doorway, opening, door, entry, ingress, gate, gateway, inlet, portal, access, admission, admittance, entrée, introduction, penetration, avenue, adit; beginning, commencement, initiation.

ANT. *Departure, egress, refusal, exit, withdrawal, ejection, exclusion, expulsion, rejection.*

Entreat. Beg, supplicate, solicit, beseech, implore, pray, appeal, petition, adjure, crave, importune, enjoin, urge.

ANT. *Command, insist, bid, enjoin, charge, direct; grant, heed, hear, answer, respond.*

Entry. Entrance, ingress, access; avenue, passage, hall, inlet; minute, note, record, register, memorandum; initiation, beginning.

ANT. *Egress, exit, departure; outlet, vent; misrecord, falsification, blank, omission; conclusion, quittance, disposal.*

Entwine. Interlace, weave, entwist, wreathe together *or* round.

ANT. *Disentwine, dissever, untwist.*

Enumerate. Compute, reckon, numerate, number, tell, cite, estimate, recount, specify, detail, calculate, rehearse, recapitulate.

ANT. *Mingle, jumble, confuse; miscount, misreckon, miscalculate.*

Enunciate. Announce, proclaim, declare; pronounce, syllable; state, propound, articulate, relate, utter, publish, promulgate.

ANT. *Mutter, babble, stammer.*

Envelop, *v.* Wrap, surround, encircle, fold, encompass, cover, hide.

ANT. *Expose, unwrap, reveal, extract; develop.*

Envenom. Poison, taint, vitiate, infect, pollute; embitter; enrage, provoke, exasperate, irritate, madden, inflame.

ANT. *Purify, disinfect; delight, please, gratify.*

Envious. Jealous, suspicious, grudging.

ANT. *Friendly, kindly, well-disposed, trustful, contented, satisfied.*

Environ. Surround, encircle, encompass, gird, belt, enclose, envelop; invest, besiege, hem in, beset.

Envoy. Messenger (*in diplomatic service*); ambassador, minister, legate, plenipotentiary.

ANT. *Scout, spy, orderly* (as messengers in military service).

Envy. Malice, ill will; jealousy, hate, spite, hatred, grudging; chagrin, discontent, mortification.

ANT. *Admiration, good will, regard, esteem, benevolence; aspiration, emulation.*

Ephemeral. Transient, momentary, daily, diurnal, fleeting, fugitive, brief, evanescent, transitory.

ANT. *Permanent, immortal, eternal, lasting, enduring, perpetual, abiding, persistent, perennial.*

Epigrammatic. Pointed, terse, laconic, concise, graphic.

ANT. *Diffuse, prolix, pointless, copious, circumlocutory, verbose, periphrastic.*

Epitome. Summary, compend, abstract, curtailment, reduction.

ANT. *Expansion, extension, amplification, dilation.*

Equable. Even, uniform, steady, regular, proportionate, smooth, easy, invariable.

ANT. *Variable, fitful, irregular, disjointed, desultory, uneasy.*

Equal. Like, equivalent, identical, tantamount; uniform, regular, even, steady; proportionate, commensurate; impartial, unbiased; competent, fit, adequate, sufficient; fair, equitable, just.

ANT. *Dissimilar, unsteady, incommensurate, irregular, disproportionate; incompetent, inadequate; unjust, unfair; variable, disparate.*

Equality. Likeness, uniformity, identity, evenness, equableness, sameness of rank.

ANT. *Dissimilarity, difference.*

Equanimity. Composure, calmness, tranquillity, steadiness, serenity.

ANT. *Impatience, perturbation, restlessness, disquiet.*

Equip. Accouter, arm, provide, furnish, fit out, supply, dress, array, garnish, arrange, invest, clothe.

ANT. *Divest, denude, dismantle, despoil, derange.*

Equipage. Carriage, retinue, vehicle, attendance, procession, suite, train; equipment, furniture, baggage, effects.

Equipment. Accouterments, apparatus, furnishings, dress, rigging, trappings, gear, outfit, provisions, equipage, arms, supplies.

Equitable. Upright, just, impartial, unbiased, unprejudiced, reasonable, fair, right, proper, honest, even-handed, proportionate.

ANT. *Unfair, unjust, unreasonable, partial, prepossessed, prejudiced, biased.*

Equity. Justice, right, uprightness, rectitude, fairness, impartiality, fair play, honesty, integrity.

ANT. *Injustice, corruption, dishonesty, partiality, unfairness, prejudice.*

Equivalent. Equal, equipollent, tantamount; synonymous, interchangeable, equiponderant.

ANT. *Unequal, incommensurate, uneven, unbalanced.*

Equivocal. Ambiguous, indefinite, enigmatical, dubious, uncertain, doubtful, questionable, perplexing, indeterminate, indistinct, suspicious.

ANT. *Evident, clear, plain, direct, manifest, obvious, indubitable, unquestionable, perspicuous, unambiguous, lucid, distinct, certain, indisputable.*

Eradicate. Abolish, extinguish, exterminate, extirpate, uproot, destroy, annihilate, excise.

ANT. *Cherish, encourage, instil, propagate, implant, inculcate, inspire, foster.*

Erase. Efface, expunge, cancel, obliterate, blot out, scratch out.

ANT. *Mark, delineate, write, inscribe, imprint, engrave.*

Erect, *a.* Upright, standing, elevated; bold, undaunted, firm.

ANT. *Leaning, lying, supine; groveling, abject; mean, servile, cowardly.*

Erect, *v.* Raise, uplift, place or set upright, build, construct; exalt, elevate, magnify; establish, institute, form, found, plant.

ANT. *Lower, incline, slant; subvert, depress, remove, destroy, demolish; debase, degrade.*

Err. Deviate, wander, ramble, rove; mistake, misjudge, blunder; sin, fall, lapse, trip, offend, trespass, misapprehend, stray, stumble, go astray.

ANT. *Succeed, prosper; correct, rectify.*

Errand. Message, mandate, commission, mission, charge, delegation.

ANT. *Misannouncement, misdelivery.*

Erratic. Wandering, nomadic, roving, rambling; planetary, moving; irregular, eccentric, abnormal; desultory, aberrant, flighty, changeful, capricious.

ANT. *Static, stationary; undeviating, steady, regular, normal; unalterable, methodical, calculable.*

Erring. Sinful, fallible, liable to err, wandering, misguided, misled.

ANT. *Virtuous, good, upright.*

Error. Blunder, mistake, misapprehension, oversight, inaccuracy; sin, fault, offense, transgression, iniquity, trespass, delinquency, misdeed, shortcoming, wrongdoing; deception, fallacy, untruth, falsity, hallucination.

ANT. *Truth, correctness, accuracy; correction, soundness,*

rectification; exactness, verification.

Erudition. Knowledge, learning, lore, scholarship, letters.

ANT. *Illiterateness, duncedom, sciolism, ignorance, stupidity.*

Eruption. Explosion, outbreak, outburst; sally, sudden excursion; discharge, eructation, exsufflation, ejection.

ANT. *Absorption, swallowing, engulfing, engrossment, irruption, inburst; consumption, devouring.*

Escape. Avoid, shun, evade, flee from, elude; pass unobserved; abscond, fly, hide.

ANT. *Incur, encounter, meet, confront; suffer.*

Esoteric. Private, secret, acroamatic, inner, inmost; abstruse, profound; special, advanced.

ANT. *Exoteric, public, popular; rudimentary, primary, elementary.*

Essence. Nature, quintessence, substance, vital part, element; volatile part, extract; perfume; scent, odor; being, existence, entity, life.

ANT. *Accident; property; garb, clothing, surroundings.*

Essential. Vital, necessary, indispensable, requisite, important; volatile, pure, diffusible, highly rectified; innate, inherent, immanent, leading.

ANT. *Accidental, induced, imported, adventitious; quantitative, qualitative; promotive, redundant, regulative, superfluous.*

Establish. Fix, settle, make steadfast; decree, enact, ordain; institute, originate, constitute, found, plant, organize, form; place, secure, set up; confirm, sanction, ratify, approve; verify, prove, substantiate; fulfil, carry out, make good; endow; demonstrate.

ANT. *Unsettle, supplant, disestablish, break up, subvert, upset; misstate, refute, confute; guess, conjecture, presume, suppose, surmise.*

Estate. State, condition; rank, position; property, possessions, fortune, effects; class, division, order; lands, demesne, domain, freehold.

ANT. *State, country, chattels, community, waste, goods, effects.*

Esteem, *n.* Estimate, favor, regard, respect, estimation; admiration.

ANT. *Aversion, hatred, dislike, contempt, abhorrence, antipathy, repugnance, loathing.*

Esteem, *v.* Estimate, hold, regard, prize, value, think, appreciate, deem, calculate, consider; price; believe, affect; revere, honor, respect, admire, venerate, love, like.

ANT. *Disregard, depreciate, undervalue, dislike, misprize, underrate, decry.*

Estimable. Appreciable, calculable, computable; worthy, excellent, good, deserving, meritorious; amiable, lovable, delectable, praiseworthy.

ANT. *Unworthy, bad, indelectable, unamiable; undeserving, unlovable.*

Eternal. Immortal, perpetual, fadeless, perennial, unfailing, imperishable, endless, everlasting, ever-living, interminable, never-ending, never-fading, unceasing, timeless, undying, unending, unfading; infinite.

ANT. *Ephemeral, transient, fleeting, mortal, temporal, transitory, evanescent, sublunary.*

Etiquette. Manners, breeding, fashion, conventionality.

ANT. *Misobservance, nonconformance, boorishness, rudeness, singularity.*

Euphonious. Euphonic, mellifluous, clear, musical, silvery, sweet-toned, melodious, harmonious, mellow.

ANT. *Harsh, discordant, dissonant.*

Euphuism. Purism, finical style, fastidious delicacy, affected elegance, high-flown diction, pompous *or* extravagantly ornate diction; affectation, factitiousness, pedantry, highflying (*used of language*).

ANT. *Simplicity, vernacular, mother-tongue, bluntness, naturalness, rusticity.*

Evacuate. Empty; eject, expel, excrete, throw out, discharge, void; quit, leave, forsake, desert, abandon, withdraw from, relinquish.

ANT. *Seize, occupy, hold, fill.*

Evaporate. Vaporize, disperse in vapor; disappear, evanesce, vanish; exhale, emit in vapor; turn to vapor; melt, colliquate, liquefy, dissolve, distil.

ANT. *Consolidate, compact, solidify, crystallize, indurate.*

Evasion. Prevarication, equivocation, quibbling, subterfuge, shuffling, sophistry, tergiversation, disingenuousness; shift, quibble, fencing.

ANT. *Answer, counter-argument, grappling; straightforwardness; challenge.*

Even. Smooth, level, flat, plane; equal, uniform, calm, steady, unruffled; fair, just, equitable; plain, flush; well-balanced.

ANT. *Variable, uneven; abrupt, inclined, rugged.*

Event. Circumstance, chance, incident, fortune, result, possibility, sequel, outcome, fact, episode, end, contingency, case, issue, consequence; occurrence, adventure, accident.

ANT. *Cause, antecedent, operation, inducement, contribution, convergence, tendency, predisposition.*

Eventful. Stirring, memorable, signal, momentous, important, critical, remarkable, marked, noted, notable.

ANT. *Ordinary, unmarked, eventless, uninteresting, unimportant, characterless, trivial.*

Ever. At any time; always, perpetually, continually, evermore, eternally, aye, for aye, forever, at all times; constantly, incessantly.

ANT. *Never.*

Everlasting. Endless, unending, perpetual, incessant, ceaseless, continual, uninterrupted, unceasing, interminable, eternal, constant, never-ending, never-ceasing; imperishable, undying, never-dying, deathless, immortal, ever-living; infinite.

ANT. *Ephemeral, transient, transitory.*

Every. All, any, both, either, each.

ANT. *None, no one, not any one.*

Evict. Dispossess, eject, throw out.

ANT. *Reinstate, admit; locate, lodge, settle.*

Evidence. Testimony, ground of belief, proof; manifestation, attraction, testimony, averment, deposition, declaration, appearance, sign, token, indication, exemplification, illustration.

ANT. *Surmise, conjecture; counter-evidence; refutation, disproof; concealment, misindication, suppression, fallacy.*

Evident. Patent, clear, palpable, manifest, transparent, visible, perceptible, obvious, open, conspicuous, apparent, distinct, discernible, indubitable, overt, plain, unmistakable, tangible; indisputable, incontrovertible.

ANT. *Doubtful, uncertain, questionable, dubious; hidden, concealed, secret, undiscovered, obscure, latent, unseen, unimagined, unknown; covert, dark, invisible; impenetrable, occult, impalpable, imperceptible, unthought of.*

Evil, *a.* Ill, noxious, deleterious, wrong, bad, hurtful, mischievous, sinful, unhappy, adverse, unpropitious, harmful, wicked, corrupt, unfair, notorious, miserable, sorrowful.

ANT. *Wholesome, right, virtuous, beneficial, holy, pure, felicitous, happy, fortunate, joyous, welcome, grateful, worthy, good, honorable.*

Evince. Prove, show, evidence, exhibit, manifest, demonstrate; establish; indicate, display.

ANT. *Suppress, negative, disprove, conceal.*

Evoke. Summon, call forth; excite, arouse, elicit, rouse, provoke, educe, produce; eliminate, extract.

ANT. *Allay, stifle, stop, silence, prevent, seal.*

Exactly. Precisely, accurately, strictly, nicely.

ANT. *Loosely, inaccurately, incorrectly, differently.*

Exaggerate. Overstate, strain, overcharge, stretch, overcolor; amplify, enlarge, magnify, overdraw, heighten, overpaint, overestimate.

ANT. *Disparage, attenuate, palliate, understate, underestimate, minimize, mitigate, qualify, soften, modify.*

Examine. Inspect, observe, investigate, scrutinize, consider, study; canvass, test, inquire into, search into, look into weigh, ponder, criticize, prove discuss, overhaul, explore.

ANT. *Conjecture, guess; discard, slur; misconsider, misinvestigate.*

Example. Model, pattern, ideal archetype, exemplar, standard sample, specimen, type, warning, ensample, exemplification prototype; copy, illustration instance; issue, development.

ANT. *Stock, material, substance, law, rule, case, system character, principle, quality.*

Excavate. Hollow, dig, scoop out, cut, trench; discover, disinter.

ANT. *Inter, inhume, bury, conceal; fill, level.*

Except, *prep.* Excepting, without, saving, unless, exclusive of.

Except, *v.* Exclude, save, bar; segregate, negative.

ANT. *Include, reckon, count, state, classify, propound, admit, affirm.*

Exception. Exclusion, omission, non-inclusion; objection; affront, offense; unusual case, anomaly; qualification, separation.

ANT. *Rule, class; statement, proposition.*

Exceptionable. Undesirable, objectionable.

ANT. *Unobjectionable, desirable, exemplary.*

Exceptional. Irregular, rare, unusual, uncommon, unnatural, peculiar, anomalous, abnormal, aberrant, exceptive.

ANT. *Common, usual, normal, ordinary, regular.*

Excess. Surplus, waste, extravagance, wastefulness, superfluity, lavishness, exorbitance, superabundance, dissipation, intemperance, profusion, prodigality, redundance; increase, debauchery.

ANT. *Frugality, economy; dearth, deficiency, defect, want, shortcoming, lack, need, poverty; failure, destitution, inadequacy, insufficiency, scantiness; temperance, sobriety.*

Excessive. Superabundant, disproportionate, undue, exuberant, superfluous; immoderate, intemperate, extreme; violent, vehement; enormous, exorbitant, overmuch, inordinate, unreasonable, extravagant.

ANT. *Insufficient, scant, inadequate, lacking, wanting, deficient.*

Excitability. Sensibility, sensitiveness; irritability, irascibility, passionateness.

ANT. *Immobility, hebetude, composure; insensitiveness, imperturbability.*

Excommunicate. Dismiss, expel, denounce, proscribe, anathematize, exscind; exclude. banish, bar, eject, blackball.

ANT. *Admit, readmit, enroll, inaugurate.*

Excrescence. Tumor, protuberance; superfluity, useless appendage; redundancy.

ANT. *Eradication, extirpation, excision, levigation, exsection.*

Excruciate. Torture, torment, rack, agonize.

ANT. *Soothe, please, tranquilize.*

Exculpate. Absolve, exonerate, acquit, clear, set right, vindicate; defend, release.

ANT. *Charge, implicate, inculpate.*

Excursion. Trip, ramble, tour, jaunt, journey, expedition.

Excusable. Pardonable, venial.

ANT. *Inexcusable, unpardonable.*

Excuse, *v.* Pardon, forgive, absolve, acquit, exonerate, exculpate; extenuate, justify; free, exempt, release, let off; overlook, regard indulgently, condone; remit, vindicate, defend, mitigate.

ANT. *Charge, condemn, inculpate, convict, sentence; exact, accuse.*

Execrable. Detestable, cursed, loathsome, accursed, villainous, hateful, abominable, damnable, diabolical, odious, abhorrent; offensive, disgusting, nauseous, obnoxious, repulsive, revolting, vile.

ANT. *Desirable, respectable, laudable, eligible.*

Execration. Curse, malediction, ban, anathema, imprecation of evil; detestation, abhorrence, horror, loathing, abomination; denunciation.

ANT. *Benediction, blessing.*

Execute. Administer, perform, enforce, carry out, do.

ANT. *Fail, be lacking, disappoint.*

Exemplary. Laudable, praiseworthy, excellent, correct, estimable, worthy, virtuous; patternlike, close, faithful, exact, scrupulous, assiduous, punctilious, rigid, punctual, rigorous; worthy of imitation, fit for a pattern.

ANT. *Detestable, objectionable, exceptionable.*

Exemplify. Illustrate, show by example; manifest, embody, exhibit, represent.

ANT. *Belie, betray, misrepresent, falsify.*

Exempt, *v.* Relieve, set free, release, grant immunity to, excuse, exonerate, except.

ANT. *Subject, render liable, bind, oblige; expose.*

Exempt, *a.* Free, irresponsible,

liberated, clear, absolved, privileged, unamenable.

ANT. *Liable, subject, amenable, responsible.*

Exemption. Immunity, privilege, exception, release, freedom from liability; dispensation, license.

ANT. *Liability, amenableness, responsibility, subjection, obligation.*

Exercise, *n.* Application, drill, employment, exertion; practice, training; occupation, use; performance, operation, act, activity, action.

ANT. *Inaction, idleness, relaxation, rest, inactivity; ease, recreation.*

Exertion. Use, exercise; effort, endeavor, struggle, trial, attempt, stretch, strain; labor, toil.

ANT. *Relaxation, rest, recreation.*

Exhalation. Evaporation; vapor, fume, steam, smoke, fog, reek; mist, damp, effluvium.

ANT. *Inhalation, exsiccation, absorption.*

Exhale. Emit, breathe out, give out, evaporate; vaporize.

ANT. *Inhale, breathe in, inspire.*

Exhaust. Drain, empty, expend, spend, waste, consume, squander, lavish, dissipate, destroy; prostrate, cripple, weaken, debilitate, enervate, disable, wear out, weary.

ANT. *Fill, replenish, augment, refresh, invigorate.*

Exhibit. Show, display; manifest, express, disclose, indicate, make known, evince; offer, present, propose; betray; demonstrate, illustrate.

ANT. *Conceal, mask, hide, secrete, suppress.*

Exhibition. Sight, representation, pageant, display, manifestation, show.

Exhilarate. Cheer, enliven, inspire, inspirit, stimulate, animate, elate, gladden; rejoice, delight, please.

ANT. *Depress, unnerve, unhinge, dispirit.*

Exhort. Urge, stimulate, persuade, incite, encourage; advise, counsel, enjoin.

ANT. *Dissuade, warn, deprecate, remonstrate.*

Exigency. Demand, urgency, need, necessity, requirement, want; pressure, crisis, emergency, juncture, quandary; conjuncture, pass, pinch, strait.

ANT. *Provision, rule, supply, course, preparation.*

Exile, *n.* Banishment, expulsion, ostracism, proscription, expatriation; separation, isolation; banished person.

ANT. *Welcome, return; remaining; cherishing, fostering, retaining.*

Exile, *v.* Banish, expatriate, ostracize, expel, proscribe, relegate.

ANT. *Welcome, reinstate, domesticate, domiciliate.*

Existence. Being, subsistence; entity, essence, creature, thing; life, animation; continuation, duration.

ANT. *Nonentity, non-existence, chimera.*

Expand. Open, spread out; dilate, enlarge, stretch, distend; swell, diffuse, extend, increase; develop, unfold, amplify.

ANT. *Contract, curtail, condense, restrict, attenuate.*

Expanse. Extent, stretch, expansion; firmament, sky, canopy, vault, welkin; vast, void, space, breadth.

ANT. *Limit, enclosure, confine, bound.*

Expatiate. Rove, range; dilate, enlarge, descant, be copious, launch out, amplify.
 ANT. *Contract, summarize, condense, epitomize.*

Expect. Await, look for; anticipate, rely upon, count upon, reckon *or* calculate upon, look forward to; look for, forecast, forebode, foresee.
 ANT. *Welcome, greet, hail, recognize; realize.*

Expectation. Anticipation, expectance, prospect, expectancy; reliance, confidence, assurance, presumption; trust, hope.
 ANT. *Recollection, remembrance, retrospect; distrust, despair, discouragement.*

Expediency. Fitness, propriety, suitableness, desirableness, advisability; advantage, utility, profit, usefulness; profitableness, advantageousness; interest.
 ANT. *Disadvantage, detriment, inutility, inexpediency.*

Expedition. Haste, speed, celerity, despatch, alertness, promptness, alacrity, quickness; enterprise, undertaking; march, voyage.
 ANT. *Delay, tardiness, procrastination.*

Expend. Disburse, spend, lay out; use, exert, consume, employ; waste, exhaust, spread, scatter, dissipate.
 ANT. *Save, economize, husband.*

Expense. Expenditure, outgo, cost, outlay; price, charge, payment.
 ANT. *Income, gain, proceeds, return, profit, product, receipts.*

Expensive. Dear, costly, high-priced; lavish, wasteful, extravagant; valuable, rich.
 ANT. *Cheap, worthless, poor; economical.*

Experience, *n.* Actual observation, feeling, *or* presentation; practice, experimental knowledge; experiment, trial, proof, test, knowledge, habit.
 ANT. *Anticipation, expectation.*

Experience, *v.* Feel, undergo, prove by trial, endure, suffer, be subject to; try, encounter.
 ANT. *Evade, escape, lose, miss.*

Experienced. Practiced, versed, accomplished, able, qualified, instructed, thoroughbred; familiar, skilled, accustomed, conversant.
 ANT. *Inexperienced, strange, unpracticed.*

Experiment. Trial, test, assay, examination, proof, touchstone, ordeal; observation, investigation, experimentation; illustration, exemplification.
 ANT. *Hypothesis, conjecture, assumption.*

Explain. Elucidate, expound, interpret, unfold, clear up, make plain; account for, make intelligible, give the reasons for, solve, warrant, trace to causes, justify; teach, decipher.
 ANT. *Mystify, bewilder, obscure, darken, misinterpret.*

Explanation. Elucidation, interpretation, exposition, illustration, description, explication; solution, warrant, justification, account, key; mutual understanding; sense.
 ANT. *Confusion, misinterpretation, mystification, obscuration.*

Explicit. Express, clear, plain, definite, positive, unambiguous, unreserved, categorical, determinate; detailed, declaratory, unobscure, stated.
 ANT. *Ambiguous, doubtful, indefinite, uncertain, vague, im-*

plied, implicit, indeterminate; hinted, suggestive, obscure.

Exponent. Index, indication, example, type, representative, illustration, specimen; advocate, interpreter, propounder.

ANT. *System, creed, principle, opinion.*

Export, *v.* Send out, carry out, send abroad, ship, produce.

ANT. *Import; consume.*

Exposed. Unprotected, defenseless, unguarded, endangered.

ANT. *Guarded, defended, protected.*

Expostulate. Object, dissuade, remonstrate.

ANT. *Abet, coincide, agree, confirm.*

Express, *v.* Squeeze out; utter, declare, assert, speak; represent, indicate, show, signify, exhibit, denote, intimate; send by express.

ANT. *Suppress, repress, conceal.*

Express, *a.* Explicit, clear, definite, plain, determinate, positive, categorical; exact, accurate, faithful, true, close, precise; special, particular; swift, rapid, fast; specific, pointed, direct.

ANT. *General; vague; leisurely; inaccurate, inexact, approximate.*

Expression. Squeezing out; assertion, statement, utterance, declaration; phrase, mode of speech, term; general tone, pervading effect, look, cast of countenance; lively representation; modulation, feeling, execution; indication.

ANT. *Suppression, restraint, repression; face, features, lineament; falsification, misstatement, solecism, enigma.*

Expunge. Erase, efface, obliterate, cancel, blot out, delete.

ANT. *Mark, write, trace, delineate.*

Exquisite. Nice, accurate, delicate, discriminating, exact, refined; precious, valuable, select, choice, rare, excellent; perfect, complete, matchless, consummate; keen, poignant, acute, intense; delicious.

ANT. *Common, coarse, ordinary; unrefined.*

Extemporaneous. Improvised, unpremeditated, extempore, impromptu, extemporary, offhand.

ANT. *Prepared, studied, premeditated, read, written, elaborated; rehearsed, recited.*

Extend. Stretch, reach; prolong, continue, lengthen, protract; expand, dilate, enlarge, widen, augment, increase; diffuse; impart, give, offer, yield; amplify, avail, apply.

ANT. *Contract, restrict, curtail, limit, narrow, reduce, condense; miss, fail.*

Extent. Expanse, amplitude, extension; volume, bulk, magnitude, size; stretch, reach, compass, length; degree, distance, quantity.

ANT. *Limitation, diminution, restriction.*

Extenuate. Lessen, diminish, reduce; palliate, mitigate, excuse, qualify, apologize for.

ANT. *Enhance, aggravate, heighten.*

Exterior, *a.* Outward, external, outer, outside, superficial; foreign, extrinsic, from without.

ANT. *Inner, internal, domestic, inward.*

Exterminate. Eradicate, overthrow, uproot, expel, extirpate, annihilate, banish, destroy, remove, root out, wipe out.

ANT. *Augment, breed, cherish, develop, increase, populate, replenish, settle, plant, foster, propagate, colonize, build up, beget.*

Extermination. Extirpation, annihilation, eradication, abolition, destruction, extinction, excision, elimination.

Ant. *Settlement, replenishment, augmentation, colonization, population, propagation, increase.*

External. Outward, outer, exterior, outside, superficial; foreign, extrinsic; visible, apparent; manifest, palpable.

Ant. *Inner, internal, intestine, inmost, hidden, non-apparent.*

Extinction. Destruction, annihilation, extirpation, extermination, abolition; extinguishment; stifling, death, suffocation, cessation, obsolescence.

Ant. *Inception, origination, birth, course, life, operation, action, exercise, continuance, prosperity, survival.*

Extinguish. Quench; destroy, suppress, put down; extirpate, abolish, eradicate, kill, annihilate, put out.

Ant. *Replenish, replant, implant, cherish, propagate, promote, invigorate, establish, confirm, secure.*

Extort. Exact, wrest, wrench, wring out, force; despoil, express, fleece, squeeze out, extract.

Ant. *Coax, cheat, wheedle, cajole.*

Extortionate. Oppressive, exacting, severe, hard, harsh; exorbitant, close-fisted, rigorous, monstrous, preposterous.

Ant. *Liberal, bountiful, indulgent, fair, moderate, reasonable.*

Extract, *n.* Selection, excerpt, passage, citation, quotation.

Extract, *v.* Draw, pull, take out; derive, select, quote, cite; determine, find; educe, elicit, gather, collect, extort.

Ant. *Insert, replace, incorporate, restore, reinsert, impose.*

Extraneous. Foreign, extrinsic; non-pertinent, not germane, unessential, superfluous; unconnected, alien, unrelated, adventitious, ascititious.

Ant. *Intrinsic, vital, internal, connected, essential.*

Extraordinary. Unusual, remarkable, uncommon, singular, signal, egregious, rare, extra; unwonted, peculiar, wonderful, unprecedented, marvelous, prodigious, monstrous, preposterous, strange.

Ant. *Common, usual, frequent, wonted, unremarkable, unimportant, ordinary.*

Extravagance. Excess, exorbitance, enormity, unreasonableness, preposterousness; wildness, folly, absurdity, irregularity; prodigality, lavish expenditure, profusion, waste.

Ant. *Carefulness, economy, frugality, saving, provision, prudence, foresight.*

Extravagant. Excessive, inordinate, unreasonable, preposterous, exorbitant; wild, foolish, absurd, irregular; lavish, profuse, wasteful, spendthrift, prodigal.

Ant. *Sound, sober, consistent, fair, rational, economical, frugal, careful, regular, usual.*

Extreme. Utmost, farthest, uttermost, outermost; greatest, highest; last, final, ultimate; extravagant, immoderate, excessive, unreasonable; remote, terminal, distant, most violent.

Ant. *Initial, primal, judicious, moderate.*

Extremity. End, verge, termination, edge, border, extreme, utmost point; close, conclusion.

ANT. *Beginning, commencement, opening, center, origin, bulk, body.*

Exudation. Ooze, drip, percolation, excretion, secretion.

ANT. *Absorption, parching, aridity.*

Exultant. Exulting, jubilant, triumphant, elated, joyous, transported.

ANT. *Mournful, dispirited, depressed.*

Exultation. Elation, joy, triumph, delight, transport, ecstasy.

ANT. *Mourning, depression.*

F

Fable. Story, myth, legend, allegory, apologue; plot, action, series of events; fiction, falsehood, lie, untruth, fabrication, forgery, invention, figment; romance, parable, novel.

ANT. *History, fact, narrative.*

Fabric. Building, structure, edifice, pile; texture, make, workmanship, conformation; manufactured cloth, woven stuff; work, construction, tissue, web.

ANT. *Destruction, dismantlement, demolition, fragment, wreck, tatters, ruin, shreds, rags.*

Fabricate. Build, frame, construct; make, manufacture; forge, invent, coin, feign; form, falsify, produce, devise, misrepresent.

ANT. *Demolish, tear, spoil, dismember, destroy, narrate, lacerate, copy, represent, repeat, portray.*

Fabulous. Invented, fabricated, feigned, unreal, coined, fictitious; incredible, pretended, imaginary, false, monstrous.

ANT. *Real, actual, historic, authentic, fair, true, reasonable.*

Facetious. Witty, jocose, jocular, humorous, waggish, funny, comical, pleasant, droll; gay, merry, sportive, lively, entertaining, sprightly; playful.

ANT. *Matter-of-fact, heavy, dull, grave, serious, saturnine, somber, lugubrious.*

Facile. Docile, easy, mild, courteous, affable, complaisant, approachable; pliant, pliable, ductile, flexible, yielding, tractable, manageable, compliant; ready, dexterous; indulgent, weak, irresolute, characterless.

ANT. *Resolute, sturdy, obstinate, determined, inflexible, crusty, self-willed, self-reliant, independent.*

Facility. Easiness, ease; readiness, dexterity, expertness, ability, knack; condescension, urbanity, affability, civility, complaisance, politeness; pliancy, flexibility, ductility; appliance, convenience, means, advantage, resource; quickness, adroitness.

ANT. *Effort, awkwardness, labor, difficulty.*

Fact. Occurrence, event, deed, incident, act, performance, circumstance; reality, actuality, certainty, truth.

ANT. *Fiction, supposition, unreality, falsehood, chimera, lie, delusion, invention, hallucination, romance.*

Factious. Turbulent, refractory, seditious, rebellious, recalcitrant, litigious, adversative, malcontent.

ANT. *Genial, complaisant, agreeable, loyal, harmonious, public-spirited, sympathetic, co-operative, auxiliary.*

Factitious. Artificial; euphuistic, affected, finical, cramped, conventional, spurious.

ANT. *Natural, genial, unaffected, pure, genuine, truthful.*

Fade. Vanish, evanesce, disappear, pass away; decline, languish, droop, decay, wither; lose color, grow dim, blanch, bleach, fall, sink, dwindle, pale, change, set, etiolate, fail.

ANT. *Rise, increase, bloom, grow, flourish, endure, abide, last, stand.*

Fag. Droop, sink, grow weary, flag; drudge, toil; do menial service, tire, fatigue, jade, exhaust; work, slave.

ANT. *Idle, lounge, dawdle; strike; bask.*

Fail. Fall short, be insufficient, be deficient; decline, sink, decay, wane, fade, break, give out; cease, disappear, become extinct; miss, miscarry, be unsuccessful, miss fire, be frustrated; omit, neglect; break, become insolvent, suspend payment; trip, lose.

ANT. *Succeed, exceed, surpass, achieve, abound, yield, excel.*

Faint. Weak, exhausted, worn, listless, languid, wearied, dim, feeble, fatigued, faint-hearted, faded, faltering, half-hearted, irresolute, purposeless, timid, ill-defined, indistinct; unenergetic; obscure, inconspicuous.

ANT. *Prominent, marked, glaring; resolute, sturdy, vigorous, strong, fresh, hearty, daring, energetic; clear, brilliant, bright, conspicuous.*

Fair. Spotless, unspotted, unblemished, unstained, untarnished; white, light, blond; handsome, comely, beautiful; pleasant, clear, cloudless, unclouded; favorable, prosperous; promising, hopeful; open, distinct, plain, unobstructed, unencumbered; frank, honest, ingenuous, candid, noble, honorable, upright, impartial; reasonable, proper, equitable, just; passable, tolerable, above mediocrity; serene.

ANT. *Lowering, dull, foul, ugly, disfigured, fraudulent, unfair, dishonorable.*

Faith. Creed, doctrine, assurance, belief, confidence, assent, credence, opinion, trust, credit, reliance.

ANT. *Distrust, disbelief, dissent, doubt, incredulity, infidelity, misgiving, skepticism, unbelief, suspicion, rejection.*

Faithful. Firm, loyal, devoted, stanch, sure, true, trustworthy, trusty, unwavering, incorruptible; attached; accurate, close, consistent, correspondent, exact, equivalent.

ANT. *Inaccurate, inexact; faithless, false, fickle, untrue, wavering, untrustworthy, capricious.*

Fall. Drop, descend, sink; lapse, droop, gravitate; fall down, be prostrated; be lowered, be depressed; decrease, decline, be diminished, die away, sin, err, transgress, trip, trespass; die, perish; empty, be discharged, flow; happen, befall, come; become, get; pass, be transferred; be dropped, be uttered carelessly.

ANT. *Rise, soar, mount, recover, climb, ascend.*

Fallacy. Illusion, deception, deceit, delusion, mistake, misapprehension, error, misconception; sophism, sophistry, paralogism, deceitful argument.

ANT. *Truth, logic, proof, postulate, argument, verity, fact, axiom, soundness.*

Fallible. Erring, uncertain, ignorant, weak, frail, imperfect.

ANT. *Certain, infallible, unerring, omniscient.*

Fallow. Pale red *or* pale yellow; untilled, unsowed, neglected; inert, inactive, dormant; quiescent, idle, uncultivated, unproductive.

ANT. *Cultivated, tilled, productive, worked, sown, prolific, operative, fruitful.*

False. Untrue, mendacious, unveracious, lying; dishonest, perfidious, treacherous, faithless, disloyal, dishonorable, disingenuous, double-tongued, false-hearted, double-faced, two-faced; untrustworthy, untruthful, unreliable, truthless; spurious, counterfeit, forged, not genuine, feigned, sham, hypocritical, make-believe; incorrect, improper, erroneous, unfounded, wrong; fallacious, deceptive, deceiving, deceitful, delusive, misleading, disappointing; sophistical, mock, bogus, fabricated, unfaithful.

ANT. *True, sound, correct, authentic, real, genuine, candid, conclusive, honorable, faithful.*

Falsehood. Falsity, lie, fabrication, untruth, fiction, fib; imposture, counterfeit, cheat; fallacy, error, sophistry, forgery, deception.

ANT. *Truth, verity, correctness, fact, genuineness, honesty, honor, reality, authenticity.*

Falsify. Misrepresent, counterfeit, belie, misstate, garble; disprove, show unsound; violate; mistake, misinterpret, betray.

ANT. *Verify, rectify, correct, check, certify, justify, expose, declare, exhibit, publish.*

Falter. Hesitate, stutter, stammer; fail, quiver, tremble, totter; waver, be undecided, show weakness; halt, slip, dubitate, demur, flinch, vacillate.

ANT. *Proceed, speed, flow, run, discourse, determine, persevere, resolve.*

Fame. Celebrity, honor, laurels, distinction, notoriety, renown, reputation, repute, glory, eminence, credit; report, tidings, rumor, bruit, news.

ANT. *Silence, suppression, hush; dishonor, discredit, humiliation, infamy, shame, obscurity, contempt, contumely, disgrace, disrepute, ignominy, oblivion.*

Familiar. Conversant, well-acquainted, well-versed; intimate, close, near, friendly, fraternal, cordial, amicable; social, accessible, sociable, affable, kindly, courteous, civil, companionable, conversible; unceremonious, unconstrained, free, easy, informal; well-known; household, frank, everyday, accustomed.

ANT. *Uncommon, rare, extraordinary, strange, unaccustomed, unacquainted, new, unfamiliar, inconversant.*

Famous. Celebrated, renowned, distinguished, remarkable, far-famed, eminent, noted, illustrious, glorious.

ANT. *Unknown, unsung, inglorious, obscure, forgotten.*

Fanatic. Enthusiast, zealot, visionary, bigot.

ANT. *Skeptic, unbeliever, cynic.*

Fanaticism. Intolerance, superstition, bigotry, credulity; enthusiasm, frenzy.

ANT. *Skepticism, cynicism.*

indifference, free-thinking, latitudinarianism; disbelief, profanity; disregard, coldness.

Fanciful. Fantastic, grotesque, visionary, imaginative, chimerical; unreal, eccentric, quaint, imaginary, freakish, erroneous, humorsome, capricious, fitful, erratic, whimsical, absurd.

ANT. *Ordinary, usual, regular, commonplace, real, accurate, literal, prosaic, reasonable, sensible, solid, sure, true, sound, calculable, calculated; natural, sober, truthful, correct.*

Fancy. Imagination, whim, vagary, caprice, belief, conceit, conception, desire, humor, idea, image, inclination, mood, liking, predilection, supposition; thought, notion.

ANT. *Certainty, fact, reality, truth, verity, actuality; object, subject, thought, law, order; aversion, horror.*

Farcical. Droll, absurd, ridiculous, ludicrous; comic, funny, nonsensical, pantomimic.

ANT. *Grave, serious, tragic, solemn, dismal, ghastly, funereal.*

Fare. Go, travel, journey, pass; prosper, be treated, prove, happen, turn out, be situated; be entertained, feed; live, speed, do.

ANT. *Toil, fast, fail, droop, sink, faint, drop, falter, halt.*

Farewell. Adieu, good-by, valedictory, leave-taking, congé, departure, parting.

ANT. *Salutation, welcome, greeting.*

Fashion. Form, shape, figure, cut, make, model, cast, mold, pattern, appearance, configuration, conformation; way, manner, sort, method; usage, custom, style, mode, conventionality; gentility; guise, character, practice, ceremony.

ANT. *Person, work, speech, dress; derangement, formlessness, shapelessness; outlandishness, strangeness, eccentricity.*

Fast, *a.* Fixed, fastened, close, tight; firm, immovable; steadfast, constant, stanch; fortified, strong, impregnable; profound, sound, deep; swift, quick, fleet, rapid; wild, reckless, thriftless, dissipated, thoughtless, extravagant; secure, stable, unyielding, unswerving; accelerated; gay.

ANT. *Insecure, loose, slow, tardy, steady, sober, virtuous.*

Fasten. Secure, bind, tie, attach; join, unite, connect, hold together; hold compact, affix, annex, grapple, fix.

ANT. *Undo, loose, sever, relax, remove, unfasten, detach.*

Fastidious. Dainty, squeamish, difficult, overnice, overdelicate, queasy, critical; overrefined, censorious, particular, punctilious.

ANT. *Indulgent, uncritical, easy; coarse; omnivorous.*

Fat. Unctuous, greasy, fatty, oily; plump, fleshy, obese, corpulent, portly, pursy; coarse, heavy, dull, sluggish, stupid; rich, profitable, lucrative; productive, fertile, fruitful; luxuriant, brawny; stout; oleaginous.

ANT. *Lean, slender, attenuated, emaciated, barren, poor, scant; marrowless; anatomical.*

Fatal. Deadly, mortal, lethal; destructive, calamitous, baleful, ruinous, mischievous, baneful, pernicious; fateful.

ANT. *Beneficial, wholesome, vitalizing, restorative, salubrious, nutritious, slight, superficial, harmless.*

Fate. Destiny, destination, inevitable necessity, fatality; lot, doom, predetermined event; destruction, death; final event, ultimate destruction; fortune, end.

ANT. *Will, choice, decision, independence, freedom.*

Fathom, *v.* Sound; divine, penetrate, reach, comprehend, understand; gage, pierce, measure, probe.

ANT. *Survey, glance, scan, miss, skin, graze, overlook.*

Fathomless. Bottomless, profound, abysmal.

ANT. *Superficial, shallow, skin-deep.*

Fatigue, *n.* Weariness, exhaustion, lassitude; labor, hardship, toil; languor, enervation.

ANT. *Freshness, vigor, indefatigability, activity.*

Fatigue, *v.* Harass, weary, tire, jade, exhaust, fag.

ANT. *Inspirit, refresh, enliven, animate.*

Fatuity. Foolishness, imbecility, idiocy; folly, madness, absurdity, infatuation.

ANT. *Wisdom, sense, soundness, sobriety, discernment.*

Fault. Defect, blemish, imperfection, flaw, weakness, failing, frailty; misdeed, misdemeanor, offense, trespass, wrong, transgression, delinquency, indiscretion; slip, error, lapse; failure, omission, want, drawback.

ANT. *Perfection, sufficiency, correctness, completeness.*

Faultless. Without blemish, perfect; innocent, guileless, blameless, sinless, spotless, immaculate, guiltless, stainless; complete, correct, accurate.

ANT. *Incomplete, imperfect, incorrect, defective, inaccurate, corrupt, faulty, erroneous.*

Faulty. Bad, defective, imperfect; blamable, blameworthy, culpable, reprehensible.

ANT. *Correct, complete, perfect, accurate; irreproachable, blameless, unassailable.*

Favor, *n.* Kindness, grace, countenance, friendliness, good will; benefit, good deed, friendly turn; patronage, championship, support; letter, communication, epistle; gift, present; decoration, knot, rosette; permission, leave, pardon; advantage, preference, boon; concession, predilection, civility, regard, condescension.

ANT. *Refusal, denial, prohibition, disfavor, withholding, withdrawal, frown, disapproval, injury, discountenance.*

Favor, *v.* Befriend, countenance, patronize, encourage; approve, regard with favor; facilitate, be propitious to; support, help, aid, assist; humor, indulge, extenuate, palliate, ease, spare; resemble, look like.

ANT. *Refuse, deny, disapprove, withdraw, withhold, prohibit, discountenance, injure, harm.*

Favorable. Kind, friendly, propitious, willing, auspicious; conducive, contributing; beneficial, advantageous, convenient, suitable, fit; permissive, indulgent, concessive, partial, fond, liberal.

ANT. *Reluctant, unpropitious, unfavorable, impartial.*

Favorite. Dear, beloved, pet, darling.

Favoritism. Partiality, invidiousness.

ANT. *Odium, prejudice; impartiality.*

Fawn upon. Flatter, wheedle, cajole, cringe, palaver, slaver.

ANT. *Insult, deride, defy, cen-*

sure, dare, satirize, rebuke, reprimand.

Fealty. Homage, loyalty, allegiance; fidelity, faithfulness, honor, good faith, devotion.
ANT. *Disloyalty, treachery, infidelity, disaffection, shame, dishonor.*

Fear. Dismay, alarm, horror, awe, apprehension, dread, terror, fright, panic, tremor, timidity, trepidation, trembling, affright, consternation, disquietude, misgiving, anxiety, solicitude, concern; veneration, reverence.
ANT. *Courage, confidence, assurance, fearlessness; trust, boldness; fortitude.*

Fearful. Afraid, apprehensive; timid, nervous, timorous, faint-hearted, cowardly; dreadful, terrible, frightful, dire; awful; shocking, terrific, horrible; hesitating.
ANT. *Venturesome, audacious, bold, confident, consolatory, inspiriting, assuring; attractive, alluring, hopeful, inviting.*

Feasible. Manageable, possible, permissible, practicable, contrivable.
ANT. *Impossible, unallowable, impracticable.*

Feast. Treat, banquet, regalement, entertainment, carousal; festival, holiday; delight, enjoyment.
ANT. *Starvation, scarcity, want, lack, bareness, scantiness.*

Featly. Neatly, cleverly, dexterously, adroitly.
ANT. *Clumsily, bunglingly, hardly.*

Feature. Lineament, cast of the face; fashion, make, aspect, appearance, conformation; prominent part, outline; characteristic, trait, point, mark, item, component, element, indication, portion, sign.
ANT. *Whole, system, countenance; arrangement, case; misindication, misinformation, falsification; blind, mask, disguise; excrescence.*

Federation. Uniting, federating, confederation, union, league, allying, alliance, coalition, federal compact, confederacy, combination.
ANT. *Secession, disunion, sedition, mutiny, disruption.*

Fee. Pay, reward, recompense, compensation, remuneration; feud, fief, fee-simple, unconditional tenure.

Feeble. Weak, not strong, enervated, debilitated, infirm, languid, sickly, languishing, declining, frail, drooping; faint, imperfect, dim; without vigor, lacking intensity; wretched, poor, dull, forceless, puny, enfeebled, nerveless; incomplete, vain, fruitless; scanty, pitiable.
ANT. *Strong, robust, active, successful, effective; abundant; powerful, muscular; forcible, cogent, telling; violent, vehement, ardent; lusty, hale, vigorous, hearty.*

Feed. Give food to, supply, contribute to, provide for; nourish, cherish, sustain; eat, take food, take nourishment; sustain life, subsist.
ANT. *Starve, refuse, deny, withhold, take away; impoverish, steal from; diet, abstain, refrain.*

Feel. Perceive, have feeling; be perceived; be moved, be excited, be stirred, be wrought up, be impressed; touch, handle; experience, suffer, *or* enjoy; be affected by, be moved by; prove, sound, try, put to the test.
ANT. *Be hard* or *callous, in-*

sensate, apathetic, dull, numb, imperceivable, indifferent, unsusceptible, or *stoical.*

Feeling. Sense of touch; sensation, perception by touch; sensibility, emotion, sentiment, affection, passion, impression; tenderness, susceptibility; contact; pathos; consciousness, sensitiveness.

ANT. *Callousness, insensibility, imperturbability, inexcitability, coldness, insensateness.*

Feign. Invent, imagine, devise, forge, fabricate; counterfeit, affect, assume, simulate, pretend to.

ANT. *Detect, test, unmask, refute, verify, substantiate.*

Felicitous. Fit, appropriate, apt, pertinent, seasonable, opportune, well-timed, happy, skilful, ingenious; prosperous, successful, fortunate, lucky, auspicious, propitious; timely, joyous.

ANT. *Unhappy, unfortunate, inauspicious, untimely, inopportune, disastrous, sad.*

Felicity. Bliss, blessedness, happiness; aptness, aptitude, fitness, propriety, felicitousness, suitableness; success, luck, fortune.

ANT. *Ill luck, bad fortune, sorrow, unhappiness, disaster, misfortune; sadness, mourning, melancholy.*

Fell, *a.* Inhuman, cruel, barbarous, relentless, ruthless, implacable, unrelenting, pitiless, malignant, malicious, malign, savage, ferocious, bloody, bloodthirsty; direful, merciless, remorseless, fierce, truculent.

ANT. *Generous, chivalrous, lenient, humane, propitious.*

Fell, *v.* Prostrate, level, bring to the ground, hurl down, knock down; cut down, hew down, lay low; hem; demolish, subvert, waste, bare.

ANT. *Plant, erect, support; stock, upraise, rear, propagate.*

Fellow. Associate, companion, comrade; equal, peer, compeer; mate, match, counterpart; adherent, colleague, member; correlative, tally; partner, friend.

ANT. *Foe, opponent, antagonist, stranger, mismatch, opposite.*

Fellowship. Companionship, familiarity, intimacy, brotherhood, acquaintance; participation, partnership, joint interest; converse, intercourse, communion; sociability, affability, kindliness; association, company; membership, society.

ANT. *Severance, disconnection, dismemberment; non-intercourse.*

Felonious. Malignant, malign, malicious, nefarious, infamous, heinous, atrocious, cruel, felon; perfidious, traitorous, disloyal, base.

ANT. *Legal, constitutional, rightful, regular; legitimate, legalized; permissible, allowable; just, proper.*

Feminine. Female, womanish, womanly, effeminate; delicate, tender, modest, soft.

ANT. *Robust, manly; indelicate, unfeminine; rough, rude; masculine.*

Fen. Marsh, swamp, bog, moor, morass, quagmire.

Fence, *v.* Enclose, guard, fortify, defend, circumscribe, protect; elude, parry, stave.

ANT. *Open, disenclose; receive, catch, suffer.*

Ferment, *n.* Yeast, leaven, fermentation; agitation, commotion, tumult; fever, heat, glow.

Ferment, *v.* Set in fermentation; excite, agitate, heat; seethe concoct, brew; warm, chafe; effervesce, rankle, fester.

ANT. *Damp, cool; dissipate; subside, evaporate, disperse; heal.*

Fertile. **Prolific,** fecund, breeding, bearing; fruitful, productive, rich, plenteous, luxuriant, exuberant, teeming; causative, conducive; pregnant; fraught, ingenious, inventive.

ANT. *Poor, sterile, barren, unproductive, ineffective, inconducive, fruitless, inoperative, uninventive, unimaginative.*

Festive. Convivial, jovial, joyous, gay, merry, mirthful, festival.

ANT. *Solitary, deserted, ascetic, gloomy.*

Fetid. Stinking, offensive, rank, rancid, malodorous, mephitic, noisome, foul, strong-smelling, corrupt.

ANT. *Inodorous, fresh, perfumed, scented, balmy.*

Fetter, *n.* Chains, bondage, custody, durance, duress, manacles, irons, shackles, imprisonment, handcuffs, gyves, bonds.

Fetter, *v.* Shackle, clog, hamper, trammel; chain, bind, tie, confine, restrain, encumber; manacle, hinder, impede.

ANT. *Free, liberate, accelerate, expedite.*

Feud. Contest, controversy, dispute, enmity, hostility, quarrel, strife, dissension, affray, animosity, bitterness, broil, contention, brawl, fray; antipathy.

ANT. *Friendliness, congeniality, sympathy, clanship, pacification, reconciliation, sociality, neighborliness.*

Fever. Heat, flush, excitement, agitation, ferment; ardor, fervor, broil, passion.

ANT. *Coolness, iciness, frigidity; composure, indifference.*

Few. Not many, small in number, hardly any, scarcely any; scant, rare, lacking.

ANT. *Many, abundant, numerous.*

Fiber. Strength, sinews, thews, toughness; thread, staple, pile, filament.

ANT. *Laxity, debility, flabbiness.*

Fickle. Wavering, unsteady, unstable, inconstant, variable, vacillating, volatile, mercurial, fitful, changeable, irresolute, unsettled, capricious, fanciful, unreliable, mutable; veering, restless, shifting.

ANT. *Sober, orderly, reliable, calculable, well-regulated, uniform, steady, trustworthy.*

Fiction. Fable, falsehood, myth, invention, novel, romance, figment, story, fabrication, legend, allegory, apologue; creation.

ANT. *History, fact, literalness, reality, truth, verity, certainty.*

Fictitious. Feigned, imaginary, invented, unreal, purely ideal, fanciful; false, counterfeit, spurious, supposititious.

ANT. *Real, true, historical, genuine, authentic, veritable.*

Fidelity. Faithfulness, devotedness, devotion, truth, loyalty, true-heartedness, fealty, adherence to duty; accuracy, closeness, exactness, truthfulness, precision, attachment, honesty, allegiance, integrity.

ANT. *Disloyalty, treachery, untruthfulness, disaffection, inaccuracy, infidelity, inexactness.*

Field. Tract of land; battle-field, scene of war; surface, expanse, range, scope; province, department, region, realm, domain; ground, arena; room, opportunity.

ANT. *Circumscription, constraint; interdiction, exclusion, debarment.*

Fierce. Ravenous, infuriate, barbarous, fell; vehement, turbulent, passionate, uncurbed, untamed, raging; furious, savage, ferocious, fiery, violent, wild, impetuous; uncultivated, untrained.

ANT. *Gentle, harmless, kind, patient, submissive, sweet, tender, docile, affectionate, mild, peaceful, tame; calm.*

Fiery. Hot, ardent, heated, fervid, flaming, glowing; impetuous, vehement, fierce, passionate, impassioned; irascible, choleric, excited, enkindled, hot-blooded, irritable.

ANT. *Cold, icy, frigid, chilly; indifferent, phlegmatic, passionless, unimpassioned, mild, tame; extinguished, quenched.*

Fight, *n.* Combat, conflict, contest, battle, struggle, engagement, encounter, action, affair, fray, affray, brush; broil, riot; spirit, fighting temper; resistance, disposition to struggle, contention.

ANT. *Pacification, reconciliation.*

Figurative. Typical, representative, emblematical; metaphorical, tropical; flowery, florid, ornate; poetical, rhetorical, symbolical.

ANT. *Literal, prosaic, unpoetical, unmetaphorical.*

Figure, *n.* Form, shape, configuration, conformation, outline; image, likeness, representation, effigy; appearance; pattern, design; metaphor, trope; diagram, drawing; price; symbol, type, emblem; digit, number, numeral, character; aspect, delineation, condition, illustration.

ANT. *Misrepresentation, deformity, disfigurement.*

Figure, *v.* Adorn, variegate, diversify; represent, signify, typify, symbolize; imagine, image, conceive, picture, represent; calculate, compute, cipher; appear, act, perform; show off, cut a dash.

ANT. *Disfigure, harm, destroy; miscalculate, mistake.*

File. Rasp, smooth, finish; place on file; polish; perfect, refine, improve.

ANT. *Roughen, jag, acuminate, denticulate, barb, notch, cusp.*

Fill. Make full, fill up; pervade, occupy; dilate, expand, stretch, distend; store, supply, furnish, replenish, stock; satisfy, content, sate, satiate, cloy, pall; occupy, hold, fulfil, perform; become full, be filled; gorge, appoint, glut; stuff; rise; swell, grow, increase.

ANT. *Exhaust, drain, dissatisfy, deprive, stint, vacate, misappoint; subside, ebb, evaporate, shrink, diminish.*

Filter. Strain, ooze, percolate, exude, transude; refine, distil, leak; purify, cleanse, depurate, defecate, clarify.

ANT. *Muddle, disturb, befoul, thicken.*

Filthy. Dirty, nasty, foul, defiled, unclean, squalid; impure, corrupt, gross; dingy, unsanitary, unwholesome.

ANT. *Pure, sweet, healthy, clean, sanitary, wholesome.*

Final. Latest, last, eventual, ultimate; decisive, conclusive, definitive; terminal; definite, developed.

ANT. *Initiative, open, progressive, continuous, incipient, current, unconcluded, inchoate, inaugural, nascent, rudimental.*

Find. Discover, fall upon, light upon, meet; obtain, get, procure, gain, arrive at, attain to; observe, remark, perceive, notice, discover; detect, catch; supply, furnish, provide, contribute; determine judicially, declare by verdict; confront, ascertain, experience, invent.

ANT. *Withdraw; miss, lose, elude, withhold, overlook, miscontrive.*

Fine, *n.* Forfeit, penalty, forfeiture, mulct, amercement.

Fine, *a.* Minute, small, comminuted, little; slender, capillary, delicate; thin, tenuous, subtile, attenuated; light, keen, sharp; exquisite, nice, refined; excellent, superior, very good; brilliant, accomplished; beautiful, handsome, splendid, elegant; clear, pure, unadulterated; gay, showy, garish, flashy, filmy, artistic, choice, finished, high, grand, noble, generous, honorable, pretentious, pretty, ostentatious; presumptuous, casuistical.

ANT. *Rough, mean, petty, unfinished; illiberal, unimposing, paltry; modest, unaffected, affable; plain-spoken, categorical; unanalytical, unreflective; coarse, great, heavy, huge, immense, large, rude, stout, thick, blunt, big, clumsy.*

Finery. Gewgaws, trinkets, ornaments, trimmings, tawdriness, decorations, trappings, bedizenment, tinsel, trash, dressiness.

ANT. *Ornament, dress, decoration, adornment; chasteness, sobriety, simplicity.*

Finical. Fastidious, dainty, overparticular, squeamish, overnice, affected, elegant; dandyish, foppish, spruce.

ANT. *Effective, unaffected, practical, energetic, real, genuine, natural; outspoken, blunt, coarse, rude.*

Finish, *v.* Accomplish, execute, complete, perform, achieve, do, get done; perfect, polish, elaborate; end, terminate, close, conclude, put an end to; shape.

ANT. *Start, commence, begin; fail, undertake; miscontrive, botch, mar, mismanage.*

Finished. Perfect, artistic, refined, high.

ANT. *Inartistic, incomplete, poor, rude, coarse, unfinished.*

Finite. Bounded, limited, conditioned, contracted, restricted, terminated.

ANT. *Infinite, unlimited, unbounded.*

Fire. Blaze, burning, conflagration, flame, combustion; discharge; heat, ardor, fervor, violence, force, passion, impetuosity, fervency, intensity, animation, vigor, spirit, enthusiasm; light, luster, radiance, splendor; vivacity, inspiration, imagination; torture, affliction, trouble, bitter trial, persecution.

First. Foremost, leading; chief, highest, principal, capital; elementary, primary, rudimentary; earliest; primitive, primeval, pristine; in the first place, at the outset, in the beginning, first and foremost; original, onmost.

ANT. *Subsequent, secondary, subordinate, subservient, lowest, unimportant, last, hindmost.*

Fit, *a.* Competent, fitted, qualified; suitable, appropriate, apt, apposite, meet, seemly, becoming, befitting, proper, good, decent, convenient, fitting, decorous, adapted, congruous, peculiar, particular, prepared, adequate, calculated, ripe, right, contrived, expedient.

ANT. *Awkward, misfitting, ungainly, ill-suited, inappropriate, unseemly, unprepared, unsuitable, inadequate, miscalculated, miscontrived, improper, unfit, inexpedient.*

Fitful. Variable, irregular, impulsive, spasmodic, unstable, fickle, whimsical, fanciful, capricious, fantastic, humorsome, odd; eventful, checkered; restless, inconstant, mutable, desultory, unequal.

ANT. *Regular, equable, orderly, systematic, calculable.*

Fix. Set, place, establish, plant, fasten, make firm; attach, tie, connect; determine, define, appoint, limit, settle; rivet, direct steadily, adjust; solidify, consolidate; link, locate, root, secure; decide.

ANT. *Displace, unsettle, remove, disarrange, uproot, transplant, transfer, weaken, shake, disestablish, reverse, disturb, change, unfix.*

Flaccid. Limber, lax, drooping, flabby, soft, limp, yielding, relaxed, inelastic, pendulous.

ANT. *Firm, braced, plump, muscular, chubby, brawny, vigorous, strong, powerful.*

Flag, *n.* Flagstone; streamer, banner, colors, standard, pennon, pennant, ensign, gonfalon.

Flag, *v.* Hang loose, droop; languish, faint, decline, pine, sink, succumb, grow weak, become dejected; pall, grow stale, lose interest, weary, tire; give in.

ANT. *Freshen, flourish; persevere, hold, brace up, struggle, persist, battle, recruit, recover.*

Flagitious. Atrocious, heinous, flagrant, scandalous, villainous, corrupt, abandoned, profligate; enormous, monstrous, disgrace ful, nefarious, aggravated.

ANT. *Creditable, honorabl noble, meritorious, justifiabl distinguished, extenuated, ex cusable, pardonable.*

Flaring. Flaming, glaring, con spicuous, bright, gaudy, over colored, flaunting, flashy, os tentatious, showy, tawdry.

ANT. *Subdued, toned, har monized, dull, dim, dingy, neu tral, dowdy, colorless.*

Flat, *a.* Level, horizontal; even plane, smooth; low, prostrate laid low; dull, lifeless, spirit less, unanimated, frigid, tame prosaic, uninteresting; point less; vapid, tasteless, insipid stale, dead, jejune; peremptory absolute, positive; downright mawkish.

ANT. *Animated, exciting, in teresting, thrilling, sensationa emotional, melodramatic.*

Flaunt. Wave ostentatiously, in solently, brazenly, *or* boldly display, vaunt, flourish, toss disport, boast; flout, flounce flutter, parade, figure.

ANT. *Conceal, suppress, re tire, skulk, recede, hide, shrivel collapse, furl.*

Flavor. Taste, savor, relish zest, smack, gusto; aroma, es sence, subtle quality, spirit soul; odor.

ANT. *Insipidity, tasteless ness, inodorousness, mawkish ness, scentlessness, flatness.*

Flexible. Pliable, pliant, lim ber, lithe, supple, crooked; af fable, tractable, compliant, doc ile, gentle; elastic; easy, indul gent, ductile, flexile, yielding.

ANT. *Tough, rigid, inelastic hard, inflexible, inexorable.*

Flicker. Quiver, flutter, falter waver, glimmer, bicker, shim mer, scintillate.

ANT. *Stream, blaze, beam, shine, gleam.*

Flight. Flying, soaring, volitation, mounting, fleeing, departure; flock; volley, shower; escape, evasion, disappearance; stampede, begira, exodus.

ANT. *Recurrence, return, reappearance; repose, perching, alighting.*

Flimsy. Gauzy, poor, transparent, thin; trifling, trivial, inane, puerile; weak, shallow, superficial, slight, unsubstantial; feeble, frivolous, foolish, light, trashy.

ANT. *Solid, sound, irrefragable, cogent, substantial.*

Flinch. Wince, swerve, recoil, blench, shrink, draw back.

ANT. *Dare, face, bare, meet, endure, challenge, defy.*

Fling. Throw, cast, toss, hurl, dart, pitch, chuck; prostrate, overthrow, throw down; wince, flounce; jeer, sneer, gibe, scoff, flaunt, taunt; emit, ejaculate.

ANT. *Snatch, grasp, hold, keep, retain, arrest, catch.*

Flippant. Fluent, voluble, glib, talkative, nimble of speech; impertinent, pert, malapert, forward, bold; superficial, saucy, thoughtless.

ANT. *Servile, considerate, obsequious, flattering, deferential; accurate; complimentary, respectful.*

Float. Waft, swim, be buoyed up; bear up, buoy up; spread, prevail.

ANT. *Sink, drown, die, vanish, founder.*

Flock, *n.* Brood, bevy, herd, lot, group, pack, swarm, set, hatch, drove, covey, litter; collection, company, congregation.

Flock, *v.* Herd, congregate, assemble, throng, crowd, troop.

ANT. *Disperse, scatter, separate, segregate, distribute, rout.*

Flood, *n.* Deluge, abundance, inundation, overflow, freshet; downrush, multitude.

ANT. *Drought, drain, ebb, scarcity, subsidence.*

Florid. Flowery; flushed, rubicund; ornate, rhetorical, figurative, embellished; overwrought, sanguine, meretricious.

ANT. *Pallid, exsanguine; bloodless, anemic, unadorned, bare, sober, nude, chaste.*

Flounder. Struggle, toss, wallow, tumble, flounce; roll, blunder, bungle.

ANT. *Emerge, course, career, speed, rise, skim, flourish.*

Flourish. Thrive, grow; prosper, succeed, be successful; vapor, boast, brag, vaunt, bluster, show off; attain one's prime, be in vigor; brandish, wave; speed, triumph.

ANT. *Fail, decline, fade, arrest, founder, miscarry; sheath, ground.*

Flow. Stream, run, pour, roll on, sweep along; melt, liquefy, be molten; issue, emanate, proceed, come, grow, arise, follow, spring, result; glide, wave, undulate, float, waver, abound, be full, flood, deluge, overflow; career, progress, course.

ANT. *Halt, stick, stop, hesitate, fail, stickle, stint, beat, recoil, ebb, regurgitate; stagnate.*

Flower, *n.* Blossom, bloom; best part; prime, vigor; figure, expression; perfection, acme, ornament, pride, gem, cream.

ANT. *Deformity, disappointment, blot, abortion; blight; scum; dregs.*

Flowing. Running; fluent, copious, smooth; abundant, exuberant, easy, eloquent.

ANT. *Dry, dribbling, meager, strained, labored, difficult, unready, forced.*

Fluctuate. Veer, waver, swerve, vacillate, vary, undulate, oscillate, hesitate.

ANT. *Abide, adhere, persist, stand fast, stay, stick, hold fast.*

Fluctuation. Oscillation, undulation, unsteadiness, variation, change, shifting, rise and fall, inconstancy, hesitation, wavering, vacillation.

ANT. *Steadiness, firmness, steadfastness, constancy, stability, fixedness, stolidity; persistence, perseverance, pertinacity, obstinacy, tenacity.*

Fluency. Smoothness, flowing quality, liquidness; copiousness, affluence, command of language, readiness of speech.

ANT. *Solidity, density, compactness, hardness; difficulty, slowness; paucity.*

Flurry, *v.* Excite, agitate, disconcert, confuse, disturb, perturb, hurry, ruffle, worry, fluster.

ANT. *Soothe, compose, quiet, calm, mesmerize.*

Flutter. Hover, flap, flirt; palpitate, tremble; flaunt; fluctuate, waver, oscillate, vacillate, be inconstant, be unsteady; flit, quiver, flicker.

ANT. *Perch, roost, nestle, settle, subside, collapse, rest, repose, pause, sink, lull.*

Flux. Flow, flowing; mutation, change, shifting, transition; fusion, melting; solvent; motion, progression, substitution, transmutation.

ANT. *Stagnation, stillness, identity, invariableness, immutability, arrestation, crystallization.*

Focus. Center; standpoint; convergence, rendezvous, nucleus.

ANT. *Circle, dispersion, divergence, dissipation.*

Foggy. Misty, hazy; confused, dazed, bewildered, muddy, muddled; absent, stupid, obscure.

ANT. *Alert, alive, awake; lucid, clear, bright; shrewd, sharp.*

Foible. Frailty, weakness, failing, defect, imperfection, infirmity, fault, weak point; peccadillo.

ANT. *Crime, atrocity, sin, enormity.*

Foil, *n.* Contrast, background, set-off; rapier; enhancement, setting; elucidation.

ANT. *Eclipse, outshining, extinction, overshadowing.*

Foist. Impose, thrust; falsify, counterfeit, palm, pass.

ANT. *Expose, detect, verify, authenticate.*

Fold, *v.* Double, enfold, enwrap, envelop, wrap, embrace, enclose.

ANT. *Unfold, expose, disengage.*

Follow. Attend, accompany, result, pursue, succeed, chase, go after, come after, copy, ensue, heed, imitate, observe, obey, practice; shadow.

ANT. *Avoid, elude, precede, quit, disobey, cause, produce, shun, abandon.*

Follower. Pursuer; attendant, retainer, supporter, dependant, companion, associate; adherent, disciple, pupil, partisan; imitator, copier.

ANT. *Leader, teacher, rival, antagonist, opponent.*

Folly. Foolishness, imbecility, fatuity, stupidity, shallowness, dulness; absurdity, extravagance, infatuation, unwisdom, imprudence, nonsense, indiscretion; slip, lapse, misstep; madness, misconduct, silliness, weakness.

ANT. *Wisdom, sanity, sense, prudence, judgment, sobriety.*

Foment. Bathe; excite, instigate, stimulate, brew, encourage, promote, abet, stir up; fan, cherish, propagate.

ANT. *Allay, extinguish, extirpate, quench, discourage.*

Fond. Foolish, silly, weak, absurd, empty, vain, senseless, baseless; doting, affectionate, loving, attached, enamored, devoted.

ANT. *Averse, unloving, unaffectionate, strong-minded, rational, austere, sensible, well-grounded, undemonstrative.*

Fondle. Caress, coddle, blandish, pet; dandle; spoil, indulge.

ANT. *Worry, annoy, tease, chafe, irritate, ruffle.*

Fondness. Delusion, folly, silliness, weakness, absurdity; tenderness, doting; liking, preference, partiality, predilection, affection; relish, appetite.

ANT. *Repulsion, aversion, dislike, antipathy; hatred, contempt; harshness, brutality, loathing.*

Food. Aliment, nourishment, nutriment, nutrition, viands, sustenance, victuals, provender, regimen, pabulum, fodder, diet, forage, feed, fare; bread, meat, provisions, cheer, commons, rations, subsistence.

Fool. Idiot, natural; dolt, witling, driveler, blockhead, simpleton, dunce; buffoon, harlequin, droll, punch, antic, jester, clown.

ANT. *Wise man, adept, expert, scholar, master.*

Foolish. Senseless, idiotic, silly, weak, daft, simple, irrational, insensate, shallow, brainless, witless; unwise, unreasonable, absurd, ridiculous, preposterous, indiscreet, imprudent; puerile, idle, trivial, trifling, contemptible, vain, childish; injudicious, objectionable, imbecile, nonsensical; crazed.

ANT. *Sensible, sane, clear-sighted, deep, strong-minded, sound, sagacious, wise, prudent, judicious, eligible, calculating, advisable.*

Footing. Foothold; foundation, basis, groundwork; standing, rank, grade, status, state, condition; settlement, establishment; sum total.

ANT. *Dislodgment, ousting, unstableness.*

Foppish. Dandyish, vain, coxcombical, dressy, dandified.

ANT. *Unassuming, modest, dowdy, unaffected, clownish, slovenly.*

Foray. Inroad, irruption, raid, invasion, incursion; sally, escapade, dragonade.

ANT. *Flight, retreat, recall, stampede, decampment.*

Forbear. Abstain, avoid, withhold, refrain, forego; stop, desist, pause, cease, stay, hold, break off, give over; be tolerant, endure, be patient; shun, decline; omit; spare, tolerate, put up with.

ANT. *Seek, indulge, gratify, yield, grant, bestow; continue, advance, progress; rebel, resist.*

Forbidding. Repulsive, repellent, unpleasant, odious, abhorrent, disagreeable, offensive; deterrent, prohibitory.

ANT. *Attractive, seductive, permissive, alluring, encouraging.*

Force, *n.* Strength, power, energy, might, vigor; efficacy, efficiency, potency, validity, virtue, cogency, agency; compulsion, violence, constraint, coercion, enforcement; army, troop, legion, battalion, host, squadron, phalanx; instrumentality, dint, vehemence, pressure.

ANT. *Weakness, feebleness, inefficiency, counteraction, neutralization, debility, inconclusiveness, pointlessness.*

Fore, *a.* Anterior, preceding, antecedent, prior, previous, former, foregoing; front, face; advanced, leading, head, foremost, first.

ANT. *Posterior, subsequent, following; rear, back, hindmost, last.*

Forefather. Progenitor, ancestor, father.

ANT. *Descendants, progeny.*

Forefend. Avert, prevent, ward off, hinder, keep off, forbid; stave, obviate.

ANT. *Remedy, rectify, cure, mend, redress.*

Forego. Relinquish, resign, renounce, surrender, cede, yield, abandon, give up, part with, let go; waive, drop, abjure.

ANT. *Claim, assume, seize, grasp, retain, vindicate.*

Foreign. Alien, external, exterior, outward, strange, exotic, from abroad; extraneous, extrinsic, adventitious, irrelevant; outlandish.

ANT. *Domestic, congenial, native, relative, germane.*

Forerunner. Precursor, herald, harbinger, foregoer, avant-courier; prelude; prognostic, sign, omen, premonition; predecessor.

ANT. *Successor, follower; postlude; fulfilment.*

Foresee. Foreknow, forecast, have prescience of; predict, anticipate, foretell, forebode, divine.

ANT. *Remember, recollect, recall, reflect.*

Foretell. Prognosticate, foreshow, foreshadow, betoken, portend, augur, bode, forebode, presage; predict, prophesy; preindicate, forewarn.

ANT. *Recite, narrate, detail, recollect, remember.*

Forethought. Foresight, anticipation, precaution, forecast, provision, prudence.

ANT. *Delay, procrastination.*

Forever. Always, perpetually, eternally, everlastingly, ever, endlessly, evermore, aye.

ANT. *Never, at no time.*

Forfeit, Forfeiture. Loss, fine, mulct, amercement, confiscation, penalty; damages.

ANT. *Bribe, premium, douceur, compensation, gratuity, reward, remuneration.*

Forge. Beat, hammer out, fabricate, frame, form; devise, invent, coin; falsify, counterfeit; work, produce, elaborate, feign, make falsely, shape.

ANT. *Shatter, batter, shiver, blast, fuse, detect, expose; misconstrue, misshape, misfabricate; verify.*

Forgery. Counterfeit; falsification, fraudulent imitation.

ANT. *Attestation, verification, signature; genuineness.*

Forget. Consign to oblivion, overlook; slight, neglect, cease to care for; unlearn, pretermit, obliterate.

ANT. *Acquire, learn, recollect, remember, retain, treasure, mind.*

Forgetful. Apt to forget; negligent, inattentive, careless, heedless, neglectful, mindless.

ANT. *Attentive, retentive, careful, mindful.*

Forgetfulness. Aptness to forget; failure of memory; negligence, inattention, carelessness, heedlessness; oblivion.

ANT. *Retentiveness, recollection, recalling.*

Forgotten. Unremembered, bygone, slighted, overlooked, obsolete, neglected, disregarded.

ANT. *Remembered, present, treasured, cherished, guarded, regarded.*

Forlorn. Deserted, forsaken, solitary, abandoned, lost, friendless; wretched, miserable, pitiable, destitute, desolate; helpless, comfortless, disconsolate, wobegone; hapless, luckless; lone, lonesome.

ANT. *Supported, cherished, attended, protected, befriended, cheered.*

Form, *n.* Shape, figure, configuration, mold, fashion, cast, cut; mode, method, formula, formulary, ritual; manner, system, sort, kind, order; regularity, arrangement; shapeliness, ceremony, formality, ceremonial; conventionality, etiquette; pattern, model; mere appearance, empty show.

Form, *v.* Shape, mold, fashion, constitute, arrange, frame, construct, contrive, conceive, make, produce, create, devise, invent, compose, dispose, combine.

ANT. *Deform, dislocate, distort, derange, disintegrate, dismember, dissipate, disorganize, analyze.*

Formal. Express, explicit, positive, strict, official; regular, set, methodical, fixed, rigid, stiff; ceremonious, precise, punctilious, starched, prim, exact; essential, constitutive; external; complete, shapely, sufficient, affected, correct, stately, dignified, pompous.

ANT. *Incomplete, irregular, informal, incorrect, inadequate, easy, unassuming, unceremonious.*

Formalism. Rigidity, parade, ceremoniousness, pomposity, externalism, punctilio.

ANT. *Simplicity, unaffectedness, unostentatiousness, unceremoniousness.*

Formality. Custom, established mode; ceremony, etiquette, conventionality, mere form; parade, affectation, punctiliousness, stateliness.

ANT. *Informality; unceremoniousness, unconventionality; originality.*

Formation. Creation, production; composition, constitution; arrangement, disposal, combination, disposition; construction, shape, structure.

Former. Anterior, antecedent, previous, prior, preceding, foregoing; quondam, late, old-time; past, bygone, foregone, previous; first-named, first-mentioned; earlier, ancient.

ANT. *Subsequent, succeeding, posterior, latter, modern, coming, future.*

Formidable. Terrible, redoubted, tremendous, dangerous; awful, alarming, terrifying, discouraging, appalling, serious, horrible, dreadful, fearful, shocking.

ANT. *Light, trivial; feeble, harmless, contemptible, powerless, despicable, weak, helpless.*

Forthwith. Instantly, directly, immediately, without delay, instantaneously.

ANT. *Hereafter, soon, by-and-by, presently.*

Fortification. Fort, stronghold, fortress, fastness, castle, citadel; bulwark, fortified place.

Fortify. Protect, surround; reinforce, brace, stiffen, strengthen; confirm, corroborate; garrison, intrench.

ANT. *Weaken, dismantle; invalidate.*

Fortitude. Endurance, heroism, resolution, courage; firmness, patience; bravery; calmness, resignation, hardihood, composure, stoicism.

ANT. *Impatience, timidity, flinching, irritation, faintness, delicacy, effeminacy, womanishness, childishness.*

Fortuitous. Accidental, casual, contingent, chance, incidental, undesigned.

ANT. *Purposed, planned, designed; anticipated, foreseen.*

Fortunate. Favored, lucky, successful, prosperous, happy, felicitous, propitious, auspicious, favorable, advantageous, providential.

ANT. *Miserable, unhappy, unlucky, ill-starred, unfortunate, wretched, woful, fallen, infelicitous, broke, crushed.*

Fortune. Chance, accident, luck, hap, casualty, fortuity; livelihood; estate, substance, property, possessions; wealth, affluence, riches, opulence; destiny, fate, destination, doom, star, lot; issue, result, event; success.

ANT. *Design, purpose; misfortune, ill luck, poverty; inception, cause, failure.*

Forward, *a.* Onward, progressive, advancing; front, fore, anterior; ready, prompt, eager, willing, zealous, earnest; presumptuous, confident, bold, impertinent, pert, assuming, flippant; early, premature; obtrusive, anxious, self-assertive.

ANT. *Tardy, reluctant, retiring, backward, slow, modest, indifferent.*

Forward, *v.* Support, foster, advance, promote, further, encourage, aid, favor, help; hasten, accelerate, quicken, speed, hurry, despatch, expedite; transmit, send on, ship.

ANT. *Retard, delay, prevent, hinder, frustrate.*

Foul. Impure, nasty, dirty, unclean, squalid, filthy, tarnished, soiled, stained, polluted, sullied; disgusting, loathsome, offensive, noisome; dishonorable, unfair, sinister, underhanded; base, scandalous, infamous, vile, wicked, dark, abominable, detestable, disgraceful, shameful; vulgar, coarse, low; abusive, insulting, scurrilous; thick, turbid, muddy; stormy, cloudy, rainy; entangled, tangled.

ANT. *Pure, uncorrupt, unstained, undefiled, uncontaminated, unsullied, stainless, fair, unspotted, spotless, unpolluted, holy.*

Found, *v.* Base, set, fix, place, ground, rest; build, construct, raise, erect; establish, institute, originate, plant, set up; cast, mold; endow, root.

ANT. *Uproot, subvert, supplant, disestablish.*

Foundation. Base, groundwork, basis, bottom, footing; establishment, settlement; endowment; institution, origin, rudiments, ground, substratum, underlying principle.

ANT. *Disestablishment; superstructure; demolition, ruin, overthrow.*

Founder. Originator, institutor, establisher, planter; molder, caster; author.

ANT. *Subverter, destroyer.*

Fountain. Spring, well, jet; source, origin, original cause, first principle.

Fraction. Part, portion, fragment, piece, bit, scrap, section.

ANT. *Whole, total, amount, sum, aggregate.*

Fractious. Cross, captious, petulant, testy, peevish, fretful, irritable, waspish, snappish; pettish.
Ant. *Good-humored, blithesome, agreeable, complaisant, genial.*

Fragile. Brittle, easily broken, frangible; infirm, frail, weak, feeble, delicate, slight.
Ant. *Tough, hardy, stout, strong.*

Fragment. Remnant, fraction, scrap, chip, detached part, bit, piece, morsel.
Ant. *Bulk, body, whole, mass.*

Fragrance, Fragrancy. Redolence, perfume, aroma, balminess, incense, grateful odor *or* smell, pleasant scent.

Fragrant. Aromatic, redolent, spicy, balmy, odoriferous, perfumed, sweet-scented, odorous, sweet-smelling.
Ant. *Inodorous, scentless, fetid.*

Frail. Fragile, brittle, frangible; weak, feeble, infirm; irresolute, erring, mutable.
Ant. *Resolute, lasting, virtuous; tough, hardy, strong, stout.*

Frame, *n.* Framework, skeleton, carcass, framing; form, structure, system, fabric, constitution, scheme; condition, state, temper, mood.

Frame, *v.* Construct, build, put together; form, compose, make, constitute; invent, devise, plan, contrive; fabricate, forge.

Franchise. Right, privilege; exemption, immunity; freedom.
Ant. *Obligation, disability, disqualification, liability, jurisdiction.*

Frank. Open, ingenuous, free, sincere, candid, artless, frank-hearted, without disguise, unreserved; familiar, honest, outspoken, easy, plain.
Ant. *Close, reserved; disingenuous.*

Frantic. Furious, raving, raging, mad, wild, infuriate, frenzied, distracted; maniacal.
Ant. *Sane, sober, calm, collected, cool, unruffled, composed.*

Fraternity. Association, circle, society, company, brotherhood, sodality, league, clan; brotherliness.

Fraternize. Harmonize, sympathize, consort, concur; associate with, coöperate with; coalesce.
Ant. *Renounce, abjure, forswear; ostracize.*

Fraud. Duplicity, deceit, deception, dishonesty, treason, artifice, trick, cheat, imposture, swindle, treachery, imposition.
Ant. *Good faith, honesty, truth, uprightness, fairness, integrity.*

Fraught. Filled, stored, laden, freighted, charged, abounding, pregnant, big; loaded, teeming.
Ant. *Devoid, divested, exempt, empty, wanting, poor, scant.*

Freakish. Whimsical, erratic, capricious, odd, fanciful, humorsome; sportful, frisky, joking, mirthful.
Ant. *Sober, steady, demure, unwhimsical, unfanciful, reliable, consistent, equable, uniform.*

Free, *a.* Independent, at liberty, unrestrained; released, emancipated, delivered, liberated; exempt, clear, allowed, permitted, open; unobstructed, unimpeded, unrestricted; frank, ingenuous, candid, artless, unreserved, sincere, frank-hearted; generous, liberal, bountiful, hospitable, charitable, munificent, openhanded; prodigal, lavish, immoderate; ready, eager, willing, prompt; gratuitous, spontaneous; loose, lax; familiar, unconstrained, easy, informal; detached, playing, operating, unoccupied, unhindered, unconditional, untrammeled, careless, unconfined, bounteous.

ANT. *Bound, shackled, subservient, restricted, obstructed, clogged; occupied; impeded, unlawful, compulsory, biased, subject, liable, amenable; conditional, qualified; stingy, niggardly.*

Freedom. Independence, liberty; scope, range, play, free swing; franchise, immunity, privilege; license, laxity, looseness, familiarity.

ANT. *Slavery, serfdom, servitude; imprisonment, captivity.*

Frenzy. Madness, rage, fury, insanity, raving, distraction, lunacy, derangement, mania, delirium, aberration of mind; fanaticism, fire.

ANT. *Calm, composure, collectedness, coolness, sanity, sobriety, equanimity.*

Frequent, *a.* Oft-repeated; common, usual, everyday; many, repeated, recurrent, general, numerous, continual.

ANT. *Few, solitary, scanty, rare, casual.*

Fresh. New, recent, novel; renewed, revived; blooming, flourishing, unfaded, unwilted, unwithered, well-preserved; unimpaired, undecayed; rosy, ruddy, fair, delicate, fresh-colored; well, hearty, florid, vigorous, healthy, hardy, strong; unworn, unwearied, unexhausted, unfatigued; vivid, lively, keen, unabated; unsalted; pure, cool, refreshing, sweet, health-giving, bracing; brisk, stiff, strong; raw, uncultivated, unpracticed, untrained, unskilled, inexperienced; young, untried, modern.

ANT. *Old, stale, weary, jaded; former; stagnant, impaired; original, ordinary, tarnished, faded, decayed, pallid, sickly, putrid, moldy, musty, fusty.*

Fretful. Touchy, peevish, petulant, testy, snappish, waspish, splenetic, spleeny, captious, irritable, ill-humored, ill-tempered; fractious, impatient, discontented.

ANT. *Patient, contented, forbearing, meek, resigned, unmurmuring.*

Friction. Attrition, abrasion, resistance, confrication, rubbing; grating, contact.

ANT. *Lubrication, non-contact, detachment, isolation.*

Friend. Confidant, intimate, associate, companion; ally, confrère, fellow-adherent; favorer, encourager, well-wisher, advocate, patron, adherent, defender, supporter; acquaintance, familiar, chum, messmate, coadjutor.

ANT. *Opponent, foe, adversary, antagonist, enemy.*

Friendly. Companionable, genial, neighborly, cordial, affectionate, brotherly, fond, favorable, kind, kindly, loving, well-disposed, social, tender, affable, accessible, sociable, amicable, complaisant, hearty, sincere.

ANT. *Adverse, estranged, ill-disposed, unfriendly, antagonistic, unkind, inimical, alienated, distant, disaffected, frigid, hostile, cold, indifferent, contentious, belligerent, bellicose.*

Friendship. Affection, good will, devotion, attachment, amity, comity, consideration, favor, friendliness, love, regard, esteem, admiration.

ANT. *Hostility, hatred, enmity, feud; contempt, disdain; antipathy.*

Frighten. Alarm, affright, intimidate, scare, terrify, daunt, appall, browbeat, depress, dismay.

ANT. *Calm, soothe, comfort, ease; reassure, encourage.*

Frightful. Terrible, fearful, terrific, dire, dread, dreadful, horrid, horrible, awful, shocking, hideous, ghastly, grim, grisly, gruesome, alarming; ugly, monstrous.

ANT. *Pleasing, fair, attractive, encouraging, lovely, beautiful.*

Frigid. Cold, dull, cool, uninteresting, lifeless, unanimated, tame, spiritless; formal, prim, stiff, forbidding, chilling, rigid, freezing, repulsive, repellent; inanimate, passionless, distant.

ANT. *Warm, ardent, impassioned; vehement, zealous.*

Frisk. Leap, skip, hop, frolic, jump, romp, gambol, wanton, dance, sport, play.

ANT. *Lie, ruminate, roost, mope, sulk, rest, repose.*

Frisky. Gay, lively, sportive, playful, coltish, wanton, frolicsome.

ANT. *Demure, sedate, pensive, meditative.*

Fritter. Slice, break, shiver, shatter; dribble, waste, dissipate, idle.

ANT. *Husband, economize, cultivate, provide, be frugal.*

Frivolous. Trivial, worthless, light, trifling, silly, petty, idle, flimsy, childish, puerile, foolish, trashy.

ANT. *Serious, earnest, important, grave.*

Frolic, *n.* Gambol, lark, escapade, prank; fun, pleasantry, drollery; merriment, merry-making; play, game, festivity, sport, entertainment, gaiety, spree.

ANT. *Study, engagement, occupation, purpose, undertaking.*

Frolicsome. Gay, lively, frisky, sportive, playful, frolic, merry, joyous; wanton, festive.

ANT. *Grave, serious, laborious, earnest, studious.*

Froward. Contrary, fractious, perverse, contumacious, refractory, untoward, unyielding, ungovernable, wayward, disobedient, peevish, cross, captious, petulant.

ANT. *Docile, amenable, favorable, agreeable, obedient, ductile.*

Frugal. Provident, economical, careful, choice, saving, chary, thrifty, unwasteful, sparing; parsimonious, abstinent, abstemious, temperate.

ANT. *Profuse, lavish, luxurious, extravagant, prodigal, intemperate, self-indulgent.*

Frugality. Parsimony, thrift, providence, prudence, economy, sparing, miserliness, parsimoniousness, scrimping.

ANT. *Liberality, luxury, opulence, waste, wealth, extravagance, bounty, affluence, abundance, riches.*

Fruit. Harvest, crop, product; production, result, effect, consequence, outcome; offspring, issue, young; produce, reward, outgrowth.

ANT. *Seed, cause, origin, operation, growth.*

Fruitful. Productive; prolific, fertile, fecund; abundant, rich, plentiful, plenteous; pregnant, fraught, causative, successful, effectual, useful.

ANT. *Unproductive, sterile, barren, fruitless, useless, abortive, ineffectual.*

Fruition. Fulfilment, enjoyment; reaping, attainment, use, possession.

ANT. *Loss, disappointment, non-attainment.*

Fugacious. Transitory, transient, evanescent, fugitive, ephemeral, fleeting.

ANT. *Persistent, perennial, permanent, perpetual.*

Fulfil. Accomplish, effectuate, effect, realize, execute, consummate, complete, perfect; obey, observe, perform, do, discharge, keep, adhere to, comply with; meet, satisfy, answer, fill, fill out; verify, achieve.

ANT. *Neglect, ignore; falsify, disappoint; render abortive; overlook, disregard, slight.*

Fulminate. Explode, detonate; utter denunciations, thunder, fulmine, hurl threats; clamor, roar, denounce, vociferate.

ANT. *Laud, panegyrize, eulogize.*

Fulsome. Gross, excessive, offensive, extravagant, nauseous, disgusting, repulsive, coarse, ribald, questionable, loathsome, sickening, fawning.

ANT. *Chaste, sober, delicate, nice, temperate, moderate.*

Fume, *v.* Smoke, reek, emit vapor, exhale; rave, rage, chafe, storm, bluster, fret, flare up, be in a rage.

ANT. *Acquiesce; smile; submit, accede, consent, concur.*

Function, *n.* Exercise, performance, execution, discharge; employment, office, duty, business, occupation, part, province; character, capacity, operation, administration, power.

ANT. *Usurpation, misdemeanor, misconduct, maladministration.*

Functionary. Office-holder, official, officer, servant, personage incumbent.

Fund. Stock, capital; supply, store; foundation, permanent fund; money, means, resources; investment.

ANT. *Expenditure, outlay, disbursement.*

Fundamental. Essential, radical, primary, organic, constitutional, indispensable, principal, important.

ANT. *Secondary, unimportant, non-essential, ascititious, adventitious.*

Funereal. Mournful, sad, lugubrious, woful, dark, plaintive, somber, melancholy, funeral, gloomy, dismal, sepulchral, solemn, deathlike.

ANT. *Joyous, festive, funny, stirring, lively, ridiculous, farcical.*

Funny. Ludicrous, droll, comical, farcical, sportive, humorous, amusing, laughable, diverting, jocose, ridiculous.

ANT. *Tedious, dull, mournful, lugubrious, grave, serious, dismal, sad, lamentable.*

Furbish. Burnish, polish, rub, scour, brighten.

ANT. *Dull, tarnish, cloud.*

Furnish. Provide, supply; fit, equip, fit up; afford, give, bestow, contribute, present, purvey, yield.

ANT. *Withhold, withdraw; dismantle; retain, keep.*

Furtive. Secret, sly, clandestine, stolen, stealthy, surreptitious, secretive.

ANT. *Open, public, undisguised, unconcealed, unreserved.*

Fuse. Melt, liquefy, smelt; intermix, amalgamate, blend, commingle, intermingle; coalesce.

ANT. *Disunite, diffuse, disamalgamate, disincorporate.*

Fuss, *n.* Hurry, worry, ado, fidget, bustle, flurry, stir, agitation, excitement, tumult.
  ANT. *Quiet, peace, sedateness, calm, composure, tranquillity.*

Futile. Trifling, frivolous, trivial; worthless, valueless, vain, idle, unprofitable, profitless, unavailing, fruitless, bootless, ineffectual; weak, ineffective, useless, nugatory.
  ANT. *Cogent, effective, potent, powerful, useful, substantial, solid.*

Future. Forthcoming, coming, advenient.
  ANT. *Past, gone, bygone.*

G

Gabble, *n.* Prate, jargon, stuff, jabber, rattle, twaddle, chatter, gibber, gibberish, babble, gab, gossip, palaver, prattle, cackle.
  ANT. *Speech, conversation, eloquence; reticence, taciturnity; mincing, mouthiness, euphuism, grandiloquence.*

Gabble, *v.* Prate, prattle, chatter, cackle, rattle, jabber, gossip, palaver.
  ANT. *Drone, drawl, murmur.*

Gag. Silence, stifle, muzzle, muffle, hush.
  ANT. *Evoke, provoke, inspire, animate.*

Gage, *n.* Measure, standard; dimensions, estimate; security; challenge, defiance.

Gage, *v.* Measure, estimate, fathom, probe.
  ANT. *Survey, conjecture, observe, view, scan, guess, mismeasure.*

Gain, *n.* Profits, earnings, increase, gainings; emolument, lucre, money-making; blessing, profit, advantage, good, benefit.
  ANT. *Loss, detriment, damage, privation, injury.*

Gain, *v.* Get, acquire, win, earn, obtain, procure, secure, carry, achieve; conciliate, enlist, persuade, prevail upon, win over, gain over, bring over; reach, attain, arrive at; profit; benefit, realize, reap.
  ANT. *Lose, forfeit, suffer.*

Gainful. Advantageous, profitable, beneficial; lucrative, paying, productive, remunerative, winning.
  ANT. *Unprofitable, disadvantageous, detrimental, injurious, losing, gainless.*

Gallant, *a.* Gay, fine, magnificent, well-dressed, showy, splendid; courageous, brave, valiant, valorous, intrepid, chivalrous, fearless, bold, daring, high-spirited; noble, lofty, honorable, magnanimous, high-minded; attentive, polite, courteous; amorous; heroic.
  ANT. *Cowardly, discourteous, churlish.*

Gambol. Frisk, frolic, romp, caper, leap, hop, skip, jump, sport.
  ANT. *Droop, tire, weary, flag.*

Game, *n.* Sport, play, amusement, pastime; plan, scheme, stratagem, strategy, adventure, enterprise, measure, undertaking; quarry, prey; recreation, frolic, diversion.
  ANT. *Toil, study, duty, labor; weariness, flagging; business.*

Garb. Dress, clothes, habit, ap-

parel, raiment, garments, vesture, costume, attire, habiliment; uniform, vestments.
ANT. *Undress; rags, tatters, shreds; nudity, nakedness.*

Garble. Mutilate, falsify, corrupt, misrepresent, misquote, pervert; cook, dress, color, distort.
ANT. *Quote, cite, extract, recite, report verbatim.*

Garnish. Adorn, embellish, decorate, deck, grace, beautify, ornament, prank, set off, trick out; furnish, furbish.
ANT. *Strip, dismantle, denude, bare, deprive, divest.*

Garrulity. Loquacity, babble, loquaciousness, babbling, talkativeness, prattle, prate; verbosity, chatter.
ANT. *Reticence, taciturnity, laconism, reserve, silence.*

Garrulous. Chattering, loquacious, verbose, talkative.
ANT. *Taciturn, speechless, laconic, reserved, reticent, silent.*

Gaud. Trinket, finery, gewgaw, trumpery, whim, gimcrack, toy, bauble, trifle.
ANT. *Ornament, gem, decoration, jewel, valuable.*

Gaudy. Flaunting, garish, glittering, tawdry, tinsel, flashy, showy, overdecorated, loud; bespangled, fine, gay, meretricious.
ANT. *Rich, simple, handsome, chaste.*

Gaunt. Lean, lank, thin, meager, emaciated, slender, attenuated, spare; grim, savage, hungry.
ANT. *Docile, tractable, well-fed, tame, sleek.*

Gawky. Awkward, clownish, ungainly, clumsy, raw, boorish, rustic, green, uncouth, loutish.
ANT. *Neat, handy, graceful, handsome.*

Gay. Showy, bright, fine, brilliant, dashing; gaudy, flaunting, flashy, garish, tawdry, glittering, tinsel; merry, lively, jovial, cheerful, gleeful, blithe, sportive, airy, gladsome, frolicsome, jolly, hilarious, lighthearted; sprightly, smart, festive, pleasuresome.
ANT. *Heavy, sad, grave, dull, dowdy, somber, melancholy.*

Gaze, *v.* Stare, scan, behold, regard, contemplate, view, gloat, glower.
ANT. *Wink, ignore, overlook, ogle, glance, disregard.*

General, *a.* Ordinary, universal, common, commonplace, customary, everyday, public, prevalent, familiar, normal, popular, habitual, frequent, usual.
ANT. *Singular, uncommon, exceptional, rare, unknown, infrequent, unusual; particular, special.*

Generality. Universality; bulk, mass, body, majority.
ANT. *Section, minority, exception, individuality.*

Generate. Beget, procreate, engender, breed, propagate; produce, form, make, cause, bring about, originate.
ANT. *Stifle, extinguish, terminate, annihilate.*

Generation. Procreation; production, formation; offspring, progeny, succession of descendants; family, stock, race, breed; contemporaries; period, epoch, age, era, lifetime; origination.
ANT. *Perpetuity, eternity, immortality; posterity.*

Generic. General, common, collective, racial, comprehensive.
ANT. *Particular, personal, specific, individual.*

Generous. Liberal, noble, magnanimous, bountiful, free, munificent, open-handed, disinterested, open-hearted, chivalrous, honorable.

ANT. *Avaricious, covetous, greedy, parsimonious, penurious, petty, rapacious, stingy, close, illiberal, ignoble, mean, miserly, niggardly, churlish, selfish.*

Genial. Fostering, cheering, enlivening, encouraging, inspiriting; cordial, hearty; cheerful, pleasant, merry, mirthful, jovial, warm, balmy, festive, joyous, revivifying, rejuvenating, restorative.

ANT. *Cold, cutting, harsh, deleterious, noxious, deadly, destructive, blighting, lethal, ungenial.*

Genius. Bent, turn, aptitude, aptness, faculty, capacity, endowment, talent, gift; ingenuity, invention, sagacity, intellect, brains, parts, wit, inspiration, creative *or* inventive power; adept, proficient, master, master hand; nature, character, disposition, constitution, characteristic; spirit, tutelary deity, guardian angel; cleverness, inventiveness, skill, creativeness, giftedness, ideality, talents.

ANT. *Stupidity, senselessness, folly, dulness, imbecility, obtuseness, stolidity, inanity.*

Genteel. Refined, polite, courteous, civil, polished, well-bred, gentlemanly *or* ladylike; fashionable, stylish, elegant; graceful, refined, aristocratic, cultivated, cultured.

ANT. *Rude, clownish, uncultivated, ill-bred, boorish, uncultured, plebeian, unfashionable, unpolished, inelegant.*

Gentle. Mild, bland, moderate, kind, tender, compassionate, indulgent, meek, soft, lenient, humane, clement, merciful, tenderhearted, gentle-hearted; tame, docile, peaceable, calm, peaceful, tranquil, tractable, pacific, quiet; light, zephyrlike; noble, high-born, well-born; cultivated, refined, courteous, wellbred, polished; placid, amiable.

ANT. *Rough, rude, coarse, fierce, savage; uneven, uncut; boisterous; shaggy, ragged, disordered; harsh, uncivil, offensive; tempestuous, stormy; inclement.*

Genuine. Pure, uncorrupt, unalloyed, unadulterated, true, authentic, real, veritable; native, unaffected, sincere; sound, natural.

ANT. *Spurious, adulterated; fictitious; apocryphal, counterfeit, false, artificial.*

Germ. Embryo, ovule, seed-bud; origin, source, first principle; nucleus, seed, bud.

ANT. *Fruit, result, development, product, produce, issue, outgrowth.*

Germane. Related, akin, cognate, allied; pertinent, relevant, appropriate, apposite, fitting, suitable; kindred, homogeneous.

ANT. *Foreign, alien, irrelevant, unconnected.*

Germinate. Bud, shoot, vegetate, sprout, push, burst forth, put forth, spring up.

ANT. *Rot, decay, spoil, die, putrefy, corrupt.*

Get. Attain, earn, achieve, acquire, obtain, procure, receive, win, secure, gain.

ANT. *Abandon, lose, forfeit, surrender, forego.*

Ghastly. Pale, wan, cadaverous, deathlike; grim, dismal, hideous, terrible, horrible, frightful, shocking, grisly; spectral, pallid.

ANT. *Blooming, fresh, ruddy, comely, buxom, seemly.*

Ghost. Spirit, soul; apparition, specter, sprite, phantom, shade, departed spirit; vision.

ANT. *Body, organism, animal.*

Gibe. Sneer, scoff, taunt, flount, jest, jeer, ridicule, deride, mock, rail at.

ANT. *Salute, compliment.*

Giddy. Dizzy, vertiginous; inconstant, fickle, changeable, unsteady, mutable, unstable, vacillating, irresolute; careless, heedless, wild, reckless, headlong, thoughtless, light-headed, flighty; whirling, hare-brained, beetling, flighty.

ANT. *Slow, ponderous, stationary; earnest, thoughtful, steady; low, wary, unelevated, circumspect.*

Gift. Bequest, benefaction, donation, boon, grant, present, largess, bribe, bounty, gratuity; endowment, talent, genius, faculty, power, capacity, capability, ability, turn, *forte;* donation, *douceur,* offering, alms, allowance, contribution, subscription, subsidy, dower, legacy, demise.

ANT. *Reservation, refusal, purchase; inanity, stupidity, forfeit, penalty, fine, surrender; earnings, wages, remuneration, compensation; reward, guerdon.*

Gigantic. Vast, huge, colossal, enormous, giant, prodigious, Herculean, Cyclopean, immense, tremendous.

ANT. *Puny, feeble, dwarfish, petty, insignificant, pigmy.*

Girdle. Gird, bind round; surround, encircle, encompass, enclose, embrace, shut in; belt, hem, environ, engirdle, begird.

ANT. *Disclose, open, disencircle, expand, ungird, disengirdle.*

Girl. Damsel, lass, lassie, miss maiden, maid, virgin, young unmarried woman.

Gist. Essence, pith, core, marrow substance, kernel, main point force, ground, foundation.

ANT. *Surplusage, additament, redundancy, environment; accessories; clothing garb; excess, overplus.*

Give. Deliver, bestow, supply, grant, cede, confer, communicate, impart, furnish; produce, yield, surrender, concede, present, afford, spare, accommodate with; pay, exchange; permit, allow, vouchsafe, deign; utter, pronounce, render; occasion, cause; devote, apply, addict, give up; sink, bend; retreat, give way, recede, retire.

ANT. *Withhold, withdraw, refuse, retain, grasp, fail, restrain, deny, take back, remove, recall; take, receive, accept; hold, support.*

Glad. Rejoiced, pleased, gratified, delighted, happy, well-contented; cheerful, joyous, joyful, gladsome, elated, jocund, playful, light-hearted, cheery, animated; exhilarating, pleasing, bright, gratifying; blithesome, gleeful.

ANT. *Unhappy, sad, sorrowful, disastrous, sorry, dismal, disappointed, discontented, uneasy.*

Gladden. Delight, cheer, exhilarate, bless, rejoice, gratify, make glad.

ANT. *Grieve, disappoint, depress, dispirit, trouble, wound, afflict, sadden, displease.*

Glare. Glitter, glisten, dazzle, flare, gleam, sparkle; glower, look fierce; beam, shine, glow, ray, radiate.

ANT. *Shimmer, scintillate, waver, glimmer, smolder, burn fitfully, flash, flicker, glister; obscure, darken.*

Glassy. Vitreous; crystal, crystalline, transparent, gleaming, lucent, brilliant, shining; smooth, polished, glacial, glabrous, brittle, pellucid, limpid, glossy, silken.

ANT. *Rough, uneven, pliant, rugged, tough, opaque, turbid, muddy, dull, dark.*

Glaze, *v.* Set glass; calender, polish, burnish, gloss, furbish; become glassy, grow dim; vitrefy.

ANT. *Roughen, corrugate, rumple, crumple, wrinkle, furrow.*

Glimpse, *n.* Glance, glimmering, sight, inkling, flash, survey, trace, tinge.

ANT. *Observation, scrutiny, investigation, inspection, exposure, analysis, examination.*

Gloom. Obscurity, darkness, dimness, gloominess, cloud; dejection, sadness, depression, despondency, melancholy; gloaming, twilight, shadow, obscuration, dulness, cloudiness.

ANT. *Light, radiance, clearness, daylight, brightness.*

Glorify. Extol, exalt, magnify, bless, honor, praise; brighten, make illustrious, elevate, ennoble, adorn; laud, signalize, aggrandize, panegyrize.

ANT. *Debase, depress, abuse, abase, defame, degrade, decry, censure, blame, rebuke.*

Glorious. Illustrious, renowned, celebrated, eminent, famed, famous, distinguished, conspicuous; resplendent, splendid, radiant, bright, brilliant; noble, lofty, exalted, supreme, high, excellent, consummate.

ANT. *Mean, debased, undistinguished, disgraced, unknown, dishonorable, inglorious.*

Glory. Honor, renown, celebrity, fame, praise; splendor, luster, brightness, brilliancy, pride, effulgence; gloriousness, nobleness, exaltation, grandeur; radiance, state, pomp, parade, magnificence.

ANT. *Obscurity, cloud, ignominy, dishonor, degradation, disgrace, shame.*

Gloss, *n.* Interpretation, comment, note, explanation, scholium, commentary, annotation; pretext, pretense, specious plea; luster, polish, shine, sheen; distortion, misinterpretation, perversion, twist, plea, speciousness.

ANT. *Haze, nebulousness; truth, literalness, representation, reality, verity, actuality, solution, exposition.*

Glowing. Shining, hot, intense, ardent, excited, fiery, fervid, fervent.

ANT. *Cool, languid, dispassionate, dull, apathetic, chilling.*

Glut, *n.* Repletion, superabundance, surplus, overplus, redundancy, overstock, superfluity.

ANT. *Scarcity, want, scantiness, dearth, failure, drainage, exhaustion.*

Glut, *v.* Cloy, sate, satiate, pall, surfeit; gorge, cram, stuff, fill, overfeed, make replete.

ANT. *Empty, void, disgorge, eject, discharge, vomit.*

Gluttony. Voracity, greed, gormandizement, deglutition.

ANT. *Abstinence, abstemiousness, temperance, frugality.*

Go. Move, pass, proceed, advance, progress; walk, travel, journey, fare; depart, set out, leave; reach, extend; contribute, concur, tend, avail; eventuate, turn out; be esteemed, be reckoned; accept, approve, endure, tolerate, swallow, bear; stir, budge.

ANT. *Stand, stay, come, remain, rest, endure, persist, lack, abide, fail.*

Good, *n.* Benefit, gain, advantage, utility, profit; welfare, weal, prosperity, interest; virtue, righteousness, excellence; abundance, riches; boon, blessing, mercy.

ANT. *Hurt, loss, detriment, injury, evil, disadvantage, ill, calamity, affliction, infliction, curse.*

Good, *a.* Advantageous, serviceable, profitable, useful, beneficial; suitable, fit, convenient, proper, well-adapted; upright, virtuous, worthy, pious, dutiful, righteous, religious; excellent, valuable, precious, sterling, admirable, capital; kind, humane, benevolent, friendly, favorable, gracious, merciful, obliging, well-disposed; fair, unblemished, untarnished, unsullied, immaculate, honorable, unimpeached; cheerful, lively, social, genial, companionable; able, skilful, expert, ready, dexterous, well-qualified; competent; pleasant, gratifying, agreeable; considerable; real, true, serious, unfeigned; right, complete, sound, propitious, efficient, sufficient, valid, actual, reputable, just.

ANT. *Bad, wrong, evil, ill, wicked, depraved, imperfect, unsound, vicious, profane, niggardly, unpropitious, unserviceable, unsuitable, inefficient, incompetent, inadequate, invalid, fictitious, supposititious, inconsiderable, mean, disreputable, disgraceful; baneful, mischievous, pernicious, injurious, hurtful; abandoned, corrupt, immoral, unprincipled, dishonest, unfair, villainous; unfortunate, unlucky, unhappy; unwelcome, sad, depressing, discouraging, distressing; wretched, sorry, abominable; inferior, defective, severe, serious, hard, heavy.*

Good-by. Farewell, adieu.

ANT. *Salutation, welcome, hail, greeting.*

Good-humored. Cheerful, buoyant, placid, amiable, good-natured, good-tempered.

ANT. *Cross, ill-humored, ill natured, unamiable, petulant, fretful, peevish.*

Goodly. Graceful, comely, beautiful, good-looking; pleasant, happy, agreeable, desirable; excellent, fair, fine; considerable.

ANT. *Unpleasant, undesirable, inconsiderable, uncomely, ungainly, clumsy, awkward.*

Gorgeous. Showy, glittering, splendid, shining, magnificent, resplendent, fine, rich, superb, dazzling; costly, grand, strong.

ANT. *Poor, naked, dingy, bare, threadbare, cheap; grimy, soiled; dull, obscure, dim.*

Govern. Manage, reign over, direct, command, control, rule, sway, influence, mold, restrain, curb, moderate, guide, supervise, conduct; regulate, steer, bridle.

ANT. *Be subject, obey, submit, comply, yield; misrule, misdirect, misconduct.*

Grace. Favor, kindness, condescension, love, benignity, good will; piety, devotion, sanctity, devoutness, faith, holiness, religion; mercy, pardon, forgiveness; elegance, polish, accomplishment, refinement; beauty, symmetry, comeliness, gracefulness, ease; short prayer; excellence, charm.

ANT. *Disfavor, deformity, pride, unkindness, gawkiness, awkwardness, inelegance.*

Graceful. Beautiful, comely, elegant, stately, easy, natural, becoming, flowing, rounded, sinuous.

ANT. *Awkward, homely, uncouth, ugly, plain, gawky, ungraceful.*

Graceless. Depraved, degenerate, corrupt, reprobate, dissolute, profligate, lost, abandoned, hardened, obdurate, shameless, incorrigible, wicked, irreclaimable; ungraceful, scampish, vicious, worthless.

ANT. *Graceful, virtuous, upright, conscientious, worthy; gracious, tender-hearted.*

Gracious. Benevolent, benign, kind, favorable, benignant, compassionate, friendly, merciful, tender, lenient, condescending, mild, gentle; affable, familiar, civil, polite, easy, courteous, beneficent.

ANT. *Haughty, discourteous, ungracious, ill-disposed, churlish, unfriendly, impolite.*

Gradation. Progress, progression, succession; graduation, precedency, arrangement, ordination, standing, rank, degree, stage, tier.

ANT. *Equality, uniformity, fraternity; abruptness, break, hiatus.*

Gradual. Regular, progressive; slow, approximate; continuous, unintermittent, step by step, gradational.

ANT. *Sudden, momentary, instantaneous, periodic, intermittent, recurrent, broken, discontinuous, disconnected.*

Grand. Stately, lordly, princely, august, exalted, majestic, elevated, illustrious, eminent, dignified, great, high; magnificent, glorious, superb, splendid, lofty, noble, sublime; principal, chief, main, leading, supreme; large, imposing, important, eventful, pompous, gorgeous.

ANT. *Little, undignified, unimposing, inferior, petty, paltry, secondary, unimportant, insignificant, mean, common, beggarly, contemptible, small.*

Grandeur. Greatness, vastness, loftiness, elevation, immensity; state, dignity, majesty, stateliness, pomp, augustness, splendor; magnificence, display, ostentation.

ANT. *Meanness, paltriness; humiliation, shame, disgrace.*

Grandiloquence. Bombast, fustian, turgidity; verbosity, pomposity, mouthiness, grandiosity, antiloquence, stiltedness, euphuism.

ANT. *Simplicity, naïveté, unaffectedness; vernacular.*

Grant. Yield, admit, concede, allow; give, bestow, confer, deign, vouchsafe; convey, transfer; allot, accord, cede, impart.

ANT. *Withhold, withdraw, reserve, resume, deny, refuse.*

Graphic. Vivid, lively, picturesque, well-drawn, striking, telling; illustrative, pictorial, descriptive, forcible, feeling; described.

ANT. *Undescriptive, unillustrative, unpicturesque; hazy, obscure, indefinite.*

Grasp. Clasp, gripe, seize, grip, grapple, catch, clutch, clinch, lay hold of; hold, retain, comprehend.

ANT. *Loose, lose, abandon, relinquish, surrender, release, miss, misunderstand.*

Grateful. Obliged, thankful, indebted, beholden; agreeable, acceptable, pleasing, pleasant, delightful, gratifying, welcome, charming, satisfying; delicious, savory, nice, cordial, luscious, refreshing, invigorating; comforting, soothing, alleviating.

ANT. *Unpleasant, unacceptable, disobliged, ungrateful, disagreeable.*

Gratification. Satisfaction, indulgence; enjoyment, delight, pleasure, fruition; reward, recompense.

ANT. *Pain, dislike, disappointment, abstinence, stinting, discipline, inurement, abnegation.*

Gratify. Please, delight, gladden; indulge, satisfy, humor, fulfil.

ANT. *Displease, dissatisfy, stint, deprive, deny, discipline.*

Gratitude. Thankfulness, obligation, gratefulness.

ANT. *Thanklessness, ingratitude, ungratefulness, unthankfulness, resentment, oblivion, indignation.*

Gratuitous. Free, voluntary, uncompensated, groundless, unwarranted, unsought, unnecessary; spontaneous, baseless, unrecompensed.

ANT. *Compulsory, involuntary, obligatory, necessitated, warranted, well-founded; unwilling, enforced, enjoined.*

Grave, *a.* Important, weighty, serious, cogent, momentous; sober, sedate, thoughtful, staid, solemn; plain, subdued, quiet, silent; sad, pressing, demure, somber, aggravated, heavy.

ANT. *Joyous, merry, unimportant, facetious, ridiculous, trivial, light, frivolous, futile, trifling, petty, slight.*

Great. Large, big, vast, huge, bulky, ample, immense, gigantic, enormous; much, excessive, high; numerous, countless; considerable, important, weighty; distinguished, eminent, exalted, prominent, excellent, elevated, celebrated, noted, famed, illustrious, famous, renowned; august, grand, dignified, noble, sublime, majestic, lofty; generous, magnanimous, chivalrous, high-minded; sumptuous, rich, magnificent; difficult, onerous, hard, burdensome, grievous; chief, principal, main, leading, grand; superior, preëminent; protracted, noticeable.

ANT. *Little, narrow, scanty, puny, few, short, mean, ignoble, weak, unimportant.*

Greediness. Avidity, hunger, voracity, ravenousness, gluttony; eagerness, longing, greed, intense desire; grasping, avarice, rapacity, selfishness.

ANT. *Generosity, prodigality, benevolence.*

Greedy. Voracious, ravenous, insatiable, gluttonous, insatiate, rapacious; eager, desirous; selfish, grasping, avaricious; hungry.

ANT. *Abstemious, abstinent, contented, apathetic, indifferent; generous, unselfish.*

Grief. Bitterness, misery, agony, anguish, heartache, heartbreak; trial, grievance; melancholy, sadness, sorrow, trouble, tribulation, woe, mourning, affliction, distress, regret.

ANT. *Happiness, joy, elation, delight, hilarity, exultation, cheer, mirth, gaiety.*

Grievance. Hardship, wrong, injury, burden, oppression; affliction, trial, sorrow, grief, distress, woe; complaint, trouble, injustice.

ANT. *Congratulation, boon, benefit, rejoicing, privilege, alleviation, riddance, disburdenment.*

Grieve. Afflict, pain, hurt, dis

tress, sadden, agonize; sorrow, mourn, lament, suffer, bewail; burden, annoy, wound, complain, deplore.

ANT. *Ease, soothe, console, please, rejoice, exult, alleviate, gratify, content, satisfy.*

Grievous. Sad, heavy, distressing, afflictive, painful, deplorable, lamentable; hurtful, injurious, noxious, mischievous, detrimental, calamitous; atrocious, heinous, outrageous, intolerable, dreadful, flagrant, aggravated; sorrowful, baleful, burdensome, unhappy, disastrous.

ANT. *Pleasant, joyous, delightful, glad, consolatory, acceptable, welcome, grateful, light, trivial, trifling.*

Grim. Fierce, ruthless, cruel, savage, ferocious; frightful, horrible, hideous, dire, horrid, appalling, terrific, dreadful; ugly, ghastly, sullen, stern.

ANT. *Mild, attractive, benign, placid, docile.*

Gross. Great, large, big, bulky; dense, thick; coarse, rough, rude, unrefined, unseemly, unbecoming; indelicate, sensual, impure, vulgar, low, broad; enormous, flagrant, shameful, outrageous, grievous; palpable, manifest, glaring; whole, total, entire, aggregate; vicious, animal, bloated.

ANT. *Partial, component; net; refined, pure; elegant, delicate, subtle.*

Grotesque. Fantastic, whimsical, fanciful, droll, odd, unnatural, strange, wild, bizarre, extravagant; ludicrous, absurd, ridiculous, antic, burlesque; quaint, old, archaic, distorted, caricatured.

ANT. *Classic, chaste, graceful, fine, severe, regular, fashionable, symmetrical, typical, formal, normal.*

Ground. Basis, base, groundwork, support, foundation; sod, soil, clod, earth, loam, turf; region, territory, country, land, domain; estate, acres, field; motive, consideration, reason, cause, account, inducement; premise, plea.

ANT. *Superstructure, statement, argument, inference, deduction; product, development, result, effect; ocean, sea, deep, main, waters.*

Grounded. Rooted, established, initiated, inaugurated, trained, prepared, fixed, set; indoctrinated.

ANT. *Ungrounded, unprepared, uninitiated, baseless, unfounded, groundless, unauthorized.*

Groundless. Vain, suppositititious, unfounded, false, baseless, fanciful, chimerical, gratuitous.

ANT. *Well-founded, authoritative, substantial, actual, authentic.*

Group. Cluster, collection, assemblage, order, bunch, knot, class, clump, assembly, collocation.

ANT. *Individual, crowd, isolation, medley, confusion; dispersion, distribution, scattering.*

Grovel. Creep, crawl, sneak, be prone, fawn, cringe, lie, grub, wallow.

ANT. *Soar, aspire, mount, rise, domineer, intimidate, dictate, browbeat.*

Grow. Enlarge, increase, swell, expand, extend, augment; vegetate, shout, sprout, germinate; advance, wax, progress, improve; adhere; raise, produce, cultivate; accrue, become, develop, amplify.

ANT. *Diminish, recede, contract, fail, stop, die, wane, decline, subside, ebb, decay, depreciate, crumble, weaken.*

Grudge, *n.* Hatred, pique, rancor, spite, malice, malevolence; grievance, aversion, dissatisfaction, discontent, refusal.

ANT. *Welcome, satisfaction, approval, contentment, benefaction, complacency, bestowal.*

Guardian. Warden, keeper, protector, defender, preserver; custodian, conservator.

ANT. *Pupil, ward; traitor, betrayer; charge, minor.*

Guess. Conjecture, divine, surmise, mistrust, suspect; find out, solve, penetrate, fathom; suppose, think, believe, fancy, imagine; hazard, risk.

ANT. *Examine, prove, investigate, establish, demonstrate, deduce, elaborate, illustrate.*

Guide, *n.* Director, conductor, pilot; mentor, monitor, adviser, instructor, counselor; clue, key; itinerary.

ANT. *Follower, disciple, imitator, pupil.*

Guide, *v.* Lead, conduct, pilot; direct, rule, manage, regulate, govern, control, steer; superintend, influence, train.

ANT. *Mislead, misconduct, misdirect, mismanage, misregulate, misguide, miseducate, betray, deceive, impose upon, disappoint, cheat.*

Guile. Cunning, craft, subtlety, artifice, artfulness, deceit, duplicity, deception, fraud, wiles trickery; treachery, insidiousness, hypocrisy.

ANT. *Frankness, simplicity, honesty, candor, generosity, sincerity, truth, veracity.*

Guilt. Guiltiness, culpability, criminality; wrong, offensiveness, wickedness, ill desert, iniquity, sin, offense.

ANT. *Sinlessness, innocence, purity, godliness, righteousness.*

Guise. Aspect, appearance, garb, dress, form, shape, figure, manner, mode, fashion; practice, habit, custom; semblance, plea, demeanor, mien.

ANT. *Character, person, individual, sentiment, disposition, opinion, life, mind, soul, self.*

Gumption. Shrewdness, discernment, sagacity, skill, cleverness, ability, capacity, power, penetration, common sense.

Gush, *v.* Burst, stream, flow, rush, spout, pour out, flow out; sentimentalize, be overeffusive.

ANT. *Drip, drop, filter, ooze, percolate, dribble, drain, strain, trickle.*

Gust. Taste, relish, zest, liking; pleasure, enjoyment, delight, delectation, gratification; turn, fancy, favor; blast, squall; fit, outburst, burst, paroxysm; puff, breeze, gale.

ANT. *Calm, tranquillity, subsidence, composure, restraint, zephyr; insipidity, tastelessness.*

H

Habiliment. Dress, garments, clothes, apparel, vesture, raiment, habit, costume, vestment, garb, robes, uniform, clothing.
ANT. *Undress, nudity, bareness, deshabille, divestment.*

Habit. Condition, constitution, temperament; way, manner; dress, garb, habiliment; habituation, familiarity, association, inurement; routine, rule, custom, fashion, practice, system, habitude, use, usage, wont.
ANT. *Dishabituation, inexperience, inconversance, desuetude, disuse, breach, infringement, disusage.*

Habitation. Abode, dwelling, lodging, domicil, headquarters, quarters, dwelling-place.

Habitual. Usual, customary, wonted, common, accustomed, regular, ordinary, familiar, everyday, perpetual.
ANT. *Irregular, extraordinary, unusual, occasional, exceptional, rare.*

Haggard. Wild, wayward, intractable, refractory, unruly, untamed; gaunt, lean, spare, meager, worn, wasted, rawboned; attenuated, wrinkled, ghastly, hollow-eyed.
ANT. *Sleek, smug, plump, chubby, comely, sightly, pretty.*

Hail. Accost, address, salute, greet, welcome, call, speak, signal.
ANT. *Ignore, avoid, pass, cut, disdain, insult, rebuff.*

Halcyon. Calm, quiet, placid, still, peaceful, tranquil, undisturbed, unruffled, palmy, serene, happy, golden, balmy.
ANT. *Stormy, tempestuous, troublous, boisterous, blustering, turbulent, violent.*

Hale. Healthy, sound, strong, robust, hearty, hardy, well.
ANT. *Feeble, sickly, weak.*

Half, *n.* Bisection, dimidiation, moiety.
ANT. *Integrity, total, whole, entirety, sum, amount, aggregate, quantity, number.*

Hallow. Consecrate, dedicate, sanctify, devote, make holy; reverence, venerate, honor, respect, pay homage to, enshrine.
ANT. *Desecrate, profane, execrate, blaspheme, abominate.*

Halt. Stop, hold, stand, pull up; limp, hobble; rest, falter, hamper, stammer, demur, dubitate, pause, stand still, hesitate.
ANT. *Advance, flow, speed; determine, decide, conclude, finish.*

Hamper. Hinder, fetter, entangle, shackle, clog, encumber, restrain, impede.
ANT. *Free, liberate, loose; expedite, hasten, speed, accelerate.*

Hand. Palm and fingers; side, direction, part; skill, dexterity, talent, ability, faculty; handiwork, workmanship; management, course; agency, share, intervention, participation; laborer, workman, operative, artificer, artisan, craftsman, employee; possession, power, control; index, pointer, indicator; chirography, handwriting; influence; handful, bunch.
ANT. *Employer.*

Handle. Touch, feel, take; manage, use, wield; treat, discuss, discourse; deal with; operate, manipulate.

ANT. *Drop, bungle, mismanage, botch, spoil, mar.*

Handsome. Comely, stately, well-formed, fine-looking; easy, graceful, becoming, appropriate; generous, liberal, noble, magnanimous, disinterested; ample, sufficient, large, plentiful; beautiful, pretty, lovely, elegant.

ANT. *Uncomely, ill-looking, ungenerous, illiberal, ugly, unsightly, ghastly.*

Handy. Dexterous, adroit, skilful, skilled, ready, clever, expert; convenient, near, at hand.

ANT. *Remote, inconvenient, unwieldy, cumbrous, awkward, useless, unhandy.*

Hang. Rest, lean, depend, poise, suspend; attach, incline, drop, decline, droop; execute; drape, adorn; dangle, be suspended, adhere, rely, stick, cling; hover, float, play; attend.

ANT. *Stand, recline, lean, lie; prop, support, uphold.*

Happen. Chance, occur, befall, bechance, betide, fall, come to pass, fall out, take place, supervene.

ANT. *Miss, omit, fail, pass, spare, pass by, neglect, discard.*

Happiness. Delight, joy, pleasure, satisfaction, comfort, bliss, triumph, mirth, gaiety, ecstasy, gladness, rejoicing, rapture, contentment, merriment, blessedness, felicity, cheer, enjoyment, well-being, light-heartedness, cheerfulness, brightness; beatitude, prosperity.

ANT. *Grief, sorrow, anguish, trouble, mourning, misfortune, affliction, disaster, woe, agony, distress, torture, torment, melancholy.*

Happy. Gay, glad, joyous, cheerful, blessed, delighted, joyful, jolly, successful, rejoicing, blissful, lucky, merry, fortunate, rejoiced, jocund, buoyant, felicitous, bright, blithesome, sunny, cheering, cheery, sprightly, delightful, smiling, mirthful, pleased, prosperous, rapturous; light-hearted, blest, gladdened, charmed; ready, expert, apt, skilful, adroit, able, dexterous; seasonable, opportune, befitting, pertinent, well-timed; auspicious, propitious, favorable.

ANT. *Unlucky, unfortunate, unsuccessful, infelicitous, sorrowful, sorry, dull, lugubrious, disappointed, desponding, unhappy.*

Harangue. Speech, public *or* formal address, oration; bombast, declamation, tirade, screed; effusion, rant.

ANT. *Mumble, drawl, insinuation, suggestion, stammering, reasoning, blandiloquence, stuttering.*

Harass. Fatigue, tire, weary, annoy, exhaust; vex, plague, worry, distress, trouble, molest, disturb, torment, harry; jade, tease, irritate, chafe, harrow, pester, perplex.

ANT. *Relieve, refresh, comfort, solace, soothe, animate, inspirit.*

Harbinger. Herald, forerunner, precursor, announcer.

ANT. *Reporter, narrator, follower, attendant, historian, relator.*

Harbor, *n.* Asylum, refuge, shelter, cover, retreat, sanctuary, resting-place; port, haven, destination, home, anchorage.

ANT. *Labor, toil, peril, exposure, roving, wandering, voyage, roaming, pilgrimage.*

Harbor, *v.* Shelter, lodge, protect; entertain, indulge, foster cherish; secrete; accommodate, encourage.

ANT. *Eject, expel, discard, discourage, stifle, exclude, banish, dismiss.*

Hard. Firm, solid, compact, impenetrable, rigid, unyielding; difficult, embarrassing, knotty, puzzling, intricate, perplexing; laborious, arduous, toilsome, wearying, fatiguing; unkind, insensible, cruel, oppressive, rigorous, severe, exacting, inflexible, obdurate, callous, unfeeling, unsympathetic; grievous, distressing, painful, calamitous, unpleasant, disagreeable; inclement, stormy, cold, severe, tempestuous; harsh, sour, acid, rough; coarse, unpalatable; unfavorable, unprosperous, unpropitious; stiff, unnatural, forced, constrained, ungraceful; excessive, intemperate; inexplicable, flinty, dense, stubborn, hardy, hardened.

ANT. *Soft, fluid, liquid, elastic, brittle, easy, penetrable, mild, lenient, tender, ductile, simple, uninvolved, intelligible, perspicuous.*

Harden. Indurate, make hard; habituate, inure, season, form, train, accustom, discipline; fortify, strengthen, steel, nerve, brace; scar, make callous, make obdurate; consolidate, compact.

ANT. *Disinure, relax, enervate, debilitate, soften, dishabituate, melt, mollify, vaporize, colliquate.*

Hardihood. Firmness, fortitude, resolution, mettle, pluck, manhood, courage, bravery, boldness, intrepidity, audacity, decision, determination; effrontery, assurance, brass.

ANT. *Weakness, effeminacy; timidity, fear; indecision; cowardice.*

Hardly. Scarcely, barely, just; severely, rigorously, unkindly, roughly, cruelly; merely, narrowly.

ANT. *Fully, amply, easily, abundantly, largely.*

Hardship. Toil, fatigue, weariness; grievance, suffering, trial, affliction, trouble, misfortune, calamity, burden, hardness; annoyance, infliction, endurance.

ANT. *Pleasure, amusement, alleviation, recreation, gratification, relief, assuagement, facilitation, treat, boon.*

Hardy. Bold, intrepid, resolute, brave, daring, valiant, heroic, manly, stout-hearted, courageous; strong, robust, firm, lusty, stout, healthy, rigorous, hale, sound, hearty; inured, vigorous.

ANT. *Weak, uninured, irresolute, delicate, debilitated, tender, fragile, frail, infirm.*

Harm. Injury, hurt, detriment, mischief, damage, prejudice, disadvantage; evil, criminality, wrong, wickedness; misfortune, ill, mishap.

ANT. *Benefit, boon, amelioration, improvement, compensation, reparation, remedy, healing.*

Harmless. Innocuous, innocent, innoxious, gentle, inoffensive; unhurt, unharmed, uninjured.

ANT. *Noxious, hurtful, nocuous, savage, cruel, deadly, mischievous, violent, pernicious, destructive.*

Harmonious. Concordant, harmonic, consonant; melodious, tuneful, musical, dulcet, mellifluous; correspondent, consistent, symmetrical, congruent; friendly, cordial, amicable, fraternal, brotherly, neighborly; accordant, proportioned, uniform, peaceful, agreeable.

ANT. *Discordant, incongruous, unshapely, harsh, disproportioned, unmelodious, sharp, grating, riotous, unfriendly, unpeaceful, quarrelsome.*

Harmony. Concord, amity, accordance, unison, consent, unanimity, unity, accord, agreement, uniformity, symmetry, union, conformity, consonance, congruity, concurrence, consistency.

ANT. *Hostility, separation, discord, warfare, battle, variance, conflict, disagreement, disunion, dissension, contention, antagonism, contest, controversy, schism, opposition, incongruity, difference, inconsistency, disproportion.*

Harsh. Rough, sour, crabbed, tart, hard, biting, sharp, corrosive, caustic; grating, discordant, jarring; morose, severe, stern, austere, acrimonious, ill-natured, unkind, unfeeling; rude, uncivil, blunt, ungracious, gruff, brutal, bearish; abusive, rigorous, rancorous.

ANT. *Smooth, lenient, melodious, genial, kindly, suave, bland, gentle.*

Harvest. Fruit, crop, increase, yield, result, return, proceeds, product, growth, ingathering, harvest-feast, harvest-festival, harvest-time, harvest-home.

Haste. Despatch, celerity, speed, promptitude, quickness; hurry, precipitation, vehemence, precipitance; expedition, excitement, heedlessness, swiftness.

ANT. *Delay, slowness, tardiness, coolness, reflection, moderation, steadiness.*

Hasten. Expedite, despatch, accelerate, speed, hurry, hustle, quicken, precipitate, press on, urge forward; haste, make haste; urge, press.

ANT. *Retard, impede, obstruct, demur, halt, hesitate.*

Hasty. Quick, swift, fleet, fast, rapid, brisk, speedy; cursory, slight, hurried, superficial; headlong, rash, reckless, precipitate, indiscreet, thoughtless; passionate, touchy, irritable, petulant, waspish, excitable, fiery, hot, irascible, peppery, fretful; impetuous, crude, incomplete, immature, undeveloped.

ANT. *Tardy, slow, leisurely, careful, reflective, developed, complete, matured, elaborate, thoughtful, deliberate.*

Hateful. Malignant, malevolent, malign; abominable, detestable, odious, execrable, abhorrent, horrid, shocking, accursed, damnable; loathsome, disgusting, nauseous, foul, repulsive, offensive, vile, obnoxious, revolting, repugnant; heinous.

ANT. *Lovely, loveable, desirable, delightful, attractive, enticing, enjoyable, tempting, pleasant.*

Hatred. Enmity, dislike, hostility, anger, abhorrence, aversion, spite, revenge, grudge, ill will, malice, antipathy, resentment, animosity, malignity, repugnance, rancor, detestation, malevolence.

ANT. *Friendship, love, benevolence, charity, beneficence.*

Have. Hold, occupy, own, possess, be in possession of, regard, consider, esteem; wish, require, desire; obtain, get, acquire, receive, gain; be obliged, be under necessity; take, accept; bear, bring forth; feel, entertain, enjoy, keep.

ANT. *Want, need, lose, discard, forego, miss, reject, covet, desire.*

Havoc. Ravage, devastation, destruction, desolation, waste, ruin; carnage, slaughter; demolition, wreck.

ANT. *Conservation, enrichment, enhancement, augmentation, development, prosperity, productiveness, luxuriance.*

Hazard, *n.* Chance, peril, venture, risk, casualty, accident, contingency, danger, jeopardy, fortuity.

ANT. *Safeguard, protection, security, surety, certainty, necessity, plan, assurance, safety; warrant, calculation, law.*

Hazy. Foggy, misty, nebulous, filmy, gauzy, cloudy, murky, gloomy.

ANT. *Clear, crystalline, diaphanous, transparent, bright, luminous, shining.*

Head. Top, summit, acme; front, fore part; rise, commencement, source, origin, beginning; chief part, principal part; person, individual; chief, chieftain, leader, commander, master, superintendent, director; first place; understanding, mind, thought, intellect; topic, subject; class, section, department, category, division; seat of the brain; crown, ruler, crisis, gathering, culmination, leadership, guide.

ANT. *Tail, bottom, foot, follower, servant, retainer, subordinate, subordination, inferiority, body, bulk, substance, continuation.*

Heal. Cure, remedy, restore; reconcile, compose, soothe, harmonize, settle; be cured, get well; repair, assuage, cicatrize.

ANT. *Harm, hurt, wound, pierce, ulcerate.*

Healthy. Healthful, sanitary, hearty, hygienic, well, vigorous, strong, sound, wholesome, hale, salutary, salubrious, invigorating, bracing.

ANT. *Unhealthy, noxious, pernicious, insalubrious; ill, sickly, unhealthful, weak, diseased, feeble, wasted, emaciated, fainting, failing, unsound, worn, frail, fragile, exhausted, delicate.*

Heart. Organ of circulation; interior, center, essence, core, kernel; disposition, mind, will, inclination, intent, passion, purpose; spirit, courage, firmness, fortitude, resolution; love, affection, feeling, emotion; conscience, character, moral nature; nucleus, hardihood, life, benevolence.

ANT. *Hand, action, aspect, exterior, manifestation, deed, conduct, timidity.*

Heart-broken. Forlorn, disconsolate, inconsolable, miserable, wretched, desolate, cheerless, comfortless, in despair, broken-hearted, wobegone.

ANT. *Cheerful, hopeful, trusting.*

Heartily. Cordially, zealously, sincerely, earnestly.

ANT. *Half-heartedly, insincerely, indifferently.*

Hearty. Earnest, warm, cordial, sincere, true, deep, profound, heartfelt, unfeigned; active, zealous, vigorous, energetic, animated; healthy, hale, sound, strong, well, robust; abundant, full, heavy; nourishing, rich, nutritious; honest, genuine.

ANT. *Delicate, infirm, unhealthy, cold, insincere, hollow, dissembling, deceptive, deceitful, hypocritical, false.*

Heat. Warmth, high temperature; excitement, flush, vehemence, impetuosity, passion, violence, fever; ardor, earnestness, fervor, zeal; contest, race, struggle; intensity, ebullition.

ANT. *Coolness, indifference, calmness, subsidence, composure, reflection.*

Heathenish. Heathen, pagan, Gentile; cruel, savage, inhuman, ferocious; unconverted, unChristian, unbelieving, uncivilized.

ANT. *Christian, believing, refined, civilized, polished.*

Heave. Lift, hoist, raise, elevate; breathe, exhale; throw, toss, hurl, fling, send; uplift, upraise, subelevate.

ANT. *Dash, sink, lower, detrude, precipitate.*

Heaven. Firmament, sky, welkin, empyrean; Paradise, bliss, Elysium; felicity, transport, ecstasy, happiness, rapture, transcendent delight.

ANT. *Gehenna, limbo, abyss, Hades, Tartarus, Avernus, infernal regions; misery, agony, torment, remorse.*

Heavenly. Celestial, divine, angelic, seraphic, cherubic, godlike, saintly, sainted, blessed, holy, beatific, beatified, glorified, blest; enrapturing, ravishing, rapturous, transporting, ecstatic, delightful, blissful, golden.

ANT. *Demoniacal, diabolical, foul, hideous, fiendish, hellish, infernal; terrene, human, terrestrial.*

Heavy. Weighty, ponderous, oppressive, grievous, severe, burdensome, cumbersome, afflictive; dull, sluggish, inert, inactive, stupid, torpid, indolent, slow, lifeless, inanimate; dejected, depressed, sorrowful, sad, gloomy, despondent, melancholy, disconsolate, crushed, downcast, crestfallen; onerous, difficult, laborious, hard; tedious, weary, tiresome, wearisome; loaded, encumbered, burdened; miry, muddy, clayey, cloggy, soggy, ill-raised; tempestuous, stormy, strong, violent, energetic, boisterous; impenetrable, stolid; loud, deep, roaring; dense, dark, gloomy, cloudy, lowering; thick.

ANT. *Light, trifling, trivial, agile, active, joyous, brisk, alleviative, quick, consolatory, buoyant, inspiriting, animating.*

Hector. Threaten, bully, menace; vex, tease, annoy, worry, fret, irritate, provoke, harass, harry; swagger, bluster, boast, vaunt.

ANT. *Cower, shrink, hide, abscond, skulk.*

Heed. Observe, regard, notice, mind, attend, harken to, listen to, obey, care, be wary *or* cautious.

ANT. *Slight, ignore, disregard, neglect, omit, overlook.*

Heedful. Observing, regardful, watchful, careful, cautious, attentive, wary, provident, circumspect, mindful.

ANT. *Heedless, careless, unobserving, thoughtless, unobservant, inattentive, negligent, regardless, unmindful, neglectful, remiss, inconsiderate, precipitate, reckless, headlong, rash.*

Height. Altitude, elevation; eminence, summit, top, apex, acme; hill, mountain; exaltation, stature, dignity, loftiness, grandeur; tallness, culmination, crisis.

ANT. *Depth, lowness, depression, base, littleness, abasement; profundity.*

Heighten. Elevate, raise; magnify, exalt, ennoble; increase, enhance, augment, improve;

aggravate, intensify; color, exaggerate, vivify, amplify, lift up.

ANT. *Lower, diminish, depress, abase, deteriorate, temper, tone, modify, qualify, extenuate.*

Heinous. Flagrant, flagitious, infamous, villainous, nefarious, wicked, atrocious, enormous, monstrous; hateful, detestable, odious, abominable, execrable.

ANT. *Excellent, laudable, distinguished, praiseworthy, justifiable, meritorious, excusable.*

Help. Foster, aid, assist, encourage, succor, uphold, sustain, support, abet, coöperate, second, stand by, befriend, remedy, prevent, avoid, promote, relieve.

ANT. *Obstruct, incur, resist, aggravate, oppose, thwart, discourage, withstand, counteract.*

Hereditary. Ancestral, patrimonial; transmitted, inherited; lineal.

ANT. *Conferred, acquired, won, achieved.*

Heresy. Heterodoxy, error, unsound doctrine, schism, unorthodoxy.

ANT. *Orthodoxy, catholicity; convention, prevailing belief.*

Heretic. Dissenter, schismatic, nonconformist, heresiarch.

ANT. *Orthodox believer, fanatic, adherent.*

Heritage. Inheritance, entailment, legacy, bequest, portion, patrimony, estate.

ANT. *Wages, acquisition, merit, compensation.*

Hermetically. Secretly, mysteriously, mystically, occultly, emblematically, symbolically; air-tight, closely.

ANT. *Loosely, misfittingly; openly.*

Heroic. Brave, valiant, courageous, bold, daring, intrepid, fearless, dauntless, noble, magnanimous, gallant; epic; violent, extreme, desperate, extravagant; undaunted, chivalrous, romantic.

ANT. *Dastardly, cowardly, cravenly, fearful, timorous.*

Hesitate. Doubt, pause, delay, demur, waver, vacillate; falter, stammer; dubitate, scruple.

ANT. *Decide, run, flow, determine, precipitate.*

Heterodox. Unsound, unorthodox, heretical, freethinking.

ANT. *Sound, orthodox.*

Heterogeneous. Unlike, variant, various, confused, conglomerate, mingled, mixed, discordant, miscellaneous, dissimilar, non-homogeneous; alien, strange, different, opposed, contrary, contrasted.

ANT. *Homogeneous, identical, like, same, pure, uniform, similar, alike, accordant, congruous.*

Hew. Cut, chop, hack; smooth, fashion, form; mold, model, engrave, carve, sculpture, turn.

ANT. *Leave intact.*

Hibernal. Wintry, brumal, arctic, glacial, frigid.

ANT. *Summery, balmy, zephyrous, halcyon, tropical.*

Hide. Conceal, secrete, mask, dissemble, protect, store, disguise, screen, cover, burrow, ensconce; suppress, shelter, withhold, cloak, veil, bury, inter, entomb, overwhelm.

ANT. *Expose, disclose, discover, exhume, show, tell, raise, reveal, unveil, unmask, uncover, exhibit, confess, betray, avow, divulge, disinter, make known, lay bare, lay open, publish, advertise, manifest, promulgate, admit; strip.*

Hideous. Frightful, dreadful,

appalling, horrible, ghastly, terrible, horrid, grim, shocking, grisly; unshapely, ugly, monstrous.

ANT. *Graceful, beautiful, attractive, captivating.*

High. Prominent, superior, distinguished, preëminent; dignified, great, admirable; recondite, abstruse, occult, profound, dark, obscure, transcendental; proud, haughty, arrogant, supercilious, lordly; boastful, ostentatious, bragging, vain-glorious; despotic, domineering, overbearing, tyrannical; turbulent, violent, strong, tumultuous, boisterous; extreme; complete, full; dear; shrill, acute, sharp, high-pitched; northerly, southerly; early, primeval; capital, principal; strong-flavored; noble, exalted, steep, tall, towering, uplifted, elevated, eminent, lofty.

ANT. *Low, base, degraded, inferior, mean, short, stunted, depressed, dwarfed, ignoble.*

Hinder. Delay, embarrass, oppose, prevent, stay, stop, retard, hamper, impede, baffle, encumber, check, bar, clog, counteract, frustrate, foil, interrupt, obstruct, resist, thwart, block, balk, debar.

ANT. *Quicken, hasten, speed, accelerate, expedite, enable, facilitate, promote.*

Hinge. Turn, depend, hang, be dependent; move, work, rotate, circulate.

ANT. *Halt, jar, grate, precipitate, abrade; give, fail.*

Hire. Engage, commission, rent, employ; bribe, buy up; lease, let.

ANT. *Buy, purchase.*

History. Annals, chronicle, recital, memoir, narrative, record, register, story, account, archives, narration, muniment, memorial, autobiography, biography.

ANT. *Fiction, fable.*

Hit. Strike; reach, attain, win, secure, gain; suit, accord with; clash, collide; succeed, be successful; chance, hazard, touch, mistake.

ANT. *Fail, err, miss, mischance, swerve, deflect, overshoot.*

Hitch. Catch, get stuck *or* impeded; go by jerks; fasten, unite, connect, tie, attach; bar, stick, stickle, jam.

ANT. *Run, glide, slide, rotate, flow, continue.*

Hoard. Store, deposit, save, garner, husband, hive, accumulate, amass, treasure.

ANT. *Waste, squander, dissipate, scatter.*

Hoarse. Husky, raucous; grating, rough, harsh, low, guttural, gruff.

ANT. *Melodious, rich, mellow, sweet, mellifluous.*

Hoary. Hoar, white, gray, silvery, frosty.

ANT. *Dark, raven, jet, black.*

Hoax. Deceive, cheat, impose upon; befool, bamboozle, trick, dupe.

ANT. *Guide, enlighten, inform, undeceive, direct, regulate, correct.*

Hobby. Nag, hobby-horse; pursuit, whim, amusement, specialty, idiosyncrasy.

ANT. *Nuisance, horror, aversion, incubus, bugbear, scarecrow.*

Hold. Possess, retain, have, occupy; clasp, grasp, clutch, clinch; restrain, confine, imprison, detain; bind, fasten, unite, connect; stop, stay, arrest, suspend, withhold; support, maintain, sustain, continue, prosecute; embrace, entertain, cherish; heed, regard, consider, notice, judge, esteem, count, reckon, deem; contain, admit; celebrate, solemnize; assemble, convene; cohere, adhere, cling, stick, cleave; be firm, be fast, persist, last, endure; be derived; think, be of opinion, believe; stand, be true.

ANT. *Drop, surrender, fail, abandon, desert, release, forego, vacate, concede, break, cease; speed, accelerate; give, dispense; disperse.*

Hollow, *a.* Empty, void, vacant, vacuous, cavernous; insincere, false, faithless, hypocritical, treacherous, deceitful, false-hearted, pharisaical; artificial, concave, insubstantial, flimsy, transparent, senseless, unsound; deep, low, rumbling.

ANT. *Full, solid, firm, sincere, well-stored, strong, true, sound, genuine, substantial.*

Holy. Hallowed, sacred, consecrated, blessed, devoted, set apart; righteous, saintly, spiritual, devout, saintlike, godly, religious, heavenly-minded, pious, pure; reverend. sanctified, divine.

ANT. *Cursed, polluted, unsanctified, unconsecrated, unhallowed, wicked, worldly, abominable, common, impure, unholy, secular, profane, evil.*

Homage. Fealty, allegiance, devotion, loyalty, fidelity; reverence, obeisance, respect, deference, duty, service, honor; worship, adoration; affiance, submission, veneration.

ANT. *Treason, rebellion, defiance, insubordination, disaffection.*

Home. Habitation, hearth, residence, house, abode, dwelling, domicil, fireside, hearthstone, ingleside.

Homely. Domestic, homelike; plain, coarse, uncomely, inelegant, homespun; rather ugly.

ANT. *Handsome, beautiful, courtly, refined, elegant.*

Honest. Honorable, fair, open, straightforward, equitable; upright, virtuous, conscientious, just, true, faithful, trusty, reliable, trustworthy; genuine, thorough; decent, reputable, respectable, creditable, suitable, proper; chaste; truthful, ingenuous, sincere, frank, unreserved, candid, good.

ANT. *Lying, unscrupulous, mendacious, untrue, deceitful, dishonest, false, hypocritical, fraudulent, disingenuous, perfidious, faithless, treacherous, unfaithful, traitorous; dishonorable, improper, wrong, insincere, vicious.*

Honesty. Integrity, uprightness, probity, justice, fairness, equity, honor, fidelity, faithfulness; truth, truthfulness, veracity; genuineness, thoroughness; chastity, virtue; sincerity, candor, frankness, openness, unreserve, ingenuousness; straightforwardness, rectitude.

ANT. *Insincerity, trickery, dishonesty, guile, fraud, deception, unfairness, chicanery.*

Honor. Veneration, reverence, respect, homage, deference, civility; dignity, elevation, distinction; majesty; reputation, repute, fame, esteem, credit, glory, consideration; integrity, probity, rectitude; pride, nobility, eminence, high-mindedness, spirit, self-respect, grandeur, renown.

ANT. *Contempt, irreverence, disrespect, slight, obscurity, demoralization, degradation, de-*

basement, disgrace, cowardice, infamy, dishonor.

Honorable. Honest, upright, high-minded, illustrious, noble, great, just, fair, trustworthy, conscientious, virtuous, estimable, reputable, right, proper, creditable, equitable.

ANT. *Dishonorable, dishonest, false, treacherous.*

Honorary. Unofficial, nominal, gratuitous, titular, unremunerative.

ANT. *Professional, official, remunerative, jurisdictional.*

Hoot. Shout; cry like an owl; denounce, hiss, execrate, cry down, decry, sibilate.

ANT. *Salute, welcome, cheer, honor, acclaim, eulogize.*

Hope. Trust, confidence, faith, reliance; expectancy, expectation, possibility; dependence; anticipation, prospect, longing, vision, desire.

ANT. *Despair, despondency, distrust, abandonment, disbelief, abjuration.*

Horizontal. Plain, flat, level, even, plane.

ANT. *Vertical, inclined, uneven, slanting, sloping, hilly, broken, irregular, rough, rolling, rugged.*

Horrible. Horrid, frightful, terrible, terrific, alarming, dire, portentous, appalling, horrific, horrifying, formidable, awful, harrowing, dreadful, hideous, fearful; abominable, ghastly, detestable, hateful, direful.

ANT. *Lovely, desirable, enjoyable, attractive, beautiful, fair, pleasant, amiable.*

Horror. Fright, alarm, dread, fear, consternation, terror, affright, dismay, panic; abomination, abhorrence, detestation, disgust, hatred, shuddering, antipathy; shrinking.

ANT. *Love, attraction, enticement, allurement.*

Horse. Steed, charger, stallion, gelding, mare, colt, pony, nag, courser, barb, filly, palfrey; cavalry, horsemen; stand, support, frame.

Hospitable. Generous, liberal, bountiful, open, kind, unconstrained, unreserved, receptive, large-minded; sociable, neighborly, charitable.

ANT. *Unsociable, exclusive, retired, recluse, unneighborly, churlish.*

Host. Entertainer; innkeeper, landlord; army, legion; multitude, horde, throng, number, assemblage.

ANT. *Handful, sprinkling, group, knot, corps, section; guest, traveler, boarder, lodger.*

Hostage. Sponsor, bail, surety.

ANT. *Dictator, conqueror.*

Hostile. Inimical, unfriendly; adverse, opposite, contrary, repugnant, opposing, opposed.

ANT. *Friendly, kindly, amicable, neighborly, cordial, congenial.*

Hostility. Enmity, animosity, hatred, unfriendliness, ill will; opposition, repugnance, variance, contrariety.

ANT. *Companionship, congeniality, sympathy, harmony, fellow-feeling, concord, alliance, kindliness, friendship.*

Hot. Burning, fiery, scalding, heated, very warm; irascible, impetuous, excitable, passionate, hasty, furious, violent; ardent, fervent, vehement, eager, glowing, animated, fervid; biting, pungent, sharp, acrid, peppery, stinging, piquant, high-flavored; choleric.

ANT. *Cold, frigid, cool, arctic, chilled, chilly, boreal, bleak, wintry, frosty, icy; apathetic, unresponsive, unfeeling, stoical, passionless, uninspiring, dull, dead, indifferent, unconcerned.*

Huge. Immense, enormous, colossal, vast, bulky, stupendous, gigantic, elephantine, Herculean, Cyclopean, large, great, monstrous, prodigious.

ANT. *Petty, pigmy, puny, undersized, small, minute.*

Human. Cosmical, ethnical, anthropological, rational, civilized.

ANT. *Inhuman, beastly, irrational, animal, brutish.*

Humane. Kind, benevolent, benignant, accommodating, tender, compassionate, charitable, sympathetic, gentle, clement, kind-hearted; tender-hearted; elevating, refining, cultivating, rational, spiritual, humanizing; benign, merciful, gracious, pitying, human, forgiving.

ANT. *Barbarous; inhuman, unkind, cruel, unmerciful.*

Humanity. Mankind; benevolence, kindness, philanthropy, tenderness, sympathy, charity, humaneness, good nature; human spirit, rationality, reason, culture; man, compassion, sensibility.

ANT. *Unkindness, cruelty, inhumanity, irrationality, bestiality, barbarity.*

Humanize. Soften, make humane; civilize, cultivate, refine, polish, improve, enlighten, reclaim, educate; ameliorate, christianize.

ANT. *Barbarize, degrade, debase, brutalize, depress.*

Humble. Meek, modest, unassuming, unobtrusive, lowly, unpretending, submissive, small, poor, low; obscure.

ANT. *High, lofty, assuming, pretentious, proud, boastful, arrogant, eminent.*

Humid. Damp, wet, moist, vaporous, dank, spongy.

ANT. *Dry, arid, moistureless, parched.*

Humor, *n.* Disposition, temper, bent, propensity, bias, predilection; mood, frame of mind, fancy, caprice, whim, freak, vagary, crotchet; pleasantry, fun, jocularity, wit, facetiousness.

ANT. *Nature, personality, mind, purpose, will, seriousness.*

Humorous. Facetious, jocular, jocose, funny, comical, sportive, comic, ludicrous, pleasant, witty.

ANT. *Grave, serious, sober, matter-of-fact, solemn, sad.*

Hurry, *n.* Flutter, flurry, precipitation, confusion, bluster, bustle, agitation, perturbation; haste, despatch, celerity, expedition, quickness, promptness.

ANT. *Slowness; composure.*

Hurry, *v.* Haste, hasten, move quickly; urge, speed, expedite, despatch, accelerate.

ANT. *Delay, retard, slow down; loiter, saunter, move slowly.*

Hurt, *n.* Damage, harm, injury, mischief, disadvantage, detriment, wound.

ANT. *Benefit, pleasure.*

Hurt, *v.* Injure, harm, damage, impair, mar; pain, wound; grieve, afflict, bruise.

ANT. *Heal, soothe, console, repair, benefit, compensate, reinstate.*

Hurtful. Harmful, injurious, mischievous, detrimental, deleterious, disadvantageous, baneful, noxious, prejudicial, pernicious, baleful.

ANT. *Helpful, beneficial, advantageous, wholesome, salubrious, good, sanative, remedial.*

Hybrid. Mixed, impure, mongrel, mule, half-breed.

ANT. *Pure, unmixed, thoroughbred.*

Hypocrisy. Formalism, Pharisaism, cant, pietism, sanctimoniousness, assumed piety; deceit, deception, dissimulation, false profession, imposture; sanctimony, pretense, sham, affectation.

ANT. *Sincerity, transparency, truth, honesty, genuineness, candor, frankness, openness, ingenuousness, truthfulness.*

Hypocrite. Deceiver, impostor, pretender, cheat, dissembler; Pharisee, formalist.

ANT. *Saint, believer, Christian; dupe, bigot, fanatic, simpleton.*

Hypocritical. Canting, Pharisaical, sanctimonious; insincere, dissembling, false, hollow, faithless, deceitful, unctuous, smug, smooth, mincing.

ANT. *Candid, truthful, sincere, plain-spoken, transparent, genuine.*

Hypothesis. Scheme, speculation, system, supposition, conjecture, guess, surmise, theory.

ANT. *Certainty, demonstration, evidence, fact, proof, discovery.*

I

Idea. Concept, conception, impression, judgment, plan, opinion, purpose, conceit, design, fancy, pattern, thought, theory, belief, image, imagination, notion, supposition, ideal, apprehension, fantasy, model, sentiment, archetype; doctrine, understanding; fiction.

ANT. *Object, form, subject; substance, fact, actuality, reality.*

Ideal, *n.* Idea, archetype, original, model, standard, prototype.

ANT. *Fact, performance, reality, practice, act, accomplishment, achievement, action, realization, attainment, development, doing, incarnation, embodiment, execution.*

Ideal, *a.* Mental, conceptional, intellectual, notional, creative, spiritual, poetical, supposititious, unreal, fictitious, imaginary, fanciful, imaginative, chimerical.

ANT. *Physical, material, visible, tangible, historical, substantial, real, actual, palpable.*

Ideality. Imagination, conception, invention, fancy, creativeness, genius.

ANT. *Imitation, uninventiveness, copyism, unimaginativeness; literality.*

Identical. Same, selfsame, not different; particular.

ANT. *Different, separate, contrary.*

Identify. Prove identical, make identical, confound; unite, integrate, incorporate, recognize, verify.

ANT. *Divide, disunite, confound, confuse, overlook, mistake.*

Identity. Sameness, unity, oneness, union, personality, individuality, convertibility.

ANT. *Difference, separateness, distinctness, contrariety, plurality.*

Idiocy. Imbecility; foolishness, fatuity, irrationality; aberration, insanity; stupidity, folly, senselessness, incapacity.

ANT. *Intelligence, sagacity, wisdom, capacity, brilliancy, astuteness, acuteness, sense, common sense, soundness; sanity, judgment.*

Idiom. Specialty, phrase, turn, peculiarity, characteristic.

ANT. *Barbarism, solecism.*

Idiosyncrasy. Peculiarity, idiocrasy; constitution, temperament, specialty, characteristic, individuality, singularity, eccentricity.

ANT. *Community, universality, generality.*

Idiot. Fool, natural, imbecile.

ANT. *Sage, authority, luminary.*

Idle. Unbusied, unused, leisure; useless, ineffectual, fruitless, bootless, unavailing, vain, abortive, futile; trifling, trivial, unimportant, trashy, foolish, unprofitable; waste, empty; indolent, inert, lazy, slothful, unoccupied, vacant, inactive, sluggish, unemployed.

ANT. *Active, busy, diligent, industrious, employed, working; occupied; tilled; filled, populated; assiduous.*

Idolize. Deify; adore, worship, reverence, venerate.

ANT. *Loathe, abominate, execrate, abhor.*

Ignoble. Plebeian, vulgar, untitled, baseborn, low, mean, rustic, peasant; worthless, insignificant, contemptible; dishonorable, disgraceful, inferior, unworthy; humble.

ANT. *Honorable, eminent, exalted, noble, lordly, illustrious, grand, notable.*

Ignominious. Dishonorable, infamous, disgraceful, shameful, scandalous, disreputable, opprobrious; despicable, base, deserving ignominy, contemptible.

ANT. *Honorable, creditable, reputable, estimable, worthy.*

Ignominy. Dishonor, disgrace, discredit, shame, infamy, disrepute, contempt, obloquy, opprobrium, scandal, abasement, odium; reprobation, reproach.

ANT. *Credit, honor, reputation, glory, luster, distinction, renown.*

Ignoramus. Smatterer, novice, wiseacre, dunce, simpleton, dullard, greenhorn, numskull.

ANT. *Savant, sage, luminary.*

Ignorance. Illiteracy, stupidity, nescience, blindness, darkness.

ANT. *Knowledge, wisdom, sense, learning, erudition.*

Ignorant. Illiterate, unlearned, unlettered, unskilled, untaught, untutored, uneducated, ill-informed, uninstructed, uninformed.

ANT. *Educated, learned, instructed, sage, wise, skilled, cultured, trained, well-informed, cultivated.*

Ignore. Disregard, neglect, overlook, not recognize; set aside, reject; disown, repudiate.

ANT. *Own, notice, recognize, mark, visit, avow, claim.*

Ill, *n.* Wickedness, depravity, evil; misfortune, calamity, affliction, misery, harm, pain.

ANT. *Good, blessing, fortune; righteousness, integrity, honor.*

Ill, *a.* Bad, evil, unfortunate, unfavorable; wicked, wrong, iniquitous, naughty; sick, ailing, diseased, disordered, poorly, indisposed; cross, crabbed, surly, peevish, hateful, malicious; ill-favored, ugly.

ANT. *Well, strong, good, vigorous, healthy, robust, hearty, hale.*

Ill-bred. Impolite, uncivil, uncourteous, uncourtly, uncouth, unpolished, rude, ill-behaved, ill-mannered.

ANT. *Polite, well-behaved, civil, refined, courteous.*

Illuminate. Light, illumine, illume; enlighten, make wise, instruct, inspire; emblazon, irradiate.

ANT. *Darken, obscure, bedim, mislead, delude.*

Illusion. Delusion, hallucination, deception, error, fallacy, mockery, fantasy, phantasm, chimera; dream, vision, myth.

ANT. *Body, substance, form, reality, actuality, essence.*

Illusive. Delusive, deceptive, deceitful, fallacious; visionary, unreal, disappointing, fugitive, erroneous, false, imaginary, illusory, chimerical.

ANT. *Substantial, real, true, satisfactory, solid, permanent.*

Illustrate. Elucidate, explain, exemplify, make clear; interpret, demonstrate, represent, embody, paint, image; adorn with pictures.

ANT. *Obscure, misinterpret, confuse, mystify, darken, misrepresent.*

Illustrious. Glorious, splendid, brilliant, bright, radiant; famous, famed, noted, renowned, distinguished, celebrated, eminent, signal, remarkable, conspicuous; deathless, noble.

ANT. *Ignominious, disgraceful, infamous, inglorious, disreputable.*

Ill will. Malevolence, unkindness, malice, enmity, hatred, hate, rancor, envy, grudge, uncharitableness, ill nature; antipathy, dislike, aversion.

ANT. *Good will, benevolence, beneficence.*

Im- or In-. This prefix, which is regularly *in-*, and which becomes *il-* before *l*, *ir-* before *r* and *im-* before a labial, means *in, into, on,* or *among*, or denotes the negative *not*, or, occasionally, has a simple intensive meaning. Such words as begin with this prefix without modification of the combined meaning of the prefix and root word will be easily derived from the antonyms and synonyms of the root words. Others of more derived meaning are found here.

Image. Statue; idol, object of worship; likeness, effigy, figure, resemblance, similitude, representation, picture; trope, metaphor; idea, copy, conception, fiction, shadow, vision.

ANT. *Person, original, substance, subject, object, reality, truth, verity.*

Imagery. Phantasm, phantom, vision, dream; tropes, figures of speech, poetry, fancy, illustration, metaphor, similitude.

ANT. *Prose, statement, fact.*

Imagination. Conception, invention, ideality, fancy, fantasy, creative power; esemplastic faculty; idea, notion; contrivance, scheme, device, plot; illusion.

Imaginative. Inventive, creative, plastic, poetical, esemplastic, poetic; conceptive, romantic, ideal, original.

ANT. *Unimaginative, unpoetical, prosaic, unromantic, literal, uninventive, matter-of-fact.*

Imagine. Conceive, think, image, fancy, picture; devise, contrive, frame, project, invent, create, mold; suppose, assume; deem, apprehend, believe; surmise, understand, fabricate, presume.

ANT. *Represent, exhibit, depict, prove, demonstrate, verify, substantiate.*

Imbecile, *a.* Weak, feeble, helpless, infirm, decrepit; foolish, witless, idiotic, driveling, fatuous.

ANT. *Shrewd, clever, sagacious.*

Imbecility. Weakness, debility, feebleness, infirmity, helplessness; foolishness, childishness, idiocy, fatuity, dotage, senility.

ANT. *Strength, energy, virility, vigor, power.*

Imbibe. Absorb, take in, suck in, swallow up; receive, gather, gain, acquire, get, pick up; assimilate, learn.

ANT. *Discard, reject, renounce, disavow, abjure, repudiate.*

Imitate. Copy, follow, pattern after; mimic, ape, mock, impersonate, take off; burlesque, travesty, parody; represent, resemble, portray, depict, repeat, counterfeit.

ANT. *Misrepresent, caricature, alter, vary, distort, remodel, differentiate, dissimilate, modify.*

Imitative. Imitating, copying, mimicking, aping, apish, caricaturing, unoriginal, servile.

ANT. *Original, creative, inventive.*

Immaculate. Spotless, unspotted, stainless, unsullied, unsoiled, untainted, unblemished, untarnished, clean, pure, undefiled; innocent, guiltless, sinless, faultless, fair, holy, saintly; virgin, unpolluted.

ANT. *Impure, corrupt, sinful, contaminated, defiled, polluted, tainted, spotted.*

Immanent. Intrinsic, inherent, internal, indwelling; empirical; innate, subjective, congenital, ingrained, natural, implicit.

ANT. *Emanant, transitive, developed, projective, exsilient, phenomenal, explicit, accidental, transcendental, transeunt.*

Immaterial. Incorporeal, unbodied, unfleshly, spiritual, supersensible; unimportant, insignificant, unessential, nonessential, trivial, trifling.

ANT. *Material, physical, important, corporeal, essential.*

Immature. Unripe, crude, raw, green, unformed, unprepared, imperfect, rudimentary, unfinished; premature, hasty, unseasonable, untimely; undeveloped.

ANT. *Ripe, complete, developed, mature, finished.*

Immeasurable. Illimitable, unbounded, boundless, limitless, measureless, immense, infinite; vast, unfathomable.

ANT. *Finite, limited, circumscribed, restricted, shallow, bounded.*

Immediate. Proximate, close, near, next; direct, unmediated; instantaneous, instant, present; contiguous.

ANT. *Distant, remote, mediate, future.*

Immediately. Presently, this instant, straightway, directly, forthwith, at once, now, right off, instantly, without delay.

ANT. *Hereafter, by and by, after a while, sometime.*

Immemorial. Olden, ancient, hoary, archaic, primitive, remote, time-honored, primordial.

ANT. *Recent, modern, late, fresh, upstart.*

Immerse. Dip, plunge, submerge, sink, douse, duck, bury;

soak, steep, macerate, drown, inundate, overwhelm.

ANT. *Dry, drain, parch, ventilate, air, ground, strand.*

Immigration. Migration, colonization, settlement.

ANT. *Exodus, emigration.*

Imminent. Impending, hovering, threatening.

ANT. *Improbable, doubtful, unexpected, unlikely, contingent, chimerical, problematical; warded, staved, escaped.*

Immunity. Freedom, exemption, release, exoneration; prerogative, privilege, right, liberty, charter, franchise; dispensation.

ANT. *Liability, obligation, jurisdiction, impost, amenability, burden.*

Imp. Sprite, hobgoblin, demon, devil, flibbertigibbet, scamp, brat.

ANT. *Cherub, angel.*

Impact. Impulse, shock, impression, stroke; collision, contact, striking, impinging; application.

ANT. *Isolation, separation, interval, removal, avoidance, non-contact, shave.*

Impair. Deteriorate, vitiate, injure, harm, make worse; lessen, diminish, decrease; enervate, weaken, enfeeble; reduce, damage.

ANT. *Enhance, improve, repair, augment, better, increase.*

Impassioned. Passionate, vehement, impetuous, animated, exciting, glowing, intense, fervid, fervent, warm, ardent, zealous; spirited.

ANT. *Cool, impassive, unimpassioned, apathetic, indifferent.*

Impatience. Uneasiness, disquietude, restlessness; haste, vehemence, eagerness, precipitation, impetuosity; heat, violence of temper, irritability, irritableness.

ANT. *Patience, calmness, endurance, composure, leniency, submission, forbearance, long-suffering.*

Impediment. Bar, hindrance, obstacle, obstruction, difficulty, clog, encumbrance, stumbling-block, check.

ANT. *Assistance, aid, benefit, help, relief, succor, advantage; aidance, support, furtherance.*

Imperative. Commanding, authoritative, peremptory; binding, obligatory; urgent, irresistible, dictatorial, inexorable, compulsory.

ANT. *Indulgent, lenient, supplicatory, mild, optional, discretional, entreative.*

Imperial. Belonging to an empire, kingly, regal, sovereign, royal; majestic, grand, magnificent, exalted, great, noble, supreme, consummate, superb.

ANT. *Ignoble, servile, slavish, beggarly, mean, paltry.*

Imperious. Magisterial, dictatorial, despotic, domineering, tyrannical, overbearing, lordly, haughty, arrogant, authoritative, exacting.

ANT. *Yielding, compliant, submissive, gentle, mild, docile, ductile.*

Impetuous. Fierce, vehement, violent, furious, passionate, precipitate, hasty, headlong, overzealous, reckless, rash, excitable.

ANT. *Careful, slow, deliberate, thoughtful, reflective, leisurely.*

Implement. Utensil, tool, appliance, instrument.

ANT. *Labor, work, science, art, agriculture, manufacture.*

Implicate. Entangle, enfold, involve, connect, associate, compromise, charge, incriminate.
ANT. *Disconnect, extricate, acquit, dissociate.*

Implication. Entanglement, involution; inference, conclusion; intricacy, complication; concealment, latency; allusion, insinuation, innuendo, adumbration.
ANT. *Arrangement, system, orderliness; manifestation, expression, exposition, demonstration, production.*

Implicit. Understood, implied, inferred, tacit; unreserved, unhesitating, firm, steadfast, unshaken, undoubting; involved.
ANT. *Expressed, explicit, developed, stated, plain, specific, unambiguous.*

Imply. Involve, import, include, signify, mean, indicate, suggest, hint, denote.
ANT. *Express, declare, state, pronounce.*

Import, *n.* Meaning, sense, purport, drift, signification, gist, spirit, bearing, tenor, intention.
ANT. *Statement, proceeding.*

Import, *v.* Bring into; purport, denote, imply, betoken, signify, mean; concern, be of significance to; introduce.
ANT. *Export, banish, exile, send abroad.*

Importance. Consequence, moment, weight, significance, momentousness, import, concern; avail; self-importance, pomposity.
ANT. *Nothingness, insignificance, unimportance, immateriality.*

Important. Grave, weighty, momentous, serious, material, significant; influential, prominent, pompous, self-important, consequential; expressive, leading, main, relevant, considerable, essential, great, dignified.
ANT. *Insignificant, trivial, inconsiderable, irrelevant, secondary, petty, mean, uninfluential, minor, unimportant.*

Importunate. Urgent, pertinacious, pressing, teasing, busy, solicitous, overurgent, overentreative.
ANT. *Modest, diffident, self-reliant, self-respecting.*

Importune. Urge, entreat, press, solicit, dun, beset, pester, tease, worry, trouble.
ANT. *Surrender, sacrifice, abandon; grant, bestow.*

Impose. Put, set, lay, place; appoint, enjoin, prescribe; obtrude, palm off, pass; inflict, subject.
ANT. *Remove, disburden, unload, free; hold up, arrest, disclose.*

Imposing. Stately, august, majestic, grand, noble, commanding, impressive; striking, effective, dignified.
ANT. *Petty, undignified, unimposing, insignificant, paltry, puny.*

Imposition. Imposing, putting, placing, laying; burden, levy, tax, constraint, oppression, injunction; deception, fraud, artifice, trickery, imposture, cheating; presumption, exaction, encroachment.
ANT. *Sanction, warrant, authority; truth, verity, fact, certainty, verification, genuineness, authenticity, honesty.*

Impost. Tax, duty, custom, excise, levy, toll, tribute, rate; imposition.
ANT. *Revenue, proceeds, exemption, immunity.*

Impostor. Deceiver, pretender, cheat, hypocrite, knave, charla-

tan, mountebank, rogue, Pharisee, trickster, dissembler.
ANT. *Guide, enlightener, detector, undeceiver.*

Imposture. Cheat, trick, deception, imposition, fraud, ruse, delusion, dodge, artifice, wile, deceit, stratagem, hoax.
ANT. *Truth, fact, verity, reality.*

Impotence. Disability, incapacity, incompetence, powerlessness, weakness, inefficiency, infirmity, frailty, imbecility, inability, incapability, helplessness, disqualification.
ANT. *Capacity, vigor, qualification, ability.*

Impoverish. Make poor *or* indigent, exhaust, deplete, rob, beggar, fleece, denude.
ANT. *Enrich, aggrandize, augment, store, enhance, endow.*

Impregnable. Invincible, unassailable, invulnerable, immovable, inexpugnable, secure, tenable, irrefragable.
ANT. *Pregnable, weak, exposed, defenseless, expugnable.*

Impregnate. Fecundate, imbue, infuse, tincture, saturate, fill, fertilize; mix, combine, insert, steep, vivify, teach.
ANT. *Remove, evolve, extricate, separate, destroy, quench, extinguish, be studious, learn.*

Impression. Printing, stamping, imprinting; stamp, impress, brand; mark; sensation, effect, influence; notion, idea, opinion, fancy.
ANT. *Concept, apprehension, comprehension.*

Impressive. Affecting, touching, moving, stirring, powerful, striking, overpowering; forcible, solemn, imposing, important.
ANT. *Weak, feeble, vapid, tame, unimpressive, dry, insignificant.*

Improve. Mend, gain, become better, get on, gain ground; increase, rise, be enhanced; better, amend, ameliorate, rectify; progress; avail one's self of, use, make productive; correct, reform.
ANT. *Debase, deteriorate, vitiate, spoil, mar, impair, injure, depress.*

Improvement. Amending, bettering, amelioration, amendment, progress, efficiency, proficiency, advancement, use, betterment; increase, correction.
ANT. *Degeneracy, retrogradation, degeneration, debasement, deterioration, retrogression.*

Impudence. Assurance, boldness, impertinence, pertness, rudeness, sauciness, effrontery, forwardness, incivility, insolence, presumption, officiousness, intrusiveness.
ANT. *Bashfulness, humility, diffidence, meekness, lowliness, modesty, submissiveness; coyness, obsequiousness, subserviency, abasement.*

Impugn. Attack, assail, contradict, oppose, resist, gainsay, controvert, deny, blame.
ANT. *Declare, state, allege, approve, commend, defend, repel; propose, propound, confront, face.*

Impulse. Thrust, push, impetus; passion, instinct, proclivity, inclination, appetite; motive, influence, incitement, instigation, incentive, force, sudden thought.
ANT. *Deliberation, premeditation, rebuff, repulse.*

Impulsive. Propulsive, impelling, moving; hot, quick, rash, hasty, passionate; wayward, impressible.

ANT. *Discreet, hesitating, reluctant, timid, calculating, wary, cautious.*

Impute. Ascribe, refer, charge, attribute, imply, insinuate.

ANT. *Withdraw, retract, recall; clear, justify, acquit.*

Inane. Empty, void; worthless, trifling, vacuous, vain, puerile, frivolous; pointless, feeble, vapid, characterless.

ANT. *Significant, pointed, powerful, sensible, forcible.*

Inanition. Emptiness, vacuity, inanity; vanity, folly, puerility, worthlessness, frivolousness; exhaustion, starvation.

ANT. *Fulness, repletion, plethora; significance, meaning.*

Inaugurate. Install, invest, induct; celebrate; commence, begin, initiate, originate.

ANT. *Divert, deprive, conclude, terminate.*

Inauguration. Investiture, installation, induction, consecration, institution, initiation; commencement, formal opening, beginning, origination.

ANT. *Dismissal, discharge; valediction, valedictory; close, conclusion, end, termination.*

Incandescence. White heat, incalescence, glow.

ANT. *Iciness, refrigeration, congelation, crystallization.*

Incantation. Sorcery, charm, enchantment, spell, magic, conjuration, witchcraft, witchery, necromancy; recitation, invocation.

ANT. *Evocation, exorcism.*

Incarnation. Embodiment, impersonation, manifestation, exemplification, personification.

ANT. *Disembodiment, abstraction, spiritualization.*

Incendiarism. Arson; conflagration.

ANT. *Extinction, quenching, annihilation.*

Incense, *v.* Enrage, exasperate, irritate, provoke, inflame, anger, excite, heat, chafe, sting, nettle, gall.

ANT. *Allay, soothe, pacify, appease, conciliate, mollify.*

Incentive. Inducement, incitement, spur, impulse, stimulant, goad, motive, cause, encouragement, rousing, excitation.

ANT. *Deterrent, prohibition, warning, discouragement, dissuasion.*

Inception. Beginning, inauguration, commencement.

ANT. *Ending, finis, conclusion, termination.*

Incessant. Ceaseless, continual, unceasing, unremitting, perpetual, constant, everlasting, eternal, uninterrupted, unintermittent.

ANT. *Periodic, occasional, intermittent, interrupted.*

Incidence. Impact, stroke, impingement.

ANT. *Reflection, resilience, rebound.*

Incident, *n.* Event, occurrence, circumstance, chance, accident, fact, adventure, casualty.

ANT. *Cause, antecedent, reason, tendency, inducement, influence.*

Incident, Incidental, *a.* Happening, liable; belonging, pertaining, appertaining, natural, relating; falling, impinging; casual, occasional, pertinent, fortuitous, concurrent, concomitant, accidental.

ANT. *Regular, systematic, disconnected, independent, irrelative, inherent, essential, immanent, invariable, uniform.*

Incipient. Beginning, inchoate, commencing, embryonic.

ANT. *Final, terminal.*

Inclemency. Harshness, severity, rigor, roughness, boisterousness, storminess, tempestuousness.

ANT. *Clemency, mildness, leniency, gentleness.*

Inclement. Harsh, tyrannical, cruel, unmerciful, severe, rigorous, stormy, rough, boisterous.

ANT. *Benign, clement, mild, genial, merciful.*

Inclination. Inclining, slope, leaning, slant; trend, verging, obliquity; disposition, predilection, bent, bias, proclivity, proneness, tendency, leaning, aptitude, propensity; desire, wish, fondness, liking, partiality; aptness, attachment, affection.

ANT. *Tangency, disinclination, divergence, ineptitude, inaptness, dislike.*

Incline, *v.* Slant, lean, slope; trend, verge, tend; be disposed, have a desire *or* propensity; dispose, predispose, turn, bias; bend, bow; bear, dip, induce, prompt.

ANT. *Deter, restrain, check; ascend, rise; indispose, disincline.*

Include. Hold, contain; comprise, embody, comprehend, embrace, take in.

ANT. *Exclude, leave out.*

Inclusive. Enclosing, encircling; including, comprehending, embracing; comprehensive, additive, implied.

ANT. *Exclusive, excepted; adversative, opposite, contrary, antithetical.*

Income. Revenue, profits, gains; proceeds, pay, allowance.

ANT. *Expenditure, disbursement, outlay, expense.*

Incongruous. Inconsistent, unsuitable, absurd, conflicting, discordant, discrepant, repugnant, mismated, incompatible, inapposite, contrary, contradictory, inappropriate, inharmonious, ill-matched, irreconcilable, mismatched.

ANT. *Consistent, harmonious, suitable, accordant, agreeing, compatible.*

Increase, *n.* Accession, growth, extension, augmentation, addition, enlargement, expansion, increment; product, produce, gain, profit; offspring, issue, progeny, descendants.

ANT. *Deduction, detraction, diminution, contraction, loss, waste, detriment, curtailment, reduction, expenditure, impoverishment.*

Increase, *v.* Advance, heighten, pile up, enhance, aggregate, dilate, magnify, spread, augment, greaten, enlarge, raise; extend, prolong; aggravate, intensify; grow; multiply, be fruitful.

ANT. *Decrease, lessen, diminish, decline, abate, lower, reduce, curtail, retrench.*

Inculcate. Infuse, impress, enforce, instil, implant, ingraft, urge, teach.

ANT. *Insinuate, suggest, abjure, disavow, denounce.*

Incumbent. Obligatory, binding, devolving; lying, leaning, reclining, resting, weighing down, prone; coercive, indispensable, urgent; threatening, impending.

ANT. *Optional, discretional, elective, voluntary.*

Incur. Contract, become liable to; bring on; meet, run.

ANT. *Avoid, shun.*

Incursion. Inroad, raid, invasion, irruption, descent, foray, sally, encroachment.

ANT. *Encampment, retreat, abode, settlement.*

Indebted. Owing, obliged, beholden, under obligation.
ANT. *Disobliged, unbeholden.*

Indeed. Truly, really, verily, positively, absolutely, in fact, veritably, certainly, in truth; strictly, in point of fact.
ANT. *By no means, not at all.*

Indefatigable. Unwearied, untiring, persevering, persistent, assiduous, sedulous, unremitting, never-tiring, unflagging; incessant, indomitable.
ANT. *Idle, indifferent, indolent.*

Indelible. Ineffaceable, indestructible, ingrained, indefeasible, irreversible, persistent.
ANT. *Mutable, evanescent, transient, effaceable.*

Indemnify. Secure, save; compensate, remunerate, reimburse, requite; satisfy.
ANT. *Fine, mulct, amerce..*

Indicate. Show, denote, mark, betoken, signify, point out, designate, specify; evidence, evince, betray, manifest, declare.
ANT. *Conceal, misdirect, falsify, misindicate, negative, contradict.*

Indication. Indicating sign, mark, note, index, symptom, token, hint, suggestion, manifestation; evidence, demonstration, proof, prognostic.
ANT. *Silence, surmise, misdirection, undemonstrativeness, misguidance, misindication.*

Indictment. Indicting, presentment; accusation, charge, impeachment, arraignment, crimination.

Indifference. Neutrality, impartiality, disinterestedness; unconcern, apathy, coolness, negligence, carelessness, inattention, heedlessness; triviality, insignificance, unimportance; inferiority; insensibility, composure.
ANT. *Importance, interest, significance, weight, gravity, affection, ardor, eagerness.*

Indifferent. Neutral, unbiased, impartial, disinterested; cool, unconcerned, unmoved, cold, inattentive, apathetic, dead, regardless, heedless, unmindful; equal, all the same, all one, just the same; passable, tolerable, ordinary, middling, mediocre, rather poor; lukewarm, careless.
ANT. *Anxious, careful, susceptible, sympathetic, sensitive.*

Indigent. Poor, needy, destitute, necessitous, reduced, penniless, moneyless, distressed, insolvent, in want; impecunious, straitened.
ANT. *Wealthy, moneyed, rich, affluent, opulent.*

Indignation. Resentment, anger, ire, wrath, fury, rage, exasperation, choler; denunciation, displeasure, protestation.
ANT. *Gratification, admiration, approval, applause, complacency.*

Indignity. Insult, outrage, affront, slight, dishonor, abuse, disrespect, contumely, reproach, opprobrium, obloquy; rudeness, contemptuousness, ignominy, disgrace.
ANT. *Deference, compliment, honor, respect.*

Indiscriminate. Undistinguishing, undiscriminating; mixed, confused, mingled, promiscuous, indistinguishable; ill-assorted, undiscerning.
ANT. *Careful, sorted, select, discerning.*

Indisposed. Averse, disinclined, unwilling, reluctant, backward, loath; ill, ailing, sick.
ANT. *Prompt, willing, eager,*

desirous, inclined; healthful, sound.

Indite. Compose, write, dictate, pen; prompt, suggest, word, describe, phrase.

ANT. *Transcribe, copy, imitate, duplicate.*

Individual, *n.* Person, personage, character, some one; unit, single instance; personality.

ANT. *Species, genus, family, kind.*

Individual, *a.* Particular, special, separate, single, unique, one; peculiar, personal; positive, decided, unconventional, independent, specific, indivisible, singular, identical, idiosyncratic.

ANT. *General, common, collective, plural, universal.*

Individuality. Personality, distinct existence; character, decision, self-direction, originality, self-determination, uniqueness.

ANT. *Generality, mediocrity.*

Indolence. Laziness, sloth, inertness, idleness, sluggishness, slothfulness.

ANT. *Activity, energy.*

Indomitable. Unyielding, unconquerable, invincible; untamable, irrepressible, indefatigable.

ANT. *Effortless, feeble, languid.*

Indorse. Superscribe; sanction, approve, vouch for, confirm, ratify; accept.

ANT. *Protest, repudiate, renounce, abjure, cancel.*

Induce. Influence, impel, move, prompt, instigate, persuade, actuate, urge, incite, spur, prevail upon; cause, produce, effect, bring on.

ANT. *Prevent, disincline, dissuade, deter, hinder, restrain.*

Induction. Introduction, installation, inauguration, institution; conclusion, inference, generalization, inductive method; collection, collation, application.

ANT. *Statement, hypothesis; deduction; subtraction; principle, class, law, proposition, argumentation, discourse.*

Indulge. Gratify, yield, satisfy; humor, pamper, favor; allow, permit, suffer, cherish, foster, harbor; spoil, revel, grovel.

ANT. *Thwart, deny, disappoint, discard, contradict, renounce, counteract, mortify, abjure, discipline.*

Indulgence. Gratification, humoring, pampering; leniency, kindness, tenderness, favor, liberality.

ANT. *Abstinence, self-sacrifice, repression, restraint.*

Indulgent. Yielding, compliant; lenient, mild, clement, tolerant, gentle, kind, tender, forbearing.

ANT. *Harsh, severe, rough, austere, self-controlled, abstinent.*

Industrious. Diligent, active, busy, assiduous, engaged, employed, sedulous, occupied, laborious, hard-working; brisk, persistent, persevering.

ANT. *Lazy, shiftless, idle.*

Industry. Diligence, labor, application, assiduity, attention, constancy, exertion, intentness, patience, perseverance, persistence, sedulousness, pains, effort, activity, toil.

ANT. *Idleness, inattention, neglect, negligence, sloth, remissness, changeableness, indolence, inconstancy, inactivity, fickleness, ease, indiligence.*

Ineffable. Unspeakable, indescribable, inexpressible, unutterable; inconceivable, unsurpassable, undeclarable, exquisite, perfect.

ANT. *Common, trivial, superficial, vulgar, commonplace, conversational, colloquial, obvious.*

Inert. Inactive, lifeless, dead, passive, motionless; dull, indolent, torpid, lazy, idle, supine, sluggish, slothful; heavy, dormant.

ANT. *Active, alert, brisk, energetic, quick, vigorous.*

Inevitable. Necessary, unavoidable, infallible, certain, fixed, irresistible.

ANT. *Uncertain, avoidable, indeterminate.*

Infamy. Dishonor, shame, disgrace, discredit, ignominy, opprobrium, scandal, obloquy, abasement; villainy, disgracefulness, wickedness, atrocity, shamefulness; despair, degradation.

ANT. *Honor, reputation, renown, glory, celebrity.*

Infantile. Young, childish, tender; babyish, weak; childlike, babylike; puerile, imbecile.

ANT. *Manly, vigorous, mature, robust.*

Infatuation. Folly, stupefaction, foolishness, prepossession, obsession; fatuity, hallucination, madness, self-deception.

ANT. *Sagacity, soundness, wisdom, sanity, clear-sightedness.*

Infection. Contagion; contamination, taint, bane, pest, poison, corruption, defilement, vitiation, pollution.

ANT. *Purification, disinfection, antidote, antisepsis.*

Infectious. Contagious, catching, pestilential, pestiferous; contaminating, corrupting, defiling, polluting, poisoning, vitiating.

ANT. *Wholesome, sanative, beneficial, antiseptic.*

Infer. Deduce, conclude, gather, collect, consider probable; derive, argue.

ANT. *State, enunciate, assume, guess, conjecture, propound, anticipate, prognosticate.*

Inference. Conclusion, deduction, corollary, consequence; generalization, induction.

ANT. *Statement, proposition, enunciation.*

Inferiority. Subordination; deficiency, imperfection, minority, poverty, subjection, servitude, depression; mediocrity.

ANT. *Superiority, eminence, excellence, majority, elevation, independence, mastery, exaltation.*

Infernal. Hellish; diabolical, devilish, fiendish, demoniacal, satanic, atrocious, nefarious, dark, accursed, abominable.

ANT. *Angelic, cherubic.*

Infest. Throng, overrun, beset, swarm in; disturb, plague, annoy, tease, harass, trouble, molest, torment, worry, pester.

ANT. *Comfort, refresh, regale, gratify.*

Infidel. Unbeliever, disbeliever, atheist, denier, freethinker, deist, skeptic, heretic.

ANT. *Believer, pietist, devotee, Christian.*

Infidelity. Unbelief, disbelief, skepticism; faithlessness, unfaithfulness, disloyalty.

ANT. *Fidelity, belief, faith, religiousness, credulity, credulousness; faithfulness, loyalty.*

Infinite. Absolute, illimitable, limitless, boundless, interminable, eternal, unlimited, unnable, unmeasured, measureless, unfathomable, unconditioned, numberless, unbounded, immeasurable, innumerable, countless.

ANT. *Brief, bounded, relative, short, limited, finite, restricted, transient, transitory, small, little, evanescent, circumscribed, measurable, moderate, narrow, shallow; infinitesimal.*

Infinitesimal. Minute, atomic, microscopic, inappreciable, inconspicuous, undiscernible, infinitely small.

ANT. *Enormous, vast, infinite, immeasurable.*

Infinitude, Infinity. Boundlessness, vastness, immensity; infiniteness; eternity, absoluteness, self-determination, self-existence.

ANT. *Relativity.*

Infirm. Weak, feeble, frail, debilitated, enfeebled, weakened; faltering, wavering, irresolute, vacillating; unsound, unstable, insecure; decrepit, lame, failing, impotent.

ANT. *Sound, forcible, firm, strong, sure, cogent, healthy, healthful.*

Infirmity. Weakness, decrepitude, debility, feebleness, frailness, frailty; foible, fault, failing, defect; disease, malady, unsoundness.

ANT. *Strength, vigor, unhealthfulness, soundness.*

Inflame. Excite, stimulate, incite, enkindle, rouse, animate, inspirit, work up, fire; irritate, exasperate, anger, nettle, provoke, enrage, incense, madden, infuriate; fan, embitter.

ANT. *Quench, extinguish, allay, cool, pacify, quiet.*

Inflate. Distend, expand, swell, bloat, blow up; puff up, make conceited; increase, enlarge.

ANT. *Exhaust, empty, flatten, squeeze, compress.*

Inflated. Distended, swollen bloated; tumid, turgid, bombastic, stilted, declamatory rhetorical, sophomorical, high flown; pompous.

ANT. *Simple, plain, unaffected, concise, laconic, explicit brief.*

Inflection. Bend, bending, curvature, flexure, crook; variation, declension, conjugation comparison; flexion.

ANT. *Straightness, directness, rectilinearity.*

Inflict. Impose, lay on, put on; afflict.

ANT. *Spare, remove, alleviate, suspend.*

Infliction. Imposition, inflicting; punishment, judgment; grievance, trouble, nuisance.

ANT. *Remission, sparing; pleasure, gratification; accommodation, condoning.*

Influence, *n.* Authority, ascendency, control, predominance, sway; reputation, weight of character, credit; influx, inflow; effect, causation, impulse, affection, power, weight, prestige.

ANT. *Inefficiency, ineffectiveness, inefficacy, nullity, inoperativeness, neutrality.*

Influence, *v.* Induce, incite, incline, persuade, move, stir, actuate, sway, compel, urge, instigate, prompt, lead, impel, excite, drive, draw, direct, bias.

ANT. *Prevent, restrain, retard, deter, discourage, impede, inhibit, hinder, dissuade.*

Influential. Potent, powerful, controlling; efficacious, persuasive, forcible, guiding, considerable; authoritative.

ANT. *Weak, ineffective, inoperative, inconsiderable, unpersuasive.*

Inform. Quicken, animate, inspire; acquaint, apprise, mention to, notify, advise, tell; educate, enlighten, instruct, impart, communicate.

Ant. *Misinstruct, misjudge, deceive, hoodwink, misinform, mystify.*

Information. Advice, notice, intelligence; knowledge; accusation, complaint, denunciation; instruction, counsel, notification.

Ant. *Concealment, mystification, ignorance, occultation.*

Infringe. Transgress, violate, break, disobey, nullify.

Ant. *Preserve, observe, conserve, maintain.*

Infuse. Instil, inspire, introduce, inculcate, implant, diffuse, shed, steep, soak, water, infiltrate, insinuate, breathe into.

Ant. *Strain, dry, drain, divert, retract.*

Ingenious. Inventive, gifted, able, clever, bright, ready, sagacious, adept, skilful.

Ant. *Unskilful, uninventive, slow, unready, unresourceful, unprepared, unapt.*

Ingenuity. Inventiveness, ingeniousness, acuteness, skill, ability, readiness, faculty, aptitude, cunning, turn, gift, genius.

Ant. *Inability, ineptitude, clumsiness.*

Ingenuous. Artless, open, candid, frank, sincere, straightforward, honest, transparent, guileless, truthful, childlike, naive, noble, generous, honorable.

Ant. *Mean, reserved, sly, insincere, disingenuous.*

Ingratiate. Commend one's self into favor, insinuate, recommend.

Ant. *Alienate, estrange.*

Ingredient. Element, component, constituent.

Ant. *Refuse, residuum, incongruity, counteragent.*

Inherent. Sticking fast, adhering; essential, immanent, inborn, inbred, native, natural, subjective, innate, intrinsic, inhering, congenital, indispensable, indwelling, infixed, internal, ingrained, inseparable, inwrought.

Ant. *Extrinsic, superficial, fortuitous, casual, accidental, external, outward, superfluous, transient, unconnected, supplemental, incidental, subsidiary, superadded; foreign, extraneous, separable, temporary.*

Inherit. Get as legacy; occupy, possess, enjoy.

Ant. *Acquire, earn, gain, squander, bequeath, leave, demise, devise; dissipate, alienate.*

Inheritance. Inheriting; heritage, patrimony; bequest, possession, legacy.

Ant. *Acquisition, purchase, donation; forfeiture, lapse; escheatment, alienation.*

Inheritor. Heir, successor, legatee, devisee.

Ant. *Testator, devisor.*

Inimical. Antagonistic, hostile, unfriendly; adverse, opposed, contrary, repugnant, noxious, pernicious, hurtful, harmful.

Ant. *Friendly, companionable, comradely; unanimous, agreeable, beneficial.*

Iniquity. Injustice, wickedness, sin, unrighteousness; crime, offense, misdeed, grievance, evildoing.

Ant. *Justice, integrity, virtue, holiness, honesty, uprightness.*

Initiation. Introduction, entrance, admission; instruction;

opening, beginning, inauguration, commencement.

ANT. *Termination, completion, finish, fulfilment, outcome.*

Initiative. Commencement, beginning; power to originate *or* begin; start, leadership, example.

ANT. *Termination, wake, rear; prosecution, progress, perseverance, accomplishment.*

Injunction. Command, order, mandate, precept, exhortation.

ANT. *Disobedience, non-observance, non-compliance, insubordination.*

Injure. Maltreat, wrong, abuse; harm, damage, spoil, mar, disfigure, wound, cripple, sully.

ANT. *Benefit, profit, advantage, advance, repair.*

Injurious. Wrong, unjust, iniquitous; hurtful, detrimental, pernicious, deleterious, noxious, deadly, mischievous, baneful, fatal, destructive, damaging, ruinous, disadvantageous; libelous, slanderous; prejudicial.

ANT. *Helpful, advantageous, beneficial, salutary, profitable.*

Injury. Blemish, damage, evil, disadvantage, detriment, hurt, loss, wrong, prejudice, injustice, mischief, impairment, outrage, harm.

ANT. *Remedy, advantage, amelioration, benefit, service, boon, help, blessing, improvement, utility.*

Injustice. Wrong, unrighteousness, iniquity, grievance, unfairness, injury.

ANT. *Equity, fairness, justice, right, rectitude, integrity, honesty, impartiality, uprightness, lawfulness, righteousness, honor, faithfulness, fair play.*

Inlet. Opening, entrance, commencement, ingress.

ANT. *Outlet, egress, d[illegible]bouchure.*

Inmate. Occupant, dweller, denizen, inhabitant, tenant, resident.

ANT. *Visitor, intruder, foreigner, stranger, traveler.*

Inn. Hotel, public house, tavern.

Innate. Inherent, inborn, natural, inbred, native, congenital, organic.

ANT. *Unnatural, adventitious, assumed.*

Inner. Inmost, within, interior, secret, close, vital.

ANT. *Outer, outermost, exterior, open.*

Innocence. Harmlessness, inoffensiveness, innocuousness; sinlessness, purity, stainlessness, simplicity, guilelessness, guiltlessness, blamelessness.

ANT. *Guilt, offensiveness, contamination, sinfulness, impurity, guile, corruption.*

Innocent. Pure, sinless, virtuous, upright, stainless, right, faultless, guileless, clear, clean, blameless, guiltless, harmless, inoffensive, righteous, spotless, immaculate, innocuous.

ANT. *Criminal, culpable, immoral, guilty, blameworthy.*

Innocuous. Harmless, innocent, inoffensive, wholesome, innoxious.

ANT. *Hurtful, deleterious, insidious, obnoxious.*

Innovation. Change, alteration, novelty, reversal.

ANT. *Archaism, conservation, maintenance, old fashion, obsolescence.*

Inoculate. Vaccinate, impregnate, indoctrinate, instil, insert, imbue, ingraft, ingrain.

ANT. *Prune, divest; disabuse.*

Inquiry. Query, interrogation,

question, interrogatory; study, investigation, research, exploration, examination, scrutiny; asking, search.

ANT. *Guess, intuition, conjecture, assumption, supposition, hypothesis.*

Inquisitive. Curious, meddlesome, intrusive, searching, prying, inquiring, meddling, peeping, scrutinizing.

ANT. *Uninterested, unconcerned, careless, heedless, apathetic, inattentive, indifferent.*

Inroad. Incursion, foray, raid, irruption, encroachment, trespass, infringement, dragonnade.

ANT. *Occupation, sally, retreat, settlement, evacuation, excursion, egress.*

Insane. Crazy, lunatic, mad, deranged, demented, crazed, delirious.

ANT. *Sane, sound, sensible, quiet, composed, sober.*

Insanity. Delirium, dementia, frenzy, lunacy, mania, aberration, madness, alienation, derangement, monomania, hallucination, craziness.

ANT. *Sanity, clearness, rationality, lucidity, good sense, reason, intellect, intelligence.*

Inscribe. Write, engrave, impress, imprint; address, dedicate; label, letter, mark, delineate.

ANT. *Erase, efface, cancel, expunge, obliterate.*

Inscrutable. Incomprehensible, unsearchable, impenetrable, unintelligible, hidden, mysterious, untraceable, insolvable, profound.

ANT. *Obvious, intelligible, explainable, self-evident, familiar.*

Insert. Set in, place in, introduce.

ANT. *Exclude, follow, add.*

Inside. Within, internally.

ANT. *Without, outside, externally.*

Insidious. Artful, crafty, scheming, cunning, intriguing, tricky, designing; secret, deceptive.

ANT. *Straightforward, sincere, undesigning.*

Insinuate. Push slily, ingratiate; infuse, inculcate; hint, intimate, suggest; introduce, insert.

ANT. *Withdraw, extract, retract, alienate.*

Insipid. Tasteless, stale, flat; spiritless, heavy, stupid, uninteresting, prosaic, tame, prosy, dull, unentertaining, characterless, flavorless.

ANT. *Racy, interesting, engaging, piquant, spirited, lively.*

Insist. Demand, maintain, urge, contend, persist, press, persevere.

ANT. *Abandon, surrender, concede, yield, waive, forego.*

Insolence. Rudeness, contempt, disrespect, contumely; impertinence, pertness, impudence; frowardness, disobedience, insubordination; arrogance, assumption.

ANT. *Consideration, deference, modesty, respect, politeness, bashfulness.*

Insolvent. Bankrupt, penniless, beggared, ruined.

ANT. *Solvent, wealthy, flush, flourishing, thriving.*

Inspect. Examine, scrutinize, investigate, oversee, superintend, supervise, overhaul.

ANT. *Overlook, connive, dismiss, glance, pretermit.*

Inspector. Examiner, critic, visitor, superintendent, censor, supervisor.

Inspiration. Inhalation; afflatus, obsession; exaltation, enthusiasm, frenzy, impulse, revelation, intuition; insight, genius.

ANT. *Study, education, acquirement, learning, elaboration, observation, deduction.*

Instance. Request, impulse, instigation, incitement; solicitation, importunity, pressure, urgency; illustration, example, citation, case, exemplification, specification; entreaty, point, prompting, persuasion, occurrence.

ANT. *Dissuasion, warning, deprecation, reluctance; rule, principle, statement.*

Instant, *n.* Moment, twinkling, second, minute, flash, trice, jiffy; particular hour *or* moment.

ANT. *Period, time, cycle, duration; eternity, permanence, perpetuity.*

Instant, *a.* Immediate, instantaneous, quick; pressing, earnest, urgent; current, present, passing.

ANT. *Continuous, continual; perpetual, eternal.*

Instantly. Immediately, forthwith, directly, at once, presently, straightway.

ANT. *In the future, after a time.*

Instigate. Incite, impel, move, urge, prompt, provoke, stimulate, rouse, influence, encourage, persuade, prevail upon.

ANT. *Repress, restrain, discourage, withhold, retard.*

Instil. Infuse, insinuate; implant, enforce, impress, inculcate, import, introduce.

ANT. *Extract, remove, eliminate, eradicate, drain, extirpate.*

Instinct, *n.* Impulse, proclivity, tendency, inclination, prompting, intuition.

ANT. *Reason, deliberation, experience, judgment, elaboration, experiment.*

Instinctive. Natural, spontaneous; impulsive, unreflecting, voluntary, intuitive.

ANT. *Rational, cultivated, logical, judicious, reasonable, reasoning.*

Institute, *v.* Found, establish, originate, appoint, settle, fix, ordain, enact, pass; begin, commence; invest, instal, appoint, induct, organize.

ANT. *Subvert, degrade, deprive, disestablish.*

Institution. Establishment, investiture, custom, practice; college, school, academy, seminary, university.

Instruct. Teach, inform, train, educate, enlighten, indoctrinate; direct, command, order; acquaint, discipline, initiate.

ANT. *Misinform, misguide, mislead, deceive, neglect; brutalize; learn, study.*

Instruction. Teaching, education, training, schooling, information, discipline, tuition, advice, counsel, direction, precept, order, command, mandate.

ANT. *Misguidance, misinformation, misdirection; pupilage, obedience.*

Instrument. Tool, utensil, implement; agent, medium, machine; document, deed, writing, charter, indenture, record.

ANT. *Obstruction, bar, stop, preventive; counteragent, opponent, neutralizer; misapplication, counteraction.*

Instrumentality. Intervention, medium, means, agency, mediation; use, employment.

ANT. *Property, quality, virtue, force, efficacy; non-intervention, spontaneity; counteragency, neutralization.*

Insult, *n.* Offense affront, indignity, outrage, abuse, rudeness, dishonor, slight, disrespect.

ANT. *Respect, homage, compliment, deference.*

Insult, *v.* Outrage, offend, dishonor, abuse; provoke, mock, ridicule.

ANT. *Respect, salute, honor, compliment, flatter, praise.*

Insure. Make secure; assure; underwrite; provide, warrant, secure, guarantee, stabilitate.

ANT. *Imperil, jeopardize, shake, stake.*

Insurgent, *n.* Rebel, malcontent, mutineer, traitor, rioter.

ANT. *Patriot, adherent, supporter; ruler, magistrate.*

Insurgent, *a.* Rebellious, disobedient, mutinous, unruly, insubordinate, seditious.

ANT. *Obedient, loyal, patriotic.*

Insurrection. Rebellion, revolt, uprising, mutiny, sedition, riot, tumult, anarchy; pronouncement.

ANT. *Law, order, peace, subjection, obedience, submission, bondage, subsidence, acquiescence; government, pacification.*

Intact. Untouched, unhurt, unharmed, uninjured, scatheless; whole, entire, unbroken, undiminished; safe, inviolate, sacred, undefiled, uncorrupted, uncontaminated.

ANT. *Defiled, hurt, touched, injured, corrupt, affected, contaminated.*

Integrate. Unite, combine, consolidate, solidify, incorporate; sum, complete.

ANT. *Analyze, dismember, detach, remove, amputate, disintegrate.*

Integrity. Completeness, entirety, wholeness; honesty, rectitude, virtue, goodness, principle; uprightness, honor, probity, candor, truthfulness, conscientiousness.

ANT. *Fraud, meanness, rascality, duplicity, unfairness, underhandedness.*

Intellect. Reason, mind, sense, brains, understanding; consciousness, instinct; ability, genius, talent.

ANT. *Matter, mechanism, force; passion; spirit, soul.*

Intellectual. Mental, psychological, inventive, learned, cultured; philosophical, metaphysical.

ANT. *Illiterate, unlearned, ignorant.*

Intelligence. Knowledge, information, understanding, apprehension, discernment, acumen, penetration, quickness, brightness, comprehension; news, announcement, tidings, report, rumor, statement, notice, notification, publication, advice, instruction; intellect, spirit.

ANT. *Misinformation, misunderstanding; ignorance, concealment, stupidity, misapprehension, dulness, suppression, silence.*

Intelligible. Clear, plain, understandable, distinct, comprehensible, explainable, familiar, self-evident, obvious.

ANT. *Inscrutable, mysterious, hidden, insolvable, impenetrable, unfathomable.*

Intend. Design, resolve, mean, propose, purpose, contemplate, determine, meditate.

ANT. *Venture, risk, hazard, chance.*

Intense. Close, severe, strict, intent, strained; extreme; forcible, energetic, powerful; ardent, earnest, vehement, excessive, immoderate.

ANT. *Relaxed, easy, moderate, forceless, impotent, indifferent, cool, languid.*

Intensity. Intenseness, closeness, severity, strictness; tension, force, concentration, attention, strain; vehemence, violence, excess; ardor, energy, eagerness, power, vigor, activity, strength.

ANT. *Laxity, relaxation, debility, languor, coolness, indifference.*

Intent, *n.* Purpose, aim, object, design, end, meaning, intention, purport, scope, drift, view.

ANT. *Chance, lot, accident, fate.*

Intent, *a.* Eager, fixed, earnest, close, bent, set.

ANT. *Distracted, diverted, indifferent.*

Intention. Design, purpose, intent, meaning, purport.

ANT. *Chance, fortune, luck.*

Intentional. Deliberate, contemplated, designed, intended, studied, purposed, premeditated.

ANT. *Casual, accidental, undesigned, fortuitous.*

Inter. Bury, entomb, inhume.

ANT. *Exhume, disinter.*

Inter-. The synonyms and antonyms of words beginning with the prefix *inter-*, signifying *between, among, amidst, mutually,* may be obtained by adding this meaning to that of the synonyms and antonyms of the root word, in such cases as are of simple derivation.

Intercede. Mediate, arbitrate, interpose, plead, make intercession, advocate, interfere.

ANT. *Abandon, excuse, incriminate, inculpate.*

Intercept. Stop, cease; arrest, catch; obstruct, interrupt.

ANT. *Send, despatch, delegate, forward, commission, interchange.*

Intercourse. Converse, communication, communion, commerce, connection, correspondence, intimacy, dealing, intercommunication.

ANT. *Cessation, suspension, reticence, disconnection, interception.*

Interdict. Prohibit, forbid, proscribe, inhibit, restrain, stop, debar, disallow.

ANT. *Indulge, grant, allow, concede.*

Interest, *n.* Advantage, benefit, profit, good; part, portion; regards, sympathy, concern, attention, curiosity, selfishness, behalf, share; authority, influence; premium.

ANT. *Disadvantage, loss, inattention, unconcern, indifference; disconnection, repudiation.*

Interfere. Intermeddle, interpose; clash, conflict, intervene, be opposed.

ANT. *Withdraw, retract, retire, recede.*

Interior. Inside, internal, inner, inward, inland.

ANT. *Outside, exterior.*

Interloper. Intruder, meddler, supernumerary.

ANT. *Member, constituent.*

Intermediate. Intervening, interposed, interjacent, included, comprised, middle, moderate.

ANT. *Surrounding, enclosing, outside, embracing, circumjacent; extreme; exclusive.*

Interment. Burial, sepulture, inhumation.

ANT. *Exhumation, resurrection.*

Intermission. Suspension, interruption, stoppage, rest, stop, pause, suspense, respite, interlude, remission, cessation, discontinuance, interval, interregnum.

ANT. *Continuity, continuance, constancy, uninterruptedness, permanence, perpetuity.*

Intermit. Suspend, interrupt, relax, discontinue, break, stop, cease, abate, subside.

ANT. *Continue, prosecute; urge, despatch.*

Internal. Inner, interior, inside; within.

ANT. *Outer, exterior, outside.*

Internecine. Destructive, exterminating, deadly, inextinguishable, irreconcilable, mortal, internecinal.

ANT. *Desultory, incursive, marauding, skirmishing, buccaneering, guerilla, freebooting.*

Interpolate. Introduce, insert, foist in, intercalate; interlard, interweave, import, garble, intersperse, gloss.

ANT. *Expunge, erase, expurgate; verify, authenticate; elide.*

Interpose. Interfere, intercede, interrupt, mediate, meddle, arbitrate, intermeddle.

ANT. *Avoid, shun, retire, withdraw, hold aloof, let be, keep clear, stand aside.*

Interpret. Explain, define, expound, elucidate, unfold, decipher; translate, render, construe; declare, represent, solve.

ANT. *Mistake, misconceive, misunderstand, falsify, misinterpret, distort, misrepresent.*

Interpretation. Exposition, explanation, elucidation; version, construction, rendering, translation; sense, meaning, definition, signification, solution.

ANT. *Misinterpretation, misrendering; problem, text, difficulty.*

Interrogate. Question, ask, examine, inquire of, catechise.

ANT. *Affirm, answer, assert, indorse, pronounce.*

Interrupt. Disturb, stop, hinder, delay, interfere with; separate, disconnect, divide, sever, sunder, cut, dissolve; suspend, discontinue, break off; intersect.

ANT. *Continue, prosecute, expedite.*

Interstice. Crevice, hole, interval, chink, cleft, cranny, gap, crack, fissure, interspace.

ANT. *Seam, suture, stop-gap.*

Interval. Interstice; spell, season, period, term, intermediate time, interim, meantime, intermission, interspace, cessation.

ANT. *Continuity, uninterruptedness, simultaneousness.*

Intervention. Interposition, interference, intrusion, intercession, insinuation; agency, mediation.

ANT. *Continuance, non-interference.*

Interview. Meeting, parley, conference, consultation, colloquy, confabulation.

ANT. *Isolation, exclusion, independence, avoidance.*

Intestate. Unwilled, undevised, unbequeathed.

ANT. *Willed, bequeathed, devised.*

Intestine, *a.* Internal, domestic, interior, inward; civil; subjective.

ANT. *External, outward, foreign, federal; objective.*

Intimate, *n.* Confidant, associate, crony, familiar, companion, friend.

Intimate, *v.* Suggest, hint, insinuate, allude to, remind of;

announce, declare, communicate, tell.

ANT. *Conceal, reserve, withhold, repress.*

Intimate, *a.* Near, close, familiar, friendly, confidential; internal, interior, inward, deep-seated, hearty; thorough, complete, direct, exact; conversant.

ANT. *Distant, strange, unfamiliar; superficial.*

Intimidate. Frighten, alarm, scare, daunt, dismay, threaten, appal, terrify, deter, dishearten.

ANT. *Calm, compose; encourage, inspirit, animate, reassure.*

Intolerable. Insufferable, unendurable, insupportable, unbearable.

ANT. *Endurable, comfortable, tolerable, supportable, possible to be borne.*

Intolerant. Bigoted, unforbearing; extreme.

ANT. *Tolerant, forbearing, large-minded, indulgent.*

Intoxication. Inebriety, inebriation, drunkenness; excitement, infatuation, exhilaration, delirium, bewilderment, hallucination, ecstasy; poison, venom.

ANT. *Antidote, sobriety, sanity, gravity, melancholy, depression; abstinence, abstemiousness.*

Intrenchment. Ditch, dike, fortification, earthwork, moat; defense, protection, shelter, invasion, inroad, encroachment, infringement, trespass.

ANT. *Wall, rampart, mole, embankment, mound, bastion; forbearance, deference, respect.*

Intrepid. Bold, brave, fearless, undaunted, courageous, valorous, unterrified, dauntless, chivalrous, heroic, undismayed, unawed, valiant, doughty.

ANT. *Cautious, timid, fearful, cowardly, dismayed, terrified.*

Intricacy. Complexity, complication, entanglement, perplexity, difficulty, intricateness, obscurity, confusion.

ANT. *Directness, obviousness; system, method; disposition, array.*

Intricate. Involved, perplexed, complicated, entangled, complex; mazy, labyrinthine, tortuous.

ANT. *Simple, direct, obvious, plain, uninvolved.*

Intrigue. Plot, scheme, cabal, conspiracy, machination, artifice, cunning, duplicity, trickery, chicanery, ruse; liaison, amour.

ANT. *Insurrection, assault, rebellion, force, violence; sincerity, candor, honesty, openness, straightforwardness.*

Intrinsic. Inward, internal, essential, real, genuine, true, inherent, native, innate, natural, immanent, inbred, inborn.

ANT. *Extrinsic, acquired, apparent, accidental, borrowed, assumed, pretended, added, external, adventitious.*

Introduce. Lead in, usher in, present, conduct in, commence, make acquainted, make known, begin, preface.

ANT. *Come after, succeed, follow; end, conclude.*

Introduction. Introducing, presentation, ushering in; preface, prelude, preamble, proem, exordium; induction, importation, insertion, commencement, preliminary; portico, gate, vestibule, entrance.

ANT. *Eduction, ejection; extraction, exportation, elimination, estrangement; completion, conclusion, end; egress.*

Introductory. Prefatory, initia-

tory, preliminary, precursory, preparatory; commendatory.
ANT. *Final, conclusive, terminal, valedictory, supplemental; alienative.*

Intrude. Obtrude, encroach, infringe, trespass, trench, interfere, meddle.
ANT. *Withdraw, retire, recede; remove, retract.*

Intrusion. Encroachment, interference, intruding, obtrusion, infringement.
ANT. *Withdrawal, removal, retirement, retraction.*

Intuition. Apprehension, cognition, perception, beholding; instinct, insight, recognition.
ANT. *Information, instruction, learning, experience, acquirement, induction.*

Inundate. Flood, deluge, overflow, submerge, cover, overwhelm.
ANT. *Drain, dry, reclaim, desiccate, parch.*

Invade. Attack, infringe, violate, encroach on, trench upon; march into, enter in, assault, assail, occupy.
ANT. *Abandon, relinquish, vacate, evacuate.*

Invalid, *a.* Week, feeble, infirm, sick, frail; null, void; unsound, baseless, untrue, unfounded, fallacious.
ANT. *Strong, well, healthy, vigorous; sound, legal, constitutional; legitimate, authorized; genuine, true, correct, exact.*

Invalidate. Nullify, cancel, annul, overthrow, make void.
ANT. *Conserve, maintain, establish, confirm, enact, institute.*

Invasion. Trespass, incursion, irruption, encroachment, inroad.
ANT. *Evacuation, abandonment, relinquishment; settlement; retreat.*

Invective. Satire, sarcasm, diatribe, railing, abuse; obloquy, denunciation, vituperation, reproach, castigation.
ANT. *Praise, commendation, encomium, eulogy, panegyric.*

Invent. Discover, find out, devise, contrive, produce; design, concoct, elaborate; conceive, contrive, fabricate, originate, forge, frame.
ANT. *Copy, imitate, reproduce; execute.*

Invention. Contrivance, construction, device; fiction, fabrication, falsehood; thought, idea.
ANT. *Material.*

Inventive. Ingenious, skilful, clever, adept, resourceful.
ANT. *Slow, unskilful, uninventive.*

Inventor. Contriver, originator, author, creator.
ANT. *Destroyer.*

Inventory. List, catalogue, register, record, enrolment, enumeration.

Inversion. Reversal, transposition, alteration, deflection, violation, permutation.
ANT. *Erectness, verticality; stability, permanence, fixity, state, order, sequence; conservation.*

Invert. Upset, overthrow, reverse, subvert.
ANT. *Restore, set up, make upright.*

Invest. Clothe, dress, array, endow; attend, surround; lay out.
ANT. *Divest, dismantle, unclothe, strip, disrobe; deprive.*

Investigate. Inquire, examine, test, scrutinize, prove, search, explore, inspect, criticize, discuss, study.
ANT. *Conjecture, guess.*

Investigation. Search, examination, inquiry, research, exploration, inquisition, sifting, scrutiny, study.

ANT. *Discovery, clue, indication; solution, thread.*

Investiture. Installation, induction, investment, habilitation.

ANT. *Divestiture, divestment.*

Inveterate. Long-established, obstinate; malignant, spiteful, virulent; besetting, confirmed, chronic, ingrain, incarnate, habitual, deep-rooted, hardened, accustomed.

ANT. *Undeveloped, incipient, unformed.*

Invidious. Hateful, offensive, odious; unfair, partial, inconsiderate; gratuitous.

ANT. *Fair, just, considerate, impartial, due.*

Invigorate. Strengthen, brace, harden, nerve, refresh, stimulate, animate, exhilarate.

ANT. *Weaken, enfeeble, debilitate, deteriorate, relax, unstring, enervate.*

Invitation. Solicitation, allurement, enticement.

ANT. *Rebuff, snub, check, repulse.*

Invite. Ask, summon, bid, request, solicit, call, attract, entice, persuade, allure; tempt, incite, challenge.

ANT. *Repel, forbid, deprecate; exclude, discard.*

Invoke. Supplicate, implore, solicit, summon, call, beseech, invite, challenge, invocate, appeal to, conjure, imprecate.

ANT. *Defy; deprecate, deter; ignore, elude; warn, inhibit.*

Involution. Complication, entanglement; envelope; implication, mingling.

ANT. *Evolution, disconnection, evolvement, extrication, separation.*

Involve. Envelop, wrap, cover; comprise, embrace, contain; connect, unite, mingle, blend twine, interweave; implicate, entangle, complicate, embroil embarrass, include, overwhelm, imply.

ANT. *Extricate, remove, disconnect, separate, disentangle, distinguish, explicate.*

Inward. Secretly, privately; internal, interior, inner; within.

ANT. *Outward, external, exterior.*

Iota. Jot, tittle, particle, atom.

ANT. *Whole, mass.*

Irate, Irascible. Hasty, angry, enraged, incensed, choleric, irritable.

ANT. *Good-tempered, calm, forbearing, gentle, mild.*

Ire. Anger, wrath, rage, fury, choler, indignation, resentment, displeasure, vexation.

ANT. *Good will, patience, forbearance, mildness, forgiveness, reconciliation, peaceableness.*

Irridescent. Prismatic; opaline, polychromatous, nacreous.

ANT. *Blanched, neutral, colorless, dingy, achromatic.*

Isolate. Separate, detach, dissociate; insulate.

ANT. *Associate, unite.*

Isolation. Separation, loneliness, segregation, detachment, disconnection, insulation; solitariness, solitude.

ANT. *Organization, community, co-membership, connection; continuity, concatenation.*

Issue. Egress, exit, outlet; delivery; copy, number, edition, impression; event, outcome, result, end, conclusion, consummation, effect, termination; children, offspring, posterity, progeny; antagonism, controversy, contest.

ANT. *Cause, principle, in-*

fluence, action, working, operation; law, system, commencement; ancestry, paternity.

Iteration. Recital, repetition, reiteration, recurrence, harping, succession.
ANT. *Single statement.*

Itinerant, *a.* Traveling, wandering, roving, roaming, journeying, unsettled, nomadic.
ANT. *Stationary, domestic, settled, fixed, local.*

Itinerary. Guide, guidebook, schedule.

J

Jade, *v.* Tire, weary, fatigue, exhaust, fag; worry, harass, oppress.
ANT. *Refresh, recruit, invigorate, inspirit.*

Jagged. Notched, indented, uneven, ragged.
ANT. *Smooth.*

Jangle, *n.* Jargon, babel, bickering, wrangle, quarrel, squabble, contention.
ANT. *Argument, discourse, debate.*

Jar, *v.* Shake, agitate; clash, interfere; wrangle, quarrel, contend, bicker, spar, squabble, jangle.
ANT. *Agree, harmonize, accord, concur.*

Jargon. Gabble, gibberish; nonsense, twaddle, flummery, trash, stuff, gabble; slang; lingo, patois.
ANT. *Speech, conversation; discourse, oration; literature.*

Jaundiced. Biased, prejudiced, warped, prepossessed; bilious.
ANT. *Unprejudiced, unbiased.*

Jaunty. Airy, showy, finical, fluttering, gay, fine, bedizened, flighty, fantastic, flaunting.
ANT. *Staid, sober, sedate, dignified, demure.*

Jealous. Envious, suspicious, resentful, covetous, invidious; anxious, apprehensive, solicitous, zealous, watchful.
ANT. *Indifferent, genial, unenvious, liberal, self-denying.*

Jealousy. Suspicion, envy, rivalry, solicitude.
ANT. *Vigilance, watchfulness, magnanimity, generousness, friendliness; certainty.*

Jeer, *v.* Scoff, taunt, jibe, sneer, flout, mock, jest, deride, banter.
ANT. *Flatter, compliment, praise; adulate, fawn, cringe.*

Jejune. Empty, barren, meager, dry, sterile, bare, lean, uninteresting, thin, scant, poverty-stricken, poor, void.
ANT. *Full, rich, exuberant, racy, interesting, overwrought, redundant, abundant.*

Jeopardy. Hazard, peril, risk, danger, venture.
ANT. *Security, safety, insurance, provision.*

Jest, *n.* Joke, witticism, quip, sally, raillery, fun, sport.
ANT. *Seriousness, gravity, earnest.*

Jest, *v.* Joke, sport, rally, banter, ridicule, mock, grin.
ANT. *Preach, sermonize.*

Jocose. Humorous, facetious, witty, droll, funny, comical, jocular, sportive, merry, waggish.
ANT. *Melancholy, serious, earnest, grave, lugubrious.*

Jocund. Joyous, joyful, merry, frolicsome, blithe, jolly, sportive, lively, playful, airy, gay, debonair, jovial, gleeful, careless, blithesome, mirthful, hilarious, sprightly, vivacious.

ANT. *Melancholy, dull, sorrowful, grave, mournful, cheerless, rueful, doleful, careworn, woful.*

Join. Add, attach, annex; connect, couple, link, unite, conjoin, cement; adjoin, be adjacent to, connect with; associate with, confederate, league.

ANT. *Separate, disconnect, disjoin, subtract, sever.*

Joint. Juncture, union; flexure, elbow, knee, articulation.

ANT. *Disconnection, continuity, uniformity, solution, disjunction.*

Jollification. Revelry, conviviality, festivity, revel, carousal, wassail, carouse, fun, carnival.

ANT. *Weariness, tedium, tediousness, soberness, monotony.*

Jolly. Merry, joyous, gay, jovial, mirthful, jocund, sportive, jocular, funny, sprightly, facetious, waggish, blithe, blithesome, cheery, cheerful; portly, bouncing, stout, plump.

ANT. *Sad, mournful, cheerless, mirthless, joyless, lugubrious, gloomy, morose.*

Jostle. Push, crowd, hustle, collide, strike against; shake, incommode, joggle, jog, jolt.

ANT. *Clear, lead, convoy, escort, pilot, precede, extricate, attend.*

Jot. Iota, whit, tittle, particle, atom, grain, bit, mite, scrap, scintilla, cipher, trifle, idea, thought, morsel, fraction.

ANT. *World, mass, volume, heap, bulk.*

Journey. Travel, transit, expedition, excursion, tour, voyage, trip, pilgrimage.

ANT. *Sojourn, tarrying, delay, stop, stay, abiding, stopover.*

Jovial. Merry, joyous, gay, festive, mirthful, jolly, gleeful, hilarious, genial, convivial.

ANT. *Ungenial, gloomy, lugubrious, melancholy, saturnine.*

Joviality. Merriment, jollity, mirth, hilarity, gaiety, frolic, fun.

ANT. *Sadness, seriousness, soberness.*

Joy. Gladness, delight, pleasure, happiness, transport, felicity, exultation, ecstasy, bliss, rapture, gaiety, hilarity, glee, beatitude, ravishment.

ANT. *Sorrow, grief, melancholy, affliction, tears, depression, despondency, pain, misery, trouble, despair.*

Joyful. Glad, joyous, merry, jubilant, jocund, happy, jolly, jovial, elate, elated, delighted, buoyant.

ANT. *Grave, solemn, mournful, sad, melancholy, lugubrious.*

Jubilant. Rejoicing, exultant, triumphant, joyous, festive, exulting, congratulatory.

ANT. *Doleful, sorrowful, remorseful, wailing, penitent, lugubrious.*

Jubilee. Festival, season of rejoicing, feast, holiday, festivity, revel, carnival, merriment.

ANT. *Fast, mourning, humiliation, penitence.*

Judge. Justice, referee, arbiter, arbitrator, umpire; magistrate, authority; critic, connoisseur.

ANT. *Criminal, novice, tyro, ignoramus.*

Judgment. Discernment, estimate, award, criticism, understanding, discrimination, intelligence, taste, sagacity, penetration, wisdom, brains, prudence, sense; determination, decision, opinion, notion, conclusion; judiciousness, intellect; verdict, sentence, reward, condemnation.

ANT. *Argument, speculation, inquiry, proposition, investigation, consideration, evidence, pleading, pronouncement; fickleness, insagacity, impulsiveness.*

Judicial. Just, well-balanced, deliberative; juridical, forensic.

ANT. *Legislative, executive,* or *administrative; impulsive.*

Judicious. Discreet, wise, prudent, sagacious, sensible, reasonable, rational, sober, sound, staid, politic, enlightened, well-considered, well-chosen; discerning, thoughtful.

ANT. *Silly, imprudent, indiscreet, ill-judged, inexpedient, rash, impolitic, blind, foolish.*

Juggle, *v.* Cheat, conjure, impose, trick, practice jugglery, deceive, defraud; bamboozle, beguile, swindle, mystify, mislead, overreach.

ANT. *Expose, enlighten, undeceive; detect, reveal, correct.*

Jumble, *n.* Confusion, disorder, hodge-podge.

ANT. *Order, system, neatness, arrangement.*

Jump, *v.* Leap, skip, bound, hop, spring, vault, caper; bounce, jolt, overleap; coincide, agree, accord.

ANT. *Walk, pace, promenade; dance.*

Junction. Joining, union, combination, coalition, connection, linking, coupling; joint, juncture, angle; fastening, attachment; alliance, confederacy.

ANT. *Division, separation, disconnection, hiatus, chasm, uncoupling, disunion; continuity.*

Jungle. Thicket, brake, wilderness, labyrinth, underbrush, entanglement.

ANT. *Open, clearing; order, arrangement, system.*

Junior. Younger; subordinate, less advanced.

ANT. *Senior, elder, older; more advanced, superior.*

Jurisdiction. Right, authority, sphere, judicature, legal power; government, control, sway, administration, magistracy.

ANT. *Immunity, exemption, freedom, independence.*

Just. Upright, righteous, honest, true, conforming to justice; exact, normal, reasonable, due; equitable, fair, impartial, right, rightful, lawful; fair-minded, blameless, honorable, straightforward, virtuous, uncorrupt; accurate, correct; deserved, fit, merited, appropriate, suitable, happy, proper, harmonious.

ANT. *Evil, untrue, unjust, dishonest, prejudiced, unfair, unreasonable, partial, unlawful, unequitable; blameworthy, corrupt, dishonorable; inaccurate, incorrect; undeserved, unfit, inappropriate, inharmonious.*

Justice. Legality, equity, rectitude, fairness, law, lawfulness, right, truth, uprightness, virtue, fair play, faithfulness, impartiality, integrity, righteousness; reasonableness, desert, propriety.

ANT. *Injustice, dishonesty, favoritism, partiality, wrong, unlawfulness, unfairness, unreasonableness.*

Justification. Vindication, defense, exoneration, exculpation; absolution; apology, advocacy, plea, maintenance.

ANT. *Censure, condemnation, conviction, implication, crimination, inculpation.*

Justify. Vindicate, maintain, defend; absolve, clear, exonerate; pardon, exculpate; adjust; excuse.

ANT. *Condemn, convict, censure, criminate.*

Justness. Exactness, propriety, correctness, accuracy, exactitude, strictness, fidelity, nicety.

ANT. *Incorrectness, inexactness, slovenliness.*

Juvenile. Young, youthful, puerile, childish, boyish, girlish, infantine, immature, adolescent.

ANT. *Mature, elderly, aged, senile, adult, manly, womanly, superannuated.*

Juxtaposition. Nearness, contiguity, adjacency, proximity, contact.

ANT. *Distance, remoteness, separateness; opposition.*

K

Keen. Sharp; acute; bitter, severe, piercing, stinging; eager, vehement, fierce; prompt, ardent, cutting, biting, sarcastic, penetrating, satirical, shrewd; poignant, acrimonious, caustic; discerning, quick, astute.

ANT. *Blunt, dull, languid, blind, indifferent, obtuse, undiscerning, slow, simple.*

Keep. Retain, hold, reserve, detain, preserve, restrain, withhold, maintain, support, sustain, continue, guard, protect, adhere to, obey, fulfil; celebrate, honor, conduct, commemorate, solemnize; haunt, frequent; observe, perform; conceal, suppress; hinder, prevent, refrain.

ANT. *Release, speed, liberate, send, dismiss; neglect, betray, abandon, discard; disregard, disobey, transgress, forsake, desert, forget.*

Keeping. Charge, guardianship, custody, care; holding, preservation, restraint; maintenance, support, feed, provision; harmony, consistency, congruity, conformity, agreement.

ANT. *Neglect, abuse, disregard; abandonment, destruction; nonsupport, betrayal; disagreement, incongruity.*

Keepsake. Souvenir, token, remembrancer.

Ken. Sight, view, cognizance, knowledge, survey, range.

ANT. *Ignorance, oversight, inexperience, inobservance.*

Kernel. Seed, grain; nucleus; core, gist.

ANT. *Peeling, meat, shell, husk.*

Key. Lock opener; clue, guide, solution, explanation; keynote, tonic; wedge, clamp; lever.

ANT. *Mystification, confusion, mystery, secret, problem.*

Kick. Strike *or* thrust at with the foot; recoil; resist, rebel, spurn, be calcitrant.

ANT. *Caress, soothe, flatter, obey.*

Kill. Murder, massacre, assassinate, butcher, execute, despatch, slay, slaughter, put to death.

ANT. *Resuscitate, vivify, reanimate, revivify, quicken, enliven.*

Kin. Family, birth, blood, consanguinity, descent, race, relationship, kind, kindred, affinity, alliance.

ANT. *Strangership, inaffinity, alienage, foreignership.*

Kind, *n.* Race, family, species, breed, class, genus; character, sort, variety, nature, fashion, description, denomination, designation.

ANT. *Dissimilarity, differentiation.*

Kind, *a.* Benign, indulgent, humane, compassionate, gentle, tender, beneficent, propitious, generous, forbearing, lenient, bounteous, clement, mild, good, obliging, bland, friendly, amicable, philanthropic, charitable, sympathetic, affectionate, tender-hearted,

ANT. *Harsh, severe, hard, cruel, unkind, rough, stern, forbidding, austere, crabbed, illiberal.*

Kindle. Light, ignite, inflame, enkindle, set on fire; excite, arouse, awaken, stir up, stimulate, incite, animate, foment; exasperate, provoke, enrage.

ANT. *Quench, suppress, extinguish, allay.*

Kindness, Kindliness. Benevolence, humanity, charity, sympathy, compassion, amiability, good nature; mildness, gentleness, softness.

ANT. *Harshness, cruelty, severity, sternness, roughness, austerity.*

Kindred, *n.* Relationship, consanguinity, affinity; relations, kin, kith and kin, relatives, kinsmen, kinsfolk.

ANT. *Disconnection, unrelatedness; strangers, foreigners.*

Kindred, *a.* Related, cognate, akin, allied, congenial; responsive, sympathetic.

ANT. *Unrelated, uncongenial, unallied; different, unresponsive.*

Kingdom. Empire, monarchy, sovereignty, domain, dominion.

Kingly. Regal, royal, monarchical, imperial, august, sovereign, noble, splendid, magnificent, imposing, grand, majestic.

ANT. *Plebeian, humble, popular, commonplace, simple, vulgar.*

Knack. Toy, plaything, gimcrack; dexterity, skill, adroitness, facility, aptness, aptitude, expertness, quickness.

ANT. *Clumsiness, awkwardness, ineptitude.*

Knave. Villain, rascal, rogue, scoundrel, cheat, scamp, miscreant, swindler, scapegrace.

ANT. *Gentleman, hero; gull, dupe, simpleton.*

Knavish. Trickish, cheating; mischievous, roguish, waggish; fraudulent, villainous.

ANT. *Honest, upright, honorable.*

Knot, *n.* Tie, bond, intricacy, connection; entanglement, complication; joint; group, band, clique, gang, crew.

ANT. *Loosening, unfastening, unraveling, dispersion; solution, simplification; evenness, smoothness; individual.*

Knotty. Knotted, difficult, intricate, perplexed, tough, hard, complicated.

ANT. *Plain, simple, obvious, easy, smooth, uninvolved.*

Know. Perceive, apprehend, understand; be convinced *or* assured; acquaint, recognize; distinguish, comprehend.

ANT. *Be ignorant* or *illiterate, overlook, misunderstand, misconstrue.*

Knowing. Intelligent, skilful, competent, well-informed, proficient, qualified, experienced, accomplished; conscious, percipient, thinking; cunning, expressive, significant; shrewd, astute, discerning, sagacious.

ANT. *Simple, innocent, gullible, stolid, silly; dull, stupid, inefficient; unresponsive, nonsuggestible.*

Knowledge. Learning, wisdom, scholarship, science, comprehension, cognition, erudition, intelligence, light, lore, perception, recognition, acquaintance, intuition, experience, information, apprehension, notice, understanding, conversance, cognizance, familiarity, instruction, enlightenment; acquirements, attainments.

ANT. *Ignorance, illiteracy, unfamiliarity, rudeness, inexperience, misapprehension, misconception, misunderstanding.*

L

Labor, *n.* Toil, exertion, work, effort, task, travail; drudgery, industry, painstaking; burden, duties.

ANT. *Ease, indolence, rest, respite, recreation, refreshment, vacation, inactivity, laziness.*

Labored. Elaborate, studied, highly wrought, overwrought, stiff, heavy.

ANT. *Easy, natural, simple.*

Laborer. Workman, operative, workingman, hand, employee, bread-winner.

ANT. *Employer.*

Laborious. Toilsome, difficult, tiresome, onerous, wearisome, fatiguing, arduous, hard, burdensome, tedious, irksome; industrious, diligent, toiling, assiduous, hard-working, painstaking, sedulous, indefatigable, active.

ANT. *Easy, light, simple, facile, feasible; lazy, indolent, indiligent, idle.*

Labyrinth. Maze, confusion, intricacy, windings; perplexity, complexity, bewilderment, involutions; difficulty.

ANT. *Simplicity, calm, perspicacity; insight, understanding.*

Lack, *n.* Deficiency, want, need, destitution, failure, scantiness, dearth, scarcity, fault, deficit, shortness, insufficiency.

ANT. *Plenty, fulness, abundance, supply, sufficiency, competence, satisfaction.*

Laconic, Laconical. Short, epigrammatic, brusk, brief, concise, pithy, sententious, terse, curt.

ANT. *Wordy, tedious, prolix, diffuse, prosy, loquacious, garrulous.*

Laggard, *n.* Loiterer, lingerer, sluggard, saunterer, dawdler, idler.

Laical. Laic, lay, unprofessional; secular, temporal; civil, non-legal.

ANT. *Clerical, professional, theological, sacred, divine, ecclesiastic, ministerial, priestly, canonical, legal, sacerdotal.*

Laity. Laymen, the people.

ANT. *Clergy, professional people.*

Lame. Hobbling, crippled, limping; inefficient, imperfect, defective; weak, feeble, poor, unsatisfactory, insufficient; halt, faltering, impotent.

ANT. *Robust, strong, potent, efficient, cogent, effective, convincing, telling, satisfactory.*

Lament, *v.* Mourn, bemoan, bewail, deplore, sorrow over, regret, grieve.
  ANT. *Rejoice, enjoy, hail, welcome.*

Language. Idiom, speech, dialect, tongue, patois, barbarism, diction, expression, vernacular, vocabulary, mother tongue, phraseology, discourse, conversation, talk; articulation, accents; style, utterance, voice.
  ANT. *Jargon, gibberish, cry, howl, roar; speechlessness, inarticulateness, muteness, dumbness.*

Languid. Drooping, indisposed, inanimate, feeble, weak, faint, sickly, pining, weary, listless, heavy, dull, exhausted, heartless; enervated, flagging, spiritless, unnerved, unbraced.
  ANT. *Strong, vigorous, robust, active, braced, healthy, energetic, animated, alert.*

Languish. To be languid, pine, droop, sink, faint, decline.
  ANT. *Luxuriate, thrive, prcsper, flourish, bloom.*

Languor. Feebleness, weakness, faintness, weariness, lassitude, listlessness, heaviness, dullness.
  ANT. *Strength, vigor, energy, freshness, lithesomeness.*

Lank. Slender, thin, shrunken, lean, loose, slim, long, lax.
  ANT. *Plump, fat, chubby, short, full, rounded.*

Lapse, *n.* Slipping, falling, slip, fault; termination, failure; escheatment, flow, flux, progress, reversion, elapsing; apostasy.
  ANT. *Stability, fixedness, retention, fixture, stoppage, uprightness; inheritance, possession.*

Large. Colossal, ample, broad, bulky, extensive, vast, massive, spacious, wide, commodious, enormous, coarse, grand, long, gigantic, immense, huge, great, big, capacious, considerable, abundant; diffuse, comprehensive, profuse, plentiful, populous, copious, liberal; enlightened, catholic.
  ANT. *Circumscribed, illiberal, contracted, niggardly, sordid, bigoted; small, little, microscopic, mean, minute, tiny, slender, trifling, trivial, diminutive, inconsiderable, slight, infinitesimal, limited, short, insignificant, scanty, petty, narrow, paltry.*

Lash, *v.* Strike, whip, scourge, flog, beat, tie, fasten; censure, satirize, castigate.
  ANT. *Soothe, smooth, caress; eulogize, compliment, extol.*

Lassitude. Languor, weariness, weakness, debility, inertia.
  ANT. *Energy, strength, robustness, vigor, freshness.*

Last, *v.* Continue, endure, persist, remain, hold, abide, live.
  ANT. *End, stop, terminate, depart, fade, cease, fail, die.*

Last, *a.* Final, hindmost, farthest; next, past; highest *or* lowest, supreme, utmost; most unlikely, least fit; latest, final, concluding, ultimate.
  ANT. *First, foremost, opening, introductory, initiatory; ensuing, next, nearest.*

Lasting. Durable, permanent, unending, enduring, abiding, perpetual.
  ANT. *Temporary, transient, ephemeral, momentary, occasional, periodic, recurrent.*

Late. Slow, tardy; deceased, departed; far advanced; recent; not long past; delayed.
  ANT. *Early, coming, present, future, forthcoming, existing.*

Lately. Recently, of late, not far past, but just.

ANT. *Formerly, remotely, distantly* in past *or* future.

Latent. Hidden, secret, invisible, dormant, unobserved, concealed, inapparent, potential, implicit, undeveloped, inherent.

ANT. *Visible, explicit, apparent, exposed, developed, active, conspicuous, manifest.*

Lateral. At the side, oblique; indirect, secondary, resultant, parallel, incidental.

ANT. *Direct, primary, immediate, lineal.*

Latter. Later, modern, more recent; last, final.

ANT. *Former, previous, ancient; penultimate.*

Laudable. Praiseworthy, commendable.

ANT. *Blameworthy, execrable.*

Laughter. Laughing, mirth, merriment, glee; derision, ridicule, contempt.

ANT. *Weeping, tears, sorrow, mourning, lamentation; respect, veneration, admiration.*

Launch, *v.* Hurl, throw, let fly; set afloat; start, propel, move; expatiate, enlarge.

ANT. *Recall, repress, retain; ignore, avoid, shun.*

Lavish, *a.* Profuse, prodigal; superabundant, excessive, extravagant, bountiful, wasteful.

ANT. *Sparing, economical, close, niggardly, chary.*

Law. Code, canon, edict, decree, order, mandate, legislation, ordinance, rule, regulation, jurisprudence, enactment, command, commandment, economy, formula, polity, principle, statute; mode, method, sequence, adjudication, jurisdiction.

ANT. *Misrule, anarchy, disorder, insubordination, rebellion; caprice, chance, irregularity, accident, casualty.*

Lawful. Conformable to law, legitimate, competent, constituted, authorized; legal, constitutional, rightful, regular; permissible, orderly, right, allowable, fair.

ANT. *Illegal, impermissible, unlawful, wrong.*

Lawless. Contrary to law, illegal; unrestrained, unregulated; wild, rebellious, savage, disorderly.

ANT. *Peaceful, law-abiding, loyal, civilized, honest, tractable, well-disposed.*

Lawyer. Counselor, attorney, counsel, advocate.

ANT. *Client.*

Lax. Slack, vague, unconfined; dissolute, licentious; incoherent; unprincipled, loose, remiss, flabby.

ANT. *Concise, strict, rigid, coherent, compact; conscientious, principled.*

Lay. Put, place, establish, deposit, arrange, spread, dispose, set down; allay, prostrate.

ANT. *Raise, erect, lift up; excite, disorder, disarrange.*

Lazy. Shirking, idle, inactive, slothful, slow, sluggish.

ANT. *Industrious, energetic, active, assiduous.*

Lead, *n.* Guidance, direction, initiative, control; precedence, priority, preëminence.

ANT. *Following, submission, subordination; inferiority.*

Lead, *v.* Guide, conduct, direct, counsel; precede, draw, induce, entice, allure; convoy; commence, inaugurate; persuade, influence.

ANT. *Follow; dissuade, mislead, misguide; leave, abandon.*

Leader. Guide, conductor; director, chief, head.
ANT. *Follower, disciple.*

League. Alliance, compact, coalition, confederacy, confederation, bond, combination, union.
ANT. *Neutrality; divorce, disruption, disunion, secession, disconnection, alienation, dissolution.*

Lean, *v.* Incline, deviate, bend, rest, rely on; conform; tend, depend, hang; slope; repose, confide.
ANT. *Support, raise, erect, stabilitate, rise, straighten.*

Lean, *a.* Slender, spare, meager, thin, lank, gaunt, skinny, bare, scant, barren, mean; shriveled, emaciated, bony, scraggy.
ANT. *Fat, plump, brawny, well-conditioned, obese, stout.*

Leaning. Tendency, proclivity, propensity, bias, liking, partiality, inclination.
ANT. *Loathing, aversion, repugnance, avoidance, dislike.*

Leap, *v.* Jump, vault, spring, bound, hop, bounce.
ANT. *Walk, dive, swim, run.*

Learn. Acquire, imbibe, attain, collect, know, gather, understand, study.
ANT. *Forget, lose; teach, instruct.*

Learned. Erudite, versed, well-informed, scholarly, skilled, literary, conversant, read.
ANT. *Ignorant, unlearned, illiterate, unscholarly.*

Learner. Pupil, scholar, student, disciple, novice.
ANT. *Teacher, professor, authority, adept, master, doctor.*

Learning. Knowledge, erudition, skill, literature, science, lore, letters, education, culture, tuition, acquirements, attainments, scholarship.
ANT. *Ignorance, illiteracy, boorishness, stupidity; inspiration, revelation.*

Least. Smallest, shortest, lowest, most unimportant, meanest, last.
ANT. *Greatest, longest, noblest, highest, most important, first, principal, main, leading, preëminent.*

Leave, *v.* Quit, abandon, give up, forego, resign, surrender, forbear; cease, stop, desist; depart, go from; bequeath.
ANT. *Persist, stay, hold, retain; continue; arrive.*

Legal. Authorized, legitimate, constitutional, licit, lawful, allowable.
ANT. *Illegal, unlawful, unconstitutional, lay, illegitimate.*

Legend. Chronicle; myth, fable; inscription, motto; hearsay, fiction.
ANT. *Fact, history, truth, verity.*

Legible. Distinct, plain, apparent, discernible, clear, manifest, decipherable, well-written.
ANT. *Illegible, cryptographic, cabalistic, undecipherable, obscure.*

Legitimate. Lawful, valid; authorized, real, genuine, licit, allowable, normal, standard.
ANT. *Illegitimate, unallowable, unfair, unauthorized, illicit, false.*

Leisure. Freedom, ease, vacation, convenience; opportunity, retirement, spare time.
ANT. *Occupation, employment, absorption, work, labor, constraint, engagement, business, toil.*

Leisurely. Deliberate, convenient, easy, sauntering.
ANT. *Hurried, hasty, difficult, speedy, industrious, assid-*

uous, eager, precipitate, expeditious.

Lend. Let, afford, furnish, loan, advance, grant.

ANT. *Refuse, withhold, retain, appropriate, withdraw; recall.*

Lengthen. Elongate, stretch, extend, prolong.

ANT. *Shorten, contract, confine, narrow.*

Lengthy. Long, drawn out, tedious, verbose, diffuse, prolix.

ANT. *Concise, comprehensive, laconic, short, brief, condensed, succinct, compact.*

Lenient. Merciful, mild, relaxing, assuasive, softening, compassionate.

ANT. *Harsh, cruel, hard, severe, stern.*

Lessen. Diminish, reduce, decrease, abate, lower, impair, degrade, weaken.

ANT. *Increase, enlarge, extend, develop, heighten, multiply, strengthen, spread, enhance.*

Lesson. Instruction, precept, doctrine, study; reproof, warning, rebuke, lecture, homily.

ANT. *Misguidance, misinformaton, deception.*

Let. Permit, allow, suffer; rent, lease, hire out; assign, grant, give, contract.

ANT. *Prevent, hinder, check, thwart; refuse, deny, withhold, withdraw.*

Lethal. Fatal, deadly, mortal, poisonous, venomous, baneful, noxious.

ANT. *Remedial, wholesome, salutary, vital, invigorating, restorative.*

Lethargy. Drowsiness, torpor, swoon, trance, stupor, oblivion; indifference.

ANT. *Alertness, liveliness, vigilance, wakefulness, life, activity, quickness; eagerness, attention, interest.*

Letter. Epistle; mark, character; note, communication, message, missive; (*pl.*) erudition, learning.

Level, *n.* Plane; surface, floor; rank, standard, degree, position; ground; horizontality, equality, platform.

ANT. *Unevenness, acclivity, inequality, verticality, declivity.*

Level, *v.* Smooth, flatten, even; overthrow; aim, direct; plane, raze, equalize.

ANT. *Roughen, furrow, graduate, grade.*

Level, *a.* Flat, horizontal, even, plane, smooth.

ANT. *Rough, uneven, broken, rolling, undulating, hilly.*

Levity. Inconstancy, unsteadiness, thoughtlessness, frivolity, fickleness; flightiness, volatility.

ANT. *Gravity, earnestness, seriousness, sobriety, dignity, importance.*

Levy, *v.* Raise, collect, assess, seize, exact; attack; tax, impose, muster.

ANT. *Pay, forego, surrender, reimburse, repay, liquidate.*

Liable. Accountable, bound, responsible, answerable, subject, exposed, obnoxious; amenable.

ANT. *Irresponsible, refractory, independent, autocratic.*

Libel, *n.* Lampoon, satire, defamation, detraction, slander, calumny, traducement.

ANT. *Retraction, vindication, apology; puff, praise, encomium, advocacy, panegyric.*

Liberal. Generous, munificent, beneficent, large, free, catholic, unselfish, unrestrained, tolerant; ample, profuse.

ANT. *Mean, grasping, greedy,*

niggardly, avaricious; narrow-minded, bigoted, prejudiced, inadequate, contracted, scanty.

Liberate. Deliver, set free, disengage, release.

ANT. *Confine, imprison, arrest; sentence, doom, condemn.*

Libertine. Rake, debauchee, dissolute person, profligate.

ANT. *Ascetic, anchorite.*

Liberty. Emancipation, choice, freedom, license, independence, leave, permission, exemption; privilege, franchise, immunity.

ANT. *Slavery, captivity, servitude, serfdom, compulsion, necessity, constraint, imprisonment, oppression, thraldom, superstition, obligation.*

License, *n.* Permission, leave, privilege, right, warrant; laxity, disorder, anarchy, lawlessness.

ANT. *Obligation, constraint, compulsion, submission, necessity, restraint, restriction, moderation, temperance.*

License, *v.* Permit, authorize, let.

ANT. *Prohibit, restrain, forbid, constrain, inhibit, interdict, withhold, withdraw; annul, disallow.*

Licentious. Excessive, abusive; unrestrained, uncurbed, unruly, lawless, immoral, lewd, riotous, ungovernable, wanton, lax, dissolute, profligate, loose, sensual, impure, unchaste, lascivious.

ANT. *Temperate, strict, moderate, controlled, self-controlled, ascetic, austere, sober, self-denying, puritanic, renunciatory.*

Licit. Lawful, legal.

ANT. *Illegal, illicit, unlawful, unlicensed, unauthorized, illegitimate, improper, forbidden.*

Lie, *n.* Untruth, fiction, fable, deception, falsehood, falsification; delusion, illusion.

ANT. *Truth, verity, reality, fact; veracity, exactness, precision, principle, honesty, sincerity.*

Lie, *v.* Utter a lie; rest, recline, be situated; abide, remain, continue; exist, belong, consist; lodge, sleep.

ANT. *Rise, stir, move, walk, be active, go, change, run.*

Life. Being, soul, spirit; affairs; animation, vivacity, energy, vigor, living being; biography.

ANT. *Death, mortality, decease, lifelessness, annihilation, nonexistence; lethargy, coma, stupor; demise, departure, dissolution.*

Lift, *v.* Raise, elevate; exalt, improve; steal.

ANT. *Lower, sink, depress, let descend; reduce, degrade, humble; crush, overwhelm; hurl, dash, fling, throw.*

Ligament. Bandage, bond, connection, ligature, strap, girth, band, brace, tie; tying, binding.

ANT. *Fracture, disconnection, dislocation, disruption, severance, laceration, splinter, rupture, break.*

Light, *n.* Gleam, shine, glitter, flame, blaze, illumination, incandescence, glow, flash, flare, sparkle, twinkle, flicker, glare, glimmer, glistening, sheen, luster, shimmer, shining, scintillation, day; open view, publicity; enlightenment, knowledge, information; prosperity, joy, happiness, felicity.

ANT. *Dark, gloom, darkness, dimness, blackness, dusk, shade, shadow, gloominess, obscurity; extinction, night, tenebrosity, death; confusion, mys-*

tification, ignorance, misunderstanding, illiteracy, blindness, nescience.

Light, *a.* Bright, clear, white; unweighty, imponderable, portable, easy, volatile, insubstantial, buoyant; small, trifling, inconsiderable, moderate, insignificant; porous, spongy; unsteady, fickle, frivolous, unsettled; empty, slight, vain, capricious, thoughtless.

ANT. *Weighty, ponderous, oppressive, grievous, burdensome; onerous, difficult, laborious, hard; dejected, depressed, despondent; dull, inert, inactive.*

Like, *v.* Be pleased with, approve, enjoy, love, relish, esteem, fancy, affect.

ANT. *Dislike, hate, loathe, detest, abhor, abominate.*

Like, *a.* Resembling, similar; equal; probable, likely; disposed to, inclined toward; correspondent.

ANT. *Different, dissimilar, counterpart; improbable, unlikely; disinclined, indisposed.*

Likelihood. Probability, semblance, appearance, verisimilitude.

ANT. *Improbability, inconceivability, impossibility, unlikelihood; distinction, difference, uncertainty, contrariety; inconsistency.*

Likely. Probable, presumable, reasonable, apt, credible, conceivable, conjectural.

ANT. *Unlikely, doubtful, incredible, dubious, improbable, questionable, unreasonable.*

Likeness. Resemblance, similarity; guise; portrait, similitude, correspondence, copy, imitation, image, representation, effigy, picture.

ANT. *Unlikeness, disparity, dissimilarity, inequality; original.*

Likewise. Also, moreover, too, besides.

ANT. *Otherwise.*

Liking. Inclination, pleasure, desire, preference, approval, affection, fondness, taste, partiality.

ANT. *Dislike, disrelish, abhorrence, hatred, loathing, repugnance, aversion.*

Limit. Boundary, termination, restriction, confine, enclosure, border.

ANT. *Expanse, space, interior, center, tract, land; void.*

Limitless. Boundless, illimitable, immeasurable, vast, immense, infinite, interminable, unrestricted, unhindered, unobstructed.

ANT. *Bounded, limited, restricted, circumscribed, defined, restrained, hindered, prevented, hampered, obstructed, conditioned.*

Limpid. Clear, transparent, lucid, pellucid, pure, translucent, bright, crystal.

ANT. *Turbid, foul, muddy, opaque, dark, black.*

Line, *n.* Thread, cord, hawser, rope; boundary, contour, outline; family, race; track, railroad, course, method; continuity, sequence, succession.

ANT. *Breadth, width; expanse, space, deviation, divergency, variation; discontinuance.*

Lineage. Ancestry, family, descendants, house, breed, race, descent, progeny.

ANT. *Ancestor, source, ancestry, origin, founder, progenitor.*

Lineament. Profile, form, feature, mark, outline.

ANT. *Face, aspect, counte-*

nance, visage. front, expression.

Linear. Direct, straight, rectilinear, lineal.

ANT. *Zigzag, wandering, divergent, crooked, hooked, incurvate.*

Linger. Lag, saunter, tarry, delay, halt, stop, hesitate, wait, pause.

ANT. *Hasten, speed, push on, go, press forward, advance, progress.*

Liquid, *a.* Fluid, flowing, fluent, running, melting, liquescent; mellifluous, soft, limpid, clear.

ANT. *Solid, hard, congealed, insoluble, solidified, concrete; harsh, discordant.*

List. Roll, catalogue, schedule, inventory, record, register, index.

ANT. *Non-registration.*

Listen. Harken, hear, attend, hark, heed, list.

ANT. *Ignore, scorn, neglect, slight, be deaf to.*

Listless. Indifferent, spiritless, heedless, careless, languid, uninterested; indolent, vacant, supine, torpid.

ANT. *Interested, eager, earnest, spirited, careful, heedful, thoughtful, alert, attentive, absorbed, curious, engaged, active.*

Literal. Unimaginative, matter-of-fact; real; accurate, correct, exact, grammatical, positive, verbal, close, plain, actual; word by word, specific.

ANT. *General, free, liberal, metaphorical.*

Literary. Learned, bookish, literate, lettered, erudite, scholarly, well-read, studious, instructed, educated.

ANT. *Illiterate, unlettered, unscholarly.*

Literature. Books, literary productions *or* works, publications, writings, belles-lettres; study, lore, reading, scholarship, attainment; inspiration, genius, intuition, the divine afflatus; science, learning, letters, erudition.

Lithe. Pliant, flexible, limber, supple, elastic, agile, flexile.

ANT. *Stiff, tough, inelastic, inflexible, unresponsive, hard, resistant.*

Litter. Clutter, disorder, untidiness, rubbish.

ANT. *Order, cleanliness, arrangement, tidiness, system, method.*

Little. Small, diminutive; insignificant, contemptible; short, brief; inefficient, weak, slight; narrow, mean, illiberal; pigmy, scanty, unimportant, inconsiderable, trivial, petty, paltry, dwarf, puny.

ANT. *Great, big, large, huge, monstrous, enormous, long, developed, bulky, full; important, momentous, grave, serious, considerable, significant; colossal.*

Live, *v.* Have life; abide, dwell, reside; survive, remain, last; enjoy; feed, subsist; vegetate, grow, continue, behave, act, exist, breathe.

ANT. *Die, perish, depart, decay, wither, fade, vanish, fail, demise, drop, languish, expire, decline, faint, sink, fall.*

Live, *a.* Alive, living, active, vigorous, earnest, energetic, animate.

ANT. *Defunct, inanimate, dead, moribund, deceased, departed, gone.*

Livelihood. Support, maintenance, sustenance, subsistence; substance, living.

ANT. *Beggary, want, starvation, penury, inanition.*

Liveliness. Sprightliness, animation, gaiety, vivacity, smartness, briskness, activity.
ANT. *Slowness, torpor, stupidity, dulness, insensibility, listlessness, languor, inertness.*

Lively. Quick, nimble, smart, active, alert, sprightly, brisk, animated, prompt, earnest, energetic, strong, vivacious, gleeful, blithe, airy, gay, jocund, keen, eager, vivid, spirited, vigorous.
ANT. *Lifeless, dull, torpid, inanimate, inert, insensate, listless, languid, indifferent.*

Livery. Release, deliverance; clothing, food, uniform, peculiar garb; ration, boarding; dependence, servitude, badge, retinue.

Living, *n.* Subsistence, estate, existence.
ANT. *Want, starvation, privation, beggary, dearth, insufficiency, paucity, poverty, indigence.*

Living, *a.* Active, lively, vigorous; issuing, flowing; quickening, invigorating; burning, ignited; vegetating, growing.
ANT. *Dead, perishable, decaying, perishing, departed, inanimate, vanishing, deceased, defunct, withered.*

Load. Burden, charge, weight, pack, lading, incubus, clog, encumbrance, cargo, freight, drag, oppression, pressure.
ANT. *Support, solace, alleviation, lightness, refreshment, emptiness.*

Loan, *n.* Advance, mortgage, hypothecation.
ANT. *Foreclosure, recall, resumption.*

Loath, *a.* Averse, unwilling, reluctant; backward, indisposed, disinclined.
ANT. *Eager, ardent, zealous, enthusiastic, anxious, desirou impatient, impetuous, earnes forward, fervent.*

Loathe, *v.* Abominate, execrat abhor, dislike, detest, hate.
ANT. *Desire, like, long fo love.*

Locality. Position, locatior town, village, city; situatio place, habitat.

Locate. Place, set; designat define; establish, settle, lodg fix, dispose.
ANT. *Remove, leave, dise tablish, dislodge, displace.*

Lock, *n.* Clasp, catch, bar, bol fastening, hasp, hook, latch.

Locomotion. Movement, trave passage, migration.
ANT. *Rest, abode, stoppag remanence, fixture, stationar ness, permanence.*

Lodge, *v.* Rest, remain, shelte stay, abide, stop.
ANT. *Remove, travel, pa on, go, move, journey.*

Lofty. Tall, sublime, exalte dignified, stately, majestic, su lime, proud, haughty, elevate towering, high, eminent.
ANT. *Low, stunted, ord nary, unimposing, unassumin undignified, depressed.*

Logical. Dialectical, reasonabl coherent, consistent, sound, a gumentative, close, discrimina ing.
ANT. *Illogical, unsound, i consistent, unreasonable, inc herent, undiscriminating, fall cious, inconclusive.*

Lonely, Lonesome. Forlorn, fo saken, dreary, wild, desolat secluded, solitary, depresse alone, retired.
ANT. *Frequented, populou companioned; cheerful, festiv gay, bustling, animated.*

Long, *a.* Drawn out, protracte extended; continued; linge

ing; distant, far away; extensive, far-reaching.

ANT. *Short, brief, curtailed, contracted, abbreviated, condensed, concise.*

Look, *n.* Appearance, aspect; manner; glance, sight, view.

Look, *v.* Behold, see, stare, scan, contemplate, view, glance, descry, watch, discern, gaze, regard, inspect, survey; consider; seem, appear; face, front, take notice; expect, anticipate.

ANT. *Be blind* or *unseeing; overlook, miss, pass, neglect.*

Loose, *a.* Unbound, untied, free, unattached, unfastened, unconstrained; vague; liberal, unchaste, dissolute; unconnected, rambling; lax; detached, flowing, scattered, sparse; inexact.

ANT. *Tight, close; bound, tied, fastened, secured; thick, compact, dense; accurate, exact, strict, logical, scientific; conscientious, self-controlled, firm, rigorous.*

Loquacity. Garrulity, talkativeness.

ANT. *Taciturnity, silence, unresponsiveness.*

Lordly. Imperious, noble, honorable; proud, haughty, lofty, majestic, magnificent.

ANT. *Humble, mean, servile, ignoble, lowly, meek, dishonorable, abject.*

Lordship, *n.* Manor; dominion, power, authority; rule, jurisdiction.

ANT. *Subjection, subordination, homage, submission, subservience.*

Lore. Knowledge; instruction, wisdom, advice, counsel.

ANT. *Ignorance, illiteracy, inexperience, folly, imprudence.*

Lose. Part with, deprive of; destroy, waste, squander, wander, miss, ruin; fail of.

ANT. *Keep, retain, hold, obtain, grasp, recover, preserve, treasure, hoard, save, husband, economize, guard, utilize.*

Loss. Failure, destruction, privation; defect, harm; waste; squandering, deprivation, forfeiture; detriment, ruin, defeat, injury, damage, disadvantage.

ANT. *Restoration, recovery, reimbursement, retention, preservation, hoarding, guarding; utilization; gain, aggrandizement, augmentation, advantage, acquisition, profit, benefit, increment, earnings.*

Lot. Chance, accident, fate, fortune, hazard; destiny, doom, allotment, apportionment; portion, division, part, parcel, land.

ANT. *Law, arrangement, design, purpose, plan, prearrangement.*

Loud. Noisy; clamorous, boisterous, vociferous; obstreperous, turbulent, blustering; ostentatious, gaudy.

ANT. *Gentle, subdued, soft, quiet, silent, inaudible; whispering, murmuring; rustling.*

Love, *n.* Friendship, liking, tenderness, regard, fondness, devotion, affection, attachment, attraction, charity, courtship; good will; kindness, delight, inclination; benevolence.

ANT. *Antipathy, hatred, enmity; alienation, dislike, disaffection, estrangement, bitterness, coldness, repugnance, infidelity; desertion.*

Lovely. Beautiful, charming, delightful, delectable, enchanting, lovable, amiable; pleasing, winning, sweet, admirable.

ANT. *Hateful, hideous, ugly, homely, unattractive, unlovely, plain, gawky, unamiable, unlovable.*

Low. Sunken; quiet; small; submissive, humble; mean, vulgar, base, ignoble, dishonorable; moderate; feeble, weak; plain, simple; reasonable, cheap, abject, servile, slavish, degraded, vile, groveling; deep; reverent; dejected, depressed, dispirited.

ANT. *High, tall, lofty, elevated, exalted; eminent, noble, illustrious, rising, strong, influential; honorable; elaborate, ornate; notable; costly, expensive, precious, dear; arrogant, haughty, proud, masterly, lordly; high, loud, violent; irreverent, sacrilegious, blatant; elated, excited; intensified.*

Lower, *v.* Depress, sink, reduce, diminish, humble; let down, drop; degrade, disgrace, debase; lessen.

ANT. *Raise, exalt, elevate, hoist; increase, aggrandize.*

Lower, *a.* Inferior.

ANT. *Higher, superior, more influential.*

Lowering. Gloomy, threatening, sullen; cloudy, overcast, murky, dark.

ANT. *Clear, bright, light; vaporless.*

Lowly. Low, humble, unimportant, meek, modest; mean, unpretending, mild.

ANT. *Lofty, eminent, proud, arrogant, lordly, haughty, elevated; supercilious, conceited, pretentious.*

Loyal. Faithful, true, constant, devoted, staunch, trusty, obedient, submissive.

ANT. *Inconstant, untrue, traitorous, mutinous, seditious, insurgent, insubmissive, rebellious, disobedient, unfaithful, disaffected, dastardly.*

Loyalty. Allegiance, fidelity, fealty, faithfulness, constancy.

ANT. *Treason, treachery, unfaithfulness, disloyalty; sedition, rebellion, inconstancy, insurrection.*

Lucid. Luminous, transparent, sane, reasonable; shining, resplendent, bright; clear; radiant, brilliant; limpid, lucent; distinct, intelligible, perspicuous, sober, sound.

ANT. *Dark, opaque, muddy, black, somber, turbid, obscure; indistinct, unintelligible, mystifying, insane, unsound, confused, involved; illegible.*

Luck. Chance, hap, fate, fortune, hazard, casualty, accident; success, good fortune.

ANT. *Rule, law, causation, purpose, design, certainty; fate.*

Luckless. Unfortunate, unsuccessful, unlucky, ill-fated, unprosperous, ill-starred, unpropitious, unhappy.

Lucky. Fortunate, successful, auspicious, prosperous, happy, favored, blessed.

Lucrative. Profitable, gainful, paying, remunerative.

ANT. *Disadvantageous, unremunerative, unprofitable, useless, fruitless, vain, unproductive.*

Lucre. Gain, profit, riches, pelf, emolument, greed, mammon.

ANT. *Loss, poverty, failure, privation.*

Lucubration. Nocturnal study, meditation, speculation, cogitation.

ANT. *Idleness, dulness, stupidity, torpor, vacuity.*

Ludicrous. Laughable, comic, burlesque, droll, sportive, ridiculous, comical, odd, funny, farcical, absurd.

ANT. *Grave, serious, important, momentous; sad, sorrowful, melancholy, tragic, mournful, lugubrious.*

Lugubrious. Mournful, woful,

pitiable, doleful, sad, sorrowful, melancholy, complaining.

ANT. *Ludicrous, droll, ridiculous, comic, witty, jovial, absurd, funny, laughable, comical.*

Lull, *v.* Compose, calm, quiet, soothe, hush, tranquilize, still.

ANT. *Excite, aggravate, incite, stimulate, exasperate, provoke, inflame.*

Luminous. Shining, brilliant, bright; illuminated; enlightened, intelligent, clear, intelligible.

ANT. *Dark, black, gloomy; unintelligible, unintelligent, involved, mixed, confused.*

Lunacy. Derangement, mania, craziness, insanity, madness, aberration.

ANT. *Sanity, intellect, reason, rationality, lucidity, intelligence, brains; mind; self-control.*

Lunatic, *n.* Insane person, maniac, madman.

ANT. *Philosopher, sage, luminary, savant, scholar, scientist, intellectual person.*

Lunatic, *a.* Insane, mad, crazy, cracked, deranged.

ANT. *Sane, rational, intelligent, reasonable, reasoning, intellectual, knowing, sound.*

Lure, *n.* Enticement, decoy; allurement, bait, temptation, attraction.

Lure, *v.* Allure, entice, decoy, tempt, attract, inveigle, seduce.

ANT. *Warn, guide, alarm, premonish, ward, instruct, conduct, guard; extricate, save.*

Lurid. Yellow, pale, wan, dismal, ghastly, gloomy, murky, lowering.

ANT. *Bright, luminous, radiant, clear.*

Lurk. Lie hid, lie in wait, hide, skulk.

ANT. *Rise, spring, emerge, appear, reveal.*

Luscious. Sweet, delicious, fulsome, cloying, savory, delightful, pleasing, grateful; sugary, honeyed; rank, nauseous, unctuous.

ANT. *Sour, sharp, tart, bitter, pungent, acid.*

Luster. Brilliancy, brightness, splendor, glitter; renown, distinction, glory; gleam, radiance, resplendence; eminence, repute, celebrity, honor.

ANT. *Darkness, tenebrosity, blackness, gloom, obscuration; detraction, derogation, infamy, disrepute, dishonor, notoriety.*

Lustration. Washing, purification, cleansing; lustrum.

ANT. *Defilement, contamination, infection, desecration; soiling, pollution.*

Lustrous. Bright, shiny, gleaming, luminous, brilliant, radiant.

ANT. *Dark, black, gloomy.*

Lusty. Stout, strong, vigorous, robust, healthful, able, lively, sturdy; bulky, large, fat.

ANT. *Weak, infirm, feeble, incapable, ailing, effete, listless, invalid, powerless, convalescent.*

Luxuriant. Exuberant, excessive, rank, abundant, profuse, plentiful, plenteous.

ANT. *Delicate, frail, scanty, scarce, feeble.*

Luxuriate. Grow exuberantly, feed luxuriously; flourish, indulge; revel, wanton; delight, indulge to excess.

ANT. *Toil, slave, drudge, labor, work; pine, waste, droop, decay, languish.*

Luxurious. Voluptuous, epicurean, sensual, intemperate, effeminate, self-indulgent.

ANT. *Austere, ascetic, hard,*

painful, self-denying, self-controlled, temperate, restrained, restricted.

Luxury. Voluptuousness, epicurism, effeminacy, sensuality; dainty, delicacy, gratification; pleasure, enjoyment, delight; treat, animalism.

ANT. *Stoicism, asceticism self-denial, austerity, hardship spirituality.*

Lying, *a.* False, mendacious, untruthful, untrue; recumbent.

ANT. *Truthful, true, veracious, upright, honest, accurate exact; erect.*

M

Macerate. Weaken, soften; attenuate, make lean, waste, wear away; harass, mortify, torture; steep, soak, digest.

ANT. *Fatten, replenish, repair, pamper, swell.*

Machinate. Plan, contrive, devise, plot, scheme, harm.

ANT. *Think aloud, speak out, be artless; counterplot, compete; expose, defeat, baffle.*

Machination. Plot, conspiracy, intrigue, cabal, stratagem, design, trick, artifice, contrivance, scheme.

ANT. *Detection, counter-action, overthrow, baffling, defeat, exposure, defiance, challenge; conflict, competition.*

Machine. Engine, instrument; tool, puppet; organization, machinery, system, supernatural agency.

Maculate, *a.* Blotched, defiled, impure, spotted, blurred, corrupt, unclean, mottled.

ANT. *Unspotted, spotless, speckless, pure, clean, immaculate.*

Mad. Crazy, insane; excited, inflamed, furious, rabid, angry; distracted, lunatic, delirious, crazed, deranged, demented, maniac; enraged, raging; exasperated, provoked, incensed, wrathful; wild, infatuated; frenzied, frantic, raving.

ANT. *Sane, sound, sensible, quiet, composed, sober, unexcited.*

Madden. Make mad, enrage; irritate, provoke, inflame, infuriate.

ANT. *Calm, pacify, assuage, mesmerize; heal, soothe, restore.*

Madness. Insanity, craziness, derangement, mania, aberration; frenzy, fury, rage, delirium.

ANT. *Sanity, calmness, rationality, soberness, reason.*

Magazine. Warehouse, receptacle, storehouse, depository, repository; periodical.

Magic. Sorcery, witchcraft, conjuration, necromancy, enchantment, incantation; fascination, witchery, charm.

Magisterial. Stately, pompous, august, lordly, dignified, lofty, official, imperious, proud, domineering, haughty, despotic, arrogant, dogmatical; dictatorial, consequential, imposing, authoritative.

ANT. *Submissive, docile, undignified, unimposing, unassuming, modest.*

Magistrate. Judge; civil *or* police officer, chief official.

ANT. *Citizen, prisoner, civilian, subject.*

Magnanimity. Generosity, disinterestedness, greatness, heroism, nobleness, forbearance.

ANT. *Meanness, pettiness, paltriness, spitefulness, spleen.*

Magnanimous. Great, elevated, generous, lofty, noble, courageous; brave, dauntless, heroic, illustrious; unselfish, exalted, chivalrous, high-minded, honorable.

ANT. *Mean, small, ignoble, base, selfish, cowardly, cringing; mediocre; parsimonious, carping.*

Magnificent. Glorious, grand, majestic, splendid, admirable, superb, sublime; imposing, gorgeous, stately, showy; august, dignified.

ANT. *Petty, mean, paltry, little, flat, beggarly, ordinary, small-minded, tawdry, unimposing, tame.*

Magnify. Enlarge, augment, increase, amplify; laud, extol; exaggerate; celebrate, glorify, bless, praise.

ANT. *Diminish, curtail, contract, palliate, extenuate, decry.*

Magniloquent. Pompous, grandiloquent, bombastic, declamatory, stilted, high-flown, turgid, inflated, boastful.

ANT. *Simple, vernacular, unaffected, plain-spoken.*

Magnitude. Extent, size; grandeur, greatness; importance; volume, dimension, mass; consequence; sublimity, loftiness.

ANT. *Smallness, diminutiveness, littleness, meagerness; insignificance, meanness, unimportance.*

Maid. Maiden, girl, damsel, virgin, lass.

ANT. *Matron, married woman.*

Maim. Disable, cripple, mangle, mar, mutilate, disfigure, lame.

ANT. *Restore, strengthen, invigorate, mend.*

Main, *a.* Bulk, majority, body, principal, trunk, chief, leading, most important, first, cardinal, capital; necessary, vital, essential, indispensable, requisite; huge, enormous; absolute, entire, mere, direct.

ANT. *Subordinate, non-essential, auxiliary, minor, tributary, inferior.*

Main, *n.* Ocean, mainland, continent; main conduit *or* pipe; force, power, might, strength; gross, majority.

ANT. *Bay, gulf; island; inability, weakness; tributaries; minority.*

Mainly. Chiefly, principally; largely, greatly, mightily, absolutely, primarily, entirely.

ANT. *Secondarily, subordinately; partially, somewhat, slightly.*

Maintain. Uphold, assert, vindicate, allege, support, sustain; defend, continue; supply; provide; affirm.

ANT. *Retract, deny, withdraw; fail, turn traitor to.*

Maintenance. Sustenance, support, vindication, defense, justification, provisions, subsistence, livelihood.

Majestic. August, sublime, magnificent, regal, royal, pompous, stately, dignified, elevated, imperial, princely, grand, imposing.

ANT. *Low, humble, mean, sordid, groveling; plebeian, vulgar, common; unassuming.*

Majesty. Dignity, power, authority, loftiness, stateliness, augustness, grandeur, elevation.

ANT. *Meanness, paltriness; humility.*

Majority. Superiority, seniority; eldership, priority; bulk, preponderance.

ANT. *Minority, inferiority, juniority.*

Make. Produce, falsify; find; acquire; travel over; cause; esteem, suppose, represent; compel, force; be; amount to; attain, reach, arrive at; manage, interfere; proceed, tend, move, go; contribute, increase, accrue, constrain, bring about, occasion, require; shape, fabricate, construct, fashion, frame, manufacture, perform, do; become, compose, constitute, create, establish, effect, execute, reach, get, render.

ANT. *Abolish, demolish, annihilate, break, disintegrate, unmake, undo; destroy, defeat, mar, disestablish, miss, lose, fail of; upset; misrepresent, mismanage; hesitate, stop; decrease, diminish.*

Maker. Creator, former, manufacturer, builder, constructor; author, composer, writer, compiler.

ANT. *Destroyer, exterminator, annihilator.*

Make up. Collect; constitute, form; reconcile, settle, adjust, compose; make good, compensate; supply, furnish, provide; determine.

ANT. *Distribute, disperse, scatter; pi; default.*

Mal- or **Male-.** A prefix denoting *ill.* For words thus compounded and not found here, see the synonyms and antonyms of the root word, from which derivatives may be readily chosen.

Malady. Disorder, distemper, disease, sickness, ailment, illness; complaint, indisposition.

ANT. *Health, sanity, vigor, robustness, soundness.*

Malediction. Curse, cursing, execration, imprecation, denunciation, anathema.

ANT. *Benediction, blessing, praise, compliment.*

Malefactor. Evil-doer, culprit, felon, criminal, convict, outlaw.

ANT. *Benefactor, hero.*

Malice. Spite, ill will, malevolence, grudge, pique, bitterness, animosity, malignity, rancor, maliciousness, virulence.

ANT. *Good will, benevolence, kindliness.*

Manacle, *n.* Handcuff, shackle, fetter.

Manacle, *v.* Handcuff, shackle, fetter, bind, chain.

ANT. *Unbind, unfetter, unchain.*

Manage. Direct, govern, control, wield, order, contrive, concert, conduct, transact; administer, regulate, supervise, superintend, handle, rule.

ANT. *Mismanage, misgovern, misconduct, upset, misuse, derange; let go.*

Manageable. Tractable, governable, controllable, tamable, docile.

ANT. *Unmanageable, untamable, uncontrollable, ungovernable, difficult, impracticable, impossible, refractory.*

Management. Conduct, administration, government, guidance, direction, care, charge, contrivance, intrigue; skill, address; economy, treatment, superintendence, surveillance; negotiations, dealings, transactions.

ANT. *Misconduct, maladministration, mismanagement.*

Manager. Director, superintendent, supervisor, comptroller, governor, overseer, conductor; economist.

ANT. *Workman, follower, workingman, employee.*

Mandate. Command, commission, order, charge, precept, injunction, requirement, edict.

ANT. *Petition, request, entreaty, suggestion.*

Maneuver (Manœuvre), *n.* Management; stratagem, artifice, scheme, plan, trick, ruse, intrigue; evolution, movement; operation, tactics, contrivance.

ANT. *Countermovement, defeat, check, bafflement, counteraction, detection, neutralization.*

Maneuver, *v.* Perform an evolution, move; scheme, plot, intrigue, manage, contrive.

ANT. *Counteract, play up to, check, checkmate.*

Mangle. Cut, bruise, mutilate, lacerate, maim, hack, tear; destroy, mar, spoil; polish, calender, smooth, press.

ANT. *Restore, heal.*

Manhood. Virility, maturity; humanity; courage, resolution, bravery, hardihood, fortitude, manliness, manfulness.

ANT. *Womanhood, femininity; effeminacy; cowardliness, cowardice, delicacy.*

Mania. Insanity, derangement, madness, lunacy, aberration, alienation, delirium, frenzy.

ANT. *Sanity, health, soundness; poise, self-control.*

Maniac. Lunatic, madman, insane, bedlamite.

Manifest, *a.* Open, clear, evident, apparent, visible, conspicuous, plain, obvious; patent, palpable, unmistakable, distinct, indubitable.

ANT. *Hidden, indistinct, inconspicuous, occult, latent, obscure, confused, hazy, foggy.*

Manifest, *v.* Reveal, declare, evince, make known, disclose, discover, display, show, exhibit, evidence, expose.

ANT. *Hide, cover, conceal.*

Manifold. Various, duplicate, multiplied; numerous, many, multitudinous; diverse, multifarious; sundry.

ANT. *Few, rare, limited, scarce, scant; uniform, facsimile.*

Mankind. Man; humanity, humankind; men; society.

ANT. *Womankind; childhood; divinity, deity, Heaven, God; earth, world, universe, nature, creation; cattle, animals, minerals, vegetables.*

Manly. Bold, daring, valorous, courageous, undaunted, hardy, dignified; intrepid, heroic, vigorous, firm, noble, chivalrous; mature, masculine, manlike.

ANT. *Womanly, childlike; timid, womanish, childish, unmanly, boyish, weak, dastardly, cowardly; effeminate.*

Manner. Mode, custom, habit, deportment, fashion, air, look, mien, aspect, appearance; behavior, conduct; method, form, style.

ANT. *Being, action, proceeding, life, work, performance, project, business.*

Mannerism. Characteristic, peculiarity, uniformity, self-repetition, self-consciousness, affectation, idiosyncrasy, specialty.

ANT. *Unaffectedness, simplicity, naturalness, character, genuineness.*

Mannerly. Civil, complaisant, respectful, courteous, polite, urbane, refined, well-behaved, ceremonious, well-bred.

ANT. *Rude, coarse, unmannerly, rough, impolite, uncivil, boorish.*

Manufacture, *n.* Making, production, fabrication; product, composition, construction, manipulation, molding.

ANT. *Use, consumption, employment, wear.*

Manumission. Release, emancipation, liberation, deliverance, enfranchisement, dismissal, discharge.

ANT. *Slavery, capture, subjugation; restraint, repression, coercion.*

Manumit. Release, liberate, enfranchise, free, emancipate.

ANT. *Enslave, capture, subjugate, enthral.*

Many. Frequent, manifold, diverse, divers, sundry, numerous, multiplied, various, abundant, multifarious.

ANT. *Few, rare, scarce, infrequent, scanty.*

Mar. Injure, mark, spoil, ruin, blemish, damage, disfigure, deface, hurt, harm, impair, maim, deform.

ANT. *Make, mend, restore, improve, reinstate, enhance, repair, conserve.*

Marauder. Plunderer, robber, ravager, pillager, outlaw, bandit, brigand, freebooter, rover, invader.

ANT. *Guard, sentry, keeper, steward, ranger, outpost.*

Margin. Border, edge, brim, lip, rim, brink, verge, confine, limit, skirt, boundary, extremity; loophole, profit, interest, leeway.

ANT. *Center, main, space; limitation, stringency, restriction.*

Marine. Naval, nautical, maritime; oceanic, salt-water, pelagic.

ANT. *Terrene, fresh-water, terrestrial, land.*

Marital. Connubial, nuptial, hymeneal, conjugal, wedded, matrimonial.

ANT. *Single, unwedded, celibate.*

Maritime. Marine, oceanic, nautical.

ANT. *Terrene, land.*

Mark, *n.* Impress, stamp, vestige, impression, imprint, track, evidence, proof, characteristic, badge, indication; distinction, eminence, importance.

ANT. *Effacement, obliteration, erasure, plainness.*

Mark, *v.* Remark, notice, regard, heed, show, betoken, characterize, denote, stamp, imprint, impress, brand; label, designate, observe, stigmatize, signalize, specify, specialize; decorate.

ANT. *Overlook, ignore, omit; mislabel, misindicate, mismark.*

Marked. Noted, notable, prominent, remarkable, eminent, distinguished, conspicuous.

ANT. *Ordinary, mean, commonplace, everyday, undistinguished.*

Marriage. Matrimony, wedlock, wedding, espousal, nuptials, conjugal union, spousal, union.

ANT. *Divorce, celibacy, virginity, bachelorhood, widowhood, maidenhood.*

Marrow. Medulla, pith, essence, quintessence; gist, substance, cream, kernel.

ANT. *Excrescence, surplusage, redundancy, superfluity; surface, exterior; amplification; body, volume, mass.*

Marsh. Fen, swamp, quagmire, morass, bog, slough.

ANT. *Solid ground.*

Marshal, *v.* Order, arrange, direct, guide, lead, rank, array, dispose, draw up; herald.

ANT. *Disarray, misguide, disarrange, disorder.*

Martial. Warlike, military, soldierly, brave.

ANT. *Peaceful, unmilitary, unwarlike.*

Martyrdom. Martyrlike state; torture, torment, persecution; confession.
ANT. *Denial, retraction; abjuration, renegation.*

Marvel, *n.* Wonder, prodigy, miracle; surprise, astonishment, amazement, admiration; portent, phenomenon.
ANT. *Commonplace, imposture, cipher, farce, trifle.*

Marvelous. Wonderful, astonishing, surprising, strange, improbable, incredible; miraculous, stupendous, extraordinary, wondrous, supernatural, portentous, prodigious.
ANT. *Commonplace, everyday, regular, normal, customary, natural, anticipated, current, calculated, expected.*

Masculine. Male, manly, virile, manlike; strong, robust, powerful, bold, hardy, courageous.
ANT. *Feminine, womanly, womanlike, female; effeminate, womanish.*

Mask, *n.* Cover, disguise, pretext, subterfuge, screen; revel, frolic, evasion, pretense, ruse, plea; redoubt; domino, blind, veil; hypocrisy.
ANT. *Truth, nakedness, candor, verity, openness; exposure, detection, unmasking.*

Mask, *v.* Disguise, cover, hide, protect, conceal, veil, shroud, screen.
ANT. *Expose, unmask, discover, detect.*

Mass. Quantity, sum, bulk, magnitude, body, size, main part, majority; aggregate, whole, totality; heap, assemblage, combination, concretion.
ANT. *Fragment, section, portion, bit, morsel, minority, segment.*

Massacre, *v.* Murder, butcher, kill, slaughter, slay.
ANT. *Preserve, spare, rescue, restore.*

Massive. Compacted, weighty, heavy, massy, ponderous, bulky, huge, immense, vast, solid, colossal.
ANT. *Slight, slender, frail, airy; petty, small, light.*

Master, *n.* Ruler, director, manager, leader, employer, owner, governor, superintendent, commander, captain; teacher, instructor, tutor; adept; possessor, proprietor; professor, head, chief.
ANT. *Servant, slave, pupil, employee, subject, learner, student.*

Master, *v.* Conquer, subdue, vanquish, overcome; acquire, learn.
ANT. *Yield, fail, surrender, succumb.*

Masterly. Imperious, domineering, arbitrary, despotic; skilful, clever, expert, dexterous, adroit; finished, excellent, artistic, consummate.
ANT. *Humble, obedient, compliant, rude, clumsy, bungling.*

Mastery. Authority, dominion, supremacy; victory, triumph, preëminence, ascendency, superiority; acquirement, attainment, acquisition; skill, dexterity, cleverness, ability.
ANT. *Subservience, tutelage, submission, guidance, obedience, inexpertness, ignorance; defeat, failure, surrender.*

Masticate. Grind, chew.
ANT. *Bolt, gobble, swallow.*

Match, *n.* Equal, mate; contest; union, marriage; competition, trial; companion; pair.
ANT. *Superior, inferior; dis-*

parity, mismatch, oddity, inequality.

Match, *v.* Mate, rival, oppose, equal; correspond; adapt, fit, suit; marry; harmonize; join, couple, combine.

ANT. *Fail, exceed, surpass, preponderate; separate, dissociate.*

Matchless. Unequaled, peerless, unparalleled, incomparable, inimitable, consummate, exquisite, excellent, surpassing, unrivaled.

ANT. *Common, ordinary, mediocre, everyday, commonplace, general.*

Mate, *n.* Companion, associate, compeer, match, equal; fellow, intimate; assistant, subordinate; peer.

ANT. *Stranger; superior, inferior; principal, chief, head.*

Material, *n.* Substance, solidity, weight, stuff, matter.

ANT. *Work, production, design; spirit, purpose.*

Material, *a.* Corporeal, physical; important, essential; momentous, vital, weighty; bodily.

ANT. *Spiritual, sublimated, incorporeal, evanescent, ethereal.*

Matrimony. Marriage, wedlock.

ANT. *Celibacy, virginity.*

Matron. Wife, widow, dame; housekeeper, head nurse; dowager.

ANT. *Girl, maid, maiden, virgin, spinster, miss, lass.*

Matter. Substance, body, material, constituency; concern, affair, business; trouble, difficulty; amount, portion, space; sense, significance, moment; import, importance; topic, subject, question; thing, event.

ANT. *Immateriality, incorporeality, spirituality; mind, soul, spirit, intellect; animus, zeal, temper.*

Mature. Ripe, perfect, ready, perfected, completed, full-grown.

ANT. *Raw, crude, blighted, immature, undeveloped, unripe.*

Matutinal. Morning, dawning, early, waking.

ANT. *Vesper, evening, late, waning, twilight.*

Maudlin. Tearful, sentimental, weak, silly; drunken; intoxicated, inebriated, tipsy, muddled.

ANT. *Dry, sober, sensible, unsentimental, unromantic.*

Mawkish. Nauseous, disgusted, squeamish; insipid, flat, stale, sickly, disgusting, loathsome, maudlin.

ANT. *Sensible, savory, fine, sound, palatable, pungent.*

Maxim. Principle, axiom, proverb, aphorism, apothegm, adage, saying, saw, dictum, precept, rule.

ANT. *Sophism, quibble, absurdity, enigma, paradox.*

Maximum. Greatest; climax, zenith, apex, acme, culmination, completion, utmost, ultimate.

ANT. *Minimum, least; morsel, fragment; initiative, commencement; decrease, wane; incompletion, abortion.*

Maybe, *ad.* Perhaps, possibly, haply, mayhap.

Maze. Labyrinth, intricacy; bewilderment, uncertainty, perplexity; embarrassment.

ANT. *Clue, elimination, explication; solution.*

Meager. Thin, lean. lank, poor, gaunt, starved, hungry, emaciated, barren, scanty.

ANT. *Stout, brawny, fat, chubby; abundant, fertile, copious.*

Mean, *n.* Middle, medium, average, intermediate point; (*pl.*) resources, property, revenue; media.
Ant. *Extreme, excess, exorbitance, enormity, extravagance; poverty, end, purpose, object.*

Mean, *v.* Purpose, intend, design; signify, import, indicate, denote, express.
Ant. *Do, perform, execute; say, state, enunciate, declare.*

Mean, *a.* Ignoble, abject, beggarly, wretched, degraded, degenerate, vulgar, vile, servile, menial, groveling, slavish, dishonorable, disgraceful, shameful, despicable, contemptible, paltry, sordid.
Ant. *Noble, kingly, heroic, princely, exalted, generous, eminent, honorable, spirited, liberal, masterly, worthy, bountiful, munificent.*

Meaning. Purpose, aim, intention, import, design, object; sense, explanation, significance, interpretation, force, purport, acceptation.
Ant. *Statement; proceeding; affidavit, declaration.*

Meanness. Stinginess, illiberality, sordidness, vileness, penuriousness, niggardliness, abjectness, baseness; destitution, poverty, lowness, scantiness, smallness, rudeness, selfishness.
Ant. *Nobleness, generosity, unselfishness, liberality, largeheartedness.*

Measure, *n.* Dimension, capacity, quantity, amount; moderation, restraint; extent, limit, proportion, degree; rule, gage, standard; meter.
Ant. *Bulk, mass; segment, section, portion; immensity, infinity.*

Measureless. Unlimited, infinite, immeasurable, immense, boundless, limitless, vast, unbounded.
Ant. *Circumscribed, finite, limited, bounded, restricted.*

Mechanic. Artificer, artisan, handicraftsman, hand, craftsman, operative, workman.
Ant. *Artist, designer, planner, architect, constructor.*

Mechanical. Approximate, empirical; machine-made; automatic, involuntary, blind; habitual, unreflective, spontaneous, effortless, unimpassioned.
Ant. *Labored, feeling, self-conscious, forced, spirited, appreciative, lifelike, lively, animated, impassioned.*

Meddle. Interfere, handle, disturb; intrude, interpose, intervene, intercede; mediate, arbitrate.
Ant. *Withdraw, retire, remove, recede, retreat.*

Meddlesome. Meddling, intrusive, officious; pragmatical, interfering; impertinent, obtrusive.
Ant. *Unobtrusive, modest, unofficious, shy, retiring, unassuming, reserved.*

Mediate, *v.* Intervene, reconcile, interpose, intercede, arbitrate.
Ant. *Retire, withdraw, let be, leave, abandon.*

Mediation. Interposition, intercession, intervention, arbitration, interference, adjustment, reconciliation.
Ant. *Indifference, neutrality; non-interference.*

Mediator. Reconciler, intercessor, interceder, advocate, umpire, propitiator.

Medicament. Remedy, specific, medicine, cure, relief, help, restorative.
Ant. *Irritant, infection, aggravation, hurt, disease.*

Medicate. Drug, treat, heal, cure.

Ant. *Harm, infect; catch, contract.*

Medicine, *n.* Drug, physic, remedy, medicament; antidote, corrective, salve, cure; therapeutics.

Ant. *Poison, virus, bane; aggravation.*

Mediocre. Moderate, indifferent, ordinary, mean, medium, average, middling, commonplace.

Ant. *Superior, inferior, extraordinary, distinguished, distinctive.*

Mediocrity. Inferiority, average, moderate *or* middle state, medium; moderation; commonplace, mean; sufficiency.

Ant. *Excellence, superiority, distinction, brilliance, rarity.*

Meditate. Consider, ponder, revolve, study, weigh, plan, contrive, devise, scheme, purpose, intend; contemplate, muse, reflect, think, cogitate.

Ant. *Execute, enact, complete, consummate.*

Medium, *n.* Middle, mean; moderation, average; proportion; mediator, intermediary; means, agency, instrumentality.

Medium, *a.* Middle, mean, middling, intermediate, medial, mediocre, central.

Ant. *Outer, extreme, distant, remote.*

Medley. Mixture, jumble, miscellany, potpourri, hodgepodge; tumult, confusion, litter, diversity, complexity.

Ant. *Order, harmony, simplicity; arrangement, classification, assortment, disposition, grouping.*

Meed. Merit, reward, recompense; worth, desert; guerdon, premium, prize, award, remuneration; gift, present.

Ant. *Penalty, punishment, brand, stigma, amercement.*

Meek. Submissive, yielding, unassuming, gentle; mild, patient, humble; lowly, modest.

Ant. *Bold, arrogant, proud, self-assertive, irritable, presumptuous, high-spirited.*

Meet, *v.* Join; confront, encounter; be present; perceive, experience, suffer; equal, satisfy; assemble, congregate; harmonize, agree, unite; fulfil, comply, gratify, answer.

Ant. *Miss, escape, elude; be absent; avoid, separate, vary, diverge, decline, part, disagree; disappoint, fall short, fail.*

Meet, *a.* Suitable, fit, proper, appropriate, qualified, convenient.

Ant. *Inappropriate, unfit, inconvenient, unsuited, improper.*

Meeting. Conference, assembly, company, convention, congregation, junction, union, confluence; interview, encounter; assemblage, concourse, gathering.

Melancholy, *n.* Melancholia; depression, dejection, brooding, gloominess.

Ant. *Happiness, gladness, sanity, merriment, mirth, cheer, hopefulness.*

Melancholy, *a.* Sad, dispirited, low-spirited, down-hearted, unhappy, hypochondriac, heavy, doleful, afflictive; dejected, depressed, disconsolate, gloomy, sorrowful, moody, desponding; grave, somber, dark.

Ant. *Happy, cheerful, gladsome, sprightly, lively, merry, mirthful, blithesome, gleeful.*

Mellifluous. Smooth, honeyed, sweet, mellow, euphonious, silvery, dulcet.

ANT. *Raucous, hoarse, discordant, harsh, rough, broken, abrupt.*

Mellow. Ripe, soft, tender; subdued, delicate; genial, jovial.
ANT. *Unripe, hard, green, acid, sour; harsh, glaring; discordant.*

Melodious. Musical, agreeable, harmonious, dulcet, sweet, tuneful, rhythmical, concordant, mellifluous.
ANT. *Discordant, harsh, dissonant, raucous, jarring, inharmonious.*

Melody. Harmony, rhythm, air, tune, music, song, sweetness of sound, descant, theme, unison, symphony.
ANT. *Discord, jarring, dissonance, harshness, discordance.*

Melt. Liquefy, fuse, thaw, mollify, soften; be dissipated, run, blend, flow, dissolve.
ANT. *Harden, combine, consolidate, unite, crystallize.*

Member. Organ, limb; constituent, part; clause, phrase; essential; portion, component.
ANT. *Whole, body, entirety, aggregate, sum, totality, community, society, association, organization, constitution.*

Memoir. Memorial, biography, record, narrative, chronicle, register.

Memorable. Important, illustrious, remarkable, extraordinary, signal, distinguished, famous, celebrated, great, conspicuous, prominent.
ANT. *Ordinary, trivial, commonplace, insignificant, mediocre.*

Memorial. Monument, record, memorandum, memento, souvenir.
ANT. *Silence, oblivion; nonobservance; erasure.*

Memory. Remembrance, recollection, reminiscence; fame, renown, reputation; monument; retrospection, retrospect; perpetuation, retention.
ANT. *Oblivion, oversight, unmindfulness, obliviousness, forgetfulness.*

Menace, *n.* Threat, evil intention, denunciation, threatening.
ANT. *Good will, benediction, blessing, kindness; protection.*

Mend. Help, amend, emend, correct, rectify; repair, improve, reform, better, restore, ameliorate.
ANT. *Impair, damage, spoil, corrupt; harm, deteriorate, pervert.*

Mendacity. Lying, deceit, falsehood, untruth, duplicity, lie, untruthfulness, deception; prevarication.
ANT. *Truth, honesty, rectitude, uprightness, veracity, accuracy, exactness.*

Menial. Servile, mean; domestic; dependent, attendant.
ANT. *Noble, independent, autocratic, supreme, superior.*

Mental. Intellectual, spiritual, metaphysical, subjective, psychological, psychical, intelligent.
ANT. *Physical, corporeal, objective, bodily.*

Mention, *n.* Reference, allusion, notice, remembrance, hint, communication, observation, declaration.
ANT. *Omission, silence, suppression, forgetfulness, neglect.*

Mention, *v.* Speak of, notice, announce, observe, remark, hint, declare, tell, state, report, disclose, allude to, name, refer to.
ANT. *Suppress, omit, be silent about, forget, silence, drop, neglect, disregard, slight.*

Mercantile. Commercial, traffic,

business; wholesale, retail; interchangeable, marketable.

ANT. *Professional; unmercantile, unmarketable, stagnant, unprofitable.*

Mercenary. Paid, hired, hireling, venal; greedy, sordid, avaricious, selfish.

ANT. *Generous, unselfish, lavish, prodigal, liberal, philanthropic, benevolent.*

Merchandise. Wares, commodities, goods; trade, traffic, commerce; stock.

Merchant. Trader, shopkeeper, dealer, tradesman, trafficker; importer.

ANT. *Shopman, salesman, retailer, pedler, huckster.*

Merciful. Compassionate, tender, humane, gracious, kind, mild, clement, benignant, lenient, pitiful, forgiving; tenderhearted.

ANT. *Remorseless, pitiless, inexorable, unrelenting, severe, cruel, hard, illiberal.*

Mercy. Compassion, grace, favor, helpfulness, clemency, forbearance, tenderness, forgiveness, gentleness, pardon, blessing, pity, kindness, mildness, lenity, benevolence, benignity, lenience, leniency.

ANT. *Harshness, rigor, severity, sternness, penalty, justice, vengeance, revenge, punishment, hardness, cruelty, implacability, ruthlessness, inhumanity, brutality, exaction.*

Mere. Unmixed, pure, absolute, unqualified, simple, bare, unaffected; unadulterated.

ANT. *Compound, mixed, impure, blended, combined, adulterated.*

Meridian, *n.* Midday, noon, zenith, height, culmination, summit, apex, pinnacle, acme.

ANT. *Midnight, antipodes, depth, profundity, base, depression, nadir.*

Merit, *n.* Desert, worth, excellence, reward, approbation; worthiness, credit, goodness.

ANT. *Worthlessness, error, unworthiness, demerit, weakness, imperfection, fault.*

Merry. Gay, jovial, sportive; cheerful, happy; blithe, lively, sprightly, vivacious, mirthful, gleeful, joyous, jocund, hilarious.

ANT. *Gloomy, sad, disconsolate, dismal, moody, dejected.*

Message. Notice, word, communication, missive, letter, intimation.

ANT. *Interception, silence, non-communication, neglect.*

Messenger. Carrier, harbinger, intelligencer, courier, forerunner, herald, precursor.

Metaphysical. Mental, intellectual, psychological, abstract, general, ideal, psychical, subjective, rational, abstruse, conceptual.

ANT. *Physical, substantial, physiological, material, practical, objective, palpable, external.*

Method. Order, system, rule, way, manner, mode, course, arrangement, process, means, regularity.

ANT. *Disorder, experimentation, guesswork, conjecture, attempt, empiricism.*

Midst. Middle, center, heart; thick; press; burden.

ANT. *Circumference, rim, surface, border, outside, perimeter.*

Mien. Aspect, manner, bearing, look, carriage, deportment, appearance.

ANT. *Character, disposition, nature, constitution, personality.*

Might. Force, energy, power, means, resources; strength, capacity, ability.
ANT. *Weakness, feebleness, infirmity, impotence; inability, inefficiency, incapability; want, lack.*

Mild. Gentle, pleasant, clement, kind, soft, bland; moderate, placid, tender, genial, meek.
ANT. *Harsh, fierce, savage, rough, wild, violent, merciless, severe.*

Mind. Understanding, intellect, soul; opinion, judgment, belief; choice, inclination, liking, intent, will; courage, spirit; remembrance, memory, recollection; reason, brain, sense, consciousness, disposition, intelligence, thought, instinct.
ANT. *Body, matter, brute force, brawn, limbs, material substance, members; feelings, emotions, heart, affections, sensibilities; conduct; forgetfulness, obliviousness.*

Mindful. Regardful, attentive, heedful, observant, thoughtful, careful.
ANT. *Inattentive, regardless, careless, forgetful, oblivious, absent-minded.*

Mingle. Combine, join, confuse, compound, mix; unite, associate; intermarry; blend, amalgamate.
ANT. *Separate, sever, segregate, dissolve, sift, sort, classify, analyze.*

Minister, *n.* Delegate, official, ambassador; clergyman, priest, parson, ecclesiastic, preacher, divine, vicar, curate; envoy.
ANT. *Monarch, master, superior, principal; layman; government.*

Minor, *a.* Inferior, less important, smaller, less, junior, unimportant, younger.
ANT. *Major, greater, older, senior, elder, main, important.*

Minute. Small, tiny, slender, diminutive, slight, little; precise, particular, detailed, critical, circumstantial, exact, fine, comminuted, specific; inconsiderable; microscopic.
ANT. *Monstrous, great, enormous, grand, huge; general, abstract, broad, comprehensive; inexact, superficial.*

Miraculous. Supernatural, super-physical; wonderful, awesome.
ANT. *Natural, ordinary, scientific.*

Mis-. A prefix used in the sense of *amiss, wrong, ill.* Words to which this prefix but adds this meaning are omitted here, and their synonyms and antonyms may usually be readily found by reference to the root words.

Misanthropy. Cynicism, hatred, egoism.
ANT. *Philanthropy, benevolence, altruism, humanitarianism.*

Miscellany. Mass, mixture, collection, medley, jumble, variety, hodge-podge, diversity.
ANT. *Selection, system, arrangement, order, group, assortment, classification.*

Mischief. Damage, harm, hurt, injury, detriment, evil, ill; mishap, trouble.
ANT. *Benefit, good, blessing, profit, gratification, compensation, favor.*

Miser. Niggard, skinflint, curmudgeon, churl.
ANT. *Spendthrift, profligate.*

Miserable. Abject, forlorn, pitiable, wretched, mean; worthless, despicable, contemptible; unfortunate, unlucky.
ANT. *Comfortable, happy,*

respectable, contented, cheerful, easy.

Misery. Unhappiness, wretchedness, woe; calamity, disaster, misfortune.

ANT. *Happiness, contentment, ease, comfort, pleasure, enjoyment.*

Misfortune. Adversity, failure, ill luck, hardship, harm, ill, affliction, calamity, blow, disaster, disappointment, trial, tribulation, sorrow, ruin, distress, stroke, misery, reverse, mischance, visitation, chastening, trouble, chastisement, misadventure, bereavement, mishap.

ANT. *Consolation, blessing, boon, happiness, joy, prosperity, relief, triumph, success, comfort, good fortune, gratification, good luck, pleasure.*

Mission. Message, errand, commission, deputation; embassy; ministry, legation; trust, office.

ANT. *Assumption, usurpation, self-appointment; faithlessness, betrayal.*

Mist. Fog, vapor; obscuration, cloudiness, perplexity, bewilderment, haze.

ANT. *Clarity, brightness; perspicuity, revelation, clearness, discernment, insight, understanding; lucidity.*

Mob. Rabble, masses, dregs of the people, the vulgar, populace, crowd, canaille, lower classes.

ANT. *Élite, aristocracy, nobility, nobles, patricians.*

Mobile. Movable, excitable, inconstant, changeable, fickle; variable, ductile, sensitive.

ANT. *Immovable, firm, set, steady, unvarying, unchangeable, inexorable.*

Model. Mold, copy, design, example, image, imitation, standard, type, representation, pattern, prototype, facsimile, original, archetype; norm.

ANT. *Imitation; work, production, execution; accomplishment.*

Moderate, *a.* Sparing, temperate, frugal, calm, mild; limited, restrained, reasonable, dispassionate, controlled; abstinent, sober; austere, ascetic.

ANT. *Immoderate, intemperate, luxurious, excessive, extravagant.*

Modern. New, novel, modish, fashionable, present, late, extant, recent.

ANT. *Past, ancient, antiquated, old, antique, obsolete, former.*

Modesty. Humility, lowliness, humbleness, meekness, shyness, reserve, coldness, bashfulness, backwardness, constraint, timidity, unobtrusiveness, coyness.

ANT. *Frankness, freedom, impudence, indiscretion, self-conceit, sauciness, abandon, arrogance, confidence, egoism, assumption, assurance, boldness, forwardness, haughtiness, loquacity, pertness, pride, vanity, self-sufficiency, openness, effrontery.*

Moment. Instant, twinkling, consequence, weight, consideration, force, value, signification, avail; second, trice.

ANT. *Age, period, decade, century, generation; insignificance, unimportance, triviality.*

Monarch. Ruler, sovereign; king, prince, emperor, queen.

ANT. *Subject, peer, plebes.*

Money. Coin, cash, currency, gold, funds, property, specie, silver, bills, bullion, notes, capital.

Monopoly. Exclusiveness, possession, privilege, appropriation, engrossment, preëmption.
ANT. *Community, partnership, competition, free trade; participation, sharing; communism; socialism.*

Monotonous. Unvarying, uniform, wearisome, dull, tedious, same, unison, humdrum, undiversified; similar, like.
ANT. *Varied, changed, diversified; harmonic; lively; divergent, variant.*

Monster. Prodigy, enormity, marvel, portent; monstrosity, wonder; demon, fiend, dragon, sphinx, colossus, leviathan; ogre.
ANT. *Pigmy, dwarf, elf; angel, beauty, cherub.*

Monstrous. Abnormal, extraordinary, prodigious, portentous, marvelous, unnatural; vast, immense, colossal, stupendous; shocking, horrible, hateful, terrible, hideous.
ANT. *Beautiful, small, reasonable, little, shapely, regular, fair, pretty, comely; ordinary, familiar, natural; charming, lovely.*

Moral, *a.* Dutiful, right, virtuous, just, worthy, ethical; intellectual, spiritual, religious, pious, righteous, ideal.
ANT. *Immoral, wrong, sinful, unjust, unworthy, vicious, gross; irreligious, impious, sensual; physical, bodily, carnal.*

Moreover. Besides, further, in addition; also, likewise, in addition to.
ANT. *Finally, lastly.*

Morose. Gruff, gloomy, crusty, crabbed, acrimonious, severe, snappish, sullen, surly, churlish, dogged, ill-humored, ill-natured, sulky.
ANT. *Bland, gentle, benignant, good-natured, kind, loving, pleasant, sympathetic, genial, amiable, friendly, tender, indulgent, complaisant, mild.*

Mortal. Deathlike; deadly, destructive, poisonous; vulnerable, vital; human, perishable, ephemeral, transient, transitory.
ANT. *Immortal, undying, everlasting, eternal, divine, celestial, life-giving, perennial.*

Motherly. Maternal, motherlike, parental; kind, loving, affectionate.
ANT. *Paternal, fatherlike, fatherly; harsh, unloving, unkind, hateful.*

Motion. Movement, change, action, act, passage, move, process, transit, transition.
ANT. *Quiescence, quiet, rest, repose, stillness, immobility.*

Motive. Incentive, incitement, inducement, reason, spur, stimulus, cause; object, purpose; argument, conviction; impulse, prompting.
ANT. *Deed, achievement, execution, action, attempt, project; deflector, preventive, dissuasion, deterrent.*

Mourn. Lament, grieve, regret, rue, bewail, sorrow.
ANT. *Exult, joy, rejoice, be joyful, triumph, make merry.*

Mournful. Lugubrious, heavy, sad, sorrowful, grievous, calamitous.
ANT. *Joyful, jubilant, gladsome, cheerful, happy, pleasant, joyous.*

Move. Stir, agitate, trouble, affect, persuade, actuate, impel, prompt, instigate, incite, offer, induce.
ANT. *Stop, stay, arrest, prevent, deter; calm, appease, deflect.*

Movement. Motion; compulsion, stimulation, incitement, agitation, arousing, instigation.

ANT. *Stoppage, stay, pause, calm, quiet.*

Much. Great; long; considerable; abundant; far; ample, plenteous.

ANT. *Little, small, scarce, few, scanty, near; narrow.*

Multiplication. Teeming, multiplicity, multitude, increase, plurality, reproduction, augmentation, swarming, multifariousness, multitudinousness.

ANT. *Diminution, division, subtraction, reduction; extinction; rarity, scantiness; unity, singularity.*

Multitude. Throng, crowd, assembly, assemblage, commonalty, swarm, populace; host, rabble, mob, concourse.

ANT. *Individual, solitude; aristocracy; oligarchy; scantiness, paucity, scarcity.*

Mundane. Worldly, terrestrial, earthly; sublunary; secular, temporal.

ANT. *Unworldly, spiritual, celestial, eternal, supramundane, stellar, solar, lunar.*

Munificent. Bounteous, bountiful, liberal, generous; beneficent, free, lavish, extravagant.

ANT. *Small, niggardly, saving, sparing, mean, close.*

Musical. Melodious, harmonious, tuneful, symphonious, mellifluous, rhythmical.

ANT. *Discordant, inharmonious, harsh, raucous, unmelodious.*

Mute. Silent, dumb, speechless; voiceless; still, unpronounced; unresponsive; taciturn.

ANT. *Talkative, chattering, garrulous, vocal, speaking, loquacious, loud, noisy.*

Mutual. Common, correlative, reciprocal, joint, interchangeable.

ANT. *Detached, distinct, disunited, separate, severed, sundered, unshared, unreciprocated, unrequited, disconnected.*

Mysterious. Abstruse, enigmatical, dark, mystical, occult, obscure, secret, transcendental, unknown, unfathomable, mystic, hidden, inexplicable, inscrutable, cabalistic, incomprehensible, recondite.

ANT. *Clear, plain, apparent, manifest, bright, light, explainable, simple, comprehensible, obvious, easy, revealed, understood.*

Mystic. Unknowable, obscure, mysterious; allegorical, enigmatical; transcendental; cabalistic, symbolical.

ANT. *Familiar, simple, ordinary, commonplace, obvious, plain.*

Myth. Fable, tradition, legend; parable, invention, fiction, allegory; falsehood, lie.

ANT. *Truth, fact, history, narrative, incident.*

N

Nabob. Millionaire, Crœsus, viceroy, governor, Dives.
ANT. *Beggar, suppliant.*

Naked. Nude, bare; defenseless, unprotected, destitute; manifest, undisguised; simple, mere, plain; unclothed, undraped, denuded; uncolored, unvarnished.
ANT. *Robed, draped, veiled, dressed, shrouded, muffled; protected, sheltered; colored, varnished, qualified.*

Name, *n.* Appellation, denomination, cognomen, designation, surname, title, style, epithet.

Name, *v.* Call, indicate, designate, specify, mention, denominate, style, nominate.
ANT. *Miscall, misname, misindicate; be nameless* or *anonymous; hint, suggest, shadow, intimate, imply.*

Narrate. Relate, tell, recount, describe, detail, rehearse, report, recite.
ANT. *Misrepresent, mistake; suppress, conceal.*

Narrative. Narration, recital, account, rehearsal, relation, description, story, tale, history.

Narrow. Not wide, straitened, limited, without margin; bigoted, illiberal; parsimonious, niggardly, selfish; close, scrutinizing, exact; slender, spare, thin, contracted, cramped.
ANT. *Wide, broad, ample, expanded, thick; generous, benevolent; unlimited; liberal.*

Nascent. Embryo, rudimental, budding, incipient.
ANT. *Grown, developed, mature; aged; confirmed, set.*

Nasty. Filthy, foul, dirty, offensive, damp, disgusting, disagreeable, wet; indecent, obscene.
ANT. *Pleasant, sweet, agreeable, savory, nice, pure.*

Nation. People, race, stock; realm, community, state, commonwealth.

Native. Innate, natal, natural, original, indigenous.
ANT. *Alien, artificial, foreign, unnatural, acquired, assumed.*

Natural. Native; essential, normal, regular, intrinsic, cosmical, spontaneous, original, artless, ingenuous; kind, affectionate; genuine, unaffected.
ANT. *Abnormal, monstrous, unnatural, improbable, adventitious, fictitious, coarse; artful, affected.*

Nature. Creation, universe; essence, constitution; kind, sort, character, quality; temper, disposition, mood; mind, intelligence; vitality.
ANT. *Thing, subject, object, man, being, creature, monstrosity, unnaturalness; art, fiction, romance, invention.*

Naught. Nothing, cipher, zero.
ANT. *Anything, everything, aught.*

Naughty. Mischievous, perverse, froward; bad, corrupt, worthless, good-for-nothing; refractory, wicked.
ANT. *Good, worthy, well-behaved, tractable, pure, docile, innocent.*

Nausea. Seasickness, loathing, disgust, qualm; repugnance, aversion.
ANT. *Enjoyment, taste, delight, relish.*

Nautical. Marine, maritime, naval, oceanic.

Near, *ad.* Nigh, not remote, almost, nearly, well-nigh, intimately, closely.

Near, *a.* Nigh, close, adjacent, adjoining, approximate; imminent, impending, forthcoming, approaching; familiar, dear, intimate; immediate; literal, accurate; narrow, parsimonious; short; proximate, contiguous, present, ready.

ANT. *Distant, remote, far; reserved, uncordial, cool, stiff; indistinct, obscure, future.*

Nearly. Almost, well-nigh, intimately, closely, approximately.

ANT. *Quite, entirely, distantly, remotely.*

Neat. Trim, tidy, prim, precise, spruce, clean, cleanly, orderly, natty, dapper, nice.

ANT. *Negligent, slack, slovenly, slouchy, dirty, soiled, disorderly, dowdy, untidy, rough, unkempt, rude, uncared for.*

Necessary. Essential, inevitable, needful, infallible, undeniable, indispensable, required, requisite, unavoidable.

ANT. *Optional, useless, contingent, worthless, casual, nonessential, needless.*

Necessitate. Force, compel, coerce, make necessary, oblige, constrain, make, drive, impel.

ANT. *Persuade, convince, induce, tempt, coax, allure; liberate, release.*

Necessity. Need, requirement, want, compulsion, fate, fatality, requisite, destiny, essential, emergency, extremity, exigency, indispensableness, urgency, unavoidableness, *sine qua non.*

ANT. *Choice, contingency, doubt, option, freedom, uncertainty, fortuity, doubtfulness, dubiousness, possibility.*

Need. Exigency, emergency, extremity, strait, distress, indigence, penury.

ANT. *Competence, affluence, choice, wealth, luxury, profuseness; superfluity, uselessness, dispensableness; casualty, accident; contingency, freedom.*

Needful. Requisite, needy, necessitous, distressful, essential, indispensable.

ANT. *Contingent, casual, unnecessary, unessential, discretional, optional, needless.*

Needless. Unnecessary, useless, superfluous, groundless, gratuitous.

ANT. *Needful, useful, helpful, obligatory.*

Nefarious. Wicked, abominable, iniquitous, execrable, atrocious, impious.

ANT. *Noble, honorable, admirable, laudable; benevolent, generous, humane.*

Negation. Denial, disavowal, disclaimer, contradiction.

ANT. *Assertion, declaration, deposition, avowal, affirmation, allegation, protestation, claim.*

Negative, *a.* Denying, indirect, unaffirmative, privative, disclaiming.

ANT. *Positive, direct, assertive, attributive, affirmative, declarative.*

Neglect, *n.* Negligence, failure, omission, disregard, oversight, indifference, remissness, slight, thoughtlessness, slackness, default, carelessness, disrespect, heedlessness, inadvertence, inattention, scorn.

ANT. *Care, attention, notice, regard, esteem, consideration, respect.*

Negotiate. Transfer, sell, pass, arrange, treat, bargain, trade, communicate, transact, effect, perform.

ANT. *Stop, quash, mismanage, misconduct.*

Neighborly. Kind, civil, social, friendly, near, adjoining, adjacent, neighboring, friendly, attentive.

ANT. *Individual, solitary, personal, distant, remote, unkind, uncivil, unfriendly.*

Nerve. Steadiness, firmness, fortitude, self-command, resolution, strength, courage, pluck, endurance, coolness, presence of mind.

ANT. *Weakness, cowardice, timidity, feebleness, nervelessness.*

Nervous. Excitable, agitated, annoyed, irritable, weak, fearful; strong, vigorous, spirited, nervy, forceful.

ANT. *Self-possessed, self-controlled, poised, calm, composed; dull, inert, phlegmatic, sluggish.*

Neutral. Neuter, undecided, indifferent, unpronounced, uninterfering, negative, impartial, unavowed, unaffiliated.

ANT. *Interested, interfering, positive, partial, active, allied, avowed, declared.*

Neutralize. Render neutral, invalidate, counteract, counterbalance, countervail, render inoperative.

ANT. *Enhance, intensify, aggravate.*

New. Fresh, modern, novel, late, recent, juvenile, upstart, young, new-fangled, youthful, new-fashioned.

ANT. *Old, antique, ancient, old-fashioned, aged, elderly.*

News. Information, tidings, intelligence, advice, word, report, account, announcement, rumor.

ANT. *Ignorance, silence, nonpublication, suppression; misintelligence, misreport.*

Nice. Exquisite, accurate, correct, precise, particular, punctilious, squeamish, finical, effeminate, silly, exact, critical, definite, strict, fastidious, cautious, scrupulous; discerning, discriminating; fine, minute, refined, delicate, dainty, pleasant, agreeable.

ANT. *Coarse, rude, rough, inaccurate, blind, undiscriminating, unscrupulous, incautious, undiscerning, careless, negligent, disagreeable, nauseous.*

Nicety. Fastidiousness, accuracy, scrupulousness, delicacy, precision, daintiness, subtlety, distinction, exactness.

ANT. *Coarseness, roughness, inaccuracy, rudeness.*

Niggardly. Avaricious, covetous, parsimonious, miserly, sordid, sparing, penurious, stingy.

ANT. *Generous, bountiful, copious, ample, profuse, abundant, bounteous, plentiful, munificent.*

Nimble. Alert, brisk, bustling, lively, prompt, quick, speedy, swift, spry, agile, sprightly, active.

ANT. *Clumsy, dilatory, dull, heavy, inert, inactive, slow, unready, sluggish.*

Nobility. Greatness, dignity, superiority, nobleness, eminence, elevation, worthiness; family, rank, title, birth; aristocracy, peerage, patrician class.

ANT. *Obscurity, meanness, serfdom, paltriness, plebeianism.*

Noble. Honorable, worthy, dignified, elevated, superior, sublime, great, eminent, stately, generous, liberal, free, aristocratic, patrician, illustrious, grand, lordly, renowned, magnificent, knightly.

ANT. *Ignoble, plebeian, paltry, vulgar, base-born, low-born, rustic, peasant, contemptible, unworthy, mean.*

Nobody. No person, no one, not anybody, cipher, nonentity.

ANT. *Somebody, notability, celebrity, colossus, star.*

Nocturnal. Nightly, dark, tenebrose, gloomy.

ANT. *Daily, diurnal, solar, brilliant, light.*

Noise. Cry, outcry, clamor, din clatter, uproar; rumor, report, rattle, tumult.

ANT. *Music, melody, harmony; silence, hush, stillness, voicelessness.*

Noiseless. Silent, quiet, inaudible.

ANT. *Noisy, uproarious, turbulent, clamorous, boisterous, brawling, tumultuous, loud.*

Noisome. Noxious, insalubrious, unwholesome, mischievous, destructive, nocuous, hurtful, pestilential, harmful.

ANT. *Wholesome, salutary, salubrious, beneficial.*

Noisy. Loud, clamorous, stunning, boisterous, turbulent.

ANT. *Noiseless, subdued, inaudible, whispering; melodious, tuneful.*

Nominal. Literal, verbal, titular; formal, avowed, pretended, ostensible, supposititious.

ANT. *Veritable, essential, intrinsic, actual, substantial, important, real, serious, true.*

Nominate. Name, specify, appoint, designate, entitle.

ANT. *Suggest, withdraw, reject, indicate, cancel, deprive, recall.*

Nonsense. Folly, silliness, absurdity, trash, inanity, platitude, pretense.

ANT. *Sense, wisdom, fact, truth, gravity, reason, science.*

Normal. Regular, ordinary, natural, standard, usual, typical, recognized, common.

ANT. *Exceptional, abnormal, uncommon, singular, unusual, monstrous, irregular, peculiar, rare, unprecedented, remarkable, unnatural.*

Notable. Plain, evident, noted, noticeable, distinguished, memorable, extraordinary, conspicuous, manifest; notorious.

ANT. *Ordinary, mean, commonplace, everyday, undistinguished, unimpressive, insignificant.*

Note. Memorandum, comment, remark, record, scholium; account, catalogue, bill; heed, observation; reputation, distinction, celebrity, fame, repute, renown.

ANT. *Misindication, misrepresentation, misleader.*

Notice, *n.* Observation, regard, cognizance, information, advice, news, intelligence, intimation, announcement, premonition, instruction, warning, attention, consideration.

ANT. *Oversight, disregard, neglect, slight, ignorance, connivance, omission, heedlessness, misinformation.*

Notice, *v.* Mark, observe, note, heed, regard, perceive, see, remark, mention, comment on, attend, mind.

ANT. *Overlook, disregard, misjudge, neglect.*

Notification. Information, notice, declaration, publication, announcement, advertisement.

Notify. Intimate, declare, publish, announce, acquaint, warn, apprise, communicate, inform.

ANT. *Withhold, conceal, suppress, misinform, misreport.*

Notion. Idea, conception, apprehension, sentiment, judgment, opinion, belief, impression, estimation, conceit, conviction.
ANT. *Misconception, misapprehension, frustration, falsification.*

Notorious. Distinguished, conspicuous, remarkable, famous, celebrated, noted, renowned.
ANT. *Suspected, reputed, reported.*

Notwithstanding, *conj.* Still, however, although, but, nevertheless, howbeit, yet, though.

Notwithstanding, *prep.* Despite, in spite of.

Nourish. Feed, foster, cherish, nurse, tend, support, maintain, train, educate, promote.
ANT. *Starve, blight, destroy, kill.*

Nourishment. Nutrition, nutriment, food, aliment, provision, sustenance.
ANT. *Poison, venom, bane, starvation, exhaustion.*

Novel, *a.* New, recent, modern, fresh, strange, uncommon, rare, unusual, fantastic, odd, upstart, new-fangled.
ANT. *Venerable, ancient, old-fashioned, time-honored.*

Noxious. Noisome, injurious, hurtful, pernicious, unwholesome, deadly, poisonous.
ANT. *Wholesome, salutary, beneficial, healthful, salubrious.*

Nucleus. Kernel, core, center.
ANT. *Exterior, face, appearance.*

Nudity. Nakedness, exposure, bareness.
ANT. *Clothing, dress, vestment, drapery.*

Nugatory. Trifling, vain, insignificant, futile, ineffectual, unavailing, trivial, worthless, useless, null.
ANT. *Important, potent, momentous, efficacious, successful, grave, serious, satisfactory.*

Nuisance. Annoyance, plague, pest, affliction, bane, trouble.
ANT. *Pleasure, delight, benefit, blessing, gratification.*

Nullify. Revoke, annul, cancel, abolish, render void, abrogate, neutralize, repeal.
ANT. *Enact, confirm, perpetuate, establish, stabilitate.*

Numb. Enfeebled, destitute, torpid, benumbed, insensible, paralyzed, deadened.
ANT. *Alive, alert, sensitive, keen, lively, animated, attentive.*

Number, *n.* Aggregation, multitude, collection, numeral, numerous, quantity.
ANT. *Scarcity, fewness, paucity.*

Number, *v.* Count, enumerate, calculate, tell, compute, reckon, estimate.
ANT. *Guess, hazard, conjecture; lump, mass.*

Numberless. Innumerable, infinite, countless.
ANT. *Few, scarce, rare, infrequent.*

Numerous. Many, abundant, diverse, multifarious, manifold, sundry.
ANT. *Few, scarce, rare, infrequent.*

Nuptial. Wedding, marriage, hymeneal, espousal, connubial, bridal.
ANT. *Bachelor, virgin.*

Nurse, *v.* Nourish, cherish, foster, attend, manage, train, educate, teach, feed, nurture.
ANT. *Starve, kill, destroy; neglect.*

Nurture. Nourish, nurse, tend, cherish, educate, train, feed,

Ant. *Neglect, deprive, disregard, slight.*

Nutriment. Aliment, food, sustenance, nourishment, sustentation, subsistence, nutrition.

Ant. *Starvation, detriment, exhaustion, poison, decay, inanition.*

Nutrition. Nutriment, feeding, sustentation.

Ant. *Poison, venom.*

O

Oath. Curse, imprecation, profanity, swearing, adjuration, affidavit, anathema, ban, blasphemy, denunciation, execration, malediction, vow, reprobation, sworn statement.

Ant. *Blessing, benediction, benison.*

Obdurate. Firm, unbending, inflexible, unyielding, obstinate, stubborn, impenitent, callous, unfeeling, insensible.

Ant. *Yielding, teachable, tender, docile, amenable, flexible, softened.*

Obedience. Submission, duty, compliance, respect, dutifulness, subservience.

Ant. *Resistance, rebellion, transgression, disobedience, antagonism, insubordination.*

Obedient. Dutiful, respectful, compliant, submissive, humble, yielding, obsequious, modest, docile.

Ant. *Disrespectful, undutiful, arrogant, hard, unyielding, obstinate, obdurate, stubborn.*

Obesity. Fatness, corpulence, fleshiness, corpulency.

Ant. *Leanness, thinness.*

Obey. Submit, yield, comply.

Ant. *Resist, refuse, disobey.*

Object, *n.* Reality, fact, existence, phenomenon; aim, intention, end, purpose, appearance, motive, design, sight, view, goal.

Ant. *Subject, idea, fancy, conception.*

Objective. Outward, external, extrinsic, concrete, universal, actual, positive, real.

Ant. *Subjective, intrinsic, abstract, notional.*

Oblation. Offering, gift, sacrifice, contribution, presentation.

Ant. *Spoliation, sacrilege, withholding, refusal.*

Obligation. Responsibility, engagement, contract, agreement, bond, covenant, stipulation, necessity, debt, duty, compulsion.

Ant. *Choice, freedom, assurance, promise, declaration, intention.*

Oblige. Bind, please, gratify, accommodate, favor, constrain, compel, force, coerce, benefit, necessitate, obligate.

Ant. *Release, acquit; persuade, induce; annoy, disoblige.*

Obliging. Civil, courteous, complaisant, kind, considerate, accommodating, compliant.

Ant. *Discourteous, inconsiderate, rude, disobliging, unaccommodating.*

Oblique. Indirect, slanting, inclined, perverse, disingenuous, diagonal, divergent, angular.

Ant. *Straightforward, rectilineal.*

Oblivion. Forgetfulness, disremembrance.

Ant. *Memory, reminiscence, remembrance, recollection, celebration, commemoration.*

Obloquy. Censure, odium, contumely, reproach, gainsaying, reviling, calumny, slander, detraction.

ANT. *Praise, acclamation, encomium, panegyric.*

Obnoxious. Odious, detrimental, blameworthy, pernicious, offensive.

ANT. *Pleasant, grateful, independent, wholesome, beneficial, salutary.*

Obscure, *a.* Abstruse, deep, involved, difficult, hidden, profound, mysterious, ambiguous, unintelligible, cloudy, complex, complicated, dark, darksome, dense, dim, doubtful, intricate, dusky, indistinct, enigmatical, incomprehensible, muddy, turbid, shadowy, misty, unknown, secluded, unascertained, remote.

ANT. *Clear, luminous, distinct, lucid, plain, plain-spoken, intelligible, prominent, eminent.*

Obsequious. Servile, cringing, fawning, compliant, submissive, deferential, sycophantic, flattering.

ANT. *Impudent, self-assertive, independent, arrogant, insubmissive, haughty, proud.*

Observance. Observation, heeding, form, practice, custom, attention, celebration, ceremony, performance.

ANT. *Inobservance, inattention, disuse, disregard, disrespect, omission, unceremoniousness, informality.*

Observant. Observing, watchful, attentive, regardful, obedient, mindful, careful, heedful.

ANT. *Unmindful, disobedient, disregardful, heedless.*

Observation. Contemplation, remark, study, notice, view, conclusion, judgment, attention, comment, note, observance.

ANT. *Inattention, oversight, silence, ignorance, inadvertence.*

Observe. Remark, note, watch, heed, see, discover, attend, comment.

ANT. *Overlook, misconceive, misunderstand.*

Obsolete. Disused, ancient, neglected, antiquated, archaic, effete, past, old-fashioned, old, rare, obsolescent.

ANT. *Fashionable, modern, current, customary, new, novel, extant.*

Obstacle. Impediment, obstruction, difficulty, hindrance, barrier, check.

ANT. *Course, proceeding, career, advancement, progress.*

Obstinacy. Pertinacity, firmness, resoluteness, inflexibility, persistency, perverseness, contumacy.

ANT. *Flexibility, docility, complaisance.*

Obstinate. Perverse, obdurate, intractable, determined, stubborn, resolved, resolute, inflexible, unyielding, intractable, indomitable, unflinching, contumacious, decided, dogged, mulish, heady, headstrong, fixed, firm, immovable, opinionated, persistent, pertinacious, refractory, unconquerable.

ANT. *Pliant, docile, submissive, dutiful, gentle, obedient, compliant, tractable, yielding, amenable, complaisant, irresolute, wavering, undecided, pliable, teachable.*

Obstruct. Bar, barricade, hinder, oppose, impede, stay, stop, arrest, check, embarrass, clog, choke, retard, interrupt.

ANT. *Aid, facilitate, accelerate, forward, promote, clear, advance, open, pave the way for, further, free, expedite.*

Obstruction. Obstacle, barrier, bar, impediment, check, clog, hindrance.

ANT. *Course, proceeding, advancement, progress, career.*

Obtain. Attain, gain, procure, acquire, earn, win.

ANT. *Lose, forfeit, surrender, forego.*

Obtrude. Intrude, force, interfere, thrust.

ANT. *Suggest, hint, insinuate; retire, withdraw.*

Obtuse. Blunt, dull, stupid, unintelligent, stolid.

ANT. *Keen, quick, sharp, intelligent, acute, clever.*

Obverse. Opposite, facing.

ANT. *Hinder, reverse.*

Obvious. Opposing; plain, evident, clear, manifest, apparent, discovered, perceived, open, explicit, patent.

ANT. *Remote, obscure, farfetched, involved, latent.*

Occasion, *v.* Cause, produce, create, induce, originate, furnish. compose, constitute, generate.

Occasionally. Sometimes, casually, rarely.

ANT. *Always, constantly, regularly, frequently.*

Occult. Secret, concealed, hidden, unknown, invisible, latent, eclipsed, unrevealed, mysterious.

ANT. *Developed, plain, exposed, patent, clear, familiar, open.*

Occupancy. Possession, occupation, tenury.

ANT. *Eviction, ejection, dispossession.*

Occupation. Occupancy, avocation, employment, engagement, vocation, calling, office, trade, profession.

ANT. *Idleness, leisure, vacancy, vacation, abandonment resignation.*

Occupy. Possess, hold, employ fill.

ANT. *Abandon, release, desert, surrender, vacate, concede*

Occur. Happen, appear, meet befall, betide, take place.

ANT. *Threaten, pass, impend.*

Occurrence. Event, happening incident, affair, adventure, circumstance, transaction, episode

ANT. *Cause, antecedent, inducement, predisposition, tendency, contribution.*

Odd. Quaint, unmatched, queer, unusual, eccentric, fantastical, droll, comical, singular, peculiar.

ANT. *Common, usual, regular, normal, matched.*

Odious. Hateful, detestable, disgusting, abominable, repulsive, forbidding, unpopular, invidious, loathsome.

ANT. *Pleasing, pleasant, acceptable, agreeable, grateful, delectable, bewitching, charming.*

Odium. Hatred, abhorrence, detestation, antipathy, unpopularity, offensiveness.

ANT. *Welcome, acceptableness, popularity.*

Odor. Scent, perfume, smell, fragrance, aroma, redolence; trail, effluvium, fume.

ANT. *Inodorousness.*

Odorous. Fragrant, perfumed, balmy, aromatic, odorant.

ANT. *Scentless, inodorous; fetid.*

Offend. Displease, affront, harm, pain, annoy, transgress.

ANT. *Please, gratify, conciliate.*

Offense. Umbrage, misdeed, delinquency, transgression, fault,

affront, indignity, outrage, insult.
ANT. *Defense, guiltlessness, innocence.*

Offensive. Disagreeable, obnoxious, distasteful, impertinent, disgusting, rude, saucy, approbrious, insulting, insolent, attacking, abusive, invading, assailant.
ANT. *Defensive, pleasing, grateful, savory.*

Offer. Propose, propound, tender, sacrifice, immolate, undertake, attempt, try, proffer.
ANT. *Withhold, withdraw, retract, retain, alienate, divert.*

Offhand. Instant, ready, extemporaneous, unpremeditated, unstudied, impromptu.
ANT. *Premeditated, elaborate, studied, thought-out.*

Office. Service, duty, custom, position, charge, authority, function, business.
ANT. *Leisure, vacancy, sinecure, resignation.*

Officer. Official, functionary, director, dignitary, manager, administrator.
ANT. *Member, servant, private, employee.*

Official, *a.* Administrative, authoritative, functional, professional.
ANT. *Private, unofficial, unprofessional.*

Officiate. Act, serve, perform.
ANT. *Witness, retire.*

Officious. Impertinent, meddlesome, interfering, forward, intrusive, pushing.
ANT. *Negligent, backward, remiss; retiring, modest.*

Often. Frequently, repeatedly, commonly, many times, not seldom.
ANT. *Infrequently, seldom, rarely.*

Old. Aged, ancient, primitive, pristine, antique, antiquated, old-fashioned, obsolete; senile; gray, hoary, olden, immemorial, time-honored, decrepit, elderly, patriarchal, remote, venerable, time-worn.
ANT. *Youthful, childlike, young; recent, modern, fresh, new-fashioned, current.*

Omen. Prognostic, augury, presage, sign, portent, foreboding.
ANT. *Fulfilment, event, occurrence, realization.*

Ominous. Significant, portentous, unpropitious, threatening, inauspicious, foreboding, premonitory, suggestive.
ANT. *Encouraging, auspicious, propitious.*

Omit, *v.* Leave out, neglect, forbear, fail, miss, overlook.
ANT. *Consider, observe, notice, attend, regard.*

Omnipotent. All-powerful, irresistible, Almighty.
ANT. *Powerless, inefficient, impotent.*

Omniscient. All-knowing, infallible, all-wise.
ANT. *Short-sighted, fallible, ignorant.*

One. Single, individual, solitary, certain, undivided, common, united, unitary.
ANT. *Many, several; few.*

Onerous. Burdensome, oppressive, heavy, toilsome, difficult, laborious, responsible.
ANT. *Light, easy, trivial.*

Only, *ad.* Solely, singly, exclusively, merely, barely, wholly.
ANT. *Among, amongst, together, collectively.*

Only, *a.* Single, sole, alone, preeminent, chief.
ANT. *Many, together, several, mixed.*

Onset, Onslaught. Assault, attack, storming, aggression, invasion.

ANT. *Repulse, resistance, protection, shelter, support, defense.*

Onward. Forward, in advance, ahead.

ANT. *Aback, astern, backward.*

Opaque. Impervious, not transparent, obscure, unintelligible.

ANT. *Pellucid, translucent, transparent, obvious, clear, intelligible, perspicuous.*

Open, *v.* Unclose, disclose, expose, explain, begin, commence, initiate.

ANT. *Close, shut, cover, conceal; conclude, terminate; misinterpret, mystify.*

Open, *a.* Unclosed, uncovered, unprotected, exposed, plain, obvious, evident, public, artless, candid, free, available, accessible, undisguised, ingenuous.

ANT. *Closed, barred, inaccessible, unavailable, reserved, shut, secreted.*

Opening. Aperture, hole, space, breach, gap, fissure; start, inauguration, commencement, initiation, beginning; opportunity.

ANT. *Obstruction, stop-gap, termination, enclosure, close, end, conclusion, inopportunity, unseasonableness.*

Operation. Agency, action, exercise, production, influence, force, performance, result, procedure, effect, execution.

ANT. *Failure, uselessness, futility, ineffectiveness, inefficiency, powerlessness, inaction, cessation, rest.*

Opinion. Persuasion, idea, sentiment, view, conviction, judgment, notion, impression, estimation.

ANT. *Evidence, argument, inquiry, speculation, investigation, pleading.*

Opponent. Antagonist, foe, adversary, enemy, rival.

ANT. *Helper, assistant, accomplice, ally.*

Opportune. Timely, seasonable, convenient, ready, suitable, auspicious, meet, appropriate.

ANT. *Untimely, unseasonable, inopportune, infelicitous.*

Opportunity. Occasion, convenience, occurrence, turn, opening.

ANT. *Lapse, omission, inopportuneness,* contre-temps.

Oppose. Combat, withstand, contradict, deny, gainsay, oppugn, contravene, check, obstruct.

ANT. *Aid, abet, support, advance, expedite.*

Opposite. Facing, contrary, repugnant, antagonistic, adverse, counter, contradictory, opposed.

ANT. *Agreeing, coincident, harmonious, conformable, suiting, fitting, accordant.*

Opposition. Restraint, defeat, resistance, hostility, obstacle, obstruction, animosity.

ANT. *Sympathy, harmony, concord, alliance, congeniality.*

Oppress. Impose, weigh down, burden, grind, persecute, overwhelm, crush, overpower, subdue.

ANT. *Encourage, assist, support, befriend.*

Oppression. Cruelty, tyranny, hardship, injustice, severity.

ANT. *Kindness, mercy, justice, clemency, leniency.*

Oppressive. Heavy, oppressing, rigorous, tyrannical, unjust, extortionate, grinding.

ANT. *Light, easy, compassionate, just, humane, generous.*

Opprobrium. Disgrace, infamy, reproach, contempt, scandal, obloquy, odium.

ANT. *Popularity, welcome, acceptableness.*

Option. Choice, preference, selection, discretion, wish, election.
ANT. *Compulsion, necessity, obligation.*

Opulence. Wealth, riches, fortune, affluence, independence.
ANT. *Poverty, impecuniosity, indigence, want.*

Oracle. Revelation; prophet, angel.
ANT. *Empiricism, pragmatism.*

Oracular. Prophetic, ominous, portentous; authoritative, positive, dogmatical; wise, grave, sage; obscure, equivocal, ambiguous.
ANT. *Cautious, modest, vacillating, diffident.*

Oral. Verbal, unwritten, vocal, spoken, traditional.
ANT. *Documentary, written.*

Oration. Address, speech, discourse, harangue, lecture, disputation, declamation, effusion.
ANT. *Reasoning, suggestion, insinuation.*

Oratory. Eloquence, rhetoric, elocution, declamation.
ANT. *Hesitation, stammering, dulness.*

Orb. Sphere, globe, ball; circle, orbit, circuit; disk; revolution.

Orbit. Revolution, path, circuit, sphere.
ANT. *Deviation, eccentricity, perturbation.*

Ordain. Set, regulate, establish, appoint, decree, constitute, institute, prescribe, dictate.
ANT. *Revoke, subvert, cancel, countermand.*

Ordeal. Test, trial, experiment, probation, proof, scrutiny, assay, investigation.
ANT. *Result, event; argument, evidence, plea, discussion.*

Order. Arrangement, system, procedure, method, rule, regulation; command, mandate, rank, direction, grade, class, character, kind, management, injunction, prohibition, requirement, instruction.
ANT. *Allowance, consent, leave, permission, permit, liberty, license.*

Orderly. Regular, obedient, systematic, quiet, peaceable, methodical, well-regulated.
ANT. *Disorderly, riotous, irregular.*

Ordinance. Statue, law, edict, decree, rescript, regulation, institute, rule.
ANT. *Custom, usage, tradition, fashion.*

Ordinary. Normal, usual, common, customary, settled, frequent, wonted, habitual, indifferent, mediocre, plain, commonplace.
ANT. *Extraordinary, superior, unusual, uncommon.*

Organic. Inherent, fundamental, essential, constitutional, radical, vital; organized, systematized.
ANT. *Non-essential, circumstantial, provisional, contingent, inorganic, secondary.*

Organization. Structure, form, construction; organism.
ANT. *Disorganization.*

Organize. Arrange, constitute, shape, adjust, frame, establish, construct, systematize.
ANT. *Disorganize, dismember, disband, break up, annul.*

Origin. Source, rise, commencement, spring, fountain, derivation, cause, root, foundation.
ANT. *Termination, conclusion, extinction.*

Original. Primitive, new, primary, pristine, genuine, inventive, peculiar, initiatory, primordial, ancient, former, first.

ANT. *Subsequent, later, derivative, modern, terminal.*

Originate. Begin, cause, commence, start, invent, create, spring, rise.

ANT. *Prosecute, conduct; conclude, finish, end.*

Ornament. Decoration, embellishment, adornment.

ANT. *Disgrace, brand, disfigurement, detraction.*

Ornate. Adorned, beautiful, embellished, decorated, elaborate, rich, ornamented.

ANT. *Bare, bald, nude, plain, naked.*

Orthodox. Sound, conventional, approved, correct.

ANT. *Heretical, unorthodox, liberal, radical.*

Ostensible. Exhibited, avowed, professed, apparent, pretended, declared, manifest, specious, plausible, outward.

ANT. *Real, actual, genuine, veritable, concealed, hidden.*

Ostentation. Display, boasting, show, boast, vaunting, flourish, pageant, pomp, parade, pageantry.

ANT. *Diffidence, modesty, reserve, timidity, shrinking, retirement, quietness, unobtrusiveness.*

Ostracism. Banishment, exclusion, expulsion, blackball, excommunication, separation.

ANT. *Admittance, enlistment, enrolment; welcome, fellowship.*

Outbreak. Outburst, eruption, tumult, commotion, rebellion, insurrection, riot, conflict.

ANT. *Quiet, order, pacification, subsidence, quelling.*

Outcast. Exile, vagabond, reprobate, castaway, pariah, vagrant.

Outcry. Clamor, tumult, vociferation, alarm, yell, scream, noise.

ANT. *Quiet, silence; acclamation, plaudit.*

Outer. Outside, outward, external, exterior.

ANT. *Inward, inside, internal, interior.*

Outlaw. Brigand, bandit, robber, highwayman, marauder, freebooter.

Outlet. Egress, exit, vent.

ANT. *Entrance, ingress.*

Outline. Contour, sketch, delineation, draft, plan.

ANT. *Form, substance, bulk, figure, field, ground, space; object, subject.*

Outrage. Outbreak, offense, violence, mischief, abuse, affront, insult, indignity.

ANT. *Favor; self-restraint, self-control.*

Outrageous. Violent, furious, excessive, exorbitant, wanton, atrocious, monstrous, nefarious, heinous.

ANT. *Moderate, reasonable, justifiable.*

Outskirts. Border, edge, outpost, precincts, environs, suburbs.

ANT. *Interior, center, bulk, mass, body, heart.*

Outstanding. Uncollected, undischarged, unappropriated, unpaid; projecting; opposing.

ANT. *Collected, appropriated, gathered, paid; supporting; reëntrant.*

Outward. Out, outer, external, exterior, public, visible, sensible, extraneous, superficial, apparent, extrinsic, ostensible.

ANT. *Internal, intrinsic, inward, withdrawn.*

Overcast. Cloudy, lowering, obscured, murky, darkened, overspread, eclipsed.

ANT. *Cloudless, clear, luminous.*

Overcome. Vanquish, conquer, surmount, excel, overthrow, subjugate, rule, domineer over.
ANT. *Lose, forfeit, surrender, fail, submit, retreat, succumb.*

Overflow, *n.* Redundancy, inundation, deluge, exuberance, superabundance.
ANT. *Subsidence, deficiency, exhaustion.*

Overruling. Governing, controlling, superior, predominant, directing, prevailing.
ANT. *Governed, controlled, inferior, subordinate.*

Oversight. Charge, superintendence, management, supervision, command, care, watchfulness, surveillance, control, inspection, direction, watch; omission, error, inadvertence.
ANT. *Mismanagement, negligence, disregard, slight; particularity, attention to minutiæ.*

Overt. Public, manifest, apparent, deliberate, open, avowed.
ANT. *Covert, secret, furtive, clandestine, implied.*

Overthrow. Upset, ruin, demolish, destroy, overcome, defeat.
ANT. *Restore, reinstate, revive.*

Overture. Proposal, proposition, offer, opening, prelude, invitation, advance, initiation.
ANT. *Inaction, quiescence.*

Overweening. Rash, arrogant, egoistic, vain, haughty, conceited.
ANT. *Affable, courteous, sociable, condescending, gracious, polite, approachable.*

Overwhelm. Submerge, engulf, immerse, overpower, extinguish, bury, crush, sink, subdue, vanquish, conquer, defeat.
ANT. *Raise, reinstate, reëstablish, rescue, extricate.*

Owe. Be indebted for, be obliged for, borrow, hypothecate, attribute.
ANT. *Repay, requite, defray, liquidate.*

Own. Possess, grant, acknowledge, admit, confess, avow.
ANT. *Lose, disown, abandon, forfeit, alienate, disinherit, abjure.*

P

Pacific. Appeasing, reconciling, tranquil, mild, calm, peaceful, conciliatory.
ANT. *Harsh, irritating, exasperating, quarrelsome, turbulent, tumultuous, warlike.*

Pacification. Conciliation, compromise, reconcilement, adjustment, reconciliation.
ANT. *Warfare, fighting, hostilities, war.*

Pact. Agreement, league, compact, covenant, bargain, stipulation, alliance, bond.
ANT. *Understanding, promise, parole, honor.*

Pæan. Jubilation.
ANT. *Dirge.*

Pagan, *a.* Gentile, heathen, idolater.
ANT. *Christian, believer.*

Paganism. Heathenism, polytheism, pantheism.
ANT. *Christianity, Christendom.*

Pageant. Spectacle, exhibition, display, show, ceremony, procession, parade.

ANT. *Illusion, mockery, fantasmagoria, dream.*

Pageantry. Pomp, parade, display, show, spectacle, splendor, magnificence.

Pain, *n.* Agony, ache, distress, suffering, torture, anguish, torment, pang, throe, paroxysm, twinge, woe, grief.

ANT. *Ease, peace, rapture, enjoyment, relief, solace, comfort, delight.*

Pain, *v.* Hurt, grieve, afflict, disquiet, trouble, distress, agonize, torment, torture.

ANT. *Please, delight, rejoice, charm, refresh.*

Painful. Disquieting, troublesome, afflictive, distressing, laborious, grievous, toilsome, arduous, difficult.

ANT. *Pleasant, pleasurable, acceptable, agreeable, grateful, desirable, delectable, delicious.*

Painstaking. Careful, diligent, attentive, faithful, laborious.

ANT. *Neglectful, heedless, unmindful, disregardful, improvident, thoughtless, careless.*

Paint. Color, picture, depict, delineate, sketch, draw, portray.

ANT. *Misrepresent, caricature, daub.*

Pair. Two, couple, span, brace, yoke.

ANT. *One, several, many.*

Pale. Pallid, white, wan, colorless, dim, sallow.

ANT. *Ruddy, high-colored, conspicuous, brilliant.*

Palliate. Cover, conceal, extenuate, hide, veil, screen, cloak, gloss over, apologize for, mitigate.

ANT. *Alleviate; aggravate, heighten, increase, intensify.*

Palm. Laurels, bays, prize, trophy, crown.

ANT. *Shame, blot, stigma, brand.*

Palpable. Perceptible, obvious, plain, gross, material, corporeal, manifest, evident, patent, distinct.

ANT. *Immaterial, intangible, ethereal, impalpable, indistinct, dubious, imperceptible.*

Paltry. Contemptible, worthless, mean, vile, pitiful, trifling.

ANT. *Valuable, estimable, admirable, worthy, grand, excellent, magnificent.*

Panegyric. Eulogy, encomium, praise, laudation, commendation.

ANT. *Satire, sarcasm, tirade, stricture, invective, philippic.*

Pang. Agony, anguish, distress, paroxysm, throe.

ANT. *Pleasure, delight, refreshment, enjoyment, gratification.*

Parable. Fable, allegory, apologue, similitude.

ANT. *History, fact, narrative.*

Parade, *n.* Ostentation, display, show, pomp, pageant, spectacle, procession.

ANT. *Modesty, humility, retirement, simplicity, plainness, seclusion, suppression.*

Paradise. Bliss, heaven, Eden, ecstasy, Elysium.

ANT. *Purgatory, hell, torture, misery, torment.*

Paradox. Contradiction, ambiguity, absurdity, enigma, mystery.

ANT. *Axiom, postulate, precept, truism, proposition.*

Parallel. Correspondent, correlative, analogous, concurrent, equidistant.

ANT. *Different, opposed, divergent, irrelative, incongruous.*

Paralyze. Deaden, benumb, unnerve, destroy, impair, enfeeble, prostrate, debilitate.
ANT. *Nerve, strengthen, restore, invigorate.*

Paramount. Supreme, preëminent, chief, superior, principal.
ANT. *Minor, inferior, secondary, subordinate.*

Parasite. Flatterer, sycophant, courtier.
ANT. *Calumniator, traducer, detractor.*

Pardon, *n.* Absolution, mercy, forgiveness, forbearance, remission, acquittal, indulgence.
ANT. *Penalty, punishment, vengeance, retribution, retaliation.*

Pardon, *v.* Condone, forgive, absolve, excuse, overlook, remit, pass over *or* by, acquit.
ANT. *Convict, castigate, condemn, chastise, correct, punish, doom, sentence, scourge, visit upon, recompense, chasten.*

Pardonable. Excusable, forgivable, venial.
ANT. *Inexcusable, unpardonable.*

Parentage. Descent, extraction, lineage, birth, stock, pedigree.

Parsimonious. Avaricious, frugal, sparing, close, stingy, penurious, niggardly, illiberal.
ANT. *Liberal, profuse, unsparing, extravagant.*

Part, *n.* Fraction, fragment, section, atom, segment, element, piece, portion, instalment, constituent, component, ingredient, member, particle, share, subdivision.
ANT. *Whole, mass, bulk, entirety, quantity, totality.*

Partake. Share, participate.
ANT. *Yield, forfeit, forego, relinquish.*

Partial. Biased, restricted, specific, limited, imperfect, incomplete, unfair, unjust, warped, interested, inequitable.
ANT. *Unrestricted, universal, general, equitable, just, unbiased, impartial.*

Particle. Atom, corpuscle, iota, grain, jot, mite, molecule, element, whit, tittle, scrap, shred, scintilla.
ANT. *Mass, quantity, sum, entirety, sum total, whole, aggregate, total.*

Particular, *n.* Detail, point, feature.
ANT. *Whole, subject, case.*

Particular, *a.* Sole, single, individual, respective, appropriate, personal, singular, important, peculiar, especial, specific, precise, critical, circumstantial.
ANT. *Universal, general, comprehensive, indiscriminate, abstract, inaccurate, inexact, undiscriminating.*

Parting. Separation, leave-taking, farewell, dividing, division, disruption, detachment.
ANT. *Union, attachment.*

Partisan. Adherent, follower, supporter, disciple.
ANT. *Opponent, antagonist, adversary.*

Partition. Division, distribution, separation, allotment, apportionment; compartment, interspace, barrier.
ANT. *Combination, inclusion, comprehension, collection, union.*

Partly. In part, somewhat, partially, not wholly.
ANT. *Altogether, entirely, completely, to the full extent.*

Partner. Associate, colleague, coadjutor, confederate, participator, partaker, comrade, mate, companion.
ANT. *Rival, competitor, opponent, adversary, alien.*

Partnership. Company, firm,

union, connection, society, interest, house, association, participation.

ANT. *Independence, disconnection, disjunction, disunion, dissociation.*

Pass. Go, move, proceed, disappear, vanish, depart, take place, occur, elapse, spend, live, experience; transcend, exceed; send, transmit, deliver; utter, promise, pledge; finish.

ANT. *Hold up; abide, wait, halt, continue, endure.*

Passable. Navigable, current, acceptable, tolerable, admissible, moderate, traversible, mediocre.

ANT. *Impassable, impenetrable, inadmissible, impervious; excellent.*

Passage. Transit, conveyance, journey, way, road, path, hall, course, progress, process, vestibule, corridor.

Passible. Susceptible, sensitive, sensible, impressible.

ANT. *Impassible, insusceptible, unsensitive.*

Passion. Feeling, emotion, susceptibility, sentiment, ardor, excitement, desire, anger, warmth, vehemence.

ANT. *Indifference, apathy, coldness, coolness, frigidity.*

Passive. Quiescent, unopposing, enduring, submissive, patient, unresisting, inert, inactive, relaxed, negative.

ANT. *Resistant, positive, impatient, vehement, active, alert.*

Past. Gone by, elapsed, ended, spent, departed, late, accomplished.

ANT. *Present; future.*

Pastime. Entertainment, recreation, sport, play, amusement, diversion.

ANT. *Business, work, task, labor, occupation, study.*

Patent. Open, expanded, evident, apparent, manifest, public.

ANT. *Ambiguous, questionable, dubious.*

Paternal. Fatherly, tender, careful, hereditary.

ANT. *Careless, rough, harsh; acquired, conferred, won.*

Path. Footway, track, pathway, route, course, road; method.

Pathetic. Affecting, emotional, moving, pitiful, tender, touching, melting, plaintive.

ANT. *Ludicrous, ridiculous, farcical, unaffecting.*

Pathless. Untrodden, impenetrable, trackless.

ANT. *Trodden, frequented.*

Patience. Composure, calmness, leniency, fortitude, sufferance, submission, endurance, forbearance, resignation, long-suffering.

ANT. *Anger, impatience, ire, passion, fury, frenzy, rage, temper, vexation, petulance, wrath, fretfulness, peevishness.*

Patient. Resigned, passive, enduring, unrepining, calm, forbearing, long-suffering.

ANT. *Impatient, insubmissive, malcontent, vehement, resistant.*

Patrician. Noble, aristocratic, high-born, well-born.

ANT. *Plebeian, churlish, ordinary, peasant.*

Patrimony. Heritage, inheritance, estate.

Pattern. Archetype, exemplar, specimen, sample, design, mold.

ANT. *Caricature, misrepresentation, monstrosity, perversion.*

Paucity. Scantiness, deficiency, fewness, lack, want, rarity.

ANT. *Fulness, number, frequency, abundance, quantity.*

Pause, *n.* Stop, cessation, interruption, suspension, hesitation, suspense, doubt.

ANT. *Continuance, continuity, perseverance, progress, progression, advancement.*

Pause, *v.* Stop, cease, intermit, wait, stay, tarry, demur, hesitate.

ANT. *Continue, proceed, persist, persevere, advance.*

Pay, *n.* Earnings, stipend, salary, wages, allowance, retainer, remuneration, payment, compensation, hire, fee, requital, honorarium.

Pay, *v.* Recompense, requite, satisfy, compensate, discharge, remunerate, fulfil, expend, liquidate, disburse.

ANT. *Deprive, defraud, retain, exact, hoard, invest.*

Payment. Pay, compensation, satisfaction, content, salary, reward, wages, recompense, requital, return.

Peace. Quiet, calm, repose, tranquillity, stillness, silence, harmony, amity, concord, reconciliation, order, pacification.

ANT. *Noise, disturbance, disorder, war, strife, discord, variance, tumult, agitation, hostility.*

Peaceable. Peaceful, pacific, undisturbed, tranquil, quiet, mild, serene, still.

ANT. *Warlike, quarrelsome, hostile, savage, fierce, violent, restless.*

Peasant. Countryman, rustic, swain, laborer, villager.

ANT. *Citizen, townsman.*

Peculiar. Special, especial, individual, particular, appropriate, unusual, singular, strange, rare.

ANT. *General, universal, ordinary, public, common.*

Peculiarity. Individuality, singularity, idiosyncrasy, distinctiveness, specialty, characteristic, particularity.

ANT. *Universality, generality, uniformity, homogeneity, community.*

Pedigree. Lineage, descent, ancestry, genealogy, birth, parentage.

ANT. *Ancestor, founder, origin; plebeianism; extinction.*

Peer. Equal, match, mate, comrade, associate; nobleman.

ANT. *Superior; subordinate.*

Peerless. Unmatched, matchless, unequaled, unique, superlative, paramount.

ANT. *Ordinary, mediocre, commonplace.*

Peevish. Querulous, cross, testy, ill-tempered, captious, discontented, petulant, irritable, ill-natured, irascible.

ANT. *Good-natured, easy, genial, mild, complaisant, gentle.*

Penal. Punitive, retributive, corrective.

ANT. *Preventive, reparatory; honorary, remunerary.*

Penalty. Retribution, forfeiture, fine, punishment, amercement, mulct.

ANT. *Reward, wages, guerdon, prize, honorarium, remuneration, compensation.*

Pendent. Pendulous, overhanging, hanging, suspended, depending.

ANT. *Supported, sustaining, propped.*

Penetrate. Enter, pierce, comprehend, discern, understand, perforate, permeate, fathom.

ANT. *Glance off, be tangent to, find impermeable; misunderstand, mistake; float.*

Penetration. Discernment, sagacity, acuteness, discrimination, sharpness, observation, insight.

ANT. *Obtuseness, shortsight-*

edness; stupidity, shallowness, dulness.

Penitence. Repentance, contrition, remorse, sorrow, regret, compunction.

ANT. *Self-approval, gratulation; obduracy, hardheartedness.*

Penitent, Penitential. Repentant, contrite, doing penance.

ANT. *Impenitent, obdurate, hardhearted.*

Pensive. Thoughtful, sad, wistful, meditative, dreamy, sober; serious, mournful, melancholy, solemn, reflective.

ANT. *Joyous, glad, happy, gay, care-free, thoughtless, unreflecting.*

Penurious. Covetous, parsimonious, stingy, avaricious, niggardly, sordid.

ANT. *Liberal, bountiful, generous, prodigal.*

Penury. Want, privation, indigence, poverty, destitution, beggary, need.

ANT. *Wealth, abundance, affluence, luxury, competence.*

People. Nation, race, population, state, tribe, community, commonwealth.

Perceivable, Perceptible. Discernible, distinguishable, cognizable, observable.

ANT. *Imperceptible, indistinguishable, insensible, inappreciable.*

Perceive. Comprehend, apprehend, conceive, understand.

ANT. *Ignore, lose, miss, fail of, overlook, misconceive, misapprehend.*

Perception. Discernment, apprehension, recognition, understanding, comprehension, feeling, sensation, sense.

ANT. *Conception, concept, imagination, idea, notion; misunderstanding.*

Percolate. Filter, strain, exude, drain, ooze.

ANT. *Flow, rush, stream, run, disgorge.*

Percussion. Shock, clash, collision, concussion, encounter.

ANT. *Recoil, rebound, reverberation.*

Perdition. Loss, ruin, destruction, overthrow, wreck, demolition.

ANT. *Restoration, recovery, rescue, salvation.*

Peremptory. Decisive, positive, absolute, final, authoritative, arbitrary, express, dogmatical, determined, resolute.

ANT. *Hortatory, mild, entreative, expostulatory, suggestive.*

Perennial. Perpetual, unceasing, never failing, enduring, continual, constant, permanent, uninterrupted.

ANT. *Occasional, intermittent, periodic, uncertain; perishing, ephemeral, transient, fleeting.*

Perfect. Finished, complete, entire, faultless, consummate, accurate, ideal, finished, absolute, completed, correct, immaculate, sinless, blameless, holy, undefiled, stainless, spotless, unblemished.

ANT. *Imperfect, bad, deficient, blemished, faulty, corrupt, poor, inferior, incomplete, perverted, worthless, spoiled, insufficient, meager, defective, short, scant, marred, defaced, corrupted, deformed, fallible, ruined.*

Perfection. Excellence, completeness, faultlessness, maturity, wholeness, consummation, perfectness.

ANT. *Defect, imperfection, incompleteness, blemish.*

Perfectly. Thoroughly, exquisitely, completely, faultlessly, entirely, fully, wholly, exactly, accurately.

ANT. *Imperfectly, faultily, partially, inaccurately.*

Perfidious. False, treacherous, faithless, disloyal, dishonest, untrustworthy.

ANT. *True, loyal, stanch, upright, faithful, honest, trustworthy.*

Perform. Complete, accomplish, execute, do, discharge, fulfil; represent, act, play, enact, consummate, achieve.

ANT. *Spoil, injure, harm, ruin, mar; fail of, misconduct.*

Performance. Completion, consummation, execution, accomplishment, achievement, work, production, act, action, deed, exploit, feat.

ANT. *Failure, defeat, omission, abortion, undoing, nonperformance.*

Perfume. Odor, redolence, balminess, fragrance, smell, aroma, scent.

ANT. *Stench, stink, fume.*

Perfunctory. Mechanical, careless, listless, indifferent.

ANT. *Animated, spirited, assiduous, careful, ardent, zealous, interested.*

Perhaps. By chance, peradventure, perchance, maybe, haply, possibly.

ANT. *Certainly, inevitably.*

Peril. Hazard, risk, jeopardy, danger, venture, insecurity, liability.

ANT. *Safety, assurance, certainty, security.*

Period. Time, cycle, age, epoch, limit, end, conclusion; era, duration, date, term, continuance, termination, conclusion, bound.

ANT. *Eternity, infinity, perpetuity, endlessness, everlasting.*

Periodical. Recurring, regular, stated, recurrent, systematic, calculable, serial.

ANT. *Indeterminate, eccentric, fitful, spasmodic, irregular.*

Permanent. Enduring, abiding, changeless, constant, durable, steadfast, unchangeable, immutable, invariable, fixed, unchanging, stable, lasting, persistent, perpetual.

ANT. *Transient, brief, fleeting, evanescent, passing, transitory, momentary, temporary, ephemeral.*

Permission. Authority, allowance, consent, liberty, leave, license, permit, authorization.

ANT. *Hindrance, opposition, objection, denial, prevention, prohibition, refusal, resistance.*

Pernicious. Mischievous, baneful, destructive, noisome, deleterious, harmful, hurtful, poisonous, noxious, pestilential, unhealthful, unwholesome, detrimental, deadly, evil, foul, injurious, insalubrious, pestiferous, perverting, ruinous.

ANT. *Helpful, invigorating, salutary, advantageous, good, favorable, life-giving, rejuvenating, useful, serviceable, beneficent, wholesome, beneficial, healthful.*

Perpetual. Continual, endless, unceasing, unfailing, incessant, constant, eternal, everlasting, perennial, permanent, enduring.

ANT. *Periodic, transient, recurrent, temporary, occasional, casual, momentary.*

Perplex. Entangle, involve, complicate, embarrass, puzzle, bewilder, confuse, distract, annoy, confound, trouble, worry, disturb, pester, bother, mystify.

ANT. *Enlighten, clear, ex-*

plicate, simplify, elucidate, illumine, unfold, explain, manifest, calm, quiet, control, please, instruct, solve, illustrate, make intelligible, account for.

Perplexity. Confusion, bewilderment, disturbance, distraction, doubt, embarrassment, astonishment, amazement.

ANT. *Composure, calmness; discernment, insight.*

Perseverance. Persistency, tenacity, steadfastness, steadiness, constancy, pertinacity, indefatigableness, resolution.

ANT. *Fitfulness, caprice, instability, variableness, irregularity, indecision, vacillation, wavering, irresoluteness.*

Perspicacity. Acuteness, keenness, discernment, penetration, perspicaciousness, insight, sagacity, astuteness, distinctness, explicitness.

ANT. *Dulness, stupefaction, obtuseness, hebetude, stolidity, inobservance, insensibility.*

Perspicuity. Plainess, lucidity, clearness, explicitness, intelligibility, transparency, perspicuousness.

ANT. *Obscurity, turbidness, unintelligibility, incomprehensibility, indefiniteness, doubtfulness, mysticism, confusion.*

Persuade. Dispose, allure, entice, urge, move, influence, prevail upon, coax, bring over, incline, convince, lead, induce, incite, win over, impel.

ANT. *Deter, discourage, restrain, hinder, repel, dissuade, hold back.*

Pertinent. Apposite, relevant, suitable, appropriate, proper, fit, adapted.

ANT. *Unrelated, unsuitable, impertinent, incongruous, alien, unconnected, discordant, inharmonious.*

Pertness. Impertinence, boldness, forwardness, sauciness, flippancy, impudence, briskness, liveliness, smartness, sprightliness.

ANT. *Diffidence, humility, modesty, shyness, bashfulness, demureness.*

Perverse. Obstinate, contrary, fractious, froward, intractable, petulant, wilful, wayward, ungovernable, stubborn, factious, untoward.

ANT. *Compliant, genial, accommodating, governable, kind, obliging, complaisant, amenable.*

Petition, *n.* Prayer, supplication, entreaty; solicitation, application, suit, appeal, address.

ANT. *Protest, claim, expostulation, demand, injunction, dictation, exaction, dissension, dissent.*

Philanthropy. Love, good will, charity, benevolence, humanity, public-spiritedness.

ANT. *Misanthropy, ill will, selfishness.*

Philosopher. Student, theorist, speculator, teacher, master, savant, schoolman, doctor; adept.

ANT. *Learner, pupil, beginner; ignoramus, dunce.*

Philosophical. Rational, wise, temperate, calm, cool, reasonable, sound, collected, composed, sedate, tranquil, Platonic.

ANT. *Popular, crude, loose, inaccurate, illogical, irrational, unsound, unscientific, thoughtless, hotheaded, impulsive.*

Physical. Material, natural, corporal, sensible, visible, tangible, bodily, corporeal.

ANT. *Mental, spiritual, immaterial, unsubstantial, hyperphysical, intangible, moral, unreal, intellectual, invisible.*

Picturesque. Graphic, vivid, artistic, beautiful, scenic, pictorial, graceful, comely, seemly.

ANT. *Unseemly, ugly, inartistic, ungraceful, tame, flat, insipid.*

Piety. Sanctity, godliness, holiness, religion, reverence, devotion, grace.

ANT. *Impiety, sacrilege, sinfulness, ungodliness, hypocrisy, formalism, sanctimoniousness.*

Piquant. Tart, sharp, pungent, stimulating, biting, racy, stinging, cutting, severe.

ANT. *Flat, tame, dull, insipid.*

Pique. Resentment, umbrage, irritation, displeasure, grudge, offense.

ANT. *Delight, gratification, pleasure, satisfaction, contentment, approval, complacency.*

Piteous. Sorrowful, mournful, affecting, doleful, lamentable, woful, rueful, sad, pitiable, pitiful.

ANT. *Joyous, glad, merry, happy, cheerful, comfortable, desirable, pleasant, agreeable, delectable.*

Pitiful. Lamentable, mournful, base, contemptible, piteous, pathetic, pitiable, touching, sorrowful, woful, wretched, despicable, moving, paltry.

ANT. *Exalted, glorious, helpful, great, grand, sublime, superior, beneficent, commanding, august, dignified, noble, lofty, mighty, superb.*

Pity. Sympathy, mercy, tenderness, condolence, compassion, commiseration.

ANT. *Cruelty, severity, mercilessness, sternness, hardness, rigor, inhumanity, brutality, barbarity, harshness, pitilessness, ruthlessness, hard-heartedness, ferocity, truculence.*

Placid. Pleased, contented, unruffled, undisturbed, peaceful, serene, tranquil, quiet, gentle, collected, calm, composed, passionless.

ANT. *Discontent, disturbed, distressed, anxious, distracted, perplexed, distrait; vehement, wild, passionate, impulsive, agitated, ruffled, excited, impassioned.*

Plain. Artless, undisguised, sincere, frank, honest, ingenuous, candid, unembellished, simple, downright, blunt, distinct, apparent, manifest, open, clear, evident, visible, obvious, unmistakable, conspicuous, level, flat, smooth; easy, natural, homely, ugly; simple, frugal.

ANT. *Unnatural, pretended, affected, assumed, feigned, artificial, insincere, vain, pretentious, conceited; ornate, ornamented, decorated, embellished; involved, obscure, hidden, invisible, inconspicuous, uneven, undulating, rugged, broken, ambiguous, abrupt, obstructed, uncertain, enigmatical, abstruse; beautiful, sophisticated, artful.*

Plant, *v.* Seed, set, sow, seed down, set out.

ANT. *Eradicate, uproot, extirpate, weed out, root up.*

Plausible. Specious, seeming, pretending, fair-spoken, passable, pretentious, ostensible, apparent; colorable, feasible.

ANT. *Genuine, transparent, true, sterling, veritable, unmistakable, authentic, sincere, unaffected.*

Plead. Advocate, ask, beg, urge, argue, solicit, entreat, implore, press.

ANT. *Grant, bestow, answer.*

Pleasant. Kindly, obliging, attractive, pleasing, pleasurable, agreeable, kind, good-natured.

ANT. *Disagreeable, gloomy, glum, harsh, hateful, repulsive, unpleasant, repellent, offensive, unkind, forbidding, dreary, arrogant, austere, grim, ill-natured, ill-humored, repelling.*

Pleasure. Satisfaction, comfort, solace, joy, gladness, delight, will, choice, purpose, command, kindness, enjoyment, gratification, happiness, self-indulgence, voluptuousness.

ANT. *Suffering, affliction, pain, sorrow, sadness, distress, misery, compulsion, force, coercion; mourning, depression, dejection, melancholy, misfortune, poverty, want.*

Plenitude. Fulness, abundance, completeness, plenty, repletion, plethora; luxury, affluence, exuberance, wealth, richness, profusion, amplitude, enough, supply, sufficiency.

ANT. *Want, need, scarcity, scantiness, dearth, insufficiency, restriction, poverty, partiality, stint, reserve, narrowness, penury, impecuniosity.*

Plentiful. Bountiful, generous, large, abundant, adequate, copious, enough, full, profuse, rich, sufficient, complete, exuberant, plenteous, replete, teeming, affluent, ample, lavish, liberal, luxuriant, overflowing, abounding.

ANT. *Deficient, drained, impoverished, scanty, insufficient, small, sparing, stingy, straitened, poor, scant, exhausted, inadequate, mean, miserly, narrow, niggardly, scarce, short, scrimped.*

Plot. Intrigue, conspiracy, cabal, contrivance, scheme, stratagem, project, combination, machination; story.

ANT. *Blunder, botch; misarrangement, miscontrivance.*

Poet. Bard, author of poems, singer, rimster, rimer, versifier.

Poetical. Metrical, rhythmical, lyric, rimed, versified; imaginative, fictitious, creative.

ANT. *Prosaic, unpoetical, unrimed, unversified, unrhythmic; commonplace, matter-of-fact, unimaginative, realistic; mathematical, historical.*

Poetry. Meter, rime, numbers, poesy, song, verse, poem, metrical composition.

ANT. *Prose, prosaic speech, prosaic writing.*

Poignant. Pricking, piercing, sharp, pungent; pointed, keen, satirical.

ANT. *Blunt, dull, obtuse, insipid, pointless, vapid, inexpressive.*

Poisonous. Venomous, baneful, corrupting, noxious, pestilential, malignant, virulent, pestiferous, deleterious, mephitic.

ANT. *Salubrious, wholesome, healthful, beneficial, sanative, genial, remedial, hygienic.*

Polite. Courteous, civil, courtly, obliging, gracious, polished, accomplished, complaisant, cultivated, cultured, elegant, genteel, urbane, well-behaved, well-mannered, well-bred.

ANT. *Awkward, clownish, unmannerly, uncouth, boorish, blunt, impertinent, brusk, bluff, impolite, insolent, coarse, ill-bred, ill-behaved, rude, rustic, impudent, ill-mannered, untutored, uncivil, untaught, discourteous, unpolished, insulting.*

Politeness. Courtesy, civility, gentility, refinement, courtliness, elegance, urbanity, good breeding, decorum, complaisance, affability.

ANT. *Rudeness, arrogance, incivility, churlishness, ungra-*

ciousness, insolence, sauciness, impertinence, effrontery, presumption.

Poor. Needy, indigent, destitute; lean, emaciated; feeble, dejected; shabby, mean; unfavorable, uncomfortable; barren; sterile; inadequate, insignificant, insufficient; meek.

ANT. *Rich, wealthy, affluent, opulent; splendid, costly, valuable, estimable; fruitful, abundant, luxuriant, productive, prolific; copious, abounding, ample, well-supplied, comfortable, favorable; adequate, sufficient; important, significant, arrogant, self-assertive.*

Popular. Cheap, common, ordinary, inferior; familiar, plain, easy, comprehensible; favorite, liked, approved, accepted, accredited; current, prevalent, general, prevailing; pertaining to the people, vulgar, plebeian; mediocre.

ANT. *Unpopular, exclusive, aristocratic, snobbish; special, excellent, unique, superior, eminent; selfish, narrow, illiberal, uncharitable; sole, only, scientific, restricted, esoteric; odious, detested.*

Position. Situation, station, assertion, place, posture, locality, site; attitude; state, condition, circumstances; principle, doctrine, proposition, dictum, affirmation, thesis; rank.

Positive. Real, actual, absolute, explicit, definite, confident, certain, dogmatic; defined, precise, clear; veritable, substantial, true; indisputable, incontrovertible; indubitable; decisive, unconditional, imperative, unequivocal, settled, assured, express.

ANT. *Negative, denying, indirect, disavowing, disclaiming, privative; relative; unreal, fictitious, imaginative, contingent, dependent, implied, conditional, dubious, unsubstantial, indefinite, equivocal.*

Possession. Control, ownership, tenure, retention, management, occupation; (*pl.*) property, estate, wealth, dominion.

ANT. *Dispossession, resignation, surrender, abandoning, renouncing.*

Potent. Powerful, mighty, puissant, strong, able, efficient, efficacious, forcible, cogent, influential, effective, active, energetic.

ANT. *Impotent, powerless, weak, feeble, infirm; inefficient, incapable, incompetent, incapacitated.*

Potential. Possible, implicit, undeveloped, virtual, immanent, inherent, intrinsic.

ANT. *Actual, explicit, real, objective, developed, express, determinate, positive, clear, definite.*

Poverty. Distress, beggary, indigence, destitution, pauperism, penury, privation, want, need, mendicancy.

ANT. *Wealth, riches, affluence, luxury, comfort.*

Power. Ability, competency, capacity, faculty, aptitude, dexterity, efficiency, might, talent, energy, skill, strength, readiness, capability, cleverness, expertness, efficacy, force, qualification, cogency, susceptibility.

ANT. *Feebleness, weakness, helplessness, impotence, incompetence, inability, inaptitude, dulness, awkwardness, imbecility, incapacity, inefficiency, unskilfulness, maladroitness, stupidity.*

Practice, *n.* Usage, habit, custom; performance, application, system; manner, method, mode, experience.

Ant. *Theory, speculation, assumption, ideal, conjecture, abstraction.*

Practice, *v.* Do, perform, exercise, carry out, execute; teach, train; habituate, try; apply, use; pursue.

Ant. *Abandon, misuse, disuse, neglect, disregard, slight, omit, pass over.*

Praise, *n.* Applause, approval, cheering, compliment, acclaim, adulation, acclamation, approbation, cheers, plaudit, eulogy, encomium, flattery, laudation, panegyric, sycophancy.

Ant. *Abuse, blame, censure, contempt, reproach, ignominy, slander, scorn, obloquy, animadversion, condemnation, denunciation, disapprobation, disparagement, vituperation, reproof, disapproval, repudiation, hissing, vilification.*

Praise, *v.* Laud, eulogize, celebrate, magnify, glorify; honor, commend; applaud, extol, compliment.

Ant. *Decry, blame, censure, reprove, disparage, depreciate, discredit, traduce, condemn.*

Pray. Ask, beg, beseech, entreat, implore, invoke, petition, supplicate, request, importune, bid, plead, call upon, conjure.

Precarious. Doubtful, dubious, hazardous, perilous, risky, insecure, uncertain, unsettled, unsteady, unstable, unassured.

Ant. *Firm, settled, stable, sure, certain, real, undoubted, unquestionable, actual, assured, immutable, incontestable, undeniable, infallible, strong, steady.*

Precaution. Foresight, prudence, forethought, providence, wariness, care.

Ant. *Thoughtlessness, improvidence, carelessness, imprudence.*

Precedent, *n.* Example, antecedent, case, instance, pattern, authority, warrant.

Precept. Commandment, law, injunction, mandate, rule, direction, principle, maxim; doctrine, dogma; order; instruction.

Ant. *Hint, suggestion, allusion, insinuation, prompting, impulse, instigation.*

Precise. Accurate, exact, correct, definite, scrupulous, punctilious, particular, nice, formal; explicit, terse.

Ant. *Inaccurate, inexact, incorrect, heedless, careless, incautious, implicit, ambiguous, circumlocutory, loose, vague, informal, unceremonious.*

Predatory. Plundering, pillaging, ravaging, rapacious, marauding.

Ant. *Protecting, guarding, watching, keeping, sheltering, shielding, saving.*

Predestination. Fate, necessity, foreknowledge, foreordination.

Ant. *Choice, freedom, free will, independence, uncertainty, accident, chance, free agency.*

Prediction. Prophecy, prognostication, foreboding, divination, augury, soothsaying, vaticination, foretelling, presage.

Ant. *Reminiscence, recollection, report; history, narration, account.*

Preface. Introduction, proem, preamble, prologue, exordium, prelude.

Ant. *Sequel, postscript, appendix, peroration, epilogue, conclusion.*

Prefer. Choose, elect, select, desire, pick out, fancy, single out, fix upon; elevate, advance, promote; offer, proffer, present, address.

ANT. *Reject, discard, decline, refuse, repudiate; degrade, depress; postpone, defer, withhold.*

Prejudice. Bias, partiality, unfairness, preconception, prepossession, presumption.

ANT. *Certainty, evidence, proof, conviction, conclusion, demonstration, reason, reasoning.*

Preliminary. Prior, introductory, preparatory, prefatory, proemial, previous, precedent, antecedent.

ANT. *Subsequent, following, consequent, appended, succeeding.*

Premium. Reward, remuneration, recompense, prize, bonus, bounty, guerdon, meed, bribe, douceur, enhancement, gratuity.

ANT. *Penalty, fine, mulct, amercement, forfeiture, depreciation, decline, fall, loss.*

Preposterous. Irrational, foolish, monstrous, absurd, perverted, extravagant, ridiculous, exorbitant.

ANT. *Reasonable, moderate, right, just, due, fair, judicious, mediocre, commonplace.*

Presence. Person, personality, individuality, port, mien, appearance, nearness, immediacy; vicinity, neighborhood.

ANT. *Absence, distance, remoteness, separation; society, world; temperament, character.*

Preservation. Security, safety, maintenance, conservation, integrity, protection, care, guardianship, watch and ward, soundness.

ANT. *Exposure, abandonment, impairment, peril, damage, injury.*

Presumption. Assumption, arrogance, effrontery, audacity, assurance; presupposition, hypothesis, guess, conjecture, belief, opinion, judgment, understanding, concession, condition.

ANT. *Modesty, deference, diffidence, bashfulness, hesitation; proof, deduction, demonstration, verification, certainty, fact.*

Pretend. Claim, represent, allege, simulate, feign, profess; counterfeit.

ANT. *Verify, substantiate, refute, detect, expose, unmask, test.*

Pretense. Disguise, excuse, affectation, mask, show, pretension, semblance, wile, trick, subterfuge, simulation, ruse, assumption, pretext, seeming, dissimulation, air, cloak, color.

ANT. *Candor, sincerity, ingenuousness, frankness, honesty, truth, openness, reality, simplicity, guilelessness, fact, actuality.*

Prevalence. Success, superiority, predominance, preponderance; influence, force, power, strength, efficacy; universality, extension, acceptation, custom, operation.

ANT. *Decay, desuetude, disappearance, evanescence, subordination, collapse, destruction, abolition, subsidence, subjection, diminution.*

Previous. Antecedent, before, earlier, precedent, preliminary, introductory, prior, preceding, front, forward, former, foregoing, anterior.

ANT. *After, concluding, following, consequent, later, posterior, latter, succeeding, subsequent, hindmost, hinder, hind.*

Price. Expense, outlay, worth, expenditure, value, charge, cost.

Pride. Arrogance, insolence, reserve, haughtiness, self-esteem, presumption, superciliousness, vanity, ostentation, conceit, self-respect, self-exaltation, disdain, vainglory, self-conceit, self-complacency.

ANT. *Humility, lowliness, modesty, self-distrust, meekness, self-abasement.*

Primary. First, fundamental, primitive, original, preparatory; chief, principal, pristine; elementary, leading.

ANT. *Secondary, posterior, subsequent, later, following; unimportant, subordinate, inferior; supplemental, auxiliary.*

Prime, *n.* Perfection, culmination, apex, zenith; dawn, opening, youth, spring, beginning; cream, flower.

ANT. *Wane, winter, evening; decadence, decay.*

Primeval. Immemorial, original, old, primal, patriarchal, native, primitive, pristine, uncreated, ancient, aboriginal, autochthonic, indigenous, prime, primary, primordial.

ANT. *Foreign, fresh, late, modern, new, novel, recent, exotic, adventitious.*

Principal. Highest, most important, chief, main; leading, foremost, preëminent, capital, essential; primary, first.

ANT. *Subordinate, inferior, secondary, auxiliary, supplemental, minor, dependent, subservient, ancillary.*

Principle. Source, cause, origin; faculty, endowment; postulate, truth, maxim, axiom; rule, law; element; doctrine, dogma, opinion; ground, motive, reason; integrity, rectitude, uprightness, probity, virtue, worth, honor.

ANT. *Result, sequence, development, issue; application, action, operation, exercise, manifestation, exhibition; iniquity, immorality.*

Prize. Trophy, honor, reward, premium, guerdon, palm, laurels; capture; gain, advantage; spoil, plunder, booty.

ANT. *Loss, failure, fine, forfeiture; brand, stigma, infamy.*

Probation. Examination, trial, ordeal, test, assay, proof, experiment.

ANT. *License, irresponsibility, non-probation.*

Proclaim. Publish, announce, declare, promulgate, herald, advertise, enunciate, utter, blaze abroad, report, make known.

ANT. *Silence, repress, suppress, conceal, secrete; retract, recall.*

Prodigal, *a.* Extravagant, profuse, lavish, bountiful, wasteful, squandering.

ANT. *Economical, thrifty, saving, frugal; close, miserly, niggardly.*

Profession. Avowal, declaration, claim; occupation, vocation, employment; law, theology, *or* medicine; assertion, acknowledgment; representation, pretense, protestation.

ANT. *Denial, concealment, suppression; retraction, recantation, disavowal; leisure, fad, hobby, avocation; trade, business.*

Proficient. Expert, adept, skilful, skilled, competent, conversant, qualified, practiced, accomplished, finished, trained.

ANT. *Unskilled, inexpert, awkward, ignorant, backward, inconversant, incompetent, untrained, unpracticed, inept.*

Profit. Gain, advantage, benefit, emolument, improvement, proceeds, utility, usefulness, returns, value, receipts, avail, expediency, good, service.

ANT. *Damage, destruction, harm, hurt, loss, injury, waste, ruin, detriment, disadvantage.*

Profitable. Lucrative, beneficial, useful, advantageous, productive, desirable, gainful, remunerative.

ANT. *Useless, vain, fruitless, unproductive, unremunerative, unprofitable, undesirable, disadvantageous, detrimental, unbeneficial.*

Profound. Deep, descending; thorough; fathomless, abysmal; mysterious, abstruse, occult, obscure, recondite; complete; penetrating, intimate, intense, philosophical.

ANT. *Superficial, shallow, commonplace, external, slight, apparent, obvious, incomplete; surface.*

Progress. Advance, advancement, attainment, increase, improvement, proficiency, progression, growth, development.

ANT. *Delay, check, retrogression, stay, stop, stoppage, falling off, relapse, decline, falling back.*

Prohibit. Forbid, hinder, inhibit, interdict, preclude, prevent, debar, disallow.

ANT. *Allow, empower, let, license, order, require, sanction, authorize, command, direct, enjoin, permit, warrant, suffer, tolerate, put up with, give permission, give consent, consent to.*

Prolific. Fertile, fruitful, productive, generating, teeming, active.

ANT. *Barren, sterile, unproductive, unfruitful, effete.*

Prolix. Long, diffuse, tiresome, prolonged, protracted; wordy, verbose, prosaic, rambling, discursive; tedious, wearisome.

ANT. *Condensed, terse, concise, brief, laconic, curt, epigrammatic.*

Prominent. Projecting, manifest, protuberant, conspicuous; eminent, distinguished, famous, celebrated, important, main, principal, leading, characteristic.

ANT. *Receding, hollowed, concave, indented, engraved; insignificant, secondary, unimportant, minor, indistinguishable, indistinct, subordinate, inconspicuous, trivial, immaterial, unessential.*

Promote. Encourage, forward, foster, push, advance, aid, assist, foment, excite, further, help, raise, urge forward, urge on, elevate, exalt.

ANT. *Abase, allay; hinder, prevent, foil, frustrate.*

Prompt. Ready, quick, agile, alert, brisk, nimble, expeditious; willing, hasty, inclined, disposed, responsive, unhesitating.

ANT. *Dilatory, slow, tardy, lingering, loitering, inactive, sluggish, unready, unresponsive, procrastinating, behindhand, backward.*

Pronounce. Deliver, speak, utter, articulate, enunciate; declare, affirm; propound, assert, express.

ANT. *Mispronounce, gabble, mumble; silence, suppress; deny, retract.*

Propagate. Increase, diffuse, disseminate, promote; spread, extend, generate, promulgate, circulate.

ANT. *Strangle, stifle, extinguish, suppress, repress, check, hush up; contract, diminish, reduce; contradict, deny.*

Proper. Own, individual, peculiar, particular; right, fit, decent; personal, constitutional, special, specific; suitable, appropriate, seemly, legitimate; decent, respectable.

ANT. *Common, universal, general; unfitting, inappropriate, unsuitable, unseemly, indecent, wrong, improper, unbecoming, unbefitting.*

Propitiation. Expiation, satisfaction, atonement, reconciliation.

ANT. *Reprobation, retribution, vengeance, wrath, alienation, estrangement, curse, penalty, punishment, offense, condemnation, chastisement.*

Propitious. Auspicious, kind, benign, gracious, friendly, benignant, clement, kindly, favorable, merciful.

ANT. *Adverse, antagonistic, hostile, repellent, unfriendly, unpropitious, unfavorable, ill-disposed, forbidding, inauspicious.*

Proportion. Ratio, symmetry, relation, harmony, share, lot; equality, similarity; adjustment, distribution; arrangement, adaptation.

ANT. *Disproportion, disparity, disorder, incongruity, discrepancy, absurdity, contrariety.*

Proposal. Bid, offer, overture, proposition.

ANT. *Acceptance, denial, refusal, rejection, repulse, disapproval.*

Proposition. Proposal, statement, offer, declaration; overture, suggestion, proffer, tender; position, thesis, dictum, assertion, affirmation, doctrine.

ANT. *Withdrawal, recantation, abjuration, disavowal, revocation.*

Prosperity. Thrift, weal, welfare, happiness, well-being, success, good fortune.

ANT. *Woe, misfortune, ill luck, failure, adversity, calamity, reverses, affliction, distress, disaster, misery.*

Protest, *v.* Assert, aver, attest, testify; affirm, declare; asseverate, avow, profess; expostulate, remonstrate, repudiate, deprecate, denounce.

ANT. *Retract, withdraw, abjure, revoke; coincide, sanction, agree, endorse, subscribe, acquiesce.*

Protract. Defer, continue, delay, extend, elongate, lengthen, procrastinate, postpone, prolong, draw out.

ANT. *Abbreviate, contract, conclude, hasten, hurry, reduce, shorten, abridge, curtail, limit.*

Proud. Arrogant, haughty, presumptuous, lordly; worthy, admirable, grand, splendid, magnificent, ostentatious; lofty, supercilious, imperious, boastful, elated, imposing, vainglorious.

ANT. *Humble, unassuming, unobtrusive, meek, lowly, mild, submissive, unpretending, deferential, affable, unpresuming, mean.*

Proverb. Axiom, byword, dictum, adage, aphorism, maxim, motto, precept, truism, saying, saw, apothegm.

Provide. Prepare, supply, afford, contribute, furnish; engage, bargain, agree; stipulate; procure.

ANT. *Neglect, withhold, refuse, mismanage, appropriate, overlook; divert, alienate, misuse; fail, disappoint.*

Provocation. Vexation, incite-

ment, stimulus, incentive; affront, insult, offense, indignity.
ANT. *Pacification, mitigation, assuagement; deference, compliment, homage, honor, respect.*

Prowess. Heroism, valor, gallantry, bravery, courage, intrepidity.
ANT. *Fear, effeminacy, timidity, cowardice, cowardliness, pusillanimity.*

Prudence. Discretion, frugality, forethought, judgment, judiciousness, providence, care, caution, foresight, wisdom, consideration, carefulness, circumspection.
ANT. *Folly, heedlessness, prodigality, recklessness, indiscretion, wastefulness, improvidence, imprudence, thoughtlessness, rashness.*

Prudent. Cautious, considerate, judicious, provident; circumspect, sagacious, wise, discreet; frugal, economical, thrifty.
ANT. *Reckless, inconsiderate, improvident, wasteful, extravagant, lavish, prodigal; indiscreet, unwise; foolish, rash, imprudent, audacious.*

Public. Common, general, popular, social, open; notorious.
ANT. *Private, individual, secret, domestic, secluded, close, personal.*

Punctilious. Exact, particular, precise, careful, nice, scrupulous, conscientious; punctual, ceremonious.
ANT. *Careless, slovenly, unscrupulous; informal, unceremonious.*

Puny. Small, feeble, inferior, petty; weak, diminutive, undeveloped, dwarfed, stunted, undersized, tiny.
ANT. *Large, great, robust, developed, fine, vigorous; colossal, gigantic.*

Pupil. Learner, disciple, student, novice, ward, tyro.
ANT. *Teacher, master, proficient, scholar, adept; guardian.*

Purchase, *v.* Buy, obtain, procure, secure, acquire, bargain for, barter for, get.
ANT. *Exchange, sell, barter, dispose of, put to sale.*

Pure. Innocent, unsullied, spotless, unspotted, stainless, true, guiltless, incorrupt, clean, genuine, chaste, guileless, classic, classical, holy, immaculate, virtuous, real, sheer, mere, simple, unmixed, unpolluted, unadulterated, unmingled, undefiled, unblemished, uncorrupted, unstained, untainted, untarnished, upright, perfect.
ANT. *Impure, indecent, polluted, foul, tainted, unchaste, immodest, lewd, obscene, indelicate, defiled, dirty, filthy, gross, mixed, stained, sullied, unclean, tarnished, adulterated.*

Purpose, *n.* Design, end, intention, aim, scope, meaning, object, plan, intention, purport, effect, project.
ANT. *Lot, chance, accident, haphazard, casualty, fate.*

Put. Deposit, place, set, lay; cause, produce, propose, state; attach, attribute, assign; assume, suppose; entice, constrain.
ANT. *Remove, raise, withdraw, displace, transpose, transfer, change.*

Putrid. Decayed, decomposed, rotten, stinking, putrefied, foul, offensive.
ANT. *Clean, sweet, wholesome, fragrant, pure, healthful, fresh.*

Q

Quaint. Odd, antique; curious, fanciful, affected, whimsical; archaic, singular, unusual; antiquated, extraordinary, droll.

ANT. *Commonplace, usual, ordinary, common; fashionable, modish, modern.*

Quality. Property, peculiarity, sort, disposition, temper; character, attribute, rank, part, position; characteristic; acquisition; nature, trait, mood, condition, station, capacity, tendency.

ANT. *Negation, heterogeneity, anomalousness, lack of distinction, nondescript, weakness, ineffectiveness, incapacity, disqualification.*

Quantity. Greatness, measure, amount, bulk, extent, size, aggregate, length, duration, content, comprehensiveness.

ANT. *Scantiness, want, deficiency, margin, deterioration, diminution, waste, wear, loss.*

Queer. Curious, bizarre, droll, comical, odd, peculiar, quaint, strange, uncommon, unusual, whimsical, singular, ridiculous, anomalous, fantastic, funny, erratic, extraordinary, ludicrous, grotesque, laughable, preposterous, unique, unmatched, eccentric, crotchety.

ANT. *Common, customary, normal, ordinary, usual, regular, familiar, natural.*

Querimonious, Querulous. Lamenting, complaining, whining, bewailing, mourning, murmuring, discontented, dissatisfied, malcontent.

ANT. *Contented, easy, uncomplaining, satisfied, complacent, cheerful, genial, good-tempered.*

Query, Question, *n.* Inquiry, doubt; point, topic, subject; dispute, discussion, debate; investigation, examination; experimentation, scrutiny, interrogation.

ANT. *Solution, explanation, answer, reply, response; concession, admission.*

Question, *v.* Ask, interrogate, catechize, doubt, controvert, dispute; examine, converse with; call in question; inquire, investigate, query, dubitate.

ANT. *Answer, reply, satisfy, respond.*

Quick. Speedy, expeditious, active, rapid, nimble, fleet, alert, lively, sprightly; alive, living, animate; agile, brisk, ready; hasty, swift; impatient, eager, passionate; fresh, bracing, keen, sharp; sensitive, perceptive, intelligent.

ANT. *Slow, tardy, inactive, inert, sluggish, dull, insensitive, deliberate, gradual, moderate, late, unready, dilatory, slack, unresponsive, lingering, heavy, stupid, wearisome.*

Quicken. Hasten, hurry, accelerate, despatch, drive, expedite, facilitate, further, speed, urge, promote, advance, make haste, press forward.

ANT. *Hinder, impede, check, obstruct, retard, clog, delay.*

Quiet, *n.* Rest, repose, tranquillity, silence, calm, peace, stillness.

ANT. *Tumult, noise, shouting, action, commotion, activity, storm; unrest, excitement, agitation, disturbance, turmoil.*

Quiet, *a.* Tranquil, unruffled, smooth, unmolested, peaceful, undisturbed, peaceable, calm, patient, contented, hushed, still, placid; gentle, mild, undemonstrative, meek.

ANT. *Turbulent, tumultuous, uproarious, disturbed, agitated, wild, excited, violent, uneasy, boisterous, restless, confused, noisy.*

Quote. Cite, recite, plagiarize, repeat, excerpt, extract, paraphrase.

ANT. *Suppress, ignore, disdain, omit.*

R

Rabble. Mob, crowd, people, populace; herd, the masses, multitudes, commonalty; scum, dregs.

ANT. *Aristocracy, nobility, élite, galaxy.*

Racy. Lively, piquant, pungent, spicy, spirited, forcible, flavorous, rich.

ANT. *Flat, cold, flavorless, insipid, stale, stupid, tasteless, dull, prosy, vapid.*

Radiant. Lustrous, brilliant, splendid, gorgeous, glittering, glaring, radiating, beaming, resplendent, shining, sparkling, luminous, effulgent, glorious.

ANT. *Dull, dark, somber, murky, lusterless, non-luminous, sunless, shadowy, lurid, cloudy, gloomy, obscure, overcast, ebon, black.*

Radical. Fundamental, innate, essential, native, natural, original, organic, primitive; entire, complete, extreme, thorough, positive, perfect, thorough-going, total; ingrained, constitutional.

ANT. *Superficial, tentative, trial; inadequate, incomplete, moderate, partial, palliative, slight; conservative.*

Raise. Lift, elevate, heave; exalt, advance, enhance; increase, excite, aggravate, intensify, heighten, set upright; awaken, arouse, originate, produce, effect, cause; build, erect; levy, collect; propagate, breed, rear; bring up, incite, start; utter, summon; cultivate.

ANT. *Depress, lower, drop, sink, let down; degrade, disgrace; debase, humble, reduce; lessen, diminish, decrease.*

Ramble. Rove, roam, wander, range, stroll, saunter, straggle, stray.

ANT. *Speed, hasten, drive, run, proceed, rush, hurry.*

Random, *a.* Chance, haphazard, fortuitous, casual, wandering, stray, wild, aimless, purposeless, unpremeditated, accidental, vague.

ANT. *Aimed, intended, controlled, purposed, deliberate, designed, intentional, regular, systematic, planned.*

Ransom, *v.* Redeem, liberate, rescue, deliver, release, emancipate, indemnify.

ANT. *Hold for ransom, kidnap, imprison, hold as hostage, indict, fine, mulct, prosecute.*

Rapid. Swift, quick, fast, fleet, hasty, brisk, expeditious, hurried.

ANT. *Slow, deliberate, cumbrous, lazy, retarded, moderate, gradual, dilatory, lingering, tardy.*

Rapidity. Rapidness, haste, celerity, speed, velocity, agility, swiftness, fleetness, quickness, despatch.

ANT. *Slowness, dilatoriness, tardiness, delay, deliberateness, moderation.*

Rare. Curious, extraordinary, incomparable, odd, peculiar, remarkable, precious, scarce, singular, strange, uncommon, unusual, unprecedented, unique, unparalleled, infrequent.

ANT. *General, usual, normal.*

Rash. Precipitate, headlong, indiscreet, foolhardy, hasty, heedless, thoughtless, incautious, careless, inconsiderate, unwary.

ANT. *Cautious, wary, discreet, thoughtful, prudent, calculating; timid, hesitating, reluctant.*

Rational. Sane, sound, intelligent, reasonable, sensible, wise, discreet, judicious; reasoning, intellectual; sagacious, equitable, enlightened.

ANT. *Irrational, insane, unsound, foolish, absurd, injudicious, unreasonable, preposterous, unintelligent, extravagant.*

Raw. Unprepared, uncooked, immature, unripe, unseasoned, inexperienced, unpracticed, untried, unwrought, unfinished; bare, galled; chilly, bleak.

ANT. *Cooked, dressed, prepared, developed, mature, ripe, mellow, seasoned, practiced, experienced, tried, tested, expert, habituated, familiar, trained; healed; genial, balmy.*

Reach. Attain, arrive, get to, enter, land, come to, gain.

ANT. *Depart, leave, set out, weigh anchor, embark, start, go, go away, set sail.*

Ready. Prompt, expeditious, speedy, unhesitating, dexterous, apt, skilled, handy, expert, facile, easy, opportune, fitted, prepared, disposed, free, willing, cheerful.

ANT. *Tardy, slow, inexpeditious, hesitating, clumsy, inept, unskilled, inexpert, hard, difficult, inopportune, unfit, ill-prepared, unwilling, reluctant, unresponsive, unaccommodating.*

Real. Actual, veritable, genuine, demonstrable, substantial, authentic, certain; developed, essential, positive; true, unquestionable.

ANT. *Illusory, imaginary, unreal, untrue, supposititious, fictitious, hypothetical, fabulous, fanciful, conceived, supposed, feigned, reported, visionary, theoretical.*

Reality. Verity, actuality, substance, truth, genuineness, authenticity, fact, substantiality, existence.

ANT. *Fiction, falsehood, untruth, myth, imagination, fabrication, fancy, supposition, unreality, chimera, vision, hypothesis, hollowness.*

Realm. Domain, kingdom, region, province, country, department, empire, state; jurisdiction, sovereignty, dominion.

ANT. *Anarchy, insurrection; independence; democracy.*

Rear. Lift, elevate, erect, raise, build, establish, exalt, foster, construct, breed, educate, instruct, train, discipline, cherish.

ANT. *Tear down, degrade, undermine, depress, overthrow; destroy, kill, demolish, subvert, stifle, extinguish.*

Reason, *n.* Cause, ground, aim, motive, account, argument, design, consideration, end, object, purpose, principle.

ANT. *Pretext, pretense, falsification; unreason, unreasonableness, irrationality, absurdity, fallacy.*

Reason, *v.* Debate, demonstrate, argue, contend, discuss, prove, establish, question, controvert, wrangle, dispute.

ANT. *Quibble, pervert, equivocate, evade, mystify; cavil, refine; misrepresent; dictate, assert.*

Reasoning. Argument, argumentation, debate, ratiocination.

ANT. *Sophistry, instinct, intuition, presentiment.*

Rebellious. Intractable, refractory, seditious, unmanageable, contumacious, disobedient, insubordinate, mutinous, ungovernable, uncontrollable.

ANT. *Deferential, compliant, docile, manageable, obedient, submissive, subservient, yielding, tractable, gentle, controllable, dutiful.*

Recant. Retract, revoke, recall, abjure, disown, disavow, renounce.

ANT. *Profess, confess, assert, declare, enunciate, maintain, hold; vindicate.*

Reception. Admission, receipt; entertainment; acceptance, credence; welcome.

ANT. *Rejection, dismissal, repudiation, denial, protest, renunciation, disavowal.*

Recite. Describe, recapitulate, detail, number; repeat, deliver, rehearse; relate, narrate, recount; quote; count, enumerate, tell.

ANT. *Misquote, garble, falsify, misrepresent, pervert; forget, fail.*

Reckless. Mindless, negligent, thoughtless, regardless, unconcerned, inattentive, remiss, improvident, rash, inconsiderate.

ANT. *Circumspect, careful, wary, thoughtful, mindful, attentive, considerate, provident, prudent, calculating.*

Recognize. Acknowledge, confess, own, allow, concede, identify, avow.

ANT. *Overlook, repudiate, disown, ignore, disavow, disclaim.*

Reconcile. Placate, propitiate, pacify, appease; conciliate, reunite, content, harmonize; adjust, settle, compose.

ANT. *Separate, sever, alienate, estrange, disaffect.*

Reconciliation. Reconcilement, reunion, pacification, appeasement, propitiation, atonement, expiation; adjustment, restoration, harmony.

ANT. *Separation, estrangement, alienation, disaffection.*

Record. Account, entry, enrolment, catalogue, enumeration, inventory, register, roll; archive, chronicle, document, history, inscription, instrument, memorandum, memorial, muniment, schedule, scroll.

Recover. Cure, heal, retrieve, restore; be cured *or* healed, recruit, recuperate, resume; reanimate, repossess.

ANT. *Relapse, sink, die, fail, grow worse.*

Recovery. Repossession, resumption; recruiting, healing, restoration; regaining, recuperation, convalescence, retrieval, redemption, resuscitation, revival; vindication, reinstatement, reëstablishment.

ANT. *Loss, forfeiture, privation, damage, ruin, destruction, waste; illness, relapse, declension, incurableness, hopelessness.*

Recreation. Sport, amusement, diversion, refreshment, reanimation; holiday, pastime, relaxation.

ANT. *Toil, labor, work, industry, employment, fatigue, weariness, lassitude, exhaustion.*

Rectitude. Justice, honesty, uprightness, fairness, integrity, straightforwardness, conscientiousness, equity.

ANT. *Iniquity, wrong, injustice, immorality, corruption, dishonesty, duplicity, underhandedness.*

Redemption. Ransom, release, rescue, retrieval, recovery, deliverance, liberation, salvation; discharge, fulfilment; atonement, compensation.

ANT. *Abandonment, forfeiture, sacrifice, betrayal, deprivation, desertion.*

Reduce. Lessen, decrease, curtail, abate, shorten, impair, lower, subjugate, subject; diminish, attenuate, abridge, contract; subdue.

ANT. *Magnify, augment, expand, amplify, exalt, raise, invigorate, promote, restore, repair, renovate, transform.*

Redundant. Exuberant, superabundant, overflowing, pleonastic; superfluous, excessive, copious, plentiful; unnecessary.

ANT. *Requisite, necessary, sufficient, enough; scanty, deficient, scarce, wanting, lacking, incomplete, inadequate, insufficient.*

Refinement. Culture, elegance, cultivation, civilization, politeness.

ANT. *Coarseness, grossness, rudeness, rusticity, barbarism, boorishness, brutality, clownishness, savagery, vulgarity.*

Reflect. Consider, think, cogitate, meditate, contemplate, ruminate, ponder, muse; animadvert.

ANT. *Idle, dream, imagine, fancy, wander, rove; disregard, neglect.*

Reform, *v.* Amend, correct, rectify, emend, repair, better, improve, restore, reclaim, mend; remodel.

ANT. *Corrupt, impair, vitiate, deteriorate, deform; spoil, deprave, pollute, defile, injure, contaminate.*

Refuge. Shelter, asylum, retreat, covert; protection, sanctuary, stronghold, defense; hiding-place, harbor.

ANT. *Exposure, peril, snare, menace, pitfall, danger, threat.*

Regard, *v.* Consider, observe, remark, heed, mind, respect, esteem, estimate, value; attend, notice; contemplate; revere, reverence.

ANT. *Overlook, disregard, miss, neglect, omit; misprize; dislike, hate, loathe; contemn.*

Regret, *n.* Grief, concern, sorrow, lamentation, repentance, penitence, self-condemnation; compunction, remorse, contrition.

ANT. *Joy, exultation, happiness, delight, self-gratulation, approbation; praise, commendation; felicitation.*

Regular. Orderly, methodical; conformable, agreeing; governed, subject; normal; constituted, selected; customary, systematic, stated, established, periodical, recognized, formal, recurrent, certain.

ANT. *Unusual, exceptional, rare, irregular, abnormal, eccentric, capricious, variable, uncertain, erratic.*

Regulation. Rule, method, principle, precept; adjustment, disposal; arrangement, ordering, disposition, government, control.

ANT. *Disorder, anarchy, license, misgovernment, misrule, non-regulation, caprice, maladjustment, derangement.*

Rehearse. Recapitulate, detail,

recount, describe, tell; narrate, repeat, recite, relate; practice.
ANT. *Misrepresent; act, perform, play.*

Rejoice. Delight, joy, exult, triumph, please, cheer, exhilarate, gladden, transport, charm, enliven, gratify, make happy.
ANT. *Mourn, grieve, weep, lament, pain, distress, defeat, sadden, deaden, vex, annoy, oppress, afflict, trouble, depress, burden, deject.*

Relation. Recital, rehearsal, account, narration, tale, narrative, detail, description; kindred, affinity, consanguinity, kinsman, kinswoman; connection, association, pertinency, relevancy, agreement.
ANT. *Action, happening, occurrence; alien, stranger, foreigner; absoluteness, disagreement, dissociation, disconnection, irrelevancy.*

Release, *v.* Discharge, extricate, disengage, quit, acquit; free, loose, liberate; exempt, indemnify; deliver, remit.
ANT. *Hold, bind, constrain, confine, fetter, shackle, fine, imprison, sentence, condemn.*

Relief. Alleviation, mitigation, aid, help, succor, assistance, redress, remedy, indemnification; exemption, deliverance, refreshment, support, comfort.
ANT. *Oppression, persecution, aggravation, severity, cruelty; weariness, discomfort, exhaustion.*

Religion. Devotion, faith, piety, righteousness, holiness, morality, godliness, pietism, worship, theology.
ANT. *Irreligion, atheism, unbelief, blasphemy, impiety, godlessness, profanity, sacrilege, ungodliness, wickedness.*

Relinquish. Resign, leave, quit, forsake, abandon, renounce, desert, forbear, forego; surrender, discontinue.
ANT. *Retain, hold, keep, detain, preserve, support, cling to, sustain, maintain; continue, be constant to, persevere, persist.*

Reluctant. Loath, slow, disinclined, indisposed, averse, backward, opposed, unwilling.
ANT. *Eager, favorable, willing, inclined, desirous, disposed.*

Remain. Wait, tarry, rest, sojourn, last, dwell; stay, abide, continue, endure; survive, outlive.
ANT. *Leave, abandon, depart, remove, go, disappear, flit; die, pass.*

Remark. Comment, note, observation, utterance, annotation.

Remarkable. Observable, rare, noticeable, extraordinary, unusual, strange, wonderful, notable, eminent; distinguished, famous, prominent, conspicuous; singular, peculiar, individual.
ANT. *Ordinary, usual, commonplace, mediocre, everyday, common, general.*

Remembrance. Memory, recollection, reminiscence; memento, souvenir, memorandum, memorial, token.
ANT. *Oblivion, forgetfulness.*

Reminiscence. Memory, recollection, remembrance; remnant, relic, trace.
ANT. *Oblivion, forgetfulness; announcement, warning, suggestion, prognostic.*

Remote. Removed, far, distant; irrelevant, not related; foreign, indirect, unconnected, alien, unallied; separate, abstract.
ANT. *Near, close, direct, related, connected, contiguous, immediate; present, pressing,*

urgent; proximate; essential, important.

Rend. Burst, break, rip, sever, mangle, rupture, sunder, tear, lacerate, rive, slit.

ANT. *Mend, reunite, secure, unite, weld, heal, join, solder, sew, stitch.*

Render. Return, pay back, restore; requite; give up, yield, surrender; furnish, contribute, deliver; translate, interpret, set forth, exhibit, try out; apportion, give, present, assign.

ANT. *Keep, withhold, appropriate, retain, refuse, use, apply, employ; alienate, misapportion.*

Renounce. Abandon, abjure, deny, disavow, disown, forswear, disclaim, retract, repudiate, revoke, recall, refuse, reject, discard, recant.

ANT. *Advocate, avow, claim, assert, defend, hold, proclaim, own, acknowledge, cherish, retain, uphold, vindicate, maintain.*

Renown. Fame, distinction, notice, repute, name, reputation, celebrity, honor, glory, eminence.

ANT. *Disgrace, shame, dishonor, disrepute, discredit, degradation, taint, stain, brand.*

Renunciation. Denial, disownment, renouncement, disclaimer, rejection, abjuration, recantation, abandonment.

ANT. *Maintenance, support, vindication, assertion, defense, apology, justification.*

Repeat. Reiterate, renew, relate, recapitulate, recite, reproduce, rehearse, renovate.

ANT. *Discontinue, drop, end, finish, stop, cease, break off, interrupt.*

Repentance. Penitence, regret, remorse, sorrow, compunction, contrition, self-condemnation, contriteness.

ANT. *Impenitence, obstinacy, obduracy; comfort, complacency, approval, hardness, content, self-approval, self-complacency, self-congratulation; stubbornness.*

Repletion. Fulness, superabundance, plethora, abundance, amplitude, sufficiency, enough.

ANT. *Scarcity, want, lack, insufficiency, need.*

Reply. Answer, respond, rejoin, replicate.

ANT. *Question, query, ask, inquire; disregard, pass, drop, ignore.*

Report. Account, description, narration, narrative, recital, rehearsal, relation, record, tale, rumor, statement, story.

ANT. *Allegory, fabrication, fiction.*

Repose, *n.* Rest, recumbency, reclination, ease, quiet, quietness, tranquillity, peace; calmness, quiescence.

ANT. *Unrest, agitation, tumult, movement, restlessness, turmoil, commotion, distraction.*

Represent. Present anew, portray, typify, delineate; personate, act; perform; depict, describe, show, exhibit.

ANT. *Misrepresent; falsify, caricature, distort.*

Reproach, *n.* Disrepute, opprobrium, discredit, dishonor, invective, contumely, reviling, vilification, abuse, scurrility, insolence, insult, scorn, contempt, ignominy, shame, scandal, disgrace, infamy.

ANT. *Approbation, satisfaction, praise, encouragement, exaltation, commendation, honor, applause, eulogy, assent, acceptance, approval.*

Reproach. *v.* Chide, rebuke, revile, condemn, vilify; blame, censure, taunt, upbraid, reprove.

ANT. *Praise, approve, commend, laud, applaud, eulogize.*

Reproof. Comment, criticism, disapproval, chiding, reproach, upbraiding, reproval, admonition, animadversion; censure, blame, condemnation, denunciation, objurgation, reprehension, rebuke, reprimand; reflection, check.

ANT. *Commendation, panegyric, approbation, applause, approval, encomium, praise, eulogy.*

Reprove. Admonish, blame, reproach, censure, condemn, reprimand, warn, upbraid, chide, check, chasten, find fault with, expostulate with, rebuke, reprehend, remonstrate with, take to task.

ANT. *Abet, applaud, encourage, cheer, countenance, incite, urge on, impel, instigate, approve.*

Repugnant. Opposite, opposed, adverse, contrary, inconsistent, irreconcilable, hostile, inimical; incompatible, loath; heterogeneous.

ANT. *Harmonious, friendly, amicable, willing, consistent, compatible, congruous; homogeneous.*

Reputable. Honorable, respectable, estimable, creditable.

ANT. *Disreputable, disgraceful, dishonorable, discreditable, despicable.*

Requite. Avenge, pay off, quit, punish, retaliate, revenge; satisfy, settle with, reward, return, repay, remunerate, recompense, compensate, reciprocate.

ANT. *Absolve, acquit, forgive, excuse, neglect, pardon, slight, forget, overlook, pass over.*

Research. Inquiry, scrutiny, examination, experimentation, exploration, discovery, investigation, study, observation.

ANT. *Ignorance, oversight, inobservance; shallowness, superficiality, sciolism.*

Reserve, *n.* Reservation, retention, limitation, backwardness, coldness, shyness, coyness, modesty; taciturnity, restraint, repression, constraint.

ANT. *Profuseness, prodigality, diffusion; affability, geniality, cordiality, abandonment, surrender, openness, frankness, transparency, indiscretion, volubility.*

Resignation. Relinquishment, forsaking, abandonment, abdication, renunciation, endurance; patience, long-suffering, forbearance; acquiescence, submission.

ANT. *Maintenance, grasp, resistance, retention, rebellion, remonstrance, contention, reservation, holding, keeping, retaining, detention; murmuring, dissatisfaction, discontent, protestation.*

Resolute. Determined, decided, fixed, steadfast, constant, persevering, firm, bold, unshaken, steady; undaunted, unflinching, stout-hearted.

ANT. *Irresolute, timid, hesitating, doubtful, wavering, vacillating, capricious, variable, weak, undetermined, undecided.*

Resources. Expedient, means, resort, contrivance; supplies, devices, money, wealth, appliances, funds.

ANT. *Destitution, poverty, indigence, bareness, want, exhaustion, inanition, lack, drain,*

Respectable. Estimable, honorable, worthy, considerable, reputable, honest; passable.

ANT. *Unworthy, bad, mean, dishonorable, dishonest, paltry, inconsiderable.*

Resplendent. Brilliant, splendid, glorious, luminous, effulgent, gorgeous, shining, glittering, burnished.

ANT. *Dull, tarnished, lusterless, somber, dimmed, sullied.*

Rest. Pause, peace, quiet, stillness, tranquillity, intermission, cessation, ease, calm, peacefulness, calmness, quiescence, stop, repose, quietude, quietness, recreation, sleep, slumber.

ANT. *Agitation, commotion, disturbance, excitement, restlessness, strain, stir, tumult, work, unrest, toil, disquiet, motion, movement, rush.*

Restive. Restless, restiff, fidgety, fretful, fractious, refractory, intractable, impatient, rebellious, skittish; resentful, recalcitrant, balky, vicious, unruly, stubborn, mulish, mutinous, obstinate.

ANT. *Docile, gentle, submissive, passive, quiet, tractable, yielding, obedient, manageable, peaceable.*

Restore. Return, replace, refund, repay, reinstate, rebuild, repair, revive, heal, cure, recover.

ANT. *Remove, steal, appropriate, abstract, destroy, shatter, injure, dilapidate, impair; deprive; wound, harm.*

Restrain. Constrain, hold in, check, repress, circumscribe, confine, curb, hinder, hold, hold back, restrict, suppress, withhold, bridle, abridge, keep back, keep down, keep in, keep under.

ANT. *Let loose, set free, release, arouse, aid, emancipate, animate, incite, excite, encourage, free, impel.*

Result. Consequence, issue, conclusion, effect; end, event, termination, product, outcome; inference, deduction; resolution, determination.

ANT. *Cause, beginning, commencement, rise, origin, antecedent, prognostic, initiation, premonition, indication.*

Retinue. Attendants, suite, followers, train, retainers, satellites, escort, cortège.

ANT. *Solitariness, non-attendance.*

Retirement. Privacy, solitude, loneliness, seclusion.

ANT. *Company, converse, society, fellowship, companionship, association.*

Retribution. Requital, retaliation, payment, recompense; repayment, compensation, reward, return; penalty, punishment, visitation.

ANT. *Remission, reprieve; pardon, condonation, sparing.*

Retrospect. Review, survey, reconsideration, reëxamination; recollection, reminiscence, memory.

ANT. *Prospect, prophecy, anticipation, forecasting, prognostication, speculation.*

Return, *v.* Turn back, come back; reply, respond; answer; restore, recompense, remit, render; reappear, recur; revert, retaliate.

ANT. *Depart, vanish, disappear, remove; retain, misappropriate; withhold.*

Revelation. Disclosure, manifestation, apocalypse.

ANT. *Concealment, shrouding, veiling, mystery, obscuration, cloud, cloudiness, hiding.*

Revenge. Retaliation, retribution, vengeance, avenging, requital.

ANT. *Mercy, pardon, reconciliation, pity, compassion, excuse, grace, forgiveness.*

Revenue. Income; taxes, excise, customs, duties, rents, receipts; produce, return, wealth, proceeds.

ANT. *Outgo, waste, expenditure, expense, deductions, impoverishment.*

Reverse, *n.* Contrary, opposite, counterpart; change, vicissitude; inversion, counter-position; derangement, alteration; rear, back; misfortune, defeat.

ANT. *Obverse, front; order, arrangement, version, position, location; continuance, perpetuation, identity, stability, regularity, uniformity.*

Revive. Reanimate, reinvigorate; restore, raise, recover, renew, recall; awake, revivify, resuscitate.

ANT. *Kill, destroy, extinguish, discourage; decline, die, droop.*

Revolution. Lawlessness, insurrection, revolt, riot, sedition, anarchy, insubordination, rebellion, mutiny, confusion, disorder, tumult, disintegration.

ANT. *Government, submission, obedience, authority, control, command, dominion, domination, law, empire, rule, sovereignity, loyalty, supremacy, order.*

Revolve. Roll, rotate, turn.

ANT. *Bind, grind, stand, slide, slip, stick, chafe.*

Reward, *n.* Recompense, compensation, remuneration, pay, requital, retribution, punishment.

Rich. Wealthy, opulent, affluent, supplied, abounding; abundant, copious, bountiful; fertile, productive; valued, sumptuous, precious, costly; high-seasoned; luscious; vivid.

ANT. *Poor, indigent, needy, impoverished, destitute, impecunious, penniless; lacking, scanty, scarce, meager; barren, sterile; trivial, worthless, unproductive, fruitless, paltry, valueless; dull, tame, dry.*

Riches. Opulence, wealth, affluence, richness, plenty, abundance.

ANT. *Poverty, want, indigence, scarcity, need, lack, impecuniosity.*

Riddle. Conundrum, paradox, problem, puzzle, enigma.

ANT. *Axiom, answer, explanation, solution, proposition.*

Ridicule. Derision, raillery, banter, burlesque, irony, satire, mocking, sarcasm, gibe, jeer, sneer.

ANT. *Respect, homage, veneration, deference, honor.*

Right, *n.* Claim, liberty, prerogative, license, privilege, exemption, franchise, immunity, duty, justice, uprightness, integrity; title, ownership; interest; rectitude, correctness, power; propriety, fitness, suitableness.

ANT. *Wrong, falsehood, incorrectness, perverseness; liability, illegitimacy, non-legality, usurpation, injustice, impropriety, unfitness, encroachment, force, violence.*

Righteous. Holy, uncorrupt, honest, equitable, rightful, upright, virtuous, just, good, conscientious.

ANT. *Unholy, corrupt, dishonest, unjust, wicked, evil, unscrupulous, vicious, false, unprincipled, profligate.*

Ripe. Mature, complete, fin-

ished; perfect, developed, full-grown; fit, consummate; prepared; full, seasoned, mellow.
ANT. *Raw, unripe, crude, fresh, green, unseasoned, unprepared.*

Rise, *v.* Arise, issue, flow, proceed, spring, ascend, emanate.
ANT. *Descend, drop, fall, go down, set, settle, sink, decline.*

Rival, *v.* Emulate, antagonize, compete with, contend, strive, oppose, equal.
ANT. *Surrender, yield, defer, retire.*

Robber. Brigand, marauder, pirate, plunderer, thief, burglar, bandit, highwayman, footpad, despoiler, depredator, raider, buccaneer, forager, freebooter.

Robust. Strong, lusty, sinewy, muscular, hale, hearty, vigorous, forceful; healthy, sturdy, sound; violent, rude, rough.
ANT. *Puny, weak, delicate, frail, sickly, emaciated, thin, slender, gentle, mild, considerate, tender.*

Romantic. Sentimental, fanciful, fantastic, fictitious, wild, extravagant, chimerical.
ANT. *Unromantic, truthful, unvarnished, unadorned, veritable, actual, real, realistic, reasonable.*

Root. Radix, radicle, stock, origin, foundation, base, source, stem, parent, commencement, beginning, radical, bottom.
ANT. *Branch, ramification, product, issue, progeny, superstructure.*

Rough. Uneven, uncut, boisterous, unpolished; coarse, disordered, shaggy, ragged; rude, uncivil, harsh; loud, offensive; tempestuous, stormy; rugged, knotty, craggy, gruff; incomplete; uncourteous, churlish, blunt.
ANT. *Smooth, plain, level, polished, flat, glossy, sleek, soft, mild, quiet, refined, tender, gentle; balmy, zephyrlike.*

Routine. Practice, custom, procedure, round, course, wont, order; gradation, rotation, sequence, tenor, system, method; regulation.

Royal. August, kinglike, majestic, munificent, princely, regal, magnificent, kingly.
ANT. *Beggarly, contemptible, mean, poor, servile, slavish, vile.*

Rude. Rough, uneven, shapeless, unfashioned, rugged, uncouth, inelegant, rustic, vulgar, raw, clownish, unskilful, untaught, illiterate, ignorant, uncivil, impolite, saucy, impudent, insolent, surly, uncivilized, brutal, barbarous, savage, violent, fierce, tumultuous, impetuous, boisterous, inclement, severe.
ANT. *Polite, urbane, accomplished, cultivated, courteous, refined, civil, affable, courtly, gracious, elegant, polished, well-bred, obliging; modest, bashful; considerate, serene, placid, genial, calm; fashionable, modern, civilized, modish.*

Rugged. Rough, uneven, rude, wrinkled, cragged, harsh, hard, crabbed; steep, precipitate; violent, sour, surly, boisterous, tumultuous, stormy, inclement, tempestuous; austere, severe; ruffled, blunt.
ANT. *Smooth, even, gentle, soft, low; pleasant, kindly; balmy, soothing; complaisant, mild.*

Rule. Regulation, law, precept, maxim, canon, order, method, direction, control, sway, empire; principle, practice; domination, mastery, government; test, criterion, formula.

ANT. *Exception, deviation, eccentricity, irregularity.*

Run. Race, hasten, speed, proceed, hurry, scamper, post; go, flow, glide, move, roll on; melt, fuse; pass, advance; course, fly, rush; hustle; pursue; cast, shape, mold; drive, force; indicate, mark out; incur, encounter, venture, risk; conduct, manage, carry on; flee.

ANT. *Delay, walk, halt, stop, saunter, rest, linger, hesitate; harden; retrograde, slip.*

Rustic. Rural, sylvan, pastoral, country, countrified, bucolic, agricultural, verdant; artless, inelegant, plain, rude, unpolished, untaught, unsophisticated; awkward, boorish, outlandish, clownish, coarse, hoydenish, uncouth.

ANT. *City-like, urban; accomplished, elegant, cultured, polite, urbane, polished, well-bred, refined.*

Ruthless. Cruel, pitiless, harsh, relentless, unsparing.

ANT. *Tender, gentle, pitiful, compassionate, lenient, regretful, long-suffering.*

S

Sable. Dark, black, ebon, somber.

ANT. *Light, white, cheerful, bright, ivory.*

Sacrament. Eucharist, Lord's Supper, communion; ceremony, rite, service, solemnity, ordinance, observance.

Sacred. Holy, divine, hallowed, consecrated, dedicated, devoted, religious, venerable, reverend.

ANT. *Secular, profane, common, unconsecrated, human.*

Sacrifice, *n.* Offering, propitiation, expiation, thanksgiving; destruction, immolation, devotion, surrender; oblation, atonement.

ANT. *Offense, transgression; retention, reservation; acceptance.*

Sad. Sorrowful, mournful, dejected, gloomy, depressed, sedate, cheerless, downcast, grievous; dull, grave, dark, somber; afflicted; calamitous; serious, staid; melancholy, disconsolate, despondent, disastrous, deplorable.

ANT. *Cheerful, joyous, glad, mirthful, jubilant, jovial, light-hearted; exultant, gay, exhilarated, happy, blithe.*

Sagacious. Sage, sensible, keen, discerning, clear-sighted, apt, acute, intelligent, sharp, wise, rational, shrewd, able, keen-sighted, keen-witted, judicious, perspicacious, quick-scented, sharp-witted.

ANT. *Obtuse, senseless, irrational, silly, stupid, simple, unintelligent, undiscerning, dull, absurd, foolish, futile, sottish, ignorant.*

Sale. Bargain, barter, deal, exchange, trade, change.

Salient. Leaping, bounding, jumping; projecting; prominent, conspicuous, noticeable, significant; strategic.

ANT. *Retreating, retiring, low-lying; unimportant, inconspicuous, unnoticeable, minor, inconsiderable, subordinate, insignificant.*

Salvation. Saving, preservation, deliverance; redemption; rescue.

ANT. *Perdition, destruction, damnation, condemnation, loss.*

Sample. Specimen, example, illustration, case, instance, exemplification.

ANT. *Total, whole, exception, aggregate; abnormality, monstrosity.*

Sanction. Authorization, authority, countenance; ratification, confirmation, approbation; approval, support, seal, allowance.

ANT. *Discountenance, disallowance, unauthorization; cancellation, nullification; disapproval, non-support.*

Sanguine. Blood-red, crimson; warm, ardent; hopeful, lively, animated, cheerful; confident, enthusiastic, buoyant; trustful.

ANT. *Pallid, cold, frigid; unresponsive, depressed, lifeless, despondent, despairing, dejected, anxious, suspicious, misgiving, distrustful.*

Sanity. Saneness, soundness, rationality; reasonableness, wisdom; amenableness.

ANT. *Insanity, aberration, derangement, unsoundness, irrationality, madness, lunacy, alienation, dementia, folly.*

Sarcasm. Taunt, gibe; scorn, contempt, satire; irony, sneer, ridicule.

ANT. *Compliment, eulogy, praise, approbation, appreciation, panegyric.*

Satisfy. Satiate, sate, compensate; cloy, surfeit, suffice, content, glut, fill, requite; relieve, reassure, convince; please, recompense, gratify, fulfil.

ANT. *Deprive, deny, starve, stint, refuse; annoy, tantalize; aggravate, tease; displease.*

Savage. Wild, uncultivated, untamed, uncivilized, rude, brutish, brutal, barbarous, cruel, inhuman, fierce, pitiless, merciless, atrocious, ferocious; murderous, violent.

ANT. *Tame, civilized, cultivated, domesticated, tender, refined, polished, gentle, humane, considerate, pitiful, merciful, protective, generous, subdued, chivalrous, clement, self-controlled.*

Save. Preserve, rescue, deliver; lay up, reserve, keep; spare, prevent; protect; be economical, hoard, husband; obviate, snatch, catch.

ANT. *Lose, destroy, abandon, imperil, expose, endanger, risk, hazard; waste, lavish, spend, fling away.*

Say. Utter, express, tell, speak, declare; repeat, rehearse, recite; assert; mention, suggest; suppose; answer; respond, reply; state, pronounce; affirm, deny; allege.

ANT. *Silence, hush, whisper, mumble; be taciturn; suppress, repress; mispronounce.*

Scarce. Rare, infrequent, deficient; uncommon; scant, sparing, meager, insufficient; unusual, unique, singular, wanting, few, precious.

ANT. *Plenty, abundant, frequent, plentiful, common, thick.*

Scheme, *n.* Plan, project, contrivance, design, purpose, plot, device; system, outline; machination, intrigue, stratagem, cabal, conspiracy; theory.

ANT. *Blunder, derangement, misarrangement, bungle, botch.*

Scholar. Learner, pupil, student, savant, disciple.

ANT. *Dunce, fool, ignoramus, illiterate person, idiot, idler.*

Science. Literature, art, knowledge; truth, facts; skill, expertness; comprehension; information, investigation, experimentation, learning, experience.

ANT. *Ignorance, error, smattering, fallacy, sciolism; inexperience, unfamiliarity, incomprehension.*

Scorn, *n.* Disdain, derision, contumely, despite, slight, mockery, dishonor; contempt, disregard; sneer, opprobrium.

ANT. *Compliment, commendation, deference, approval, esteem, respect, regard, approbation.*

Scruple, *n.* Unwillingness, hesitation, doubt; particle; qualm, reluctance, misgiving.

ANT. *Confidence, assurance, recklessness, heedlessness; daring, self-complacency.*

Scrupulous. Cautious, careful, conscientious, hesitating; exact, nice; questioning, unwilling, punctilious, precise; diffident, dubious.

ANT. *Reckless, confident, careless, unconscientious, self-complacent, heedless, unwary, incautious, daring.*

Scrutiny. Examination, inspection, observation, search, sifting, exploration, inquisition, inquiry.

ANT. *Oversight, misobservance, disregard, slight, inattention.*

Season. Time, period, term, interval, spell, while; occasion, opportunity, timeliness, seasonableness.

ANT. Contretemps, *unseasonableness, untimeliness, unsuitableness.*

Seasonable. Opportune, suitable, timely, fit, convenient, appropriate, normal; periodical; welcome.

ANT. *Inopportune, unsuitable, unfit, untimely, inconvenient, inappropriate, unwelcome, unexpected, abnormal.*

Secure, *a.* Undisturbed, assured, heedless, inattentive; easy, unanxious, trustful, insured; obtained, acquired; fast, firm; defended, guarded, protected, certain, sheltered, safe.

ANT. *Disturbed, endangered, imperiled, insecure, hazardous; anxious, distrustful, suspicious, careful, precarious; loose, drifting, doubtful, dubious.*

Sedate. Settled, composed, calm, quiet, tranquil, still, serene, unruffled, undisturbed, contemplative, sober, serious; passive.

ANT. *Flighty, disturbed, uneasy, restless, excited, discomposed, agitated, indiscreet; active, moving; frivolous.*

Sedition. Riot, rebellion, revolt, insurrection, mutiny; outbreak, uprising, secession, treason; insubordination; tumult, turmoil, anarchy.

ANT. *Peace, pacification, order, quiet, orderliness, obedience, allegiance, fealty, union, patriotism, fidelity.*

See. Perceive, behold, descry, view; observe, discern, understand, comprehend; watch, look after; interview, visit; associate, meet; accompany, escort; attend, heed, be attentive; gaze, glance at.

ANT. *Be blind; overlook, mistake; misunderstand, miscomprehend; pass, ignore, neglect; disregard, misconceive.*

Seek. Search, try for, solicit, inquire for, strive after, hunt, follow, trace, prosecute, attempt, endeavor, investigate.

ANT. *Shun, elude, ignore, neglect, disregard, avoid, relinquish, drop, abandon, discard.*

Seldom. Rarely, not often, infrequently; hardly ever, occasionally.

Ant. *Often, frequently, generally, commonly, regularly, habitually, invariably, uniformly, systematically.*

Selection. Choice, pick, preference, election, option.

Ant. *Repudiation, rejection, discarding, refusal; exclusion.*

Self-abnegation. Self-renunciation, self-sacrifice, self-control, self-devotion, self-immolation, self-denial.

Ant. *Self-indulgence, self-gratification, self-will, selfishness, self-seeking.*

Selfish. Self-seeking, mean, ungenerous, narrow, illiberal, mercenary, greedy, egoistical, self-indulgent.

Ant. *Generous, liberal, altruistic, philanthropic, beneficent, self-denying, public-spirited, magnanimous, unselfish, considerate.*

Send. Sling, throw, fling, hurl, lance, launch, propel, project, cast, dart, despatch, discharge, drive, emit; forward, transmit, impel, dismiss, delegate, depute.

Ant. *Receive, keep, retain, hold; bring, carry, hand, get, give, convey.*

Sensation. Emotion, sense, feeling, perception.

Ant. *Apathy, non-sensibility, non-perception, indifference.*

Sense. Understanding, reason; cognition, apprehension; deduction; perception, feeling; recognition, discernment; reasoning; opinion, judgment, notion, meaning, import, signification.

Ant. *Nonsense, misunderstanding; stupidity, non-apprehension; non-comprehension; stolidity, inertness, non-observance; fancy, folly, unsoundness.*

Sensibility. Feeling, sensitiveness, susceptibility, impressibility.

Ant. *Coldness, deadness, unconsciousness, hardness, numbness, insensibility.*

Sentiment. Thought, opinion, notion, sensibility, feeling; susceptibility, impressibility, impression, conviction; emotion; maxim, saying, toast.

Ant. *Nonsense, conjecture, vacuity; assumption, prejudice, preconception.*

Separate, *v.* Disunite, divide, sever; come between, part; disjoin, divorce; disengage, detach; sunder; withdraw, eliminate, remove, segregate.

Ant. *Unite, consolidate, integrate, connect, join, attach, link, weld, engage, wed; gather, convene, collect.*

Sequence. Succession, following, consequence, arrangement, order; series, progression, continuity.

Ant. *Precedence, introduction, priority; disorder, disconnection; intermission, irregularity.*

Serious. Sober, earnest, momentous, grave; thoughtful, sedate, solemn; important, weighty; dangerous.

Ant. *Gay, thoughtless, frivolous, laughing, joking, jocose, careless, trifling, trivial, unimportant, light, insignificant,*

Serve. Obey, minister to, subserve, promote, aid, help, abet, assist, benefit, succor.

Ant. *Command, order, manage; obstruct, counteract, retard, defeat, injure, thwart, oppose.*

Set. Put, seat, place, fix; affix, attach; fasten, make stable *or* firm; obstruct, embarrass; determine upon, fix upon; plant; frame; stiffen, solidify; adjust, regulate, adapt; prepare; replace; spread; stud, variegate; value at, rate at; establish, furnish, prescribe, strengthen, stabilitate, ground, confirm, determine, appoint, assign.

ANT. *Remove, uproot, transfer, eradicate, transplant, unsettle, weaken, soften, destroy, demolish; disperse, discard; denude, disarrange, divest, strip; misvalue, under-* or *over-rate; abolish, frustrate.*

Settle. Regulate, arrange, compose, decide; establish; still, calm; clear; restore; depress, sink, lower, make compact, harden; determine, adjust, make up, pacify; liquidate, balance; colonize, people.

ANT. *Disturb, confuse, derange; agitate, unsettle, excite, uproot, overturn; obstruct; elevate, upheave, break up; discompose, disorder, rise, ascend, move; misregulate, aggravate.*

Severe. Stern, strict, austere, hard, relentless, rigorous, unrelenting, inexorable, harsh, inflexible, rigid, morose, stiff, uncompromising, unmitigated, unyielding; critical, grave, serious.

ANT. *Lenient, clement, unexacting, mild, easy, gay, cheerful, joyous; loose, slack, inexact, indulgent, uncritical, moderate, kind, considerate.*

Shade. Shadow; darkness, obscurity; screen, shelter, protection; body, spirit, ghost; umbrage, adumbration; degree, minuteness; seclusion.

ANT. *Light, illumination, sunshine, brightness, daylight; glare, radiance, exposure; publicity; quantity, amount; defenselessness.*

Shake. Agitate, fluctuate, flutter, oscillate, quake, quiver, quaver, rock, shiver, shudder, totter, tremble, waver, wave, sway, swing, vibrate, thrill, jar.

ANT. *Fasten, fix, set, secure, settle, confirm.*

Shame. Disgrace, reproach, dishonor, ignominy; degradation, contempt, infamy; diffidence, modesty, discredit; humiliation, abashment; decency, decorum.

ANT. *Fame, honor, glory, approval, renown, credit; impudence, shamelessness, indecency, immodesty, indecorum, impropriety.*

Shape. Appearance, figure, aspect, form, guise; outline; embodiment; character, fashion, mold, pattern, cast, model.

ANT. *Imitation, reproduction, copy; deformity, disfigurement.*

Sharp. Quick, sagacious, witty, discerning, shrewd, ingenious, sour, acid, tart, acrid, biting, poignant, acrimonious, sarcastic, bitter, painful, afflictive, violent, fierce, ardent, fiery; acute, keen, trenchant, astute, subtle, penetrating, discriminating, inventive, piquant; severe, vigilant, attentive; caustic, cutting; eager, hungry; thin, emaciated; shrill, high; exacting, close.

ANT. *Dull, blunt, slow, obtuse, undiscerning, unresourceful, sweet, honeyed, cloying, saccharine, mellow; soft, gentle, mild, tender, considerate, kindly, lenient, clement; uninventive, indifferent, sluggish, inactive, tame, characterless, spiritless, careless, inattentive; thick; generous, unexacting.*

Shelter. Defend, guard, harbor, protect, shield, screen, ward, cover, conceal.

ANT. *Expose, betray, imperil, endanger, exhibit, lay bare, discover, attack.*

Short. Brief, contracted, inadequate, limited, scanty; insufficient, incomplete, imperfect; abrupt, petulant, quick; near, direct, straight; succinct, concise, condensed, compendious; terse, pithy, laconic, curt, sententious; severe, uncivil; narrow; destitute.

ANT. *Long, protracted, extended, adequate, ample, sufficient, plentiful, abundant, copious; perfect, complete; civil, suave, complaisant; circuitous, indirect; tedious, prolix, verbose, extended, wordy; broad; provided for.*

Show, *v.* Exhibit, present, display; tell, reveal; direct, conduct; clear, prove, manifest, explain, evince; bestow, confer; appear, look, seem; demonstrate, unfold, inform, teach; evidence.

ANT. *Conceal, hide, withhold, suppress, obscure, mystify, cloak, wrap; contradict, deny, refute, disprove, falsify; misinterpret.*

Shrewd. Keen, critical, subtle, arch, astute, sagacious, acute, discerning, penetrating; malicious, evil, vicious; wily, artful, cunning; clever, sharp, able; discriminating, intelligent.

ANT. *Stolid, stupid, unintelligent, dull, thick, unsagacious, undiscerning, undiscriminating; plain, blank, blunt, frank; kindly, sincere, benevolent; fair, open.*

Sick. Diseased, ill, disordered, distempered, indisposed, weak, ailing, feeble, morbid; imperfect, impaired, weakened, corrupted; disgusted, surfeited.

ANT. *Healthy, whole, well, sound, strong, robust, salubrious, vigorous, hale, wholesome, salutary.*

Side. Margin, edge, verge, border, boundary; party, sect, faction, interest, cause, policy, behalf; face, aspect, plane; slope, declivity; half.

ANT. *Center, interior, body, heart, core; opposition, secession, neutrality.*

Sight. Vision, show, representation, exhibition; faculty of seeing, view; visibility, spectacle; inspection, examination; opinion, judgment; perception, ken, cognizance; contemplation, survey; insight; appearance.

ANT. *Blindness, non-visibility, obscuration; non-appearance; oversight, neglect; disappearance; vanishing; impression, prejudice.*

Sign. Mark, manifestation, indication, presage, symbol, type, token, emblem, note, omen, signal, prognostic, symptom.

Significant. Expressive, suggestive, important; weighty, momentous; manifest, intimating, declarative, betokening, implying, meaning, denoting; telling, speaking; forcible; conspicuous.

ANT. *Insignificant, meaningless, inconspicuous, mute, inexpressive, expressionless, unsuggestive.*

Silence. Stillness, hush, restfulness, quiet, muteness, noiselessness, calm, peace, tranquillity; dumbness, taciturnity; obscurity, secrecy, oblivion.

ANT. *Noise, sound, tumult, clamor, roar, storm, din, unrest, babel, commotion, reverberation, resonance, agitation, clatter; talkativeness, loquacity, garrulity; publicity, fame, rumor, repute, celebrity.*

Similar. Corresponding, like, resembling, uniform, homogeneous; congruous, harmonious.

ANT. *Dissimilar, unlike, different, alien, discordant, heterogeneous, incongruous.*

Simple. Silly; single, uncombined; plain, unadorned; mere; sincere, artless, unaffected, natural; direct, clear, perspicuous; credulous, foolish; humble, undistinguished, lowly; innocent; elementary.

ANT. *Complex, double, compound, combined, mixed; ornate, adorned; blended, fused, multiform; artful, affected, artificial; indirect, complicated, circuitous, skeptic, pragmatic; proud, haughty, distinguished, celebrated; various, organized, elaborate; designing, insincere, double-minded; developed, perfect.*

Sin. Evil, crime, guilt, offense, wickedness, fault, vice, criminality, misdeed; viciousness, ungodliness, wrong, wrong-doing, unrighteousness, iniquity, transgression, immorality, depravity, delinquency.

ANT. *Virtue, godliness, rectitude, uprightness, sinlessness, excellence, blamelessness, goodness, holiness, innocence, morality, integrity, purity, righteousness, right.*

Sing. Chant, carol, chirp, hum, warble, chirrup.

Singular. Unexampled, eminent, unprecedented, extraordinary, remarkable, uncommon, rare, unusual, peculiar, strange, odd, eccentric, fantastic; individual, unique; conspicuous, consummate, exceptional, particular; curious, queer.

ANT. *Common, everyday, ordinary, commonplace, general, universal, usual, regular, customary, frequent, numerous; unnoticeable, normal, typical, inconspicuous, humdrum.*

Sink. Subside, drop, droop, decay, lower, lessen; submerge, immerse, engulf; depress, degrade, debase, diminish; fall, descend; decline, dwindle, decrease; weary, flag, abate; reduce; drown; attenuate.

ANT. *Rise, ascend, mount, increase, augment, aggrandize, swell; flourish, exalt, heighten, promote, enhance; encourage, perpetuate.*

Situation. Site, station, post, case, plight, state; location, position; place, office; condition; locality, seat, ground, spot; circumstance, predicament; category; employment; footing, aspect; birth, standing.

ANT. *Absence, dislodgment, displacement, non-assignment.*

Skeptic. Agnostic, doubter, freethinker, infidel, unbeliever, deist, atheist, disbeliever.

ANT. *Christian, believer.*

Sketch, *n.* Outline, picture, design, drawing, draft; skeleton, plan, brief.

Skilful. Expert, dexterous, apt, handy, adroit, clever, deft, proficient, skilled, trained, accomplished, happy, ingenious, practiced; adept, masterly, cunning.

ANT. *Unskilled, clumsy, inexpert, unskilful, unintelligent, awkward, incompetent, unprepared, untrained, unable, untaught, bungling, helpless, maladroit, shiftless.*

Slander, *v.* Defame, disparage, depreciate, malign, asperse, calumniate, libel, vilify, revile, traduce, decry, backbite.

ANT. *Extol, eulogize, laud, praise, vindicate, defend.*

Slang. Vulgarity, cant, colloquialism, vulgarism.

ANT. *Diction, language.*

Slender. Small, narrow, slim; weak, feeble, slight; moderate, trivial, inconsiderable, meager; spare, abstemious, frugal.

ANT. *Thick, stout, robust, broad, ample, deep, bulky, considerable, massive, weighty; giant, colossal.*

Slippery. Smooth, glib; mutable, uncertain, fickle, inconstant; unstable, changeable; wanton, loose, unchaste; icy, glassy, insecure, perilous, unsafe; shifty, elusive; deceptive, evasive; unprincipled.

ANT. *Rough, firm, safe, secure, stable; constant, certain, dependable, upright, sincere, outright, trustworthy, sound.*

Slow. Deliberate, dilatory, lingering, gradual, moderate, procrastinating, tardy; inert, inactive, sluggish, drowsy, dull, delaying, dawdling.

ANT. *Nimble, active, brisk, alert, lively, prompt, speedy, quick, spry, swift, agile.*

Small. Little, diminutive, inconsiderable; inconsequential, uninfluential, trivial, insignificant; paltry, mean, incapable, unable; short; weak, slender, gentle, low; tiny, puny; unimportant; scanty, moderate; sordid, selfish; inferior, unintellectual, ungifted, unintelligent.

ANT. *Large, great, big, extensive, enormous, bulky, massive, weighty, ample, spacious, broad, strong, stout, generous, liberal, munificent; important, significant, notable, influential, distinguished, gifted, magnanimous, intelligent, intellectual, superior, competent.*

Smart. Acute, quick, lively, brisk, clever, dashy, showy; pungent, pricking; keen, severe, poignant; vigorous, sharp; active, shrewd; efficient, witty; pretentious, spruce; fresh.

ANT. *Dull, heavy, blunt, obtuse, dense, stupid; aching; slow, inactive, sluggish, inefficient, shabby, dowdy, boorish, clownish.*

Sneer. Jeer, mock, gibe, taunt, fling, scoff.

ANT. *Smile, laugh; flatter, compliment; cheer.*

Sober. Abstinent, abstemious, moderate, regular; steady, collected, quiet, cool, staid, somber; temperate; dispassionate, self-controlled, calm, self-possessed, solemn, sedate.

ANT. *Intemperate, intoxicated, drunk, impassioned, excited, heated, furious, passionate; unreasonable, immoderate, uncontrolled, agitated, extravagant; erratic, eccentric.*

Socialism. Communism, collectivism, fabianism.

Society. Companionship, fellowship, company; participation, connection; association, partnership; community, sodality, communion, intercourse.

ANT. *Solitude, solitariness, privacy, separation, segregation; individuality, personality; disconnection, dissociation, unsociability.*

Soft. Yielding, impressible, malleable; smooth, delicate; agreeable, gentle, flowing; flexible; mild, tender, conciliatory, kind; effeminate, weak; easy; quiet, peaceful, tranquil.

ANT. *Hard, unyielding, impervious, tough, stubborn, impermeable; non-resilient; disagreeable, harsh, brusk, gruff, unkind; strong, manly; virile;*

rough, coarse, rigid, rigorous, abrupt; resolute, determined.

Solemnity. Gravity, formality, ritual, ceremonial, sobriety, seriousness, reverence, devotion; celebration, observance; sanctity, awfulness, sacredness; impressiveness.

ANT. *Levity, triviality, gaiety, vulgarity; secularity, desecration, profanity; meaning, unimpressiveness, unimposingness; simplicity.*

Solid. Hard, sound, real, valid, weighty, profound; compact, resistant, dense; heavy; strong, firm, stable; substantial; impenetrable; cubic.

ANT. *Hollow, yielding, soft, resilient, malleable, fluid, flexible, impressible, liquid; brittle, frail; light, trifling, frivolous; invalid, weak, fallacious, unsound.*

Solitude. Loneliness, solitariness, loneness, recluseness, retiredness; withdrawal, remoteness, destitution, absence; seclusion, retirement; desertion, retreat, wilderness, desert, privacy, isolation.

ANT. *Populousness, society, popularity, throng, crowd, intercourse, meeting, convening, populace, multitude.*

Solution. Disruption, separation, breach; disentanglement, explanation, clearing up; resolution, disintegration; release, discharge; solvency; disconnection, discontinuance; key, answer, elucidation.

ANT. *Union, amalgamation, conjunction, connection, combination, entanglement, complication; continuity; integration; obscurity, confusion, perplexity, mystification.*

Soothe. Soften, allay, compose, tranquilize, pacify; humor, flatter, please; assuage, calm, mollify, comfort; lull; mitigate, relieve.

ANT. *Rouse, excite, disturb, disquiet; aggravate, displease, scold, irritate, exasperate, annoy, infuriate; dissatisfy.*

Sordid. Vile, base, gross; mean, avaricious, covetous, niggardly; greedy; low, degraded; stingy, close, ungenerous, penurious; illiberal.

ANT. *Pure, noble, honorable, refined; generous, unselfish, liberal, broad, munificent, uncovetous; prodigal, profuse, lavish; high-minded.*

Soul. Spirit, life, courage, fire, ardor; vitality, animus; leader, inspirer; passion, fervor, affection; person; reason, intellect, emotions; ghost, specter.

ANT. *Lifelessness, soullessness; body; coldness, spiritlessness; irrationality, unintellectuality.*

Sound, *n.* Noise, note, tone, report; impulse, vibration.

ANT. *Silence; taciturnity; stillness, hush, lull, muteness.*

Sound, *a.* Whole, unbroken, unharmed, free, perfect, healthy; firm, strong, solid, safe; correct, true, orthodox; deep, profound, undisturbed; right; legal, valid, undefective; entire, thorough, substantial, irrefutable.

ANT. *Unsound, broken, partial, harmed; imperfect, soft, diseased; weak, mellow, unsafe; incorrect, untrue, heterodox; light, trivial, fragile; illegal, illegitimate, invalid, defective; insubstantial, fallacious, hollow, unfounded.*

Sovereign, *n.* King, prince, potentate, monarch, emperor; ruler.

ANT. *Subject, peasant, serf.*

Sovereign, *a.* Supreme, paramount, superior, chief; independent, unlimited, absolute; controlling, efficacious; princely, royal; primary, principal, regal, imperial; predominant.
ANT. *Inferior, subordinate, subservient, ministerial, secondary, subject; popular, menial; inefficient, unefficacious, uncertain, weak.*

Space. Extension, room; interval, duration, time; capacity, distance, measure, quantity; boundlessness, illimitableness; immeasurableness, immensity.
ANT. *Confinement, proximity, limitation, restriction, contiguity, continuity.*

Spare, *a.* Scanty, sparing, frugal, wanting, lacking, parsimonious, needed, chary; superfluous; lean, meager, thin, gaunt.
ANT. *Ample, abundant, profuse, plentiful, liberal, bountiful, unsparing, unstinted, unrestricted, generous; plump, fat, corpulent, portly.*

Sparse. Scattered, sprinkled, infrequent, thin, scanty, meager, few.
ANT. *Dense, thick, plentiful, many, populous, crowded, numerous, frequent, multitudinous.*

Speak. Say, talk, tell, utter, discourse, articulate, converse, express, chat, chatter, enunciate, pronounce; announce, declaim, declare, deliver.
ANT. *Be mute* or *dumb; keep silence, be taciturn; suppress; recall.*

Speculation. Venture; theory, view, notion, conjecture; consideration, meditation, contemplation, thought, weighing; hypothesis, scheme.
ANT. *Certainty, fact, verity, proof, realization, verification.*

Speech. Address, discourse, language, speaking, talk, oration, utterance, sermon, harangue, dissertation, oratory, disquisition.
ANT. *Hush, silence, stillness, taciturnity, speechlessness.*

Spirit. Life, soul; ghost, specter; fairy, sprite; energy, vivacity, ardor, courage, enthusiasm; intellectuality; meaning, intent; vapor; distilled liquid; air, breath; intelligence, immateriality, essence, disembodiment, apparition; activity, earnestness, zeal; temper, disposition; principle, motive.
ANT. *Substance, body, corporeity, flesh, frame, materiality, embodiment, organization; spiritlessness, timidity, lifelessness, soullessness, deadness, torpor, dejection, slowness.*

Spiritual. Immaterial, incorporeal, mental, intellectual; holy, divine, heavenly-minded; ecclesiastical, sacred; moral; religious, ethical.
ANT. *Carnal, fleshly, material, sensuous; gross; unspiritual.*

Splendid. Shining, showy, magnificent, sumptuous, pompous; illustrious, brilliant, famous; gorgeous, grand, glorious; imposing; superb, heroic, noble.
ANT. *Dull, tame, obscure, tarnished, tawdry, somber, beggarly, gloomy, poor, ordinary, ineffective, inglorious, insignificant, mean, low.*

Spontaneous. Free, intentional, voluntary, willing, unbidden, impulsive, automatic, instinctive, deliberate.
ANT. *Forced, compelled, coerced, unwilling, reluctant.*

Spread, *v.* Open, unfurl, disperse, distribute, scatter, circulate, disseminate, dispense; extend, stretch, expand, amplify; divulge, propagate, publish, diffuse.

ANT. *Collect, condense, contract, furl, gather, close, shut; confine, suppress, restrict, recall, conceal, hush, localize.*

Spring, *v.* Leap, bound, jump; shoot, fly, dart, start; emerge; bend, warp; proceed, issue, result; burst, emanate, flow; rise, originate, germinate.

ANT. *Settle, alight, arrive, land, drop; end, terminate, debouch, finish, eventuate.*

Spy. Scout, emissary, detective.

Stable, *a.* Steady, abiding, firm, strong, durable; fixed, established; constant, resolute, unwavering; secure, stanch, permanent; solid, lasting, perpetual; immobile, rigid, unmovable.

ANT. *Vacillating, wavering, unsteady, toppling, weak, tottering, infirm, insecure, precarious, frail, unstable; transient, ephemeral, evanescent, vanishing, non-durable.*

Stain, *v.* Blot, spot, sully, tarnish, tinge, tint, color, discolor, disgrace, dishonor, dye, soil.

ANT. *Preserve inviolate* or *unspotted.*

Stand, *v.* Rest, continue upright *or* erect, be situated *or* located; cease, stop, pause, halt; endure, last; maintain, be fixed *or* steady; be, consist; agree, accord; endure, sustain, bear; withstand; submit to.

ANT. *Advance, move, proceed, progress; fail, fall, die, depart, run, yield, succumb, drop; give up, surrender; retaliate, avenge, resent.*

Standard, *n.* Flag, colors, banner, ensign; criterion, test; support, frame; model, type, norm; gage, measure, scale; upright; exemplar.

ANT. *Misrule, mismeasurement, misadjustment, misfit, non-criterion.*

State, *v.* Declare, tell, assert, affirm, asseverate, allege, testify, assure, swear, set forth, protest, predicate, pronounce, specify, propound, maintain, inform, express, depose, claim, avow, avouch, aver, certify.

ANT. *Deny, contradict, controvert, disprove, refute, repudiate, waive, contravene, dispute, gainsay, oppose, retract.*

Station. Depot; place, spot, position, stand; office, sphere; state, rank, condition, occupation, business.

ANT. *Removal, departure; dislodgment, ejection, displacement; locomotion.*

Stay, *v.* Stop; prop, hold up, support, sustain; hold, restrain; hold back, hinder, delay; check; fasten, secure; continue, abide, remain; dwell, tarry, linger, wait; forbear; rest, depend, rely.

ANT. *Loose, liberate, free; fail, let fall; expedite, speed, accelerate; proceed, advance, progress, go on; move, depart; oppress, burden; overthrow.*

Steadfast. Established, firm; constant, resolute; grounded, rooted, placed; resolved, unwavering, stanch.

ANT. *Unsteady, unattached; vacillating, wavering, weak, insecure, irresolute, inconstant, unreliable.*

Steep. Sharp, sheer, high, precipitous, abrupt.

ANT. *Gradual, level, slight, flat, easy, gentle, horizontal, low.*

Stiff. Rigid, inflexible, strong, obstinate, pertinacious, rigorous, constrained, affected; unbending, unpliant; starched; formal, ceremonious, difficult, punctilious, stately; austere, peremptory, inexorable, uncompromising.

ANT. *Flexible, pliant, unaffected, amenable, easy, yielding, affable, genial, unceremonious, informal; pliable, malleable; considerate, compromising.*

Still. Noiseless; inert, stagnant, serene; motionless, restful, quiet; silent, calm, soundless, low; hushed, mute, placid, quiescent; stationary; gentle, soft, mild, pacific, peaceful.

ANT. *Disturbed, agitated, moved, restless; noisy, moving, loud, resonant, turbulent; unquiet, rough, harsh.*

Stop. Suppress, discontinue, delay, interrupt; close, obstruct; arrest, impede; restrain, hinder, repress; cease, halt, stay, tarry; bar, seal; suspend, end, terminate.

ANT. *Assist, advance, continue, expedite, speed, hasten, promote; clear, open; improve, push, benefit; progress; facilitate; initiate, commence, begin.*

Storm. Agitation, disturbance, tempest.

ANT. *Calm, hush, peace, serenity, stillness, tranquillity, fair weather.*

Story. Narrative, legend, anecdote, account, tale, record, recital, incident, myth, narration, novel, relation.

ANT. *Annals, chronicle, biography, history, memoir.*

Stout. Corpulent; portly; vigorous, strong, lusty, robust; firm, resolute, bold; tough; large, bulky; brawny; valiant, courageous, redoubtable.

ANT. *Thin, slender, weak, lean, frail, feeble, attenuated, emaciated; timid, irresolute, cowardly.*

Strange. Outlandish, wonderful, astonishing, marvelous, uncommon, irregular, queer, odd, eccentric; foreign, new, novel, unusual; reserved, distant; unfamiliar, unaccustomed, inexperienced.

ANT. *Familiar, usual, common, general, universal, accustomed, ordinary, home, domestic, regular, customary, habitual, commonplace.*

Strength. Robustness, toughness, hardness, stoutness, spirit, lustiness, puissance, authority; force, vigor, power; endurance, resistance; security, validity; firmness; intensity; virtue; energy, nerve, sinew, fiber; soundness.

ANT. *Weakness, thinness, frailty, softness, delicacy; imbecility, feebleness; spiritlessness, impotence, inability; insecurity, invalidity; wavering.*

Strenuous. Eager, pressing, urgent; zealous, ardent, earnest; bold, intrepid; strong, determined, resolute; vigorous, energetic, vehement, forceful.

ANT. *Weak, irresolute, vacillating, wavering, enervated, undetermined.*

Strong. Powerful, cogent, muscular; robust, lusty, sinewy, hale, hearty, vigorous, forceful; enduring, resistant; violent, forcible; ardent, zealous, vehement, earnest, solid, nourishing; firm; capable, potent, effective, influential, sound; pungent; hardy, tenacious.

ANT. *Weak, feeble, infirm,*

sickly, exhausted, debilitated, wanting, pliant, frail, soft; low, faint; spiritless, foolish; wavering, impotent, powerless, defenseless, insecure, delicate; unefficacious, unconvincing, unsatisfactory, unavailing, flaccid, nerveless.

Stubborn. Obstinate, inflexible, obdurate, headstrong, harsh, intractable, firm, contumacious, heady; unbending, unyielding, persistent, refractory.

ANT. *Yielding, pliant, mild, gentle, docile, tractable, manageable, flexible, pliable; vacillating, wavering, irresolute, undecided.*

Studious. Contemplative, observant; sedulous, earnest, diligent; studied; absorbed, meditative, thoughtful, attentive, pondering, devoted, musing, cogitative; careful, literary, reflective, assiduous.

ANT. *Illiterate, unliterary, idle, indulgent, careless, inattentive, thoughtless, negligent, regardless, indifferent.*

Study, *n.* Application, learning, acquisition, meditation, contemplation; diligence, consideration, thought, research, endeavor, knowledge, purpose, intention, attention, concentration.

ANT. *Idleness, dawdling, illiteracy, ease, indifference, indiligence, negligence, carelessness, unstudiousness, thoughtlessness.*

Stupid. Simple, insensible, sottish, sluggish, senseless, doltish, heavy, dull; stolid, insensate, obtuse, prosy.

ANT. *Quick, bright, sharp, intelligent, responsive, clever, sensible, eager, animated, penetrating.*

Stupidity. Slowness, dulness, obtuseness, insensibility, sluggishness, stupor, apathy.

ANT. *Intelligence, animation, brilliancy, acuteness, sensibility, cleverness, sense, sagacity, quickness, readiness, alertness, keenness.*

Stupor. Apathy, swoon, torpor, lethargy, coma, fainting, unconsciousness, stupefaction, asphyxia, swooning, insensibility, syncope.

Sublime. Exalted, lofty, noble, majestic, grand, stately, magnificent, dignified, elevated, august, pompous, high, eminent, glorious.

ANT. *Low, ignoble, debased, degraded, inglorious, ordinary, mean, undignified, inconspicuous, unimposing, ridiculous.*

Submissive. Obedient, compliant, yielding, obsequious, subservient, humble, modest, passive, docile, acquiescent.

ANT. *Disobedient, haughty, proud, arrogant, unyielding, conceited, active, rebellious, reluctant, defiant, refractory, resistant.*

Subsidy. Aid, allowance, gift, bounty, reward, tribute, support, subvention, pension, bonus, premium, grant, indemnity.

Substantial. Real, solid, true, existing, essential; corporeal, material; strong, stout, resourceful, massive, tangible, bulky; sensuous.

ANT. *Imaginary, unreal, insubstantial, fictitious, supposititious, immaterial, weak, chimerical, visionary, spiritual, disembodied, ghostly.*

Subtle. Artful, crafty, cunning, shrewd, sly, wily; astute, guileful, discriminating, insinuating, sophistical.

ANT. *Frank, honest, open,*

sincere, artless, undiscriminating, undiscerning, simple, direct, blunt, unsophisticated.

Subvert. Destroy, ruin, supplant, suppress, supersede, extinguish, overthrow, overturn.

ANT. *Conserve, preserve, uphold, sustain, keep, perpetuate.*

Succeed. Follow, pursue; ensue, result, be subsequent; descend, devolve; gain, acquire, attain, obtain, achieve, accomplish; supervene; flourish, prosper, thrive.

ANT. *Precede, anticipate, antecede; fail, deteriorate, be lacking, lose, miss, disappoint, be deficient in; decline, wane, decay.*

Succession. Succeeding, series, sequence, order; lineage, descent; following, continuity, consecution, rotation, regularity.

ANT. *Antecedence, precedence, anticipation, forerunning, prevention; disorder, irregularity, non-sequence, intermission, gap, failure, inconsecutiveness.*

Sudden. Unexpected, unusual, abrupt, unlooked for, hasty, unanticipated, unforeseen, unprovided for; rash, quick, heedless, reckless.

ANT. *Anticipated, foreseen, expected; slow, gradual, transitional, moderate; wary, cautious, careful, provident.*

Suffer. Support, sustain, tolerate, permit; allow, let, grant, consent to; endure, bear, submit to, undergo, be affected by, experience.

ANT. *Resist, rebel, repel, withstand; forbid, disallow, refuse, reject, expel, repudiate; fight, antagonize, challenge.*

Sufficient. Competent, satisfactory, full, ample; equal, adequate, enough; qualified, capable, responsible; efficient; adapted, fitted.

ANT. *Inadequte, incompetent, unsatisfactory, lacking, wanting, unequal, unfit, incapable, unqualified, insufficient, unsuited, meager, short, deficient, scanty.*

Suggestion. Hint, innuendo, intimation, insinuation, implication.

Suitable. Proper, competent, correspondent, consonant, compatible, congruous, consistent; fitting, accordant, becoming, adapted; seemly, appropriate, agreeable, convenient; harmonious, uniform; homogeneous.

ANT. *Improper, divergent, incompetent, incompatible, dissonant, incongruous, inconsistent, unfit, discordant, unbecoming; unseemly, inappropriate, inconvenient; unharmonious, different, heterogeneous.*

Sum. Aggregate, quantity, magnitude, amount; compendium, substance, gist; height, completion; total, whole, computation; example, problem; collection; drift, bearing.

ANT. *Part, portion, half, fraction, item, particular; incompleteness, imperfection, discrepancy; article, detail, fragment, component, constituent, element.*

Superb. Grand, magnificent, august, stately; rich, elegant; showy, excellent; princely, gorgeous, splendid; proud.

ANT. *Mean, shabby, poor, undignified, dingy; meager; tawdry, impoverished; ordinary, common; humble, plain, unimposing.*

Superior. Elevated, higher, upper; surpassing, greater; preeminent, excellent, ascendent, predominant, prevalent, advantageous, beneficial.

ANT. *Inferior, lower, worse, deeper, meaner, subordinate, lesser, mediocre, ordinary, average, common, unremarkable, inconspicuous, detrimental, disadvantageous; declining, deteriorating.*

Supernatural. Miraculous, preternatural, superhuman.

ANT. *Common, natural, ordinary, commonplace, everyday, usual.*

Supple. Pliant, flexible, bending; fawning, soft; yielding, compliant, submissive; flattering, obsequious, subservient, servile, cringing, adulatory; lithe, limber, elastic.

ANT. *Firm, stiff, unyielding, obstinate, inflexible, hard, dominant, domineering; abusive, scolding, tyrannous; unbending, stubborn, independent, self-assertive, supercilious, arrogant, haughty.*

Support. Maintain, sustain, uphold, cherish, keep, bear, prop, carry, tolerate, hold up, keep up.

ANT. *Demolish, abandon, betray, destroy, drop, desert, wreck, break down, cast down, overthrow, let go, throw down.*

Suppose. Deem, guess, imagine, think, conjecture, surmise.

ANT. *Conclude, ascertain, discover, prove, know, be sure.*

Suppress. Repress, subdue, restrain, overthrow, quell, overwhelm, conceal, stifle, smother, stop; overpower, extinguish, destroy.

ANT. *Excite, fan, increase, augment, strengthen, raise, aggravate; publish, promulgate, advertise, spread, disseminate; intensify.*

Sure. Unfailing, infallible, permanent, steady, stable, strong, indisputable, confident, positive, firm; certain, safe, secure, assured, believing, trusting, unquestioning; abiding, fast.

ANT. *Insecure, fallible, unsteady, inconstant, wavering, indeterminate, dubitable, uncertain, questionable, impermanent, doubtful, hesitating, distrustful, precarious, disputable, loose.*

Surrender. Abandon, give over, relinquish, resign, waive, yield, alienate, capitulate, cede, let go, sacrifice, give one's self up.

ANT. *Resist, withstand, oppose, thwart, baffle; die.*

Suspense. Uncertainty, expectation, apprehension, anxiety, indetermination, indecision; solicitude, intermission, protraction, abeyance, doubt; pause, stop.

ANT. *Decision, settlement, determination, finality, execution; achievement, termination, accomplishment, end; uninterruption, continuance, continuity, regularity, sequence.*

Sustenance. Subsistence, food, provision, maintenance, support; supplies, aliment, nutriment, nourishment; livelihood, living, nutrition, sustentation.

ANT. *Starvation, want, indigence, poverty, hunger, lack, thirst, inanition, exhaustion; non-subsistence, non-support.*

Sweet. Sugary, saccharine, dulcet, luscious; agreeable, pleasing, fragrant, soft, melodious; beautiful, mild, fair; fresh; amiable, winning; wholesome.

ANT. *Sour, bitter, sharp, acid; discordant, inharmonious, dissonant; disagreeable, displeasing; fetid, malodorous; plain, homely; stale, unwhole-*

some, spoiled; offensive, repulsive, unlovely.

Swift. Quick, fleet, speedy, expeditious, rapid, prompt; accelerated, nimble, alert, ready, headlong, eager, fast.

ANT. *Slow, tardy, delaying, late, unready, laggard, deliberate, sedate, reluctant, lingering, lazy, loitering, inactive, sluggish, inexpeditious.*

Symmetry. Proportion, grace, conformity, uniformity, similarity, regularity, shapeliness, harmony, agreement; comeliness.

ANT. *Disproportion, disharmony, incongruity, irregularity, disagreement, disparity, shapelessness; interdisparity.*

Sympathy. Pity, compassion, commiseration, tenderness, condolence; fellow-feeling; agreement, conformity, reciprocity; congeniality.

ANT. *Antipathy, harshness, antagonism, unkindness, coldness, mercilessness, pitilessness.*

Synonymous. Similar, correspondent, like, identical, interchangeable, alike, same, corresponding, synonymic, equivalent.

ANT. *Antonymic.*

System. Order, mode, method, regularity, rule, manner.

ANT. *Confusion, chaos, disorder, derangement, irregularity, disarrangement.*

T

Tacit. Silent, implied, granted, unexpressed, understood, implicit.

ANT. *Mentioned, expressed, explicit, declared.*

Taciturn. Mute, silent, speechless, reserved, close, dumb, uncommunicative, reticent.

ANT. *Communicative, free, garrulous, loquacious, talkative, unreserved.*

Take. Lay hold, seize, grasp, obtain; capture, fasten on; attack; gain, captivate, charm; choose, turn to; employ, use, demand, require; copy, delineate; assume, adopt; acquire; engage in, indulge in; carry, convey, conduct; remove, withdraw, deduct; acknowledge, accept, receive, admit; partake of, swallow; undertake, clear; tolerate, endure; consider, interpret, suppose; receive, submit to, bear.

ANT. *Drop, reject, abandon, surrender, miss, lose, repel, refuse, decline, repulse, spurn.*

Talent. Ability, gift, endowment, genius, faculty; capacity, cleverness, aptitude, forte.

ANT. *Inability, ineptitude, incompetence, imbecility, stupidity.*

Tangible. Perceptible, tactile, palpable; apprehensible, evident, manifest, clear; material, substantial, sensible, obvious.

ANT. *Impalpable, spiritual, intangible, incorporeal, immaterial, incomprehensible.*

Tart. Sharp, acid, sour; keen, severe; harsh, caustic, petulant, acrimonious.

ANT. *Gentle, mild, genial, kindly, polite; mellow, sweet.*

Taste, *n.* Savor, relish, flavor, sensibility, judgment; discernment, nicety, perception, zest, choice, elegancy, refinement.

ANT. *Disrelish, insipidity, ill-savor, coarseness, indelicacy, non-perception, indiscrimination.*

Tasteful. Delicate, artistic, elegant, dainty, esthetic, exquisite, fastidious, fine, chaste, nice, tasty, delicious, esthetical.

ANT. *Coarse, rough, rude, harsh, hideous, clumsy, disgusting, deformed, displeasing, fulsome, gaudy, grotesque, distasteful, horrid, inartistic, inharmonious, meretricious, offensive, ragged, tawdry.*

Taunt, *v.* Ridicule, mock, jeer, deride, revile, flout, scoff, scorn, insult; reproach, rebuke, censure.

ANT. *Compliment, flatter, approve of, congratulate.*

Teach. Discipline, instruct, tutor, school, train, educate, enlighten, drill, inculcate, give lessons, give instructions, indoctrinate, inform, initiate, instill, nurture.

ANT. *Learn, study, practice, investigate, experiment, try, develop, receive, drink in, acquire, attain, imbibe, understand, glean, gather, collect.*

Tedious. Wearisome, fatiguing, irksome, tiresome; prolix, dull, slow, monotonous, tiring, trying.

ANT. *Interesting, exciting, amusing, charming, delightful, stirring, bright, entertaining.*

Tell. Enumerate, communicate, impart, reveal, disclose, report, acquaint, repeat, rehearse, discover; count, number, reckon, recount; narrate, divulge; inform, teach; order, command, request.

Temerity. Audacity, foolhardiness, rashness, presumption, recklessness, hardihood, hastiness, heedlessness, precipitation, overconfidence, precipitancy, venturesomeness.

ANT. *Care, caution, hesitation, cowardice, timidity, wariness, circumspection.*

Temporal. Transient, fleeting, transitory, temporary; terrestrial, worldly, secular, mundane.

ANT. *Eternal, permanent, everlasting; religious, spiritual.*

Tendency. Proneness, drift, aim, disposition; direction, course; influence; inclination, leaning, bent, bias; proclivity, aptitude, propensity, liability.

ANT. *Aversion, repulsion, repugnance; opposition, reluctance, divergence, tangency, deviation.*

Tender. Effeminate, soft, sensitive, compassionate, humane, kind, merciful, pitiful, dear, delicate; gentle, mild, susceptible.

ANT. *Hard, pitiless, callous, careless, heedless, rough, coarse, unkind, inhuman, unmerciful, unfeeling; hardy, strong, sturdy.*

Tension. Strain, stretch, effort, stretching, tensity, tenseness, rigor, severity, harshness, stiffness, tightness.

ANT. *Relaxation, release, relief, laxity, slackness, looseness.*

Term. Boundary, limit; expression, phrase, word, name; member, condition, denomination.

Termination. Limit, end, conclusion, bound, result; completion, consequence, effect; fulfilment, consummation, accomplishment, achievement, finis, finality, exit, issue.

ANT. *Beginning, initiation, inception, commencement, rise, start, origin, source, cause, process, course.*

Terrible. Terrific, fearful, horrible, shocking, awful; dreadful, formidable, frightful; tremendous; astounding, startling.
ANT. *Insignificant, amusing, pleasing; unastonishing.*

Terse. Concise, pithy, succinct, short, brief, laconic, compact, sententious, condensed, compendious, neat.
ANT. *Long, lengthy, tedious, wordy, diffuse, prolix, verbose.*

Testimony. Affirmation, certification, deposition, proof, evidence, witness, affidavit, attestation, oath.
ANT. *Demonstration.*

Theory. Hypothesis, speculation; doctrine, conjecture, explanation; assumption, scheme, postulate, plan; science, philosophy; exposition, rationale; supposition.
ANT. *Fact, truth, verity, actuality.*

Therefore. Consequently, then, hence, thence, whence, wherefore, accordingly.
ANT. *Because, as for, inasmuch as, since.*

Thick. Dense, close, compact, solid, coarse, gross; muddy, turbid, misty; crowded, abundant; indistinct; dull; numerous; inarticulate.
ANT. *Thin, rare, sparse, infrequent; pure, limpid, crystalline, clear, distinct, incompact, shallow, articulate.*

Think. Cogitate, contemplate; remember, reflect, muse, meditate, ponder, consider, deliberate, judge, conclude, believe; purpose, intend, design, mean; presume, venture; imagine, apprehend.
ANT. *Guess, hazard; dream, idle, stargaze, wander, rove.*

Thought. Imagination, fancy, conceit, notion, consideration, supposition, contemplation, deliberation; reflection, cogitation, meditation, conception solicitude, care, concern; reasoning; idea, opinion, concept judgment, purpose, intention provision.
ANT. *Thoughtlessness, giddiness, carelessness, inconsideration, dreaminess, dulness, stupidity, rashness, impulsiveness, vacuity, dream, hallucination, aberration.*

Threat. Menace, denunciation, threatening, intimidation.
ANT. *Promise, encouragement, allurement, enticement, anticipation.*

Thrifty. Economical, saving careful; sparing, frugal, industrious, prosperous, thriving; provident, foresighted.
ANT. *Wasteful, prodigal, uneconomical, lavish, spendthrift, extravagant; slack, lazy; improvident, unprepared.*

Throng. Concourse, crowd, host, jam, mass, multitude, press.
ANT. *Solitude; wilderness, desert, waste.*

Tidings. Message, information, intelligence, news, rumor, report, advices, announcement.
ANT. *Suppression, censorship, misinformation, canard.*

Time. Epoch, era, period, date, age, eon, season, term, while, succession, sequence, duration.

Timid. Fearful, timorous, cowardly, afraid, pusillanimous, faint-hearted, shrinking, retiring, shy; diffident, bashful.
ANT. *Bold, confident, venturesome, courageous, adventurous, heedless.*

Tip. Incline, lean, list, slant, slope, tilt, cant, careen, dip, heel over.

Tire. Exhaust, fag, weary, fatigue, jade, harass, wear out.

ANT. *Refresh, recreate, rest, relax, relieve, repose, restore, invigorate.*

Title. Epithet, name, appellation, designation, cognomen, denomination; address, inscription, heading, style.

ANT. *Nondescript, namelessness.*

Together. With, in company, associated, conjoined, unitedly, simultaneously, contemporaneously, coincidently.

ANT. *Separately, variously, independently.*

Toil. Labor, drudgery, work, exertion, employment, occupation, task, travail.

ANT. *Rest, relaxation, recreation, ease; amusement, pleasure, enjoyment, fun.*

Tolerable. Endurable, bearable, supportable; passable, medium, ordinary, mediocre, indifferent.

ANT. *Intolerable, unendurable, insufferable, unbearable, insupportable.*

Tool. Appliance, implement, apparatus, mechanism, utensil, machine, weapon.

Topic. Head, division, motion, point, proposition, question, issue, subject, theme, matter.

Torment. Pain, misery, agony, anguish, torture, distress.

ANT. *Enjoyment, pleasure, comfort, ease, gratification, delight.*

Total, *a.* Whole, entire, full, absolute, complete, undivided.

ANT. *Partial, imperfect, incomplete, divided, fractional, sectional.*

Trace. Mark, remains, sign, vestige, track, token, trail, footmark, footprint, footstep, impression, memorial, remnant.

Trade. Profession, occupation, office, calling, avocation, employment, commerce, dealing, traffic.

ANT. *Stagnation, inactivity, dulness, embargo; leisure, vacation, idleness, vacancy.*

Tragedy. Mournful drama; catastrophe, calamity, adversity, disaster, affliction.

ANT. *Comedy, happiness, mirthful drama, prosperity, luck, good fortune.*

Traitor. Betrayer, turncoat, renegade, rebel, deceiver, apostate; insurgent, deserter, mutineer.

ANT. *Patriot, adherent, defender, supporter.*

Tranquil. Quiet, calm, undisturbed, peaceful, unagitated; unruffled, composed, poised, collected, cool.

ANT. *Agitated, excited, uneasy, anxious, troubled, restless.*

Transact. Conduct, carry on, perform, act, accomplish, do, negotiate, treat.

ANT. *Leave alone, rest, stop, refrain, desist, cease.*

Transaction. Business, action, deed, proceeding, doing, affair, act, negotiation, performance.

ANT. *Inactivity, quiescence, rest, neglect, inaction, passivity.*

Transgression. Infringement, misdemeanor, misdeed, affront; violation, breach, fault, crime, offense, sin.

ANT. *Innocence, guiltlessness; purity, righteousness; observance, obedience, fulfilment.*

Transient. Fleeting, temporary, transitory, ephemeral, evanescent, brief, flitting, flying, momentary, passing, fugitive, short.

ANT. *Permanent, perpetual, lasting, enduring, abiding, immortal, everlasting, unfading, undying, persistent, eternal, imperishable.*

Transparent. Translucent, pellucid, clear, lucid; diaphanous; open, porous; crystalline, limpid, bright; perspicuous.

ANT. *Opaque, thick, turbid; mysterious, questionable, dubious.*

Travel. Go, pass, journey, migrate, move, traverse, wander, roam.

ANT. *Dwell, reside, stay, remain, settle.*

Treasure. Wealth, abundance, plenty; money, jewels, cash, valuables, hoard, riches, bullion; reserve.

ANT. *Refuse, trash, offal; dregs, trifles.*

Treaty. Negotiation, compact, agreement, covenant, alliance, convention, contract.

ANT. *Neutrality, non-interference, non-intervention.*

Tremendous. Frightful, terrific, horrible, awful; fearful, appalling, alarming, horrifying, dreadful.

ANT. *Unappalling, inconsiderable, unimposing.*

Trial. Attempt, endeavor, essay; effort, exertion; experience, proof, test; examination, experiment; criterion, ordeal, assay; temptation, trouble, affliction, distress, grief, suffering, tribulation.

ANT. *Non-attempt; ease, facility; acceptance; oversight, disregard; trifle, triviality.*

Trick. Stratagem, wile, fraud, cheat, juggle, finesse, sleight; deception, imposture, delusion, imposition; artifice, machination, contrivance, legerdemain.

ANT. *Exposure, revelation, examination; blunder, botch, bungling, fumbling, maladroitness, mishap; genuineness, artlessness, openhandedness.*

Triumph. Success, conquest, victory; ovation, celebration, jubilee, jubilation, exultation; achievement, attainment.

ANT. *Defeat, failure, disappointment, discomfiture, abortion, baffling.*

Trouble. Affliction, sorrow, disturbance, perplexity, vexation, molestation, annoyance, inconvenience, calamity, misfortune, adversity, misery; tribulation, distress, disaster, torment, difficulty, anxiety.

ANT. *Blessing, peace, composure, alleviation, appeasement, pleasure, fortune, boon, affluence, happiness, joy, success, gladness, ease, facility, amusement, recreation.*

True. Correct, accurate, precise, exact; unwavering, faithful, loyal; actual, pure, real, genuine; veritable.

ANT. *Untrue, false, fictitious, unreliable, incorrect, inaccurate, inexact; vacillating, disloyal, faithless; counterfeit, impure, unreal, factitious, untrustworthy, adulterated, spurious, fickle, treacherous.*

Trust, *n.* Confidence, belief, expectation, faith, hope; reliance.

ANT. *Doubt, misgiving, distrust, skepticism, suspense; despair.*

Truth. Fact, reality, fidelity, conformity, exactness; steadfastness; veracity, verity; accuracy, precision, faithfulness.

ANT. *Falsehood, falsity, lie, untruth, fabrication, fiction; fallacy, mistake, sophism.*

Tumult. Ferment, disturbance, turbulence, disorder, bluster, hubbub, bustle, brawl, riot; excitement, distraction, confusion, turmoil, noise.

ANT. *Peace, order, orderliness, pacification, quiet, subsidence.*

Turn, *n.* Revolution; alteration, vicissitude; winding, bending, meandering; stroll; succession, alternation; chance, occasion; convenience, purpose, exigence; form, cast, shape, manner, fashion; rotation, recurrence; opportunity; deed, office, treatment, act; tendency, talent, gift; crisis.

ANT. *Fixity, unchangeableness, immobility, uniformity, stability, continuity; independence; malformation, shapelessness.*

Turn, *v.* Revolve, reverse, deflect, change; divert, transfer, use, employ, apply, devote; alter, metamorphose, transform, convert; shape, mold, adapt; whirl; hinge, depend; eventuate, issue, terminate.

ANT. *Stick, stop, remain; adhere, hold to; persist, continue; stabilitate, perpetuate, arrest, stereotype.*

Tutor. Teacher, instructor, professor, preceptor, master, savant, guardian, governor.

ANT. *Pupil, student, novice, disciple, scholar, ward, learner.*

Twist, *v.* Contort, writhe, convolve; pervert, distort; wind, wreathe; insinuate; encircle.

ANT. *Straighten, untwist, rectify, unwind, disentangle, unravel; verify, substantiate.*

Type. Mark, stamp, sign, emblem; style, semblance; representation, similitude, figure, symbol, token; character, pattern, archetype, model, norm; cast, mold, fashion.

ANT. *Caricature, monstrosity, abnormity; falsification, deviation; misrepresentation.*

U

Ubiquity. Omnipresence; universal presence, all-pervasiveness.

ANT. *Localization, limitation.*

Ugly. Loathsome, unsightly, repulsive; ill-natured, quarrelsome; unpleasant; plain, ordinary, homely, hideous, frightful; cross, vicious.

ANT. *Attractive, handsome, fair, pleasant, agreeable, beautiful, shapely, comely; lovely, kindly, good-natured, gentle.*

Ultimate. Final, last, conclusive, farthest, extreme, most remote; elemental.

ANT. *Initial, nearest, beginning, primary.*

Un-. A prefix meaning *not* or *without,* or simply intensive, which is prefixed to nouns, adjectives, adverbs, and the participles of verbs. Words whose meaning is simply that of the root word with negative or intensive emphasis are omitted here, and their synonyms and antonyms may be formed from those of the root word.

Unction. Anointing, ointment; power, fervor, animation, fervency, ardor, enthusiasm, energy, spirit, emotion.

ANT. *Tameness, perfunctoriness, coldness, lifelessness.*

Unctuous. Fatty, oily, greasy; bland, suave, tender, fervid; obsequious, fawning, servile, sycophantic.

ANT. *Blunt, brusk, abrupt; cynical, sarcastic; harsh, unmannerly, uncomplimentary.*

Under-. A prefix meaning *beneath* or *below.* Words whose meaning is simply that of the root word with the meaning of the prefix added are omitted in this place, and their synonyms and antonyms may be formed in many cases from those of the root word.

Under, *prep.* Below, beneath, underneath.

ANT. *Above, upon, over.*

Understand. Know, comprehend; learn, be informed, hear; recognize, interpret; imply, assume; apprehend, discern, see, perceive, conceive, penetrate.

ANT. *Misunderstand, miscomprehend, misinterpret; declare, state; express, inform.*

Understanding. Sense, intelligence, conception, perception, discernment, knowledge, intuition, cognition, reason; interpretation; mind, brains.

ANT. *Insensibility, stupidity, dulness, obtuseness, senselessness, slowness, irrationality, sluggishness, ignorance, unintelligence.*

Undertake. Engage, enter, set about, attempt; covenant, contract; guarantee, promise, affirm; project, commence; stipulate.

ANT. *Abandon, drop, desist, discontinue, decline; complete, finish, end, terminate.*

Undertaking. Enterprise, engagement, attempt, adventure, business, effort, endeavor; experiment, venture, interest, affair, matter, concern.

ANT. *Leisure, inactivity; recreation.*

Undulation. Waving motion; vibration; wavy outline; pulsation; oscillation, swelling; wave, ripple.

ANT. *Equilibrium; arrestation, standing; plain, tableland.*

Uniform. Unchanging, equable, consistent, homogeneous; consonant; regular, constant, invariable, steady; similar, unvaried, alike.

ANT. *Heterogeneous, variable, varying, diverse; irregular, inconsistent, erratic, eccentric, unsymmetrical.*

Union. Unity, connection, concord, combination, confederacy, alliance; coalition, conjunction; harmony, concert, agreement; league, confederation, consolidation; oneness, juncture, unification.

ANT. *Disconnection, separation, disjunction, disunion, divorce, severance, analysis, dissociation, contrariety, decomposition, division, schism, partition, discord, disagreement, secession, disruption; multiplication, diversification.*

Unique. Sole, only, unmatched, unequalled, unparalleled, singular, peculiar, exceptional, rare.

ANT. *Common, universal, everyday, commonplace, ordinary, familiar, vulgar, mean.*

Unison. Harmony, agreement, concord, union, accordance.

ANT. *Discord, variance, disagreement, divergence.*

Unit. Oneness, unity; one; integral; item, individual.

ANT. *Sum, mass, total, aggregate, whole, collection.*

Unite. Add, join, attach, annex; combine, connect; agree, harmonize, associate, coalesce; incorporate, consolidate, amalgamate, blend, embody, merge;

concur, coöperate, league, confederate.

ANT. *Disjoin, sever, separate, divide, resolve, disconnect; disintegrate, dissociate, sunder, diverge; multiply, split, disrupt.*

Unity. Oneness, concord, conjunction, agreement, junction, uniformity, harmony, union; singleness, unanimity.

ANT. *Separation, disunion, disconnection, division, disagreement, divorce.*

Universal. General, unlimited, all-reaching; total, whole, entire; catholic, common; comprehensive, exhaustive, complete.

ANT. *Specific, special, individual, particular, limited, local, partial, exclusive, exceptional.*

Up-. A prefix giving the idea of elevation or an intensive value. Words whose meaning is derived quite simply from that of the root plus that of the prefix are omitted here. Their synonyms and antonyms may be readily formed from those of the root word.

Upbraid. Reproach, censure, blame, condemn; taunt, chide, reprove.

ANT. *Approve, commend, praise, eulogize, compliment, applaud.*

Upon. On; about, concerning; with, immediately after, forthwith.

ANT. *Under, beneath, below; before, after, without.*

Upper. Higher, superior, on top.

ANT. *Lower, inferior, below, beneath.*

Upright. Erect, perpendicular, vertical; honest, just, honorable, conscientious, virtuous, good, faithful, true, trustworthy.

ANT. *Inclined, slanted; inverted; unprincipled, dishonest, unscrupulous, corrupt, unconscientious.*

Uproar. Tumult, disturbance, confusion, bustle, clamor, commotion, turmoil, racket, noise, din.

ANT. *Peace, calm, quiet, silence, order, tranquillity.*

Urbane. Courteous, polite, refined, suave, elegant; civil, polished.

ANT. *Discourteous, uncivil, unrefined, impolite, rude, boorish.*

Urge. Animate, instigate, stimulate, encourage, arouse; impel, press, drive; beseech, entreat, importune; goad, spur, incite; hasten, accelerate, expedite.

ANT. *Hold back, hinder, obstruct, prevent, retard, inhibit, restrain; defy, challenge, dare; oppose, object.*

Urgent. Urging, pressing, importunate, immediate, important, imperative, grave, momentous, serious, cogent, solicitous, critical, emergency, necessitous.

ANT. *Trivial, insignificant, unimportant, immaterial, inconsiderable.*

Usage. Custom, wont, habit, use; mode, method, manners, behavior; practice, procedure; fashion.

Use. Employment, application, occasion, necessity, usefulness, utility; practice, usage, custom, manner, habit; service, advantage; profit, avail, need; benefit.

ANT. *Uselessness, misapplication, superfluousness, worthlessness, disuse, non-observance, desuetude.*

Useful. Advantageous, profitable, serviceable, beneficial; fruitful, effectual, suitable, effective, adapted, helpful, good, convenient, valuable, available.

ANT. *Useless, profitless, unprofitable, valueless, unserviceable, fruitless, inconducive, ineffectual, unavailing, retarding, hindering, preventive, obstructive, cumbersome, burdensome, unusable.*

Usual. Familiar, frequent, ordinary, regular, wonted, prevalent, accustomed, common, customary, everyday, general, normal, habitual, prevailing, public.

ANT. *Exceptional, infrequent, extraordinary, strange, uncommon, unparalleled, unusual, out-of-the-way, singular, rare.*

Usurp. Arrogate, assume, appropriate, seize.

ANT. *Inherit, accept, receive.*

Utility. Profit, expediency, use, usefulness, avail, benefit, advantage, service, usableness.

ANT. *Futility, inutility, inadequacy, inexpediency, uselessness, folly, impolicy, disadvantage, worthlessness, unprofitableness.*

Utmost. Farthest, extreme, remotest, last, most distant; uttermost; greatest.

ANT. *Nearest, next; least.*

Utter, *v.* Issue, deliver, liberate, discharge; circulate, pass; express, publish, disclose, speak, pronounce; promulgate.

ANT. *Suppress, recall, check, stifle, hush, repress; retract, disavow.*

Utter, *a.* Complete, perfect, total, entire, absolute; peremptory, unconditional, unqualified; thorough.

ANT. *Imperfect, incomplete; conditioned, qualified; partial.*

Utterly. Fully, totally, thoroughly.

ANT. *Partially, imperfectly, specifically.*

V

Vacancy. Emptiness; leisure, intermission, idleness; vacuum; chasm, gap; interval; vacuity, space, void.

ANT. *Fulness, plethora, repletion; business, occupation, employment.*

Vacant. Blank, empty, void, unoccupied, waste, unemployed, untenanted, vacuous, unfilled, devoid, unencumbered, disengaged, idle, uncrowded; inane, silly; free; thoughtless, unreflective; abandoned; inane; leisure; unmeaning.

ANT. *Full, filled, occupied, replenished, diligent, busy, engaged, employed; reflective, thoughtful, meaningful; brimful, busy, crammed, inhabited, packed, replete, brimmed, overflowing, brimming, jammed, gorged, crowded.*

Vacate. Empty, make vacant, quit, resign, surrender; annul, abrogate, cancel, invalidate, abscind, abolish, overrule, neutralize.

ANT. *Fill, occupy, employ, hold, retain, substantiate.*

Vacation. Interval, intermission, holidays, rest, leisure.

ANT. *Worktime, term, business.*

Vacillate. Fluctuate, waver, be unsteady, stagger, reel, sway, rock, hesitate, be inconstant, dubitate.

ANT. *Adhere, abide, determine, be steadfast, stay.*

Vacillation. Wavering, fluctuating, swaying, reeling, rocking, fluctuation, hesitation, inconstancy, unsteadiness.

ANT. *Steadiness, firmness, inflexibility, determination.*

Vacuity. Emptiness, vacancy, void, vacuum; inanity, nihility, inanition, unreality; space.

ANT. *Fulness, bulk, matter, substance; occupation, actuality, reality; contents.*

Vagabond. Wanderer, vagrant, tramp, rascal; outcast, loafer, nomad, idler, beggar, rogue.

ANT. *Worker, laborer.*

Vagary. Whim, freak, crotchet, whimsicality, caprice, fancy.

ANT. *Purpose, idea, determination, judgment, seriousness, conviction.*

Vagrant, *a.* Wandering, erratic, unsettled, strolling, itinerant, roving, sauntering, nomadic.

ANT. *Domestic, local, established, resident, abiding, dwelling.*

Vague. Unsettled, undetermined, indefinite, ambiguous, lax, uncertain, dim, doubtful, obscure, indistinct, unfixed, general, intangible, equivocal, pointless; unwarranted, unauthorized.

ANT. *Determined, limited, strict, specific, pointed, definite, distinct, scientific, settled, clear, fixed, manifest, perspicuous.*

Vain. Futile, trivial, vapid, visionary, worthless, abortive, unsatisfying, fruitless, empty, deceitful, baseless, delusive, bootless, idle, ineffectual, shadowy, trifling, unserviceable, unsubstantial, profitless, inconstant, unprofitable, null, nugatory, unavailing, unimportant, unreal; showy, useless; conceited, arrogant, ostentatious.

ANT. *Adequate, solid, useful, effective, powerful, worthy, important, sufficient, serviceable, potent, competent, advantageous, beneficial, efficient, expedient, profitable, real, sound, substantial, valid, valuable, essential, cogent, availing, satisfactory, modest.*

Valediction. Farewell, valedictory, leave-taking, adieu.

ANT. *Salutation, welcome, hail, reception, recognition.*

Valiant. Strong, powerful, intrepid, courageous, brave, valorous, heroic, gallant, chivalrous, daring, dauntless, bold, fearless, redoubtable, undaunted, stout-hearted.

ANT. *Timid, cowardly, fearful, timorous, recreant, craven.*

Valid. Sound, good, justified, trustworthy, well-grounded, efficacious, weighty, powerful, efficient, conclusive, logical, solid, cogent, important, grave, substantial, sufficient.

ANT. *Weak, invalid, null, void, unsound, baseless, fallacious, unfounded, untrue; unavailable, inoperative, superseded.*

Validity. Soundness, justness, efficacy, force, weight, cogency, importance.

ANT. *Weakness, impotency, ineffectiveness, lightness, futility.*

Valor. Bravery, courage, prowess, intrepidity, heroism, boldness, daring.

ANT. *Timidity, fearfulness, cowardice, pusillanimity.*

Valuable. Worthy, estimable, costly, precious, expensive, useful, dear, serviceable.

ANT. *Worthless, valueless, cheap, inexpensive, silly, useless, trifling, trivial.*

Value, *n.* Worth, utility, desirability, importance, power; import, signification; esteem, regard, excellence; price, cost, equivalent.

ANT. *Cheapness, reduction, depreciation.*

Value, *v.* Compute, esteem, respect, regard; be worth, rate, appraise, estimate; appreciate, prize, treasure, account.

ANT. *Cheapen, reduce, contemn, despise, undervalue, underestimate; disregard, disesteem, misprize.*

Vanish. Disappear, fade, pass away, dissolve, melt away, be annihilated.

ANT. *Appear, approach, be manifest, loom up, arrive.*

Vanity. Pride, conceit; unreality, worthlessness, emptiness; hollowness, triviality, futility, unsubstantiality, falsity; egoism, self-sufficiency; show, ostentation.

ANT. *Reality, truth, worth; simplicity; modesty, humility, self-distrust; substance, solidity.*

Vanquish. Conquer, overcome, subdue, defeat, surmount, confute, silence; subjugate, overthrow, master, foil, discomfit, quell; disprove, confound.

ANT. *Succumb, yield, fail.*

Vapid. Dead, spiritless, flat, insipid, dull, unanimated; tasteless, stale, tame; languid, prosaic, feeble, prosy.

ANT. *Pungent, spirited, animated, pithy, trenchant.*

Vapor, *n.* Fume, steam, reek, exhalation, smoke, fog, mist; vagary, phantom, whim, dream, vision; flatulence; fantasy.

ANT. *Inhalation, absorption.*

Variable. Changeable, fickle, inconstant, mutable, shifting, unsteady, vacillating, wavering, fluctuating, versatile, capricious.

ANT. *Unchanging, immutable, constant, firm, unwavering, steady, invariable, unalterable.*

Variance. Variation, dissension, disagreement, discord, difference, alteration, strife; hostility, antagonism, discrepancy, estrangement.

ANT. *Harmony, agreement, assimilation, reconciliation, accommodation, peace.*

Variation. Modification, alteration, mutation, change, diversity, vicissitude, variety, deviation; departure, difference, discrepancy.

ANT. *Fixity, harmony, continuance, uniformity, rule, law, agreement.*

Variegated. Streaked, dappled, particolored, diversified, varied, checkered, figured, mottled.

ANT. *Unspotted, spotless, speckless.*

Variety. Diversity, difference, assortment, species, class, multifariousness, medley, miscellany, multiplicity, kind.

ANT. *Type, species, specimen, uniformity.*

Various. Different, diverse, several, manifold, changeable, uncertain, inconstant, variable, variegated, sundry, diversified.

ANT. *Identical, few, same, uniform, similar, single.*

Varnish, *v.* Gloss, palliate, conceal, cover, embellish, disguise, lacquer, extenuate, excuse, mitigate, glaze over.

ANT. *Simplify, divest; reveal, bare, manifest.*

Vary. Alter, change, modify, alternate, diversify, variegate,

differ, deviate, depart, be diverse, swerve, disagree, transform, metamorphose.
ANT. *Stereotype, perpetuate; conform, assimilate, harmonize.*

Vast. Spacious, huge, immense, great, mighty, transcendent, measureless, boundless, colossal, enormous, stupendous, prodigious, gigantic, monstrous, remarkable, extraordinary.
ANT. *Moderate, limited, confined, circumscribed, narrow, close, small.*

Vaticination. Prediction, divination, prophecy, prognostication, augury.
ANT. *Fulfilment, ratification, realization, verification, accomplishment.*

Vault. Jump, spring, bound, leap; tumble, turn.
ANT. *Crawl, creep, grovel.*

Vaunt. Boast, brag, display, show off; advertise, flourish, parade.
ANT. *Conceal, disparage, decry, detract, repress, suppress.*

Veer. Shift, turn, change, trim, vacillate.
ANT. *Stand, stick, adhere, persist, remain.*

Vegetate. Sprout, grow, germinate; bask, idle, hibernate.
ANT. *Decay, fade, wither, pine; bustle, energize, work, stir.*

Vehemence. Impetuosity, violence, fury, frenzy, ardor, fervor, fervency, warmth, zeal, enthusiasm, passion, force, intensity.
ANT. *Passivity, inertia, quiescence, coldness, stoicism, indifference, unconcern, apathy, inattention.*

Vehement. Raging, hot, ardent, fervid, burning, passionate, eager, violent, impetuous, furious, urgent, mighty, forcible, powerful, sanguine, enthusiastic.
ANT. *Cool, impassive, indifferent, feeble, mild, controlled, subdued, cold, stoical, passionless, weak, inanimate.*

Veil, *v.* Cover, invest, hide, conceal, screen, mask, shroud, envelop.
ANT. *Expose, disclose, strip, denude, unveil, make manifest.*

Velocity. Celerity, fleetness, rapidity, speed, swiftness; impetus, momentum.
ANT. *Inertia, sluggishness, inertness; resistance; passivity, languor, inactivity.*

Venal. Mercenary, hireling, sordid, purchasable, salable, prostitute.
ANT. *Honest, honorable, incorruptible, public-spirited, patriotic, unpurchasable, generous, disinterested.*

Vend. Barter, trade, sell, hawk, retail.
ANT. *Buy, purchase, bribe, subsidize.*

Venerable. Worthy, honorable, estimable; dread, awful; sage, wise, grave.
ANT. *Despicable, dishonored; informal, free, intimate, easy; foolish, silly.*

Venerate. Honor, respect, revere, reverence, adore, admire, worship.
ANT. *Dishonor, disregard, scorn, scoff at, slight, spurn, detest, disdain, despise, contemn, abhor, execrate.*

Veneration. Reverence, adoration, respect, awe, worship, esteem, dread.
ANT. *Irreverence, loathing, disrespect, contempt, disdain, dishonor, scorn.*

Vengeance. Punishment, retribution, revenge, retaliation.

ANT. *Forgiveness, pardon, reprieve, indulgence, amnesty, remission, absolution.*

Venial. Excusable, justifiable, pardonable, slight, trivial.

ANT. *Inexcusable, heinous, unpardonable, flagrant, mortal, infamous, unjustifiable, inexpiable.*

Venom. Virus, bane, poison; spite, malice, malignity, hate, ill will, maliciousness, rancor, grudge, bitterness, acrimony.

ANT. *Medicine, remedy; benevolence, kindness, good will.*

Venomous. Poisonous, malignant, noxious, mischievous, virulent, spiteful.

ANT. *Wholesome, remedial, salubrious; kindly, compassionate, genial.*

Vent. Outlet, escape, emission, utterance, discharge, opening, hole, passage; market, sale.

ANT. *Close, stop-gap, end, termination, obstruction, stoppage.*

Venture, *n.* Chance, risk, hazard, speculation; accident, contingency; stake, adventure, experiment; luck, hap; danger, jeopardy.

ANT. *Certainty, surety, security, inevitableness, assurance; safety, protection; law, method; caution, calculation.*

Venture, *v.* Dare, hazard, adventure, risk, jeopardize, imperil, chance.

ANT. *Calculate, warrant, secure, guarantee, protect.*

Venturesome. Bold, daring, adventurous, hardy, courageous, intrepid, enterprising, doughty, fearless.

ANT. *Fearsome, timid, reluctant, averse, loath, unwilling.*

Venturous. Bold, daring, fearless, venturesome.

ANT. *Timid, fearful, diffident, shy.*

Veracious. True, truthful, reliable, trustworthy, straightforward, honest, credible.

ANT. *False, deceitful, mendacious, lying, dishonest, perfidious.*

Veracity. Honesty, truthfulness, reality, candor, truth, ingenuousness, frankness, verity, exactness, correctness, accuracy.

ANT. *Deception, duplicity, falsehood, fiction, guile, mendacity, untruth, lie, delusion, fabrication, deceit, error, falseness, falsity, imposture.*

Verbal. Spoken, oral, literal, parole, vocal, unwritten, unrecorded.

ANT. *Written, recorded, epistolary, documentary.*

Verbose. Wordy, prolix, diffuse, prosy, tedious.

ANT. *Laconic, terse, concise, succinct, curt.*

Verdict. Decision, judgment, opinion, pronouncement, finding, sentence.

ANT. *Indecision, indetermination.*

Verge, *n.* Border, limit, boundary, edge, margin, brink; circumference, circle, ring; rim, brim, confine, skirt.

ANT. *Center, midst, heart, depth.*

Verge, *v.* Tend, incline, slope, lean, trend, bear, border, approach, approximate.

ANT. *Deviate, recede, revert, return, depart, retrocede.*

Verify. Prove, correct, establish, confirm, authenticate, affirm; corroborate, attest, substantiate; fulfil, demonstrate, warrant.

ANT. *Falsify, misrepresent, subvert, misstate, fail, disestablish, mistake.*

Verisimilitude. Likelihood, probability, consistency.
ANT. *Improbability, inconsistency, unlikelihood.*

Veritable. Actual, real, genuine, true; positive, absolute; original, authentic.
ANT. *False, fictitious, sham, spurious, untrue, feigned, supposititious.*

Verity. Fact, truth, reality, actuality, existence, truthfulness.
ANT. *Falsity, unreality, delusion, fancy, dream, conjecture, hypothesis.*

Vernal. Spring, balmy, genial, youthful.
ANT. *Wintry, aged, autumnal, decadent, brumal, harsh, cutting.*

Versatile. Changeable, inconsistent, variable, many-sided, capricious, erratic, fickle, unstable; mobile, plastic, ready.
ANT. *Fixed, uniform, one-sided, immobile, immutable, unvaried.*

Versed. Experienced, studied, practiced, skilled, acquainted, conversant, proficient, familiar, clever, indoctrinated.
ANT. *Unskilled, ignorant, unpracticed, untaught, uninitiated.*

Version. Account, description, translation, rendering, interpretation, reading; statement.
ANT. *Text, problem, difficulty; misinterpretation.*

Vertical. Perpendicular, plumb, upright.
ANT. *Inclined, slanting, sloping.*

Vestige. Trace, mark, footstep, track, sign, remains, trail, token, remnant, record.
ANT. *Misindication; obliteration, effacement.*

Veteran. Old soldier; expert, adept, proficient; habitué.
ANT. *Novice, recruit, tyro.*

Veto. Prohibit, forbid, negative, withhold assent to.
ANT. *Pass, approve, assent to, promulgate, endorse.*

Vex. Agitate, disquiet, harass, afflict, tease, weary, jade; torment, worry, hector, distress, annoy, trouble, perplex, bother, persecute, fret, irritate, offend, provoke, affront, disturb, tantalize.
ANT. *Please, soothe, quiet, allay, appease.*

Vexation. Chagrin, agitation, mortification, uneasiness, grief, trouble, sorrow, distress, irritation, displeasure, affliction, plague, torment.
ANT. *Pleasure, enjoyment, gratification, satisfaction.*

Vibrate. Swing, oscillate, fluctuate, quiver, waver, undulate, quake.
ANT. *Rest, be still.*

Vice. Crime, sin, fault, iniquity; defect, error, blemish, imperfection, immorality, depravity, wickedness; evil, corruption.
ANT. *Virtue, goodness, perfection, righteousness, nobility, honor.*

Vicinity. Neighborhood, vicinage, nearness, proximity, propinquity.
ANT. *Distance, remoteness, separation, removal.*

Vicious. Faulty, wicked, corrupt, depraved; foul, noxious, defective, unruly, refractory, spiteful, malignant, mischievous, immoral.
ANT. *Virtuous, pure, good, upright, noble, moral, perfect.*

Vicissitude. Change, alternation, mutation, interchange, variation, revolution.
ANT. *Fixity, changelessness, stability, perpetuity, immutability.*

Victorious. Conquering, triumphant, winning, successful, exultant, elated, boastful, vanquishing, subduing, prevailing, overcoming, mastering, subjugating.

ANT. *Defeated, worsted, humiliated, beaten, baffled, discomfited, conquered, overcome, vanquished, routed, repulsed, foiled, disconcerted.*

Victory. Success, supremacy, triumph, achievement, advantage, conquest, mastery.

ANT. *Defeat, disaster, destruction, overthrow, miscarriage, retreat, rout, failure, disappointment, frustration.*

Victuals. Food, provisions, viands, sustenance, meat.

View, *n.* Sight, look, survey, inspection; perception, examination; reach, range; scene, prospect; sketch; conception, judgment, opinion; object, aim, purpose, design; vista, perspective; picture, intention, scope, drift; estimate; apprehension.

ANT. *Blindness, darkness, obscuration, mistiness; prejudice, misconception, misrepresentation, deception, error, delusion, aimlessness, non-intention, occultation.*

View, *v.* See, behold, look at, survey, examine, inspect, explore, consider, contemplate, regard, scan, witness, study, reflect upon, reconnoiter.

ANT. *Overlook, neglect, pass by, miss, slight, ignore; misestimate, misjudge.*

Vigilance. Sleeplessness, wakefulness, watchfulness, circumspection, attentiveness, wariness, cautiousness, caution, activity, lookout, alertness, observation.

ANT. *Torpor, dulness, inattention, somnolence, carelessness, drowsiness, indifference, apathy.*

Vigilant. Alert, awake, careful, on the alert, on the lookout, wary, watchful, wakeful, wide-awake, sleepless, cautious, circumspect.

ANT. *Negligent, thoughtless, unwary, oblivious, drowsy, inattentive, careless, dull, heedless, inconsiderate, neglectful, incautious.*

Vigorous. Full of vigor, strong, lusty, robust; forcible, energetic, powerful, sturdy, hearty, thrifty, flourishing, spirited, lively.

ANT. *Weak, impotent, incapacitated, feeble, inactive, debilitated, powerless, effete, enervated, indolent.*

Vile. Low, base, worthless, despicable, mean, depraved, impure, sinful, wicked, bad, dishonorable, ignoble, degraded, sordid, infamous, low-minded.

ANT. *Noble, exalted, honorable, upright, estimable, great, worthy, eminent, liberal, free, generous, superior, dignified, sublime, stately.*

Villain. Scoundrel, knave, rascal, scamp, ruffian, rogue; malefactor.

ANT. *Gentleman, man of refinement, polish, delicacy,* and *honor.*

Villainous. Base, vile, mean, depraved; sorry, mischievous, infamous, knavish; heinous, sinful, outrageous, atrocious.

ANT. *Gentlemanly, noble, refined, honorable, worthy, upright.*

Vindicate. Maintain, defend, justify; assert, protest, pronounce, declare, asseverate; uphold, claim, substantiate, support, advocate.

ANT. *Surrender, yield, give*

up, resign; abandon, forego, waive; destroy, annul, vitiate; accuse, charge, impute, tax, slur.

Vindictive. Revengeful, unforgiving, implacable, spiteful, unrelenting, malicious.

ANT. *Forgiving, generous, merciful, long-suffering, magnanimous.*

Violate. Injure, disturb, interrupt, transgress, desecrate, debauch, dishonor, outrage, profane, abuse, infringe, ravish.

ANT. *Respect, protect, reverence, honor, value, prize, foster, shelter.*

Violence. Vehemence, impetuosity, fierceness, force, violation, infraction, infringement, transgression, profanation, assault, outrage.

ANT. *Preservation, defense, protection; mildness, self-control, gentleness, respect, obedience, conservation.*

Violent. Fierce, vehement, outrageous, boisterous, turbulent, impetuous, passionate, severe, extreme.

ANT. *Sane, sober, calm, collected, unruffled, composed, cool.*

Virgin, *n.* Maid, maiden, girl, damsel.

ANT. *Wife, mother, married woman; prostitute, whore.*

Virgin, *a.* Chaste, maidenly, modest; pure, undefiled, fresh, new.

ANT. *Married, matronly, motherly; defiled, polluted.*

Virile. Mature, masculine; masterful, forceful; robust, vigorous.

ANT. *Feminine; feeble, effeminate, puerile, emasculate.*

Virtual. Potential, efficacious, energizing, implicit, indirect, practical, essential, equivalent.

ANT. *Stated, direct, definite, expressed, explicit, emphatic, categorical.*

Virtue. Energy, strength, potency, efficacy; value, merit, excellence; worth, meritoriousness; integrity, purity, virginity, chastity; goodness, morality, uprightness, rectitude, probity, righteousness; force, power, capacity; honor, worthiness, honesty, truth, duty, virtuousness, faithfulness, justice.

ANT. *Inability, weakness, impotency, inefficacy; badness, corruption, impurity, unchastity, depravity, wickedness, laxity, dishonesty.*

Virtuous. Excellent, upright, righteous, pure, chaste; good, honest, exemplary, blameless, worthy, modest.

ANT. *Wicked, bad, wrong, unrighteous, impure, dishonest, worthless, immodest, blameworthy.*

Virulence. Malignancy, virus, contagion, poison, venom; bitterness, malevolence, acrimony.

ANT. *Mildness, blandness, salubriousness, abatement, assuagement; potency; benevolence, virtue.*

Visible. Perceptible, noticeable, apparent, open, conspicuous, obvious, manifest, evident, clear, plain, observable, palpable, discernible.

ANT. *Invisible, unseen, imperceptible, concealed, eclipsed, indistinguishable, impalpable, microscopic, indiscernible.*

Vision. Sight; apparition, creation, phantom, fancy, specter, appearance, chimera, illusion, phantasm.

ANT. *Material, substance; reality, fact, actuality.*

Visionary. Fanciful, fantastic, unreal, imaginary, ideal, chimerical, fantastical, wild, whimsical, capricious, illusory, romantic, shadowy, dreamy, unsubstantial, fabulous.

ANT. *Actual, real, true, substantial, genuine, palpable, authentic, veritable.*

Vital. Living; mortal; important, necessary, essential; animate; indispensable, material, paramount.

ANT. *Mortal, lifeless, inanimate, secondary, separable, unessential, unimportant, immaterial.*

Vitiate. Impair, contaminate, annul, spoil, void, destroy, injure; cause to deteriorate, taint; invalidate.

ANT. *Adhere to, corroborate, support, confirm, substantiate, justify, sanction, vindicate; refresh, improve, remedy.*

Vivacious. Animated, sportive, gay, jocund, light-hearted; merry, sprightly; brisk, frolicsome, spirited, cheerful, mirthful.

ANT. *Inanimate, dead, lifeless, spiritless, heavy, somber, melancholy, mournful, sad, inert, dull, stolid.*

Vivid. Clear, lucid, striking, active, lively, quick; fresh, intense, animated, bright, strong, spirited, sprightly; brilliant, lustrous, radiant, glowing, scintillant, sunny.

ANT. *Dull, opaque, lurid, obscure, rayless, somber, cloudy, dark, colorless, dim, pale, wan, dusky, non-luminous.*

Vocation. Call, summons, citation; business, profession, employment, calling, occupation, trade; function, mission, office.

ANT. *Leisure, non-employment; avocation, hobby.*

Vogue. Mode, custom, way, use, fashion, practice, usage.

ANT. *Disfavor, desuetude, disuse, unfashionableness, abolition.*

Voice, *n.* Sound, utterance, tone; language, words, speech, judgment, expression, vote; command, precept; opinion.

ANT. *Dumbness, silence, inexpression, muteness, inarticulation, obtumescence.*

Void, *a.* Empty, vacant, devoid, wanting, ineffectual, destitute, lacking; unoccupied, unused, unfilled; null, invalid, nugatory; vain, unreal, imaginary, unsubstantial.

ANT. *Occupied, solid, substantial, possessed, endued; effectual, valid, operative, good, efficacious, furnished.*

Volatile. Light-hearted, airy; changeable, fickle; lively, evaporating, vaporable, vivacious, buoyant, jocund; inconstant, flighty, whimsical, capricious, unsteady, reckless.

ANT. *Fixed, steady, established, determined, solid, settled; persistent, resolute; involatile; somber, demure.*

Volition. Will, choice, preference, determination, purpose; discretion, free will, election, deliberation.

ANT. *Necessity, force, predestination, fate, coercion, foreordination.*

Voluble. Rotating; nimble, glib, active; fluent, loquacious, talkative, rapid, running, coursing.

ANT. *Direct; slow, deliberate, hesitating, stuttering, torpid, stammering, creeping, lazy.*

Volume. Book, tome; convolution, coil; dimension, mass, capacity, bulk, size.

ANT. *Minuteness, smallness.*

Voluntary. Spontaneous, willing, uncompelled; free, impulsive; unconstrained, deliberate, intentional, optional, gratuitous, by choice; discretional.

ANT. *Coerced, forced, involuntary, compulsory, necessitated, constrained.*

Volunteer, *v.* Offer, bestow, *or* act freely, proffer, tender, present.

ANT. *Levy, draft, requisition, request, demand, suborn, confiscate.*

Voluptuous. Sensual, sensuous, epicurean, luxurious, pleasurable, licentious, self-indulgent.

ANT. *Self-sacrificing, abstinent, ascetic, self-denying, austere, puritanical, renunciatory.*

Voracious. Hungry, greedy, rapacious, eager, ravenous, gluttonous, insatiate, omnivorous.

ANT. *Fastidious, dainty, refined, delicate, nice.*

Vouch. Declare, affirm, attest, support, asseverate, aver, protest, assure, promise, warrant, guarantee.

ANT. *Repudiate, abjure, renounce, protest against, demur, decline, abnegate.*

Vouchsafe. Grant, concede, bestow; condescend, deign, stoop, descend, yield.

ANT. *Deny, refuse, withhold.*

Vow, *n.* Promise, pledge; oath, asseveration.

Vow, *v.* Devote, promise, consecrate, dedicate; assert, asseverate, swear.

ANT. *Release, absolve, free; pollute, defile, profane.*

Vulgar. Common, general, ordinary, public; vernacular; plebeian; popular; rustic, boorish, low, coarse, base, underbred.

ANT. *Noble, aristocratic, patrician, high-born, refined, polite, high-bred, stylish, select, choice, cultivated, strict, scientific, philosophical, technical, accurate.*

Vulnerable. Susceptible, liable, subject, assailable, weak, tender, exposed.

ANT. *Impregnable, unassailable, unexposed, concealed, fortified, defended.*

W

Waft. Bear, convey, transmit, carry, transport, make to float on waves (*of air or water*).

ANT. *Sink, weigh down, depress.*

Wages. Salary, stipend, allowance, remuneration, fruit, hire, pay, compensation; earnings; reward, emolument.

ANT. *Gratuity, bonus, premium, grace, douceur, gift, boon.*

Wait. Stay, tarry, delay, stop, abide, remain, linger; rest; expect, watch, await, look for.

ANT. *Hasten, hurry, speed, press on; go, depart.*

Waive. Relinquish, forbear, refuse, forego; throw away, cast off, reject, desert; abandon, remit, quit claim, cancel, drop, renounce, surrender.

ANT. *Urge, assert, press, enforce, claim, defend, vindicate.*

Wake. Be awake, watch; excite, arouse, stir; reanimate, revive; call, evoke, summon, provoke.

ANT. *Soothe, hush, tranquil-*

ize, quiet; mesmerize; allay, appease, calm.

Wakeful. Vigilant, awake, sleepless; watchful, observant, wary.

Ant. *Drowsy, sleepy; heedless, careless, incautious, unwary.*

Walk. Move on foot, proceed; be stirring, be abroad; behave, pursue, conduct one's self; perambulate, pass, traverse; step, stride, march, stalk, tramp, plod, trudge, tread.

Ant. *Halt, stop, stand still; ride, drive.*

Wan. Pale, sickly, languid, pallid; ashen, colorless, haggard, cadaverous; livid, bloodless.

Ant. *Fresh-colored, bright, rosy, lively, sanguine, incarnadine.*

Wander. Straggle, stroll, range; turn aside; be delirious, rave; be crazed; expatiate; depart, saunter; navigate, travel; deviate, diverge, err, ramble, go astray, rove, stray, veer, roam, swerve, digress.

Ant. *Remain, stay, settle, rest, stop, pause, moor, anchor, perch, bivouac, halt, alight, repose.*

Wane. Be diminished, decrease; decline, fail, sink; fade, pale; ebb; pine, droop, deteriorate, attenuate, contract, recede.

Ant. *Wax, increase, rally, improve, brighten, expand, develop, advance.*

Want, *n.* Defect, failure, dearth, indigence, absence, scarcity, deficiency, lack; destitution, poverty, need, shortness, insufficiency, scantiness.

Ant. *Supply, sufficiency, allowance, provision, abundance, production, adequacy, supplement.*

Ward, *n.* Watch, guardianship, guard; garrison, defender, protector; defense, protection; custody; keeper, guardian, warden; pupil, minor; division; apartment.

Ward, *v.* Watch, guard; defend, protect; repel, turn aside; be vigilant; keep guard, avert, repel, parry, fend.

Ant. *Betray, surrender, admit.*

Warfare. Hostilities, war; contest, struggle; strife, discord; belligerence, antagonism; campaign, battle, skirmish, engagement.

Ant. *Peace, truce, armistice; amity, pacification; neutrality; reconciliation; tranquillity, friendliness, harmony, order, quiet, concord.*

Warlike. Military, martial, hostile, soldierly, inimical, bellicose, unfriendly, belligerent.

Ant. *Peaceful, civil, unmilitary, friendly, pacific, amicable.*

Warm. Ardent, zealous, fervent, cordial, hot, glowing; violent, vehement, furious, excited, passionate; warm-blooded, warm-hearted; sunny, mild, genial, pleasant; close, oppressive; fervid, earnest, eager, enthusiastic, hearty; lively, interested; irascible.

Ant. *Cool, cold; dispassionate, collected, composed, calm, unruffled, placid, sedate, quiet, staid; unconcerned, frigid, apathetic, chilling; repellent.*

Warmth. Fervency, glow, earnestness, cordiality, animation, eagerness, excitement, vehemence; interest, zeal, ardor, enthusiasm, passion, fervor, heat, intensity, spirit; emotion, life.

Ant. *Coolness, calmness, indifference, frigidity, torpidity, apathy, impassiveness; calm, chill, obtuseness, frost, iciness.*

Warn. Make ware, notify, admonish, caution; advise, mention to, inform, apprise; dissuade, deter, alarm, premonish.

ANT. *Encourage, embolden, inspirit, hearten, induce, instigate, prompt, impel.*

Warrant, *n.* Guaranty, security, voucher; commission, credentials.

Warrant, *v.* Secure, guarantee, support, justify, sanction, assure; empower, engage, undertake, authorize.

ANT. *Invalidate, nullify, repudiate, cancel, make void; endanger, imperil.*

Wary. Circumspect, watchful, cautious, vigilant, prudent, discreet, heedful, thoughtful, careful, guarded, scrupulous, chary.

ANT. *Unsuspecting, unwary, incautious, negligent, heedless, inattentive, indifferent, remiss.*

Wash, *v.* Cleanse, wet, scrub, moisten, bathe, lave; overflow, fall on; waste, abrade; stain, tint, color; overlay, cover; cleanse, rinse.

ANT. *Soil, stain, pollute, defile, contaminate, bemire.*

Waste, *n.* Squandering, devastation, loss, decrease; void, desert, wilderness; refuse; prodigality, diminution, dissipation, destruction, havoc, desolation, ravage; solitude, expanse; consumption, expenditure, extravagance.

ANT. *Restoration, renovation, reimbursement, renewal, recovery, restitution, reparation; accumulation, frugality, economy, thrift, hoard, store, accretion.*

Waste, *v.* Squander, dissipate, lavish, desolate; ruin, devastate, destroy; wear away, impair, use up, consume, spend; damage, injure.

ANT. *Restore, renovate, repair, renew; develop, multiply, augment; economize, hoard, accumulate, treasure, husband, protect.*

Waste, *a.* Desolate, devastated, stripped, bare, dreary, dismal, gloomy, cheerless; worthless, valueless, refuse, rejected, unused, superfluous.

ANT. *Populated, occupied, cheerful, lively; valuable, useful, essential, necessary.*

Wasteful. Destructive, ruinous; lavish, prodigal, profuse, extravagant.

ANT. *Careful, economical, frugal, protective.*

Watch, *v.* Be awake, keep vigil, be on guard, tend; heed, observe, expect.

ANT. *Sleep, drowse, slumber; be careless, neglect, overlook.*

Watchful. Circumspect, wakeful, heedful; vigilant, awake, attentive, wary, cautious, observant.

ANT. *Drowsy, slumbrous, inobservant, careless, heedless, inattentive, unwary, incautious, remiss, distracted, inadvertent.*

Waver. Reel, totter, vacillate, fluctuate, hesitate, dubitate, be undetermined, alternate, be perplexed, scruple.

ANT. *Decide, choose, settle, determine, dispose of, be steadfast.*

Wavering, *n.* Fluctuation, hesitancy, indecision, vacillation; uncertainty, irresolution.

ANT. *Decision, determination, resolution, promptness.*

Way. Path, road, route, street, track, alley, avenue, channel, course, highway, pathway, highroad, driveway, lane, pass, passageway, passage, thoroughfare, roadway; distance, interval; motion, progression, journey;

means, scheme, device, plan; manner, method, mode, fashion, style; practice, habit, habitude, custom, wont.

ANT. *Deviation, error, discursion; deflection, divergence, rambling, wandering; exception, variation.*

Wayward. Disobedient, headstrong, froward, perverse, wilful, obstinate, stubborn, unruly, capricious, contrary.

ANT. *Amenable, docile, manageable, compliant, obedient.*

Weak. Feeble, infirm, sickly, exhausted, unable; deficient; soft, pliant, frail; low, faint; spiritless; foolish, wavering, lacking; debilitated, unsound, invalid, fragile, delicate, tender; exposed, unguarded, defenseless; pliable, irresolute; simple, silly, witless, shallow, imbecile, childish; injudicious, unwise; insipid, tasteless, thin, diluted, watery; imprudent, indiscreet, erring; flimsy, slight, frivolous; unsafe, unsubstantial, untrustworthy; ineffectual.

ANT. *Strong, sturdy, vigorous, hardy, robust, powerful; sound, hale, healthy, stout, able; efficient, capable, potent, mighty; firm, compact, secure, impregnable; forcible, intense, energetic; biting, sharp, racy, pungent; rank; tough, tenacious, cohesive, resisting; strenuous, ardent, eager, zealous, hearty; vivid, brilliant; solid, substantial; valid, confirmed, binding.*

Weaken. Debilitate, enfeeble, enervate; invalidate; depress, impair, reduce, lower, sap, dilute, attenuate.

ANT. *Strengthen, empower, invigorate; confirm, corroborate, substantiate; augment, increase, mend, improve; enhance.*

Weakness. Feebleness, debility, languor, imbecility, infirmity, decrepitude, faintness, frailty.

ANT. *Strength, vigor, tone, health, power, efficiency, nerve, spirit.*

Wealth. Riches, affluence, opulence, abundance, plenty, fortune, competence, estate, treasure, money, funds, cash, property; luxury, satiety.

ANT. *Poverty, scarcity, indigence, lack, want, need, impecuniosity.*

Wear. Carry, bear, have on; use up; impair, waste, diminish, consume; last; don, exhibit, sport.

ANT. *Doff, abandon; renew, renovate, repair; increase, augment, swell.*

Weariness. Fatigue, languor, exhaustion, lassitude, prostration, depression.

ANT. *Strength, vigor, force, energy, restedness.*

Wearisome. Tiresome, tedious, irksome, vexatious, fatiguing; trying, wearing; prosy, monotonous, annoying, uninteresting; toilsome, laborious.

ANT. *Easy, pleasing, comfortable; invigorating; facile; interesting, exciting, fascinating, delightful, amusing, stirring.*

Weary, *a.* Fatigued, tiresome, irksome, wearisome; tired, sick, exhausted.

ANT. *Energetic, strong, refreshed, invigorated; pleased, interested.*

Weave. Interlace, unite; compose, fabricate; intwine, plait, braid, plat.

ANT. *Disentangle, unravel, untwist, disunite, untwine; extricate, simplify.*

Wed. Marry, espouse; unite, attach.

ANT. *Separate, divorce.*

Wedding. Marriage, bridal, espousals, nuptials, nuptial ceremony.

ANT. *Celibacy, bachelorhood, virginity.*

Wedlock. Marriage, matrimony, nuptial state.

ANT. *Celibacy, bachelorhood, virginity.*

Weep. Cry, shed tears, lament, complain; drip, be soaked; sob, bewail, bemoan; droop.

ANT. *Laugh, smile; rejoice, be cheerful, enjoy.*

Weight. Heaviness; pressure, burden; importance, influence, consequence, moment; ponderousness, gravity, load, power; efficacy, impressiveness.

ANT. *Lightness, levity, volatility; insignificance, triviality, weakness, inefficacy, worthlessness; portableness, ease, facility.*

Weighty. Heavy, ponderous, burdensome, onerous; forcible, momentous; efficacious, impressive, cogent.

ANT. *Easy, light, unencumbered; active, swift; slight, unimportant; frivolous, volatile, unsettled, giddy.*

Welcome, *n.* Greeting, salutation, reception.

ANT. *Farewell, adieu, parting, good-by, leave-taking; repulse, repudiation.*

Welcome, *a.* Grateful, pleasing, gladly entertained, acceptable, agreeable, gratifying; gratuitous, free.

ANT. *Unwelcome, unpleasant, disagreeable, unacceptable.*

Welfare. Prosperity, happiness, well-being, enjoyment, success, weal, advantage, benefit, profit, luck, thrift.

ANT. *Adversity, misfortune, reverses, failure, ill luck, unhappiness.*

Well, *a.* Good, desirable, fortunate, advantageous; healthy; favored, lucky; hale, sound.

ANT. *Ill, sickly, diseased, unwell, poorly; unlucky, unfortunate.*

Well, *adv.* Justly, rightly, abundantly, fully, adequately, thoroughly, satisfactorily, advantageously, conveniently, properly.

ANT. *Ill, wrongly, poorly, imperfectly, improperly, badly.*

Wet. Damp, moist, rainy, humid; nasty; dank; showery; lively, interesting.

ANT. *Dry, parched, thirsty, arid; plain, unvarnished; shrewd, sharp, quaint.*

Wheedle. Cajole, flatter, entice, coax, inveigle, fawn upon.

ANT. *Deter, undeceive, detract, decry; chide, scold, rebuke, blame.*

Whereas. Since, considering; when in fact, while, although; seeing that; inasmuch as.

Whimsical. Capricious, fanciful, queer, strange, freakish, quaint, fantastic.

ANT. *Staid, serious, sober, matter-of-fact, steady, sedate.*

White. Snowy, pale, pallid; unblemished, innocent, pure; gray, hoary; fortunate, happy, favorable.

ANT. *Black, dark, colorless, negro, sooty, coallike; dismal, gloomy, forbidding, threatening, sullen, foreboding; impure, sullied.*

Whole. All, total, complete, entire, undivided, uninjured, unbroken; unimpaired, integral; sound, perfect, faultless, strong, well, healthy.

ANT. *Partial, imperfect, unsound, ill, sick; divided, fractional.*

Wholesome. Salubrious, salutary, healthy, healthful, nourishing, **nutritious**, strengthening, invigorating; beneficial, good; fresh, sound, uncorrupt.

ANT. *Detrimental, deleterious, prejudicial, hurtful, pernicious, noxious.*

Wholly. Entirely, completely, perfectly, totally, fully, altogether, utterly.

ANT. *Partially, imperfectly, incompletely, separately, in part.*

Wicked. Sinful, criminal, guilty, immoral, ungodly, profane, unrighteous, atrocious, unholy, vicious, nefarious, heinous, abandoned, iniquitous, depraved, unprincipled, irreverent, vile, abandoned, bad, evil, unjust, ill, outrageous, monstrous, villainous.

ANT. *Good, righteous, just, godly, virtuous, fair, honorable, unsullied, pious, benevolent, upright, reputable, true, excellent.*

Wickedness. Crime, sin, vice, iniquity, evil, depravity, immorality, enormity; badness, vileness, corruption.

ANT. *Goodness, piety, godliness, righteousness, honor, virtue, benevolence.*

Wide. Broad, spacious, vast, extensive, comprehensive, liberal; remote, distant, far; ample, expanded.

ANT. *Narrow, contracted, confined, cramped, constricted, limited; bigoted, parsimonious; close, near.*

Wife. Married woman, consort, spouse, helpmate.

ANT. *Sweetheart, maiden; widow.*

Wild, *a.* Untamed, uncultivated, undomesticated; savage, uncivilized, rude, ferocious; violent, turbulent; disorderly, crazy, ungoverned; visionary; unsheltered, exposed.

ANT. *Tame, domesticated, cultivated, civilized; populated, frequented; polite, gentle, refined; rational, orderly, sane, controlled, sober, collected.*

Wile. Trick, snare, artifice, beguilement, allurement, stratagem, cheat, fraud, imposture, deceit, deception, contrivance, device.

ANT. *Artlessness, openness, candor, straightforwardness.*

Wilful. Self-determined, voluntary; obstinate, perverse, stubborn, refractory; self-willed, headstrong; wayward; intentional, prepense, preconceived, premeditated, designed, deliberate, purposed.

ANT. *Concessive, compliant, amenable, obedient, docile, manageable; adventitious, accidental.*

Will, *n.* Choice, determination, preference, volition; decree, desire, command, purpose; control, disposal; testament; resolution, decision, self-reliance, force; inclination, pleasure, disposition; behest, order, direction.

ANT. *Indecision, vacillation, indeterminateness, indifference; sensibility, perception.*

Will, *v.* Bequeath, devise, direct; choose, decide, determine, decree; wish, desire, incline to have; be willing.

ANT. *Die intestate; be indifferent.*

Willing. Inclined, consenting, ready, complying; chosen, desired; disposed, minded, desirous; voluntary.

ANT. *Loath, disinclined, reluctant, averse, backward.*

Win. Gain, get, procure, earn; be victorious, prevail; obtain; acquire, achieve; conquer; succeed, accomplish.

ANT. *Lose, fail of, miss, forfeit, be deprived* or *bereaved of.*

Wind, *v.* Coil, twine, wreathe, twist, turn; enfold, encircle; direct; insinuate.

ANT. *Straighten, unravel, untwist.*

Winding. Twisting, circuitous, bending, curving, meandering, flexuous, serpentine, sinuous.

ANT. *Straight, rectilinear, direct, undeviating, unswerving.*

Winning. Charming, attractive, alluring, pleasing, bewitching, winsome, fascinating, delightful, lovely, captivating, prepossessing, enchanting.

ANT. *Repulsive, unpleasing, repellent, disagreeable, offensive, repugnant, revolting, disgusting, odious.*

Wisdom. Judgment, prudence, reason, understanding, sense, skill, sagacity, attainment, discernment, depth, discretion, information, foresight, learning, profundity, reasonableness, prescience, knowledge, insight, judiciousness, erudition, enlightenment.

ANT. *Folly, imbecility, stupidity, error, foolishness, fatuity, idiocy, absurdity, imprudence, indiscretion, miscalculation, nonsense, misjudgment, silliness, senselessness.*

Wise. Knowing, erudite, wary, learned, sagacious; crafty; judicious, discreet; skilled, intelligent, rational; sage, sensible; logical; deep, discerning, profound, philosophical.

ANT. *Senseless, idiotic, irrational; nonsensical, imprudent, irrational, indiscreet, ridiculous, preposterous, insensate.*

Wish, *v.* Long for, hanker after, desire; invoke, imprecate.

ANT. *Despise, dislike; disrelish, be averse to, displease.*

Wit. Ingenuity, humor, satire, sarcasm, irony, burlesque; intellect, mind, understanding, sense; man of genius *or* humor; penetration, discernment, insight, acumen; facetiousness, drollery, waggery, jocularity, sparkle, repartee, joke, playfulness, fun, witticism, pleasantry, banter, jest, raillery.

ANT. *Stupidity, inanity, obtuseness, vapidity, dulness, commonplace, matter-of-fact; irrationality, platitude; dolt, dullard; sobriety, solemnity, seriousness, gravity, stolidity.*

Witchcraft. Sorcery, enchantment, magic, necromancy, conjuration, incantation, charm, spell, thaumaturgy.

Witchery. Sorcery, witchcraft; fascination, enchantment, spell, entrancement, ravishment.

ANT. *Reality, actuality, disillusionment, bald facts.*

With. By, on the side of, by the help of; attending, accompanying, close; against; according to; in contrast with; upon, immediately after.

Withdraw. Take back, recall, retire; draw back, remove; recede, depart.

ANT. *Offer, afford; produce; repeat, reiterate, confirm; renew; furnish, propose, give.*

Withhold. Hold back, restrain, impede, hamper; retain, refuse; suppress, check, rein in, inhibit, stint, forbear; detain.

ANT. *Let go, give, bestow, confer; admit, yield; furnish, allow, provide, permit; encourage, embolden, cheer, hearten, animate.*

Within, *a.* Inside, inwardly, internally, indoors, in the limits of.

ANT. *Without, outside, outwardly, externally, outdoors.*

Without, *prep.* Out of, beyond, out of the limits of, in the absence of, in separation from; independently of; exclusive of, omitting.

ANT. *Within, inside of, in the limits of, including, embracing.*

Without, *conj.* Unless, except.

Withstand. Oppose, resist, confront, thwart, combat, prevent, contradict.

ANT. *Concede, grant, assist, submit, acquiesce, abet, countenance, encourage, support.*

Witness, *n.* Attestation, testimony, evidence, proof; one who attests *or* is directly cognizant of; eye-witness; deponent, corroborator; spectator, auditor, voucher.

ANT. *Belief, hearsay, rumor, report; invalidation, refutation.*

Witty. Acute, sharp, smart, facetious, arch, keen, amusing, humorous, satirical, taunting, ironical.

ANT. *Dull, stupid, obtuse, dry, prosaic, prosy, tiresome, tedious, serious.*

Woe. Grief, sorrow, misery, calamity; curse, malediction; disconsolateness, tribulation, melancholy, agony, depression, unhappiness.

ANT. *Joy, delight, pleasure, prosperity, enjoyment, bliss, felicity, welfare, cheerfulness, merriment.*

Woful. Sorrowful, distressed, wretched, afflicted, unhappy, sad; paltry, poor, piteous, disconsolate, miserable, burdened, troubled.

ANT. *Joyous, light-hearted, cheerful, merry, rejoiced, glad, delighted, gay, blessed.*

Womanhood. Muliebrity, maturity in woman, feminality; womanliness; woman, womankind.

ANT. *Manhood, manliness, masculinity; man, mankind.*

Womanish. Effeminate, weak, foolishly feminine.

ANT. *Mannish, aping a man, foolishly masculine.*

Womanly. Becoming a woman, feminine, delicate, refined.

ANT. *Manly, strong, virile, becoming a man.*

Wonder, *n.* Astonishment, admiration, amazement, surprise, awe, bewilderment, curiosity; portent, miracle, prodigy, marvel; phenomenon, sight, rarity, spectacle.

ANT. *Expectation, anticipation; familiarity, apathy, indifference; foreknowledge, prescience; ennui; satiety; platitude, truism, commonplace.*

Wonderful. Amazing, astonishing, marvelous, surprising, improbable, strange, incredulous; startling, awesome, portentous, extraordinary, prodigious, wondrous.

ANT. *Commonplace, familiar, expected, ordinary, wonted, hackneyed, customary, habitual.*

Wonted. Accustomed, usual, habitual, customary, habituated, used, conventional, regular, frequent, common.

ANT. *Exceptional, unusual, unused, unconventional, infrequent, irregular.*

Wood. Forest, grove, thicket; timber, trees; copse, woodland, forestland.

ANT. *Open, prairie, clearing.*

Word. Term, expression, accents, tongue, vocable; account, tidings, message; statement, declaration, affirmation, promise; (*pl.*) contention, dispute, wrangling, altercation; speech, talk, discourse, language.

ANT. *Idea, conception, suggestion; sentence, unit of composition, paragraph.*

Work, *n.* Exertion, activity, effort, toil, employment, labor; business, duty; product, fabric, production, performance, manufacture; act, deed, service, result, effect, achievement, feat; composition, structure; management, treatment, operation, issue, fruit; occupation; action, drudgery.

ANT. *Frustration, abortion, hodge-podge; failure, deficiency, defect, fault; miscarriage; rest, inertia, fruitlessness, inoperativeness; inefficiency, futility; repose, relaxation, ease, vacation, idleness, leisure, recreation.*

Work, *v.* Exert one's self, labor, be engaged, toil; operate, act, perform; effect, affect, conduce, influence; strain; use, utilize; produce, accomplish; prevail upon, manage, lead; ferment.

ANT. *Rest, recreate, stop, repose, halt, relax, be at ease, lie, recline, sleep, slumber; fail, miscarry, be wanting, lapse.*

Workman. Worker, artificer, laborer, artisan, mechanic. operative, craftsman; toiler, hand; master.

ANT. *Employer, superintendent, inspector, supervisor, director, overseer.*

Workmanship. Handicraft, execution, skill, art, manipulation, handiwork.

ANT. *Bungling, botching.*

World. Earth, universe, creation; affairs, interests, life, action, occupation; inhabitants, people, mankind; globe, cosmos, planet, nature; public, society, human race.

ANT. *Heaven; atom, individual.*

Worldly. Human, common; secular, temporal; mundane, terrestrial, earthly; fleshly, carnal; universal; sublunary; sordid, selfish, ambitious, earthborn, groveling.

ANT. *Spiritual, ethereal, celestial, heavenly, lunar, solar; incorporeal, ghostly; ideal, abstract, mental, intellectual; sacred, holy, pure.*

Worry, *n.* Care, anxiety, fret, solicitude, torment, vexation, trouble, annoyance, plague, disquiet; perplexity, concern, fear, apprehension, uneasiness, misgiving.

ANT. *Trust, calm, courage, serenity, tranquillity, placidity, quiet, ease of mind, resolution, dauntlessness.*

Worship, *n.* Reverence, homage, adoration, submission, obsequiousness, honor, abjectness.

ANT. *Detestation, hatred, abhorrence, loathing, disgust, antipathy, assertion, defiance, challenge.*

Worship, *v.* Adore, reverence, revere, idolize, respect, defer, venerate, deify, honor, exalt.

ANT. *Defy, dare; abhor, detest, hate, disdain, abominate, contemn, loathe.*

Worth. Desert, merit, excellence; price, rate; value, quality, equivalence; virtue, character, worthiness, integrity; credit, cost, estimate.

ANT. *Demerit, worthlessness, cheapness, uselessness, futility, poverty.*

Worthless. Undeserving, useless, valueless, vile, mean, miserable, poor, wretched, abject, unworthy, ignoble, abandoned, depraved; refuse, waste.

ANT. *Costly, valuable, dear, high-priced, expensive; sumptuous, splendid, rich, precious; useful, excellent, estimable, virtuous, worthy.*

Worthy. Valuable, deserving, estimable, virtuous; suitable, adapted, meritorious, exemplary, upright, righteous, honest, honorable.

ANT. *Worthless, valueless, ignoble, defective, unsuitable.*

Wound, *v.* Hurt, injure, damage, harm, cut, stab, rend, lacerate, pain; annoy, mortify, offend.

ANT. *Heal, allay, cure, remedy, soothe, repair; appease, assuage, comfort, harmonize.*

Wrap, *v.* Wind, fold, cover, envelop, enfold, involve, conceal, hide, muffle.

ANT. *Unwind, unfold, lay bare, reveal, develop, expose.*

Wrath. Fury, ire, resentment, passion, anger, rage, exasperation, indignation, choler, irritation.

ANT. *Calmness, control, restraint, composure, placidity, serenity.*

Wrathful. Furious, raging, indignant, passionate, choleric, ireful, angry, exasperated, incensed, irate, wroth, mad, provoked, resentful.

ANT. *Calm, collected, controlled, repressed, masterly, restrained, good-tempered.*

Wreath. Garland, chaplet, festoon, crown, bays, diadem.

Wreck, *n.* Ruins, remains, rubbish, wreckage, débris; havoc, destruction, shipwreck, ruin, desolation, perdition, demolition.

ANT. *Preservation, conservation, saving, protection, security.*

Wrench, *v.* Pull, twist, wrest, force, strain, sprain; pervert, distort, wring.

ANT. *Straighten, untwist; rectify.*

Wretched. Miserable, calamitous, afflicted, unhappy, degraded, woful; worthless, paltry; forlorn, wobegone, comfortless, distressed; shocking, deplorable, depressing, sad; contemptible, mean, pitiful, debased, humiliated.

ANT. *Prosperous, flourishing, fortunate, happy, enviable, felicitous, successful, thriving; valuable; honored, noble, exalted.*

Wrong, *a.* Injurious, unjust, faulty, detrimental, unfit; improper, incorrect; mistaken, erroneous; illegal, immoral.

ANT. *Right, upright, lawful, equitable, fair, just, becoming, proper, suitable, appropriate, fit; correct, true, actual, real.*

Wrought. Worked, elaborated; performed, done, effected, executed, produced, manufactured.

ANT. *Rough, crude, coarse, raw, unpolished.*

Wry. Twisted, distorted; misdirected, perverted, wrested; askew, contorted, deformed, deranged; crooked, awry.

ANT. *Straight, rectilinear, direct, upright, erect; perpendicular, shapely, comely, symmetrical, proper, well-formed.*

Y

Yawn. Open wide, gape; desire, be eager.
ANT. *Close, shut, engulf.*

Yearly. Annual, happening each year, per annum, every year, year by year.
ANT. *Perennial, everlasting, evergreen.*

Yearn. Long, desire, be eager, covet, crave, hanker.
ANT. *Loathe, revolt, recoil, shudder at, despise.*

Yell, *v.* Cry out, shriek, scream, holler.
ANT. *Keep silence, subdue, silence.*

Yet. Besides, nevertheless, notwithstanding, however, still, eventually, ultimately, at last, so far, thus far, hitherto, at present; over and above; further; now.

Yield. Furnish, produce, afford, bear, render; relinquish, give in, let go, forego; accede, acquiesce; resign, surrender, concede, allow, grant, submit, succumb; comply, consent, agree.
ANT. *Withdraw, withhold, retain, deny, refuse, vindicate, assert, claim, disallow, appropriate, resist, dissent, protest, struggle, strive.*

Yielding. Conceding, producing, surrendering, supple, pliant, submissive, unresisting, obsequious, attentive, flexible, compliant, accommodating.
ANT. *Defiant, resisting, obstinate, firm, stiff, hard, perverse.*

Yoke, *n.* Bond, chain, link, tie; servitude, bondage, vassalage, service, thraldom, subjection, subservience.
ANT. *Freedom, liberty; authority, command.*

Yoke, *v.* Couple, conjoin, connect, link; enslave, subjugate.
ANT. *Dissever, divorce, disconnect, liberate, release, manumit, enfranchise.*

Young. Juvenile, immature; inexperienced, innocent, ignorant; youthful, boyish, girlish, childlike.
ANT. *Old, mature, adult; experienced, knowing; senile, aged, decrepit, venerable; antique, antiquated, obsolete; superannuated.*

Youth. Adolescence, childhood, infancy; youthfulness, juvenility; minority; lad, boy, girl, youngster.
ANT. *Age, senility, maturity.*

Youthful. Puerile, juvenile, immature, young, fresh, vigorous, unripe, callow, childish, boyish, childlike, girlish, adolescent.
ANT. *Mature, adult, full-grown, ripe, ripened.*

Z

Zeal. Ardor, eagerness, earnestness, fervor, enthusiasm, energy, feeling, devotion, intensity, passion, spirit.
ANT. *Apathy, indifference, coldness, carelessness, sluggishness, torpor.*

Zealot. Partisan, bigot, enthusiast, fanatic, devotee, visionary, dreamer.
ANT. *Renegade, traitor, deserter; lukewarm person.*

Zealous. Ardent, anxious, earnest, enthusiastic, fervid, eager, steadfast, keen, fervent, devoted, prompt, ready, fiery, passionate.

ANT. *Lukewarm, indifferent, cold, apathetic, passionless, phlegmatic.*

Zenith. Height, pinnacle, acme, summit, culmination, maximum, apex, top.

ANT. *Nadir, lowest point, depth, minimum.*

Zephyr. West wind, breeze, gentle wind.

ANT. *Gale, furious wind.*

Zero. Naught, cipher, nothing.

ANT. *Something, existence, creation; infinity.*

Zest. Flavor, appetizer, pleasure, gusto, gust, enjoyment, relish, sharpener, enhancement, savor, taste, smack, sauce, appetite.

ANT. *Distaste, disrelish, detriment.*

Zone. Girdle, belt, girth, cincture, band, baldric; region, climate, clime; circuit, circumference; zodiac; orbit.

ANT. *Sphere, universe.*